THIRD EDITION

Reading Diagnosis and Remediation

William H. Rupley

Timothy R. Blair

TEXAS A & M UNIVERSITY

LIBRARY

Merrill Publishing Company
A Bell & Howell Information Company
Columbus Toronto London Melbourne

Cover Art: Jim Jackson

Published by Merrill Publishing Company
A Bell & Howell Information Company
Columbus, Ohio 43216

This book was set in Bookman Light.

Administrative Editor: Jeff Johnston
Production Coordinator: Carol Driver
Cover Designer: Brian Deep
Text Designer: Connie Young

Library of Congress Catalog Card Number: 88-61661
International Standard Book Number: 0-675-20932-3
Printed in the United States of America
1 2 3 4 5 6 7 8 9—93 92 91 90 89

To our families—Agnes, Billy, Donald, Jeanné, Tim, and Billy—
for their patience, support, and continued understanding

Preface

A knowledgeable, thinking, and caring teacher of reading is a key variable in whether or not children will be successful in learning to read. This book is based on this assertion. Designing and implementing instruction in relation to what students need is the challenge and responsibility of all teachers of reading, whether they are regular classroom teachers or reading resource teachers. In the last 15 years, teacher and school effectiveness research studies have highlighted this important fact and have identified instructional variables that often promote student learning. Those variables of teacher beliefs, attitudes, knowledge, and behaviors that contribute to student achievement in reading from the heart of this book.

Teachers of reading have always known the importance of diagnosing their students' needs and then planning instruction based on their findings. Teacher effectiveness research has reaffirmed the importance of the diagnostic process. It has also brought to light additional considerations for teachers to ponder, especially in the area of group diagnostic techniques (whole class and small group). These additional diagnostic strategies will be discussed throughout the text as they apply to specific areas in the teaching of reading.

Along with the emphasis on identifying what makes an effective teacher of reading, there has been an equal emphasis on basic research of the reading process itself, especially in the area of reading comprehension. This particular line of research has produced significant information that affects how teachers teach reading and what strategies readers use while interacting with text. This new information in the area of comprehension instruction is emphasized throughout the text with implications for both classroom and resource teachers of reading. In addition to the research emphasis on teacher effectiveness, the new considerations in the areas of group diagnosis and correction, and the new thinking in the reading comprehension area, important features of this revision include new and revised discussions on comprehending expository materials, computer-assisted instruction, exceptional children, culturally divergent children, reading materials, and teacher decision making.

Throughout the book, practical examples, case studies, and exercises for the reader to complete (field-based, sharing and brainstorming, role-playing, discuss and debate, and library) are given to heighten the reader's involvement. While recommendations for corrective and remedial instruction are given, readers are continually asked to think of alternatives to fit their own situations. The children in every classroom deserve thinking teachers who are constantly striving to provide them with an appropriate education.

ACKNOWLEDGMENTS

We wish to express our appreciation to Rick Erickson, University of Southern Illinois, and Michael Rowls, University of Tennessee at Chattanooga, for their constructive reviews of the text. We also wish to thank Viola Florez for her major contributions to chapter 14.

Our sincere appreciation also goes to our excellent and patient typists, Sherry Ealoms and Norma Hinojosa.

Writing a book is certainly a team effort. We thank our many students, public school teachers, and colleagues for their insights into and suggestions for several parts of this revision. Finally, we would like to extend our appreciation to the staff at Merrill Publishing, especially Jeff Johnston, for their help and expert guidance throughout the preprartion of this book.

William H. Rupley

Timothy R. Blair

Contents

PART ONE

Foundations of Reading Diagnosis and Remediation

1

Reading Ability and the
Role of Reading in the
Elementary School

Typically, one period during the school day is set aside for a subject called "reading," but reading serves a broader purpose than as just a subject of instruction for a specific part of the school day. Reading integrates the elementary curriculum; it enables students to learn better in nearly all content areas.

Students who experience reading problems are at a disadvantage in school and in later life. In school they often find reading frustrating; it is something to avoid. As a result, such students often do poorly in other learning areas and may demonstrate behavior problems. If their reading difficulties are not corrected or remediated, these students may be limited in future achievements both in and out of school.

The importance of reading, as Strang (1968) has pointed out, is of international concern. "Reading is the key to communication and contributes to the solution of world problems of poverty and animosity. From a personal viewpoint, reading is the key to continuing education, employment, and enjoyment. These goals may be achieved through the effective teaching of reading" (p. 15).

The demands of reading in today's society are continually changing. Rapid developments in such areas as computer technology, electronics, and transportation bring with them greater demands for competent reading. Although one may argue that the role of reading wanes in a highly technical society, a rival argument states that the demand for capable reading increases in this situation. Brandt (1981) makes this case for the importance of competent readers in the computer age: "Computers are especially prolific, printing out enormous quantities of information and analysis, which someone has to read" (p. 11).

It is well known that some students have problems learning to read. Newspapers carry major headlines such as the following: "Are We Becoming a Nation of Illiterates?"; "Why Can't Johnny Read?"; and "Back to the Basics of Teaching Reading." Widespread interest in improving students' reading abilities is evidenced by the large number of states that have legislated minimum competency requirements in reading. Because this text focuses specifically on the role of the teacher in corrective and remedial reading instruction, its primary purpose is to help teachers become more effective in teaching corrective and remedial reading.

After reading this chapter, the teacher should be able to

☐ describe reading as it relates to the instructional responsibilities of the teacher.
☐ define facilitative and functional reading factors.
☐ analyze facilitative reading factors and their role in reading instruction.
☐ identify and understand the purposes served by the ability to read and the instructional responsibilities of the teacher in relation to each purpose.
☐ identify the diagnostic responsibilities of the teacher for each purpose served by the ability to read.

CONSIDERING THE VARIABLES RELATED TO READING

Mature, capable readers take reading for granted; it seems as natural as talking. In reality, however, reading is a complex process. Most reading authorities agree that *reading is comprehension* (getting meaning from written text). **Comprehension** has been further defined by several reading authorities. Tierney and Pearson (1981) define reading comprehension as "an active process that involves the activation, focusing, maintaining, and refining of ideas toward developing interpretations (models) that are plausible, interconnected, and complete" (p. 9). Wittrock (1987) conceptualizes comprehension as a process of "learners constructing relations among the words and sentences of the text, and between the text and their knowledge bases, to build a sensible structure for the text" (p. 735). Reading instruction does not mean the teaching of isolated skills, but rather the building on and continual development of students' abilities to comprehend what they read.

An important question for the teacher to ask is "How is the ability to read related to *my instructional practices and responsibilities* as a teacher?" The teacher's role in reading instruction can be better understood by considering the variables that lead to reading ability.

Facilitative Reading Factors

The variables that lead to reading ability can be classified for instructional purposes as either facilitative or functional. **Facilitative reading factors** are skills and abilities that facilitate reading ability, but by themselves are not reading. Examples of such factors are word-recognition skills, speaking and listening vocabularies, and experiential/conceptual background. None of these individual factors can be called reading—they must be integrated in their use within a reading situation where getting meaning is the focus. An excellent analogy is found in *Becoming a Nation of Readers* (Anderson, Hiebert, Scott, & Wilkinson, 1985) where reading is compared to the performance of a symphony orchestra.

> First, like the performance of a symphony, reading is a holistic act. In other words, while reading can be analyzed into subskills such as discriminating letters and identifying words, performing the subskills one at a time does not constitute reading. Second, success in reading comes from practice over long periods of time, like skill in playing musical instruments. Indeed, it is a lifelong endeavor. Third, as with a musical score, there may be more than one interpretation of a text. The interpretation depends upon the background of the reader, the purpose for reading, and the context in which reading occurs. (p. 7)

Similarly, an analogy can be made to basketball players who are practicing and sharpening their ability to pass the basketball. These players are not playing the game of basketball; they are developing facilitative abilities that will transfer to an actual basketball game. There is no guarantee, however, that such facilitative factors will improve each player's ability to play the game. The same holds true for facilitative reading factors—neither the presence nor the absence of facilitative reading factors guarantees students' success or failure in learning to read. However, the likelihood of success is enhanced when teachers realize that instruction in reading should lead students to the orchestration of facilitative factors to get meaning, not the learning or enhancement of isolated skills.

Examples of Facilitative Factors   Students' level of language development, or **language competency**, is an important facilitative factor that can affect their success in reading development, although language competency is not reading. Students' intuitive understanding of **oral language features** facilitates their understanding of the relationship between spoken and written language. Students who demonstrate an understanding of **syntax** (how words are ordered in English) and **semantics** (meanings associated with words) in their oral language may be more successful in their reading development than students who lack such an understanding. However, when teachers build on and enhance this understanding of language in their reading instruction, this ability becomes a facilitative factor to better enable students to read for comprehension.

Oral language development facilitates a child's ability to read. (Pat McKay)

Vocabulary background is a facilitative factor similar to oral language or language competency. Students' vocabulary backgrounds give meaning to the words they speak, hear, write, and read. Both vocabulary background and language competency relate directly to facilitating students' understanding of concepts and to giving meaning to what they read. Although a broad vocabulary background does not guarantee reading ability, it does facilitate the ability to read. The more words students use and understand, the more likely they are to be successful in reading acquisition and development; however, isolated drill and practice on learning new vocabulary words is not teaching reading. It is when students are instructed and provided opportunities to *apply* their vocabulary knowledge to reading text, where the focus is on comprehension, that such knowledge facilitates reading development.

As we consider other facilitative reading factors, their relationship to developing reading ability becomes more apparent. Students' **experiential/ conceptual backgrounds** contribute significantly to their level of language development, breadth of vocabulary, and understanding of the thoughts communicated through language. **Visual and auditory abilities**, other facilitative factors, are the abilities to see clearly, to discriminate between shapes and parts of words, and to integrate auditory representation of letters and words with their graphic representations—all of which facilitate learning to read.

Word recognition is another factor that facilitates the ability to recognize words and apprehend meaning. Through the automatic use of such word-recognition skills as phonics, structural analysis, configuration, whole word, and context, students can get at meaning. However, as stated before, it is our belief that the identification of individual words is *not* reading; until the synthesis of words is accomplished and meaning is apprehended, reading has not occurred.

Facilitative factors enhance a reader's ability to comprehend and learn from text. Competence in or a high level of development of one or all of these factors, however, does not guarantee reading. As teachers consider factors related to the acquisition and development of reading ability, they need to determine how each of these factors aids reading comprehension. Some of the essential facilitating factors associated with reading comprehension are prior knowledge, knowledge that stories and text have a basic structure, experiential/conceptual background, orchestration of many skills, automatic word identification, and the flexible use of knowledge (Valencia & Pearson, 1987). By knowing students' strengths and weaknesses in such facilitative areas, teachers can plan instruction that builds on these. Such instruction would provide students opportunities to apply their facilitative strengths to get at meaning and would increase the possibility that reading comprehension will occur.

Functional Reading Factors

The previously discussed definition of reading focuses on getting meaning from what is read. Reading occurs only when a reader comprehends written text. The earlier discussion of facilitative factors emphasized that these factors can assist reading acquisition when they are used to acquire and build **functional reading factors**, which deal with the development and enhancement of reading comprehension. Functional reading factors pertain to actual reading, where the intent of the reader is to get meaning (comprehension) from what is read. Once it has been determined through diagnosis which facilitative and functional reading factors a student brings to the reading instruction setting, the teacher can build on these and focus on the continued development of reading for meaning. Figure 1–1 illustrates this relationship between the teacher and facilitative and functional reading factors.

The key to functional reading factors is that they involve the application of facilitative factors to get meaning. Thus, the focus is not on demon-

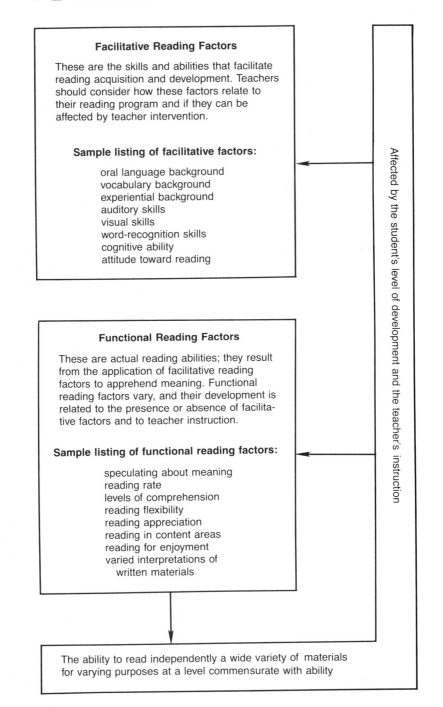

Facilitative Reading Factors

These are the skills and abilities that facilitate reading acquisition and development. Teachers should consider how these factors relate to their reading program and if they can be affected by teacher intervention.

Sample listing of facilitative factors:

      oral language background
      vocabulary background
      experiential background
      auditory skills
      visual skills
      word-recognition skills
      cognitive ability
      attitude toward reading

Functional Reading Factors

These are actual reading abilities; they result from the application of facilitative reading factors to apprehend meaning. Functional reading factors vary, and their development is related to the presence or absence of facilitative factors and to teacher instruction.

Sample listing of functional reading factors:

      speculating about meaning
      reading rate
      levels of comprehension
      reading flexibility
      reading appreciation
      reading in content areas
      reading for enjoyment
      varied interpretations of
         written materials

Affected by the student's level of development and the teacher's instruction

The ability to read independently a wide variety of materials for varying purposes at a level commensurate with ability

FIGURE 1–1 The Ability to Read as It Relates to the Teacher's Domain of Instructional Responsibilities

strating mastery of isolated reading skills, but on applying such skills in order to comprehend. Some examples of functional reading factors are the ability to vary reading interpretations of written materials, speculation about meaning, flexible meaning, reading for enjoyment, and reading in content areas (Wixson, Peters, Weber, & Roeber, 1987). The key feature that defines these as functional reading factors is that comprehension is the major component. For example, through the orchestration and application of facilitative reading factors, students can read a selection for a specific purpose. They could read in order to speculate about the author's purpose for writing a story, to identify the main ideas in a story, or for enjoyment. But whatever the reason for reading, it is based on the assumption that comprehending is the primary focus.

None of the functional reading factors is independent of the others, nor are they independent of the facilitative factors. Depth of comprehension is dependent not only on the purposes for reading, but is also limited by such facilitative factors as oral language background, experiential/conceptual background, and word-recognition skills. Students who read a selection to speculate about the author's purpose must be able to automatically apply word-recognition skills, to "read between the lines" or infer, and to make predictions to comprehend the text (Sheridan, 1981). The absence of one of these facilitative factors could interfere with the development of functional reading and, as a result, meaning would be lost.

The facilitative reading factors that students bring to reading situations, coupled with those that the teacher introduces or enhances, lead to the growth or functional reading factors. Instruction that takes into account students' capabilities in the facilitative areas can enhance students' capabilities in functional reading. Functional reading factors lead to independent reading at a level equal to students' abilities. As the teacher's instruction focuses on both of these areas, each student's ability to read for meaning should continue to develop.

IMPLICATIONS FOR DIAGNOSIS AND REMEDIATION/CORRECTION OF READING ABILITY

As noted earlier, many facilitative factors have been shown to aid reading ability. However, it is impossible to list a specific set of factors that are unquestionably related to reading development of all children. The importance of facilitative reading factors to the enhancement of reading comprehension relates to two major considerations. First, the level of development in these factors is important only to the degree to which they contribute to the development of functional reading. Isolated drill and practice of the facilitative skills will not lead to functional reading because there is no opportunity to apply them when comprehension of meaning is the purpose. Second, many facilitative reading factors fall outside the domain of teachers' influences and competencies.

Both of these considerations are important for diagnosing and improving the reading ability of students experiencing reading problems. For example, most beginning reading programs emphasize auditory and visual discrimination. Students' levels of development frequently are assessed with standardized readiness tests and informal measures, and the results should be used in making instructional decisions (Durkin, 1987). Students who have weaknesses may be given instruction by the classroom or reading resource teacher to strengthen these facilitative skills. Such instruction is important because these skills facilitate word identification which, in turn, can lead to comprehension. However, when students are not instructed in how to apply these skills to comprehend meaning, the skills become an end in themselves rather than a means of acquiring functional reading ability. Reading instruction should provide students with numerous opportunities to acquire all of the elements necessary for constructing meaning (facilitative factors) and have as its ultimate goal making students aware that reading is always involved with comprehension (Anderson, Hiebert, Scott, & Wilkinson, 1985).

Each student's facilitative and functional reading strengths and weaknesses will vary. Thus, classroom and resource teachers should analyze a student's reading strengths and weaknesses in facilitative reading skills to determine what course of instruction to follow to develop functional reading ability. What students bring to the reading tasks determines their probability of success. In addition, there are varying levels of development *among* students. Teachers should strive to accommodate individual needs and should utilize each student's particular strengths as they work toward correcting and remediating areas of weakness.

PURPOSES SERVED BY THE ABILITY TO READ

In a school setting the ability to read serves three major purposes. First, instruction in developmental reading builds on the application and development of existing reading ability; second, the ability to read is an important learning tool in content areas; and third, reading is a means of personal enjoyment.

These purposes are not independent of each other or applicable solely to the classroom. For example, instructional purposes in reading are introduced, extended, and reinforced in the content areas where reading is an important learning tool. Recreational reading requires students to apply skills learned in reading instruction. In recreational reading students may also employ their reading ability as a learning tool to pursue areas of special interests. Outside of the classroom, the ability to read continues to serve these three purposes. Children or adults who encounter difficult reading material apply their existing reading ability and, in a sense, instruct themselves when they ask others for help, consult a dictionary, or struggle through the material. Readers who use a book to learn how to refinish furniture or how to repair a bicycle are employing their reading abilities as a learning tool. Also, individuals who read for enjoyment are realizing one of the purposes served by the ability to read.

Developmental Reading Instruction

Developmental reading instruction is the phase of the reading program, designed for all students at all levels, that is "a systematic guided series of steps, procedures or actions intended to result in learning or in the reaching of a desired goal by students" (Harris & Hodges, 1981, p. 157). In this phase of a reading program students' reading is usually based on externally established purposes. For example, the teacher selects the materials to be read, establishes purposes for reading, and sets the time frame for completion. The texts used in developmental reading are most often narrative in nature. They are likely to include character stories, fables, poems, fantasy stories, and fairy tales.

The conceptualization of the ability to read presented earlier stressed the importance of considering individual students and taking into account the facilitative and functional reading capabilities that each brings to the developmental reading instruction settings. Instructional practices and reading approaches must accommodate students who have weak facilitative reading skills by taking advantage of those individuals' strengths. As students' reading abilities improve, the uses of reading need to be reinforced, extended, and modified.

The development and application of comprehension abilities make future developmental reading instruction possible. As the ability to read develops, its application provides a foundation for further reading instruction. The instructional purposes of reading are cyclical. Their goal is the continued improvement and development of functional reading.

Reading as a Learning Tool

The ability to read serves the purpose of enabling students to read informational materials. Reading is used as a learning tool in other content areas such as science, social studies, and mathematics. A major instructional focus of teaching students to apply their reading skills in the content areas is to enable them to achieve content-area learning objectives (Harker, 1981). Reading skills for use in the content areas can be taught during the developmental reading period as well as during the time devoted to teaching each particular subject. Content-area texts, however, are more expository than narrative and should explain information specific to the content area.

Every content area deals with a unique configuration and application of reading skills. Each has its own vocabulary, requires different thinking strategies, and varies in organization. The relationship between facilitative and functional reading factors plays an important role in the use of reading as a learning tool. Students' vocabulary backgrounds can be enhanced in a developmental reading instructional setting, but may need to be expanded for use as a learning tool. For many students, however, reading in content-area textbooks is a real problem.

> Not uncommonly, up to 50 percent of the students in an upper-grade class cannot read their textbooks. This is not to suggest that these students cannot read; on the contrary, most are quite literate. Literacy, however, does not guarantee success with all types of reading assignments. Because a student can read some materials successfully does not ensure that he or she is proficient enough to learn effectively from a content area textbook. (Estes & Vaughan, 1985, pp. 9–10)

Students' growth in functional reading as a learning tool depends on what they bring to the reading task. What students bring depends on their facilitative and functional reading factor skills and development. Ensuring that the ability to read becomes a learning tool requires teachers to focus on individual students' reading abilities in relation to the demands of the learning task. If a student's reading ability does not match the learning task, then the task should be modified as instruction is provided to improve the student's ability.

Reading in the content areas requires students to apply their functional reading abilities with greater precision than does reading story-type materials. For such application students must be able to use efficiently the facilitative reading factors most appropriate to the content areas in which they are reading. The learning demands that the teacher places on students influence their success in using reading as a learning tool. These demands must relate to the students' competencies in facilitative reading abilities that can enhance their reading comprehension in the content areas. Background knowledge, purposes for reading, vocabulary familiarity, and conceptual awareness are types of facilitative factors that have a major influence on readers' development of meaning in content-area textbooks (Estes & Vaughan, 1985; Tierney & Pearson, 1981). Once students begin to make progress in their use of reading as a learning tool, their acquired skills and abilities can serve an instructional purpose. This progress allows teachers to provide a reading instruction environment aimed at continued development of students' abilities to use reading as a learning tool. As noted in *Becoming a Nation of Readers* (Anderson et al., 1985), "Teachers must instruct students in strategies for extracting and organizing critical information from text" (p. 71).

Reading for Personal Enjoyment

The ability to read serves a third purpose—reading for personal enjoyment. This purpose is related to the previously discussed instructional and learning purposes. Because a student who reads for personal enjoyment applies both facilitative and functional reading abilities, these reading skills are further developed and future reading instructions can build on this development. Students who frequently engage in recreational reading are getting more practice in the whole act of reading and such practice leads to an increase in their automaticity of word-identification skills (Anderson, 1984). In fact, recreational reading can reinforce the use of reading as a learning tool as students pursue specific areas of reading interests (e.g., reading about fossils, how to repair a bicycle, Indians, care and feeding of horses, etc.).

There is an important difference, however, in teacher roles for these different purposes. Instructional and learning purposes involve improving students' reading abilities and are generally under the direct supervision of the teacher. Encouraging students to read for personal enjoyment places the teacher in the role of facilitator rather than director. This role is no less important, but it is considerably different. Features of a reading program that encourage independent reading by students include making books readily available to students, guiding students in selecting books to read, and making time available to students for independent reading (Becker & Gersten, 1982).

Developing positive recreational reading attitudes and interests is the teacher's primary responsibility in encouraging students to read for enjoyment. Although a child's attitudes and interests are often determined largely by the home environment, they are not irreversible. Attitudes and interests can be changed by new experiences. Careful planning can involve students in many reading activities that will contribute to the development of positive attitudes and interests.

Recreational reading should not be viewed as something for students to do only when time allows—it should be an integral part of the total reading program. Overemphasis on skill development can affect a student's view of reading. Reading for enjoyment allows students to apply acquired reading skills. A better understanding of the purposes that the ability to read serves may emerge from recreational reading. A student who views reading as only the development of facilitative reading factors may never fully understand that these skills and abilities are a means toward understanding and enjoying what is read.

It is best to plan for and capitalize on classroom opportunities to develop positive attitudes and interest in reading. Occurrences within the classroom that can negatively affect students' attitudes and interests in reading should be avoided. Overemphasis of reading skills and abilities that students have already mastered can cause them to dislike reading. Attitude toward reading is an important facilitative reading factor that affects students' acquisition of functional reading ability. This point is best made by Strickler and Eller (1980):

> Anyone who has heard the statement made by a child that he "hates reading" cannot help wondering whether the child is referring to the instruction he

receives in school, or to the process of learning, discovering, and experiencing through the medium of print. In most cases he is probably referring to the former and has, unfortunately, been provided with very little assistance in truly discovering the latter. (p. 381)

IMPLICATIONS FOR DIAGNOSIS AND REMEDIATION

Reading diagnosis and remediation procedures differ for all three purposes of reading. In reading instruction, diagnosis and remediation focus on the student's ability to apply facilitative reading factors in comprehending the materials used in developmental reading instruction. Diagnostic findings help teachers to better determine what the student brings to the instructional tasks of reading. After determining a student's strengths and weaknesses, the teacher uses the information to build an instructional program that accommodates the individual needs.

Reading for learning in the content areas requires different skills and abilities than does reading in story-type materials. Thus, diagnostic procedures appropriate for one may not be appropriate for the other. Strong reading skills and abilities in a reading instructional setting do not guarantee successful use of reading as a learning tool. Students who cannot use their reading abilities as a learning tool have a reading difficulty. Those who have limited ability in using reading to learn need special help from the classroom or reading resource teacher. Each student's needs are determined from individual diagnostic findings for that student. Facilitative factors, such as vocabulary, experiential background, and word-recognition skills, must be extended as they relate to content-area reading. Additional meanings for words are necessary in content areas because students often do not know the meanings that fit various situations. Experiential background often needs to be extended to ensure comprehension of the intended meaning. Teachers may need to emphasize the use of context clues, structural analysis, and language structure in order to help students figure out the many new words they are likely to encounter.

Diagnosis of students' abilities to use reading as a learning tool focuses on facilitative factors as they pertain directly to content-area reading. In fact, content-area reading materials should be used to evaluate a student's ability to use reading as a learning tool. Corrective or remedial reading instruction is then based on the diagnostic findings. Content-area reading materials should also be used for instruction.

No test is needed to uncover a student's attitude toward and interest in recreational reading. Students who dislike reading are identified easily; the difficulty is in finding a method to involve the student in actively reading for enjoyment. Reluctance to read for pleasure may result from a reading difficulty. Not knowing the majority of words in stories of interest or not being familiar with the author's language does little to interest students in recreational reading.

□ SUMMARY

Reading has been defined as comprehending and learning from written materials. Facilitative reading factors facilitate the ability to read but by themselves are not reading. Functional reading factors are actual reading abilities, and their level of development depends on the facilitative factors that a student brings to a reading situation and the instruction offered by the teacher. Teachers must analyze facilitative factors and determine if those factors are in the domain of their influence and responsibility. The areas over which the teacher has an influence should be strengthened through instructional practices.

The purposes that reading serves in a school setting include instructional purposes, recreational purposes, and learning-tool purposes.

Instructional purposes are found in a reading instructional setting. As students progress in reading ability, subsequent instruction builds on this reading growth. Students who have reading problems cannot be expected to progress in reading ability if reading instruction does not build on their strengths. Such students need corrective or remedial instruction to improve their reading skills so that future instruction can build on their ability to read.

The use of reading as a tool for learning focuses on reading in the content area. Skills used in developmental reading often differ from those used in content-area reading. If students' reading abilities are not sufficient for the content-area learning tasks, then the task should be modified and reading instruction should be provided to improve students' abilities to use reading as a learning tool. The ability to read also serves the purpose of recreational reading. Reading for enjoyment is an important part of the reading program because it allows students to apply their reading skills in actual reading situations and fosters a positive attitude toward reading. Although attitudes toward reading are often a result of home environment, teachers have a responsibility to foster interest in reading.

□ IN-TEXT ASSIGNMENTS

LIBRARY ACTIVITY

Look at the teacher's edition of a basal series for primary-level reading instruction and one for intermediate-level reading instruction. Analyze each instructional component (review and introduction of vocabulary, purposes for reading, questions, etc.) and classify them as either focusing on facilitative reading variables or functional reading variables. Upon completion of your review of each teacher's edition, compare and contrast the focus of the primary and intermediate levels. Questions to guide your analyses could focus on concerns such as: Does reading appear to be defined as comprehension? Is there a balance between the emphasis given to facilitative and functional reading variables? Are recommendations given to assist the teacher in illustrating for the students how to apply their facilitative skills in actual reading situations? Does it appear that teaching suggestions build on students' existing capabilities? Once you have completed your analyses, share this information with your classmates and determine if there appear to be common strengths and weaknesses across different basal reader series.

FIELD-BASED ACTIVITY

Visit an elementary classroom and observe the teacher during reading instruction. During your classroom visit evaluate the teacher's emphasis on facilitative and functional reading variables. Some questions to guide your observation might be the following: What facilitative reading factors does the teacher emphasize? Is the teacher attempting to force all the students to develop the same strengths in facilitative areas or emphasizing individual strengths and weaknesses? Does the teacher instruct the students on how to use facilitative factors to comprehend what they read? Does comprehension of written materials appear to be the focus of reading instruction? Does it appear that the teacher is building on students' strengths?

SHARING AND BRAINSTORMING

Reflect on your own elementary school reading experiences regarding reading for enjoyment. Share with your classmates your experiences related to the number of books in your classrooms, your opportunities to read for enjoyment, your favorite books, whether or not your teacher read aloud to the class, your reactions to stories read aloud by the teacher, the quality of the school library, how your teachers used the school library, and so forth.

DISCUSS AND DEBATE

Either discuss as a class or divide into two groups and debate the following: (1) In most primary grade classrooms, less than 10 percent of any given school day is devoted to silent reading. (2) Both parents and teachers should establish as a major priority increasing the amount of time children spend in reading books. If you wish to debate these issues, one group could try to provide reasons to support these facts and another group argue their point for why changes must occur.

☐ *REFERENCES*

Anderson, L. (1984). The environment of instruction: The function of seatwork in a commercially developed curriculum. In G. G. Duffy, L. R. Roehler, and J. Mason (Eds.), *Comprehension instruction: Perspectives and suggestions* (pp. 93–103). New York: Longman.

Anderson, R. C., Hiebert, E. H., Scott, J. A., & Wilkinson, I. (1985). *Becoming a nation of readers: The report of the commission on reading.* Washington, DC: The National Institute of Education.

Becker, W. C. & Gersten, R. (1982). A follow-up of follow-through: The later effects of the direct instruction model on children in fifth and sixth grades. *American Educational Research Journal, 19,* 75–92.

Brandt, A. (1981). Do we care if Johnny can read? In F. Schultz (Ed.), *Education 81/82* (pp. 4–11). Guilford, CT: Dushkin.

Durkin, D. (1987). Testing in the kindergarten. *The Reading Teacher, 40,* 766–771.

Estes, T. H. & Vaughan, J. L., Jr. (1985). *Reading and learning in the content classroom: Diagnostic and instructional strategies.* Boston: Allyn & Bacon.

Harker, W. J. (1981). Does content area reading teach content area learning? *Reading Horizons, 22,* 25–28.

Harris, T. L. & Hodges, R. E. (Eds.). (1981). *A dictionary of reading and related terms.* Newark, DE: International Reading Association.

Sheridan, E. M. (1981). Theories of reading and implications for teachers. *Reading Horizons, 22,* 66–71.

Strang, R. (1968). How successful readers learn: A global view. In R. Staiger and O. Anderson (Eds.), *Reading: A Human Right and a Human Problem* (pp. 15–22). Newark, DE: International Reading Association.

Strickler, D. & Eller, W. (1980). Reading attitudes and interest. In P. Lamb and R. Arnold (Eds.), *Teaching reading: Foundations and instructional strategies* (pp. 375–406). Belmont, CA: Wadsworth.

Tierney, R. J. & Pearson, P. D. (1981). *Learning to learn from text: A framework for improving classroom practice.* Reading Education Report No. 30, Center for the Study of Reading, University of Illinois at Urbana-Champaign.

Valencia, S. & Pearson, P. D. (1987). Reading assessment: Time for a change. *The Reading Teacher, 40,* 726–733.

Wittrock, M. C. (1987). Process oriented measures of comprehension. *The Reading Teacher, 40,* 734–737.

Wixson, K. K., Peters, C. W., Weber, E. E., & Roeber, E. D. (1987). New directions in statewide reading assessment. *The Reading Teacher, 40,* 749–755.

2

Characteristics of Effective Reading Instruction

□ OVERVIEW

There is more empirical evidence concerning the psychology of reading and methodological approaches to reading instruction, diagnosis, and remediation than there is for any other area of the curriculum. Nevertheless, major studies of teacher effectiveness claim that the teacher is a primary factor in determining whether students will learn to read successfully (Rupley, Wise, & Logan, 1986). The 1970s and 1980s saw numerous inquiries (Hoffman, 1986) focused on identifying both the teacher characteristics that make such a difference and the relationship that exists between teacher performance and student reading achievement. These investigations have confirmed the importance of effective instruction to both the affective and cognitive growth of students. This chapter places the information on teacher effectiveness in reading instruction into a meaningful framework for the diagnostic-remedial teacher.

After reading this chapter, the teacher should be able to

□ summarize research on teacher effectiveness as it relates to reading instruction.
□ identify specific teacher characteristics that could lead to better instruction in particular teaching situations.
□ critically evaluate motivational strategies in relationship to students' attention to task.
□ discuss the role of the teacher in "motivating" students to read.

□ incorporate motivation techniques into corrective and remedial reading instruction.

THE TEACHER VARIABLE

The statement "It's the teacher who is the single most significant factor in determining whether children will be successful or not in learning to read" is a popular pronouncement repeated by educators. In the early 1960s in an evaluation of three grouping procedures for teaching reading, Ramsey (1962) concluded:

> The thing that the study probably illustrates most clearly is that the influence of the teacher is greater than that of a particular method, a certain variety of materials, or a specific plan of organization. Given a good teacher other factors in teaching reading tend to pale to insignificance. (p. 151)

Almost a decade later, in a major study sponsored by the President's Commission on School Finance, the Rand Corporation assessed the current state of knowledge regarding the determinants of educational effectiveness (Averch et al., 1971). Perhaps the commission's most revealing conclusion was that research has yet to find anything that consistently and unambiguously makes a difference in student achievement. The entire research area of teacher effectiveness was included in the evaluation. The report indicated that there is considerable evidence that nonschool factors may be more important in determining educational outcomes than school factors. In another study, Coleman and his associates (1966) found that little of the variance in student achievement could be assigned to the schools themselves. They concluded that socioeconomic background of the student was the most important factor connected with school success and student achievement.

The relationship between nonschool factors and student achievement is significant, yet studies of this nature have been attacked on theoretical and methodological grounds. In addition, research done prior to the mid-1970s overlooked some factors relating to teacher characteristics that might have had an effect on student achievement. Indeed, a reversal of earlier findings on the effects of teacher and school on student achievement has been verified by a multitude of investigations conducted since 1975 (Hoffman, 1986). These studies have confirmed that the quality of the teacher and of the school *do* make a difference on student learning. The following section presents selected reviews of teacher effectiveness findings.

Research Findings

In a synthesis of the findings on teacher effectiveness in reading, Blair (1984) concluded that the effective teacher of reading is characterized by exhibiting the following traits:

□ Provides adequate instructional time to teach reading and ensures students are engaged in learning.
□ Diagnoses students' strengths and weaknesses and teaches to students' needs.
□ Teaches basic reading skills using the direct-instruction method.
□ Provides independent practice of targeted reading skills to ensure transfer of skills to actual reading situations.
□ Uses predominantly group instruction to increase student time-on-task.
□ Believes his or her teaching will make a difference and expects students to be successful.
□ Manages the classroom efficiently to minimize wasted time.

Time The amount of time allocated for teaching reading and how that time is actually used partly determine student achievement (Fisher et al., 1978 and Anderson, Evertson, & Brophy, 1987). Time scheduled for daily reading instruction is sometimes called **allocated or allotted time.** Adequate time must be allocated for reading instruction. This time affords teachers the opportunity to teach and affords students the opportunity to learn the content. This "opportunity to learn" is a very important variable in education. Obviously, if students are not given sufficient time to learn or are not exposed to important topics, it is unreasonable to expect them to learn. While teachers have little control over the amount of time allocated for reading instruction, they do have control over whether or not the total instructional time is used for reading and if reading skills are indeed covered or taught during the reading period. Surprisingly, in the Beginning Teacher Evaluation Study (BTES), Fisher and others (1978) reported vast differences in the amount of allocated time given to teaching reading. For example, in fifth-grade reading instruction the researcher discovered that the amount of allocated time averaged from 60 to 140 minutes per day. Likewise, Durkin (1978–1979) reported considerable variation in the time allotted to instruction on reading comprehension.

Of more importance, teachers have direct control over exactly *how* allocated time is used in their classrooms. This aspect—how teachers use the time given for instruction—has been shown to be a strong indicator of student achievement in reading. Classrooms in which students have been involved in learning for a high percentage of time have yielded better-than-average gains on reading achievement tests. Central to this involvement is ensuring that students know the purpose of each reading activity.

The amount of time students spend actually working productively on the task at hand is sometimes called **time-on-task or academic engaged time.** Studies on teacher education have indicated it is much easier to maintain student time-on-task if the teacher is directing the learning. Fisher, Marliave, and Filby (1979) extended the concept of time-on-task to include student success rate. Students should not only be on-task, but should be completing their work with a high rate of success (i.e., at least

80 percent correct in answering the teacher's questions and in working independently) (Anderson, Hiebert, Scott, & Wilkinson, 1985). This concept, referred to as **academic learning time** (ALT), is "the amount of time a student spends engaged in an academic task he/she performs with high success" (Fisher, Marliave, & Filby, 1979, p. 52). The three factors of allocated time, student engagement, and student success rate compose academic learning time. All three factors have been shown to contribute to increased student achievement. Collectively, academic learning time occurs when a student is given the time or opportunity to learn, is actively engaged with the task at hand, and is experiencing success with the task. Classrooms exhibiting more academic learning time or student time-on-task than other classrooms produce higher reading achievement scores.

It is important to underscore that this concern for a task-oriented, closely supervised utilization of instructional time is related to basic skill mastery in reading. Most of the research on teacher effectiveness in reading has centered on achievement of measurable skills on standardized tests; the whole area of critical and creative reading abilities have rarely been the topic of studies in this area. Recent research on critical thinking suggests that a lesser concern for time-on-task and more time devoted to student exploration are necessary for developing critical and creative reading abilities.

Diagnosis Reading teachers have long believed in the importance of diagnosis to delivering effective instruction, and research on teaching has verified this belief (Heilman, Blair, & Rupley, 1986). Diagnosis in reading means a student's current level of performance is assessed (i.e., his or her instructional level) and specific strengths and weaknesses are determined. Using this information, effective teachers are able to teach students those skills and abilities on their own instructional levels which will advance their reading abilities. While the benefits of teaching students at a level equal to their abilities seems to be automatic, misplacement of students at a level too difficult is a common occurrence in our schools. It is admirable to hold high expectations for students (more will be discussed on this topic later in the chapter), but these expectations should be based on reasonable diagnostic data. Expecting a student on a second-grade instructional level to be successful in a fifth-grade-level reader will potentially cause several problems (i.e., student failure, low self-esteem, embarrassment in front of peers, and so forth).

The importance of diagnosis is further advanced when viewed as an integral component of academic learning time. In fact, without an accurate diagnosis of a student's reading ability, high ALT is virtually impossible. ALT is dependent upon students being on-task and making few errors. For this to occur, students must be placed on an instructional level—that level which is not too difficult or too easy—for the reading of any text, and placed on an independent level—an easier level—for practice activities. For this match to be made, teachers must diagnose their students' current level of performance both before and during instruction.

The notion of diagnosis is not only important for initial placement of students; it is crucial to formal and informal diagnosis of students' reading abilities throughout the year. Students vary in a multitude of ways, including learning rate. As students grow in their abilities, it is necessary to make adjustments in the reading program. If such adjustments are not made, student progress may be seriously impeded. Thus, the quality of instructional time is directly dependent upon the diagnostic process.

Direct Instruction   Research on the effective teaching of basic skills in reading overwhelmingly supports the use of the direct-instruction method (Rosenshine & Stevens, 1984). As one might suspect after discussing the importance of student time-on-task, the direct-instruction method promotes more student involvement in reading and thus better usage of time. At the heart of this approach to teaching is directly explaining a reading skill in a step-by-step manner with a great deal of teacher-supervised practice. Summarizing teacher practices that lead to higher student achievement, McDonald (1976) stated:

> There is a theme in these "promising teacher practices" if a classroom organizational structure or a teaching performance provides for direct instruction by the teacher, learning will be improved. The critical problem is not whether a teacher teaches in a group; it is whether such teaching provides direct instruction to pupils. When a particular teaching practice is found to be ineffective, it should be examined to find out what is missing from the process of direct instruction. (p. 14)

Agreeing with McDonald, Rosenshine and Stevens (1986) concluded that effective teaching is characterized by the pattern of direct instruction. According to these authors, direct instruction has an academic focus and is teacher-directed in nature. It has several other salient characteristics: making goals clear to students, reviewing past learning, presenting new material in small steps, providing sufficient teacher-supervised practice with a high student success rate, monitoring student performance by asking several questions, providing feedback with corrections, providing independent exercise, and reviewing the lesson's goals.

Summarizing the research studies on direct instruction, Rosenshine and Stevens present the direct-instruction method as comprising six functions (see figure 2–1). It is important to reiterate that this approach has been shown to be effective with respect to direct, explicit, or structured learnings (i.e., the word-recognition skills in the areas of phonics, structural analysis, vocabulary, and context; literal and some inferential comprehension skills; and study skills such as reference, library, graphs, tables, and maps). These basic reading skills are usually assessed on standardized reading achievement tests and state mandated criterion-referenced tests. While the development of higher level reading skills has

1. Daily Review and Checking Homework
   Checking homework (routine for students to check each other's papers)
   Reteaching when necessary
   Reviewing relevant past learning (may include questioning)
   Review prerequisite skills (if applicable)
2. Presentation
   Provide short statement of objectives
   Provide overview and structuring
   Proceed in small steps but at a rapid pace
   Intersperse questions within the demonstration to check for understanding
   Highlight main points
   Provide sufficient illustrations and concrete examples
   Provide demonstrations and models
   When necessary, give detailed and redundant instructions and examples
3. Guided Practice
   Initial student practice takes place with teacher guidance
   High frequency of questions and overt student practice (from teacher and/or materials)
   Questions are directly relevant to the new content or skill
   Teacher checks for understanding (CFU) by evaluating student responses
   During CFU teacher gives additional explanation, process feedback, or repeats explanation— where necessary
   All students have a chance to respond and receive feedback; teacher insures that all students participate
   Prompts are provided during guided practice (where appropriate)
   Initial student practice is sufficient so that students can work independently
   Guided practice continues until students are firm
   Guided practice is continued (usually) until a success rate of 80% is achieved
4. Correctives and Feedback
   Quick, firm, and correct responses can be followed by another question or short acknowledgement of correctness (i.e., "That's right")

FIGURE 2–1 Instructional Functions

(From "Teaching Functions" by B. Rosenshine and R. Stevens, in Handbook of Research on Teaching *[pp. 377– 391] edited by M. C. Wittrock, 1986, New York: Macmillan. Copyright 1986 by the American Educational Research Association. Reprinted by permission.)*

not been the subject of many teacher effectiveness studies, evidence is beginning to emerge that indicates a form of direct instruction (with somewhat less teacher control and monitoring) is conducive to fostering critical (indirect, inquiry implicit, or unstructured) reading skills (Paris, Cross, & Lipson, 1984, and Raphael & Pearson, 1985).

Independent Practice Although technically a part of the direct-instruction method, the provision of a multitude of interesting and varied practice activities in promoting reading development demands special consideration. It is one matter to successfully complete a workbook page or unit test on a particular reading skill, but it is quite another to be able to

Hesitant correct answers might be followed by process feedback (i.e., "Yes, Linda, that's right because . . .")
Student errors indicate a need for more practice
Monitor students for systematic errors
Try to obtain a substantive response to each question
Corrections can include sustaining feedback (i.e., simplifying the questions, giving clues), explaining, reviewing steps, giving process feedback, or reteaching the last steps
Try to elicit an improved response when the first one is incorrect
Guided practice and corrections continue until the teacher feels that the group can meet the objectives of the lesson
Praise should be used in moderation, and specific praise is more effective than general praise
5. Independent Practice (Seatwork)
   Sufficient practice
   Practice is directly relevant to skills/content taught
   Practice to overlearning
   Practice until responses are firm, quick, and automatic
   Ninety-five percent correct rate during independent practice
   Students alerted that seatwork will be checked
   Student held accountable for seatwork
   Actively supervise students, when possible
6. Weekly and Monthly Reviews
   Systematic review of previously learned material
   Include review in homework
   Frequent tests
   Reteaching of materials missed in tests

Note: With older, more mature learners, or learners with more knowledge of the subject, the following adjustments can be made: (1) the size of the step in presentation can be larger (more material is presented at one time), (2) there can be less time spent on teacher-guided practice, and (3) the amount of overt practice can be decreased, replacing it with covert rehearsal, restating, and reviewing.

FIGURE 2–1 *Continued*

independently use one's reading skills in various reading situations. This ability to ensure that students have both mastered what they have been taught and have transferred reading skills to actual reading situations can be handled by teachers. Samuels (1981) hypothesizes that students complete the stages of utilization and automaticity during the independent practice stage. The **stage of utilization** is that time in which students are trying out the skill and are expending much of their energy in practicing the skill. The **stage of automaticity** is reached after much practice, and is characterized by students not consciously thinking about the skill while they are performing it. At this stage, students can focus more on comprehending the author's message. **Mastery** implies that a student knows the skill at the automatic level (i.e., application of the skill without thinking about it). Once reading skills are mastered, students need interesting and varied practice activities to transfer these reading skills to other reading situations.

This practice is achieved through the proper use of instructional materials. Materials selected for use should be on the proper level, match the student's preferred learning style, capitalize on the student's interests, be self-corrective in nature as much as possible, and relate directly to the skill being addressed (Rupley & Blair, 1988). Directly in line with research on academic learning time, this independent practice should be on a student's instructional-independent level to ensure a high success rate, and this practice should be monitored by the teacher as much as possible. It is foolhardy to have students practicing skills independently and completing only a low percentage of the practice items successfully. The higher the success rate (without having the practice items too easy) the greater the student involvement and the probability that skills will transfer to other reading situations. Also, this independent practice needs to be monitored as much as possible to ensure that an appropriate success rate is maintained and to allow adjustments to be more readily made to meet the changing needs of students.

Research has shown that grouping students together for instruction has a positive affect on student achievement. (Phillips Photo Illustrators)

In summary, the provision of interesting, meaningful, and varied independent practice activities is crucial to the diagnostic-remedial process. Following a diagnosis of student strengths and weaknesses and a proper sequence of direct instruction, carefully thought-out independent practice is necessary to complete the teaching-learning cycle. Effective teachers plan independent activities to ensure that their students can apply new skills in other reading situations.

Group Instruction For years, teacher education students at the undergraduate and graduate levels were told that the optimum type of grouping for reading instruction was one-on-one, one teacher for one student. Research on teaching has not supported this age-old belief; surprisingly, group (large and small) instruction was a positive factor in increased student achievement in learning basic reading skills (MacDonald, 1976).

Grouping students for instruction allows for a larger percentage of academic learning time because students are more likely to be engaged or working at the task at hand when the teacher is directing the learning. In an "individualized program," the teacher can hardly see each student daily for a significant portion of time, but grouping students allows for using the maximum amount of time allocated for actual instruction and increases total time-on-task for students. In addition, grouping students is an organizational plan conducive to using the highly successful direct instruction.

The concept of ability grouping, however, has been called into question by several researchers (Allington, 1984; Hiebert, 1983). A major finding of this research is that the low-ability group typically receives considerably less instruction due to slower paced lessons. In addition, students in these low groups have less opportunity to read orally or silently and thus have fewer opportunities to apply words in context (Anderson, et al., 1985). Such problems can be minimized by not always forming groups on the basis of ability. Interest, research, partner, cooperative, skill, and whole-class groups are alternatives to always using ability grouping in reading instruction.

The research findings on grouping have direct implications for the diagnostic-remedial process. After the teacher collects diagnostic data, interprets and synthesizes the information, and prescribes instruction based on student needs, it is advantageous to form groups, for example, skill groups based on particular reading skill or whole-group instruction. Instructing students in groups helps keep students attentive to the task at hand and helps promote learning. Teachers of reading can have confidence in using groups because grouping capitalizes on a teacher's most precious commodity—instructional time with one's students. Whether in a small or a large group, more students are able to be given the opportunity to learn targeted skills through a teacher's step-by-step direct explanation. This discussion is not meant to imply that one-on-one instruction is not to be used. On the contrary, effective teachers work individually with students during each day for a variety of reasons. What the research is saying, however, is that if mastery of basic reading skills is one's goal, then a large percentage of time should be spent in working with students in groups.

Teacher Expectations Much of the research on the effective teacher of reading has centered on the use of instructional time and instructional behaviors in the direct-instruction approach. However, results of this research have also reemphasized the importance of teacher expectations for students' learning and of teachers' own perceptions of their importance in student learning. Effective teachers believe their students can and will learn to read and they communicate this expectation to them (Brophy & Everston, 1976). In addition, effective teachers have faith that their own efforts will pay off in increased student achievement. While holding high expectations for students is necessary, it is also important that these expectations are reasonable and are based on diagnostic data, not socioeconomic level or physical characteristics. Thus, it is perfectly acceptable to have different expectations; in fact, it would be harmful *not* to hold different expectations for different students. The negative effects of having low expectations for students and manifesting these expectations directly to them, however, have been well-documented. Among the results of communicating low expectations to students are that these children receive more criticism; are seated farther from the teacher; interact less frequently with teachers; are smiled at less often; and receive less wait-time, praise, eye contact, and practice time (Brophy, 1983).

Guarding against communicating low expectations for certain students and thus perpetuating a self-fulfilling prophecy should be a major concern for teachers of reading. Reading teachers can eliminate an undesirable bias by basing their instruction on what students need to know as evidenced by formal and informal measures, by providing sound instruction based on these diagnoses, by communicating goals and positive expectations to students, and by making sure that all students participate in the learning process. These instructional bases imply that teachers will monitor their instructional effectiveness and modify their teaching decisions based on their ongoing diagnosis of student needs as well as their own instruction.

Brophy (1981) has studied the whole area of praise and its effects on student achievement. Contrary to opinions that there are no negative side effects of praising students, his findings indicated that ineffective praise was global and not specific to the task at hand. Effective praise, on the other hand, is task-oriented and focuses directly on student performance.

Classroom Management In summarizing studies on teacher effectiveness, Berliner (1981) concluded that "elementary school teachers who find ways to put students into contact with the academic curriculum and keep them in contact with that curriculum, while maintaining a convivial classroom atmosphere, are successful in promoting reading achievement" (p. 218). This statement highlights a teacher's managerial as well as instructional techniques. Knowing the reading process and the techniques and strategies required to teach reading are certainly prerequisites of effective reading instruction; however, knowledge of effective managerial techniques is equally important to ensure a high percentage of student time-on-task. Studies have shown clearly that teachers of high-achieving students are good classroom managers (Rosenshine & Berliner, 1978 and Otto, Wolf, & Eldridge, 1984). Instructional techniques and managerial techniques go hand in hand in promoting student learning.

In light of the importance of a teacher's managerial ability and of the use of small- and large-group instruction to increase direct-instruction time, teachers should apply specific managerial skills in their reading class to ensure student learning. Aside from common-sense recommendations passed down through the years, the research literature on classroom management has just begun to reveal some specific guidelines. Weber (1977) defined classroom management as "that set of activities by which the teacher promotes appropriate student behavior and eliminates inappropriate student behavior, develops good interpersonal relationships and a positive socioemotional climate in the classroom, and establishes and maintains an effective and productive classroom organization" (p. 286).

The most meaningful work in this area has been completed by Kounin (1970), Brophy and Putnam (1978), and Emmer, Everston, and Anderson (1980). According to these authors, many of the characteristics of a good classroom manager deal with preparation. Successful teachers devote the necessary time and energy at the beginning of the school year to get to know their students, to set instructional goals, and to make sure students know what is expected of them. Also in the earlier part of the year, successful teachers plan their lessons in advance, breaking them down into small, concise parts for presentation to students, and use large group activities to facilitate the monitoring of student progress (Emmer, Everston, & Anderson, 1980).

Kounin (1970) identified the following group-management techniques that successful teachers use to increase and sustain student engagement:

Withitness: Ability to know what is going on in the classroom at all times and to communicate this knowledge to students

Overlappingness: Ability to carry out or attend to more than one thing at a time in the classroom

Smoothness: Ability to change from one activity to another without undue disruption or wasting time

Group alerting: Ability to keep the attention of students in a group during a lesson

Momentum: Ability to provide well-paced instruction, avoiding slowdowns

Logan and Rupley (1982) reviewed Kounin's and others' work related to effective large-group management techniques. They recommended that classroom reading teachers attempt to minimize disruptive transistions during reading instruction and to incorporate the use of activity file folders, help signs, positioning of students, and behavior-monitoring techniques to enhance on-task reading behaviors. These strategies, described in the following list, also enable teachers to attend to individual reading needs.

Classroom transitions: To minimize disruptions teachers can make sure that reading materials are prepared in advance and organized and distributed before the reading class begins. Also, to ensure smooth transitions from one activity to another, teachers should have already explained to their students how the class will run and what the daily schedule will be.

Activity file folder: Using individual student activity folders during the reading lesson can minimize disruptive transitions and can aid in keeping students on-task. These file folders may contain work to be completed by students on a daily basis. The teacher should collect, evaluate, and return the folders to the students daily. The benefits of this procedure are many—it promotes close monitoring of student work, provides daily feedback to students, and eliminates time wasted on the distribution and collection of daily work.

Help signs: The help signs are small signs that students may display on their desks to signal for teacher assistance (Berliner, 1978). Students should be told to use the signs when they cannot solve a problem themselves. The use of such a device cuts down on the amount of time wasted when a problem arises as well as on student interruption of a lesson when the teacher is busy elsewhere in the room.

Positioning of students in the classroom: By making sure all students are positioned so that they can be seen by the teacher at all times, teachers can more easily monitor student engagement in learning activities. When this common-sense factor is overlooked, it often leads to decreased student time-on-task and frequent interruptions by both teacher and students.

Behavior-monitoring techniques: One way to help minimize disruptive behavior is to gather helpful information about disruptive students. Such information can be gathered by teachers asking themselves questions such as:

□ When does a student usually exhibit disruptive behavior?
□ Is there a pattern to such occurrences?
□ To what extent does an interruption cause other students to become off-task?

These reflections can help teachers understand the problem and take steps to correct it.

Summary of Research Findings Related to Teacher Effectiveness

One frequently hears that professional educators do not know what factors make an effective teacher of reading; yet, a great number of studies in the 1970s and 1980s have identified the same characteristics of effective instruction. It must be acknowledged that these studies concentrated on teaching basic reading skills. Also, the application of these characteristics depends upon the specific grade level taught, student characteristics, the nature of the task being addressed, and teachers' individual styles. Still, it

Research related to teacher effectiveness has delineated the important role of the teacher in delivering instruction. (Kevin Fitzsimons/Merrill)

A teacher effective in basic-skill instruction

depends on

student opportunity to learn

affected by

quality of instruction

Teacher knowledge and preparation for teaching
Promotion of academic learning time
Diagnosis of student strengths and weaknesses
Use of direct-instruction method
Use of small- and large-group instruction
High expectations for student learning
High expectations for teacher success
Efficient classroom organization and management
Proper use of materials during independent practice to ensure transfer
Self-monitoring attitude to continually adjust instruction
Maintain fast-paced lessons in relation to students' ability and the difficulty of materials

FIGURE 2–2 Summary of Research Findings

must be said that some characteristics of the effective reading teacher are known. If teachers want their students to achieve in reading, they should concentrate their efforts on the characteristics stated in figure 2–2.

MOTIVATION AND READING

Motivating students to read is important in all phases of instruction in elementary schools. A major concern of most elementary teachers is how to motivate students to learn the basic reading skills, to apply these skills in their reading, and to read for personal enjoyment. The success of corrective and remedial reading instruction is determined in large part by the teacher's skill in motivating students—lack of motivation is frequently identified as a major contributor to students' reading difficulties.

Ideally, all children should be intrinsically motivated to read. **Intrinsic motivation** occurs when the engagement in reading tasks brings satisfaction by itself. Children who are intrinsically motivated realize that reading is an important skill needed to be an informed and productive member of society as well as a means for personal enjoyment. In the real world of school, however, many elementary students find learning to read frustrating, anxiety-producing, and something to avoid. Students who do not find satisfaction in reading and in reading instruction (intrinsic motivation) often need extrinsic rewards to sustain their behavior. **Extrinsic motivation** is the control of desired behaviors by the use of rewards such as stars, smiling faces, and teacher praise—all of which students value. Properly monitored and controlled, extrinsic motivation can often lead to intrinsic motivation.

A cursory review of the literature reveals a general tendency to attempt to motivate students to read by suggesting several activities to make learning more fun or interesting; however, the usefulness of such an approach should be questioned. Although it is important to identify activities that are interesting to students, what some students find interesting others do not. Furthermore, increasing students' interest is not sufficient by itself to sustain motivation if students are not capable of successfully engaging in the learning task.

If interest alone is not the solution, how do we motivate students to read? There is no simple answer to this question. Despite many theories of human motivation, there have been few attempts to apply these theories to the teaching of reading. Research and the expert opinion of learning psychologists do, nevertheless, offer a foundation on which educators can begin to build.

Motivational Functions of Teachers

The following four achievement-oriented behavior concepts—arousal, expectancy, incentive, and discipline—can be viewed as functions that teachers can use to guide their motivational strategy (DeCecco & Crawford, 1974).

Arousal **Arousal** refers to an individual's state of activity in relation to internal and external stimuli. This state of activity can range from a low level (boredom) to a high level (emotional excitement). Within this range the intermediate level of arousal is most appropriate for classroom instruction since either extreme of arousal can interfere with learning and may not provide a student with a motive to learn. Hence, reading instruction should generally be neither too boring nor too exciting. An important function of the reading teacher is to engage the students in reading instruction at the appropriate arousal level.

Expectancy Teachers can further motivate their students by telling them what they will be able to accomplish after completing a reading activity. Setting purposes for student learning is the function of the teacher called **expectancy**. Telling students why they are learning a reading skill, what they will be able to do with the skill, and how they can apply the skill to actual learning situations serves to motivate. Specific ways to increase the relevancy of reading tasks and enhance student motivation include setting and illustrating specific purposes for learning; illustrating the application of reading skills in meaningful comprehension tasks; building instruction in small, highly related instructional steps; and making students aware of their progress in reading for meaning (Heilman, Blair, & Rupley, 1986).

Teachers who know the entering behaviors of students can ensure that all students will experience some success in reading. The adage "Nothing breeds success like success" could read "Nothing breeds motivation like success." Students who continually meet with failure in a reading program may tend to lower their levels of achievement expectancy or try to minimize their probability of failure by not engaging in reading activities at all. Knowing the level of reading development for each individual allows the teacher to set learning goals that ensure that all students will experience some success in learning to read. If students are to aspire to achieve the goals set by the teacher, these goals must be set in accordance with the entering abilities of students. Only under these circumstances can there be any certainty that such goals are realistic and that students will be continually motivated to achieve. Ensuring success in reading can also be examined by monitoring the student success rate during supervised or independent activities. As shown in the BTES study, a high success rate (80 to 90 percent) on practice items is necessary to promote quality time or academic learning time. By allowing students to self-monitor their performance during reading lessons with regard to success rate and then using the results to adjust instruction accordingly, teachers are raising the probability of success and are thus motivating their students.

Incentive (Reinforcement) Establishing instructional goals and setting purposes for students facilitates motivation. As students are motivated in reading instruction, their reading behavior must be reinforced. **Reinforcement**, or strengthening a desired response in specific situations, has long been recognized as a means for encouraging and extending students' reading efforts—the incentive function of the teacher centers on providing student reinforcement. Educators tend to view reinforcement as appropriate only if it *rewards* student behavior. A promise of a material gain such as a token, a free-choice activity, a party, candy, and so forth are considered motivating rewards for students. Rewards, however, do not have to be of a material nature. Teachers can reinforce reading efforts by using verbal or written praise, by discussing performance in an instructional setting, and by providing feedback on student performance. In addition to teacher-controlled reinforcement, students can monitor their own reading behavior to note their progress.

The incentive function of the teacher is extremely important. To ensure that students are motivated to read, their appropriate reading behavior must be reinforced and extended. The degree to which various reinforcers reward reading behavior is related to the experiences of individual students. Teachers must—and this cannot be stated strongly enough—know their students not only in terms of reading skill development but also in terms of their overall experiences. Students who have not learned to associate certain stimuli, such as praise or record keeping, with specific behaviors will not view these stimuli as rewarding. Knowing how individual students react to specific reinforcing stimuli enables the teacher to identify the rewards that are most likely to motivate appropriate reading behavior.

Discipline   The disciplinary function of the teacher and its relation to motivation may seem obvious—student behavior in the classroom must be appropriate to the learning situation. **Discipline**, in terms of reading, is the directing and monitoring of the student behavior in reading situations. This function focuses not only on disorderly behavior but also on subtle behavior patterns that interfere with learning. Improper behaviors, such as talking instead of listening or walking around the room rather than reading, are easily identified. Less obvious student behaviors are more difficult to identify but are equally important if students are to achieve instructional objectives. Marginal listening, feigning reading, and hurriedly completing assignments without thinking are examples of student behaviors that interfere with achieving instructional objectives. Teachers can use discipline to regulate student behaviors to minimize inappropriate behavior and thus facilitate motivation.

Motivation Guidelines and Evaluation

Many teachers are aware of the need to support students' reading behaviors extrinsically and they recognize the practical value of extrinsic motivation. Extrinsic approaches combine motivation with the desired learning outcomes and focus on reading behaviors as they relate to motivational strategies that enhance students' engagement in learning.

The necessity for extrinsic motivation to sustain students' attention to instructional reading tasks is apparent in many beginning reading activities, since these beginning tasks often lack immediate relevance for students. Many students find little satisfaction in associating letters with the sounds they represent or in learning to recognize words on sight. Teachers can enhance students' engagement and satisfaction in such beginning reading tasks by using extrinsic motivation.

If a student does not demonstrate the desired learning behavior, then teachers should evaluate the motivation schemes, the instruction, or both. Based on this evaluation, appropriate adjustments can be made to accommodate students' needs and to enhance their participation in learning (Rupley, Ash, & Blair, 1982).

Evaluating the effects of motivation strategies on students' reading appears to be the key to successfully motivating learning. Regardless of whether one leans toward an intrinsic or an extrinsic approach to motivating classroom reading, the teacher must find out how the approach is influencing learning. Following are some basic criteria for evaluating motivation as it relates to reading instruction:

□ Students who are instrinsically motivated to complete a reading activity because they find it satisfying and meaningful will probably not show increased engagement if an extrinsic reward is employed. In many cases the introduction of an extrinsic reward will decrease students' motivation in a task they find satisfying. The use of extrinsic rewards might best be delayed as long as students' satisfaction persists; however, if their desire to engage in the task begins to decrease, teachers may wish to introduce some extrinsic rewards to restimulate students' motivation.

□ Participation in relatively unsatisfying reading tasks may be enhanced by extrinsic motivation strategies, but extrinsic rewards will probably lose their effectiveness in sustaining students' engagement over time. That is, students may begin to associate less value with a reward as it is used over some length of time. Teachers must pay close attention to how extrinsic motivators are sustaining desired behaviors in order to make necessary adjustments to elicit students' active participation.

□ It appears that the *lack* of appropriate extrinsic motivators is more damaging to developing intrinsic motivation than is their use (Bates, 1979). If extrinsic rewards are removed or changed substantially, student motivation can be negatively affected. In terms of classroom reading instruction this suggests that for tasks where students already have developed some association with extrinsic rewards, lack of these rewards could negatively influence student motivation. Teachers must carefully evaluate the interaction of rewards with students' motivation in terms of specific reading tasks to ensure continued motivation.

□ Not all reading behavior is associated with extrinsic rewards. Social reward systems, such as group membership, public praise, and peer recognition can positively affect students' motivation in reading if they associate value with these social factors. Teachers can provide opportunities within their classrooms for social reward systems to function. Student response to such systems should be closely monitored to determine how these systems impact students' motivation.

□ SUMMARY

This chapter synthesized a selection of research findings related to teacher effectiveness in reading instruction. Despite the inherent difficulties of performing teacher effectiveness research and the complex nature of the teaching-learning situation, research has specified some teacher characteristics that differentiate the effective teacher of reading from the ineffective one. Researchers indicate a pattern of desirable teacher practices conducive to student growth. (Figure 2.1 summarizes those effective teaching practices.)

Motivation is a wonderful tool that teachers can use to make learning to read a marvelous and meaningful experience for each student. Criteria for making motivation a concern throughout the curriculum are outlined. These criteria support the idea that lessons and activities can be designed to motivate students by establishing what the students are to learn, helping them to understand why such learning is important, and illustrating for them how to apply what they learn in reading for meaning.

☐ IN-TEXT ASSIGNMENTS

LIBRARY ASSIGNMENT

Using your university curriculum lab or Chapter I reading resource room, select three different types of materials (textbooks, supplemental kits, games, recreational materials, or other practice materials). For each material, list its primary purpose, assumptions underlying its use, and advantages and disadvantages in its use with students experiencing difficulty in learning to read (as opposed to students performing satisfactorily or students who are gifted readers). Also, describe the teacher's role in effectively using each material.

FIELD-BASED ACTIVITY

To gain insight into the motivational characteristics of students at particular grade levels, use the following questions to interview a regular classroom teacher or Chapter I teacher in the local school system. (These questions are based on the discussion in the chapter of the motivational functions of teachers.)

☐ What are the main interests of students in your grade level?
☐ In what ways do you try to capitalize on these interests?
☐ In what ways do you try to encourage the low-achieving students to actively participate during the reading class (raising student's expectancy level of success)?
☐ In what ways do you reinforce student learning? Do you use extrinsic rewards (tokens, stars, free-choice activities, candy, and so forth)?
☐ What are some ways you minimize classroom disruptions that interfere with students working on their seatwork assignments?

SHARING AND BRAINSTORMING

Divide into small groups representing either primary (1–3) or intermediate (4–6) grade emphases. Using figure 2–1 as your guide, brainstorm as many specific ways as you can to implement in reading instruction those charac-teristics that have been identified as effective to teaching. These character-istics should serve as the basis for studying the effective teaching of corrective and remedial reading; however, these characteristics are applied differently depending on the grade level being taught. Each group should share their ideas and then as a whole group pinpoint similarities and differences.

□ REFERENCES

Allington, R. (1984). Content covered and contextual reading in reading groups. *Journals of Reading Behavior, 16,* 88–96.

Anderson, L. M., Evertson, C. M., & Brophy, J. E. (1987). An experimental study of effective teaching in first-grade reading books. In T.F. Hutchins (Ed.), *Effective classroom instruction.* (pp. 75–105). Bloomington, IN: Center on Evaluating Development, Research, Phi Delta Kappa.

Anderson, R. C., Hiebert, E. H., Scott, J. A., & Wilkinson, I. A. (1985). *Becoming a nation of readers.* Washington, DC: National Institute of Education.

Averch, H. A., et al. (1971). *How effective is schooling? A critical review and synthesis of research findings.* Santa Monica, CA: Rand.

Bates, J. A. (1979). Extrinsic reward and intrinsic motivation: A review with implications for the classroom. *Review of Educational Research, 49,* 557–576.

Berliner D. C. (1978). *Changing academic learning time: Clinical interventions in four classrooms.* Paper presented at the meeting of the American Educational Research Association, Toronto, Canada.

Berliner, D. C. (1981). Academic learning time and reading achievement. In J.T. Guthrie (Ed.), *Comprehension and teaching: Research reviews* (pp. 203–226). Newark, DE: International Reading Association.

Blair, T. R. (1984). Teacher effectiveness: The know-how to improve student learn-ing. *The Reading Teacher, 38,* 138–141.

Brophy, J. (1981). Teacher praise: A functional analysis. *Review of Educational Research, 51,* 5–32.

Brophy, J. (1983). Research on the self-fulfilling prophecy and teacher expecta-tions. *Journal of Educational Psychology, 75,* 631–661.

Brophy, J. & Putnam, J. (1978). Classroom management in the elementary grades. Research series no. 32, The Institute for Research on Teaching, Michigan State University.

Brophy, J. E. & Everston, C. M. (1976). *Learning from teachers: A developmental perspective.* Chicago: University of Chicago Press.

Coleman, J. S., et al. (1966). *Equality of educational opportunity.* Washington, DC: Government Printing Office.

DeCecco, J. & Crawford, W. (1974). *The psychology of learning and instruction* (2nd ed.). Englewood Cliffs, NJ: Prentice-Hall.

Durkin, D. (1978–1979). What classroom observation reveals about reading comprehension instruction. *Reading Research Quarterly, 14,* 481–533.

Emmer, E. T., Evertson, C. M., & Anderson, L. M. (1980). Effective classroom management at the beginning of the school year. *Elementary School Journal, 80,* 219–231.

Fisher, C. W., et al. (1978). *Teaching behaviors, academic learning time, and student achievement: Final report of phase III-B, Beginning Teacher Evaluation Study.* San Francisco: Far West Educational Laboratory for Educational Research and Development.

Fisher, C. W., Marliave, R., & Filby, N. N. (1979). Improving teaching by increasing academic learning time. *Educational Leaderships, 37,* 52–54.

Heilman, A. W., Blair, T. R., & Rupley, W. H. (1986). *Principles and practices of teaching reading.* Columbus, OH: Merrill.

Hiebert, E. H. (1983). An examination of ability grouping for reading instruction. *Reading Research Quarterly, 18* 231–255.

Hoffman, J. V. (1986). *Effective teaching of reading: Research and practice.* Newark, DE: International Reading Association.

Kounin, J. S. (1970). Discipline and group management in classrooms. New York: Holt, Rinehart & Winston.

Logan, J. & Rupley, W. H. (1982). Classroom reading practices to increase active learning during reading instruction. Unpublished manuscript, Texas A&M University.

McDonald, F. I. (1976). Beginning teacher evaluation study, Phase II Summary. Princeton, NJ: Educational Testing Service.

Otto, W., Wolf, A., & Eldridge, R. G. (1984). Managing instruction. In D.D. Pearson (Ed.), *Handbook of Reading Research,* (pp. 799–828). New York: Longman.

Paris, S., Cross, D., & Lipson, M. (1984). Informal strategies for learning: A program to improve children's reading awareness and comprehension. *Journal of Educational Psychology, 76,* 1239–1252.

Ramsey, W. Z. (1962). An evaluation of three methods of teaching sixth grade reading. In J.A. Figurel (Ed.), *Challenge and experiment in reading.* Proceedings of the International Reading Association. New York: Scholastic Magazines, 7, 151–153.

Raphael, T. E. & Pearson, D. P. (1985). Increasing students' awareness of sources of information for answering questions. *American Educational Research Journal, 22,* 217–237.

Rosenshine, B. & Berliner, D. (1978). Academic engaged time. *British Journal of Teacher Education, 4,* 3–16.

Rosenshine, B. & Stevens, R. (1984). Classroom instruction in reading. In P.D. Pearson (Ed.), *Handbook of Reading Research* (pp. 745–798). New York: Longman.

Rosenshine, B. & Stevens, R. (1986). Teaching functions. In M.C. Wittrick (Ed.), *Handbook of research on teaching* (pp. 376–391). New York: Macmillan.

Rupley, W. H., Ash, M. J., & Blair, T. R. (1982). Motivating children to actively engage in learning to read. *Reading Psychology, 3,* 143–148.

Rupley, W. H. & Blair T. R. (1988). *Teaching Reading: Diagnosis, Direct Instruction, and Practice* (2nd ed.). Columbus, OH: Merrill.

Rupley, W. H., Wise, B. S., & Logan, J. W. (1986). Research in effective teaching: An overview of its development. In J. V. Hoffman (Ed.), *Effective teaching of reading: Research and practice* (pp. 3–36). Newark, DE: International Reading Association.

Samuels, S. J. (1981). Some essentials of decoding. *Exceptional Education Quarterly, 2,* 11–15.

Weber, W. A. (1977). Classroom management. In Cooper, J. M. et al. (Ed.), *Classroom teaching skills: A handbook* (pp. 284–348). Lexington, MA: D.C. Heath.

3

Individualizing Corrective and Remedial Reading Instruction

☐ OVERVIEW

Anyone who teaches reading should realize the importance of matching its instruction to the needs of the student. Individualization of reading instruction does not imply that a teacher works with only one student at a time, but that the reading instruction offered to an individual student is what is needed by that student.

Individualization of students' reading is important in all phases of the reading program—developmental, corrective, and remedial. **Corrective reading instruction** is "supplemental, selective instruction for minor reading difficulties, often within a regular classroom by the regular teacher, an aide, or peer tutor" (Harris & Hodges, 1981, p. 77). **Remedial reading instruction** is "any specialized reading instruction adjusted to the needs of a student who does not perform satisfactorily with regular reading instruction" (Harris & Hodges, 1981, p. 276). This type of instruction demands careful attention to developing programs based on students' needs. Remedial reading instruction is intensive and more specialized than corrective instruction. Students who have remedial reading problems read considerably below their expected level. Furthermore, remedial reading is most often taught by a reading resource teacher in a special classroom, clinic, or school.

Diagnostic and remedial procedures employed by any teacher of reading must take into account the unique characteristics of the student's learning situation. Instruction should take into account that reading is an

41

interactive process involving the reader, the text, and the conditions under which reading is to take place (Lipson & Wixson, 1986). This chapter serves as the *core of this book* and encourages the development of an analytical and reflective approach to individualizing corrective and remedial reading instruction.

After reading this chapter the teacher should be able to

□ understand that reading is an interactive process and that reading problems vary in relation to the demands of learning to read.

□ develop an individualized corrective or remedial reading program.

□ evaluate how well he or she has individualized a corrective or remedial reading program.

□ understand the importance of developing a cooperative effort on the part of both the classroom and the reading resource teacher to help students improve in reading.

WHAT IS INDIVIDUALIZED INSTRUCTION?

Individualized reading instruction ensures that the subject matter taught to students is appropriate to their needs. This instruction is more a process than a product. It is a process that a teacher uses to match reading instruction to student needs by determining students' strengths and weaknesses, identifying what instruction is most appropriate to build on students' strengths, specifying how much instruction should be offered at any given time, and determining how the instruction should be structured. This process provides the most appropriate instruction for students' reading needs and ensures that the product—student learning—is the most likely result.

Individualized reading instruction can be whole-class, large-group, small-group, or individual. As previously mentioned, the number of students with whom the teacher is working does not determine individualization; if the instruction offered is what is needed in terms of students' strengths and weaknesses, then it is individualized. To illustrate how individualized instruction is a function of the text, the task, and the context of reading, let us use the following example: A teacher discovers that seven students are experiencing difficulties in determining the main idea in the stories they read. Such difficulties, however, may vary in relation to what the students read and what their purposes are for reading. Based on this understanding, the teacher finds that two students have a limited concept of the meaning of *main idea*, two students lack the experiential background for the content of the stories they read, and three students are not able to integrate the story content of stories that are several paragraphs long. What these findings imply is that these students *have* the abilities to comprehend main ideas, but need appropriate instruction that builds on their strengths to further develop their abilities.

Based on the students' identified strengths and weaknesses in identifying the main idea, the teacher forms three groups: (1) students who do not fully understand what is meant by the main idea concept, (2) students who have difficulty relating to the content of stories they are asked to read, and (3) students who exhibit problems in integrating story content for stories of any length. The implication for developing individualized instruction for these groups is that if the task, text, and demands of learning are matched to the needs of these students, then reading development will occur. The teacher's responsibility is to now identify instruction that will enable the students to use their existing knowledge and skills (reading strengths) as building blocks (Samuels, 1984) for further reading development in the area of identifying main ideas. Essentially, the teacher is identifying conditions in which this particular ability will occur and is then continuing to offer quality reading instruction that builds on students' growth.

Individualized instruction should be based on students' capabilities, the resources available for instruction, teacher competencies, and the **appropriate learning product**, that is, what students are to learn and the behavior indicative of that learning. As students' reading develops, they can move to advanced groups, be regrouped in other areas of reading instruction, or be given individual instruction.

The previous example illustrates how individualized instruction is a process of matching instruction to the needs of the students rather than attempting to mold the students to the instruction. Students who learn more rapidly than others are allowed to move into different instructional settings that extend their learning. Students who exhibit difficulty in one instructional setting may be regrouped to allow for modifications in teaching that better meet their needs. As emphasized earlier, a major understanding that teachers must have about their individualized instruction is that reading ability varies in relation to the text, the reader, the task, and the conditions (Wixson & Lipson, 1986); therefore, students' reading strengths and weaknesses, *not* the content of materials, determines what and how students are taught.

A MODEL FOR CONSIDERING INSTRUCTIONAL VARIABLES

The four instructional variables to consider when developing an individualized instructional reading program are learner style, task conditions, resource attributes, and teacher style (see Figure 3–1). Both classroom and resource teachers should focus on each of these four variables as they plan their individualized instruction. They must decide what to teach, when to teach, how to teach, and how much to teach. Such decisions must be related to the teacher's instructional competencies, learners' needs, materials available, time, and group size. Logically analyzing these variables

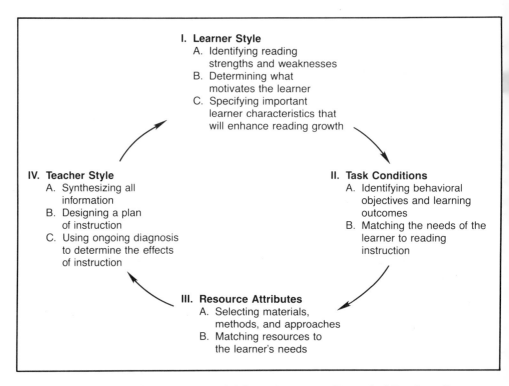

FIGURE 3–1   Individualization Model for a Corrective/Remedial Reading Program

allows the teacher to match the external conditions of a learning task (learning environment) with the internal conditions of the learner (product) of instruction).

Applying the Model to Individualized Reading Instruction

The instructional variables model can be used to individualize all phases of a total reading program; however, the focus here is on the corrective and remedial phases alone. The first area of concern to a teacher is **learner style**, which focuses on what students bring to the reading-instruction setting. Thus, information about learner style should deal specifically with the students—not with instruction. Data collected by the teacher from various sources (see chapter 5) are analyzed to identify students' reading strengths and weaknesses, attitudes, and motivational characteristics. The types of diagnostic procedures and the interpretations employed will depend on the teacher's competencies and the assessment strategies available. Assessment and interpretation, however, should concentrate on the individual learner's strengths as well as weaknesses.

As mentioned, teachers must also assess motivational characteristics and attitudes. Information about what motivates students and about their attitudes toward reading provides the teacher with a basis for planning instruction that will keep students actively engaged in learning activities. Diagnosis in these areas can help to answer a number of important questions: Would students learn better individually or in groups? Are particular students easy or difficult to keep engaged in learning activities? Can students be paired with other students so that both students can learn from each other? The answers to these and similar questions have a strong impact on the selection of a method of instruction and on the strategies used for teaching.

After collecting and analyzing information about the learner, teachers must look at this information in relation to the task conditions. **Task conditions** are the products of instruction that specify what the learner should be able to do as a result of corrective or remedial reading instruction. The most well-known example of task conditions are behavioral objectives. Analyzing information about learner style helps teachers to relate the needs of the learner to the learning task. This information helps to identify appropriate learning outcomes that meet the students' needs. Thus, rather than fitting students to the curriculum, students are taught the reading skills and abilities they need as individuals.

Resource attributes are the materials, methods, and approaches available to the teacher for corrective or remedial reading instruction. It is important to determine not only what is available, but also how well the resources meet the student's reading strengths and motivation/attitude characteristics. Answers to the following questions will enable the teacher to choose the best resources to individualize corrective or remedial reading instruction.

1. Is the intent of the instruction to *introduce, reinforce,* or *diagnose* a reading skill or ability?
2. Should the instructional organization be small-group, large-group, or individual?
3. Does the student learn best when instruction emphasizes relationships or differences?
4. Will the instructional resources influence the student's attitude and attention so as to motivate participation in instruction?
5. Does the student learn best with concrete or vicarious examples (e.g., films, filmstrips, pictures, audiotapes, videotapes, etc.)? Should these examples be a combination of visual and auditory?
6. Are there instructional limitations, such as cost, time, equipment, or space?
7. Are the instructional resources ones with which the teacher is familiar and competent?

Answers to these questions allow teachers to select and design resource materials that best suit the reading needs of their students. When resources are related to both the students and the learning tasks, those resources are more likely to enhance reading improvement.

The last instructional variable in an individualized program involves the synthesis of information from the other three variables. **Teacher style** involves designing direct-instruction lessons that integrate the information gained from diagnosis, task conditions, and resources. As lessons are developed and taught, they incorporate the teacher's instruction methods and chosen strategies. Ongoing diagnosis helps the teacher to determine if instruction is appropriate and effective in terms of students' reading development. The teacher then makes changes when the analysis of diagnostic information suggests the instruction effect is lessening.

Learner needs will change as reading growth becomes apparent. Materials used for instruction may lose their effectiveness if students become bored or confused. Learning tasks that are too difficult will need to be modified. For individualized instruction to operate effectively, all three instructional variables (learner style, task conditions, and resource attributes) must be continuously analyzed in relation to the teacher style variable, and then necessary changes must be made promptly.

EXAMPLE OF AN INDIVIDUALIZED READING INSTRUCTION PROGRAM

The following example shows how a teacher might develop an individualized corrective reading program. This program illustrates each of the four variables discussed earlier.

Learner Style

Reading strengths as identified through the use of diagnostic tests, observation, informal diagnostic instruments, and teacher-made assessment instruments include the following:

□ Is able to recognize and recall specific story facts
□ Appears to be able to recall and recognize stated character traits found in narrative (story-type) text (This needs to be further substantiated through observation.)
□ Exhibits well-developed word-recognition and word-analysis abilities
□ Possesses a well-developed sight vocabulary

Reading weaknesses as identified through use of the previously mentioned diagnostic procedures are as follows:

□ Has difficulty making inferences and understanding relationships among story events
□ Sometimes overrelies on word analysis to identify words without giving attention to whether or not the words make sense in context
□ Has problems with the concept of inferences in narrative text

The following **motivational characteristics and attitudes** were identified through observation of class performance:

☐ Responds well to sincere, task-specific verbal and written praise
☐ Works best when specific instruction goals are presented and are illustrated with familiar examples
☐ Enjoys art activities
☐ Is interested in sports and athletes
☐ Works well with peers in group instructional settings
☐ Is not easily frustrated when instructional tasks are well-structured and teacher supervised

Task Conditions

Behavioral objectives would include the following:

☐ Given stories with familiar content, the student will infer whether or not given events would most likely occur.
☐ Presented with familiar pictures of scenic and sporting events, the student will develop the concept of what it means to make inferences.
☐ Given a familiar story which lacks an ending, the student will infer additional story events or a logical ending.

Resource Attributes

Instructional materials, approaches, and formats include the following:

☐ Pictures, filmstrips, and student-made drawings for building background and setting purposes for reading
☐ Easy-to-read sports stories and biographies
☐ Language-experience stories
☐ Highly structured instruction that builds on previous experiential background and specifies a purpose for learning

Teacher Style

As noted earlier, the category of teacher style encompasses the synthesis of learner information, resulting in a set of direct-instructional plans (see the following example of a direct-instruction lesson based on teacher-style information) that match students' needs with appropriate instruction.

The following instructional procedures and strategies can be identified:

☐ The teacher will select sports stories that have topics with which students are familiar.
☐ Instruction will build on students' existing background and will illustrate with examples how students' present knowledge relates directly to what they will be learning.
☐ The teacher will state and illustrate with familiar examples the purpose of the instruction, that is, why students are learning this ability, what they are to do, and how they will apply the learning in both small-group and individual activities. He or she will also structure these learning activities in a step-by-step fashion to maximize students' attention.

□ Instruction will build on students' ability to identify story facts by relating this ability to making inferences about other story events.

□ Instruction will include sports-related visuals, familiar pictorial scenes, sports stories, language-experience stories, and content-familiar stories.

□ Classes will utilize instructional procedures that closely relate to motivation and attitude concerns, such as setting and illustrating purposes for learning, and building on students' past learning.

□ The teacher will complete several practice examples with students before they independently complete instructional activities.

EXAMPLE OF A TEACHER-DIRECTED INSTRUCTIONAL LESSON BASED ON THE INDIVIDUALIZED INSTRUCTIONAL PLAN

The following is one example of a direct-instruction lesson that illustrates how a teacher might utilize information from the previously discussed individualized instructional plan. (This format is adapted from *Teaching Reading: Diagnosis, Direct-Instruction, and Practice* [2nd ed.] by William H. Rupley and Timothy R. Blair, Merrill, 1988.)

□ AREA OF NEEDED READING INSTRUCTION

Development of the concept of inferences in relation to written text.

□ TASK CONDITION (INTENDED LEARNING OUTCOME)

Given a set of pictures taken from sports magazines, students will infer the content of a part of each picture that the teacher has covered with a blank sheet of paper.

Given a series of pictures that represent a story event, students will dictate different endings by making inferences from their interpretations of the pictures.

□ PAST LEARNING RELATED TO STUDENTS' LEARNER STYLE

Students should understand the information represented in the pictures (i.e., it should relate to their interests and experiential backgrounds).

Students should have well-developed word-recognition capabilities in relation to the text used for instruction. (Students will generate their own text through the use of the language-experience approach.)

Students learn best when instruction is structured and is able to build on their past learning.

□ BUILDING BACKGROUND

This step in the direct-instruction lesson is intended to help students understand what they will be learning and uses information obtained from learner style (reading strengths and motivation), resources (materials appropriate for the area of instruction and within students' background of experiences), and teacher style (how to structure the lesson).

Display several sports pictures to students and call on them to tell what sport they think each picture represents. As students respond, write their responses on the chalkboard. After all students have responded, point out to them that they used their background knowledge about each sport and the information represented in the pictures to make good guesses about what sports were represented in the pictures. Explain to students that their good guesses are called *inferences*, and they make inferences often—use written examples of this concept, such as "Sweat was dripping from his head," "Joe hid his report card," and "'Many presents were on the table" to illustrate how students can also make inferences when they read. Call on individual students to make inferences for each written phrase. As students respond, write their responses on the chalkboard and discuss with them how they arrived at their conclusions.

Explain to students, by referring back to their responses for the pictures and short phrases, that they already know a lot about inferences; in this lesson they will be learning more about what inferences are and how they can use inferences in their reading. Explain to them that after working as a group on inferences, they will practice making inferences with familiar pictures. Show them an example of the pictures and very briefly discuss what they will be asked to do after the lesson. (This will help establish a purpose for learning.)

☐ TEACHER-DIRECTED INSTRUCTION

This part of the lesson is concerned with the actual teaching. Because the diagnostic data indicate that students learn best when instruction is structured, the teacher will proceed in a highly structured manner, use much verbal praise, and use sporting event pictures to motivate students' attention to task.

Again demonstrate how inferences can be made about pictures or events by showing students a large picture representing a sporting event while covering a major feature of the picture.

For example, if the picture shows a baseball game, cover the pitcher and batter with a piece of paper and ask the students to infer what features are missing. Ask students to explain their answers.

Provide a second example using the same procedure. For example, show a picture of a basketball game. Cover the section of the picture that contains the ball and one or two players. Ask students again to make inferences about the missing sections. Discuss students' responses with them.

Remove the papers covering the picture sections and direct students to make up a story for one of the pictures. (Students can either select the picture they want to tell a story about or the teacher can select one of the pictures.) As students respond to the picture, write their responses on the chalkboard. Discuss with them how the story fits together to make sense. After students have finished telling their story, instruct them to think about which parts of the story are inferences and which parts are facts. (If they are describing actual events depicted in the picture these can be identified as facts. Information in their story that is not solely based on pictorial information can be discussed as inferences.)

□ INDEPENDENT STUDENT PRACTICE

This portion of the direct-instruction lesson should be based on diagnostic data and should closely match the direct-instruction phase of the lesson. It is essential that students be extremely successful with independent practice to ensure that they will engage in the activity and that it will reinforce their learning.

Provide each student with several cartoon-like series of pictures that each tell a story, but for which there is no given ending. Direct them to look at each frame of the first story and then infer what the last picture frame could be. Do one example with the group to determine that each student understands the task. After each student has had an opportunity to discuss his or her inferences about the ending for the cartoon series of pictures, direct them to take their cartoon strips back to their seats and draw an ending frame for each series. Tell students that they will discuss their inferences for each cartoon series tomorrow and that the inferences will be used to better understand how they use inferences as they read.

□ ONGOING DIAGNOSIS

Ongoing diagnosis of students' progress is an important feature of individualized reading-instruction programs. For the previous lesson, teacher evaluation of students' drawings for the cartoon series and of the group experience story they compose will provide valuable information about the effectiveness of this lesson. If students' performances suggest that they are experiencing difficulty, then the task needs to be modified to better meet their needs.

The previous example of a direct-instruction lesson illustrated how information from the individualized instructional plan is used to provide corrective or remedial reading instruction. The reading strengths of the students were used to enhance their reading development, and many features of the lesson were built on information about students' motivational factors. The resources used for instruction were based on students' interests, and the instructional strategies selected by the teacher were those most appropriate for this group.

TEACHERS' COOPERATIVE RESPONSIBILITIES

Students who are experiencing reading problems may receive special help from the classroom teacher or from both the classroom and the reading resource teacher. When instruction is provided by the classroom teacher, it is usually referred to as **corrective reading instruction**. When instruction is offered by a specially trained reading resource teacher, it is often defined as **remedial reading instruction**. Before deciding whether a student would benefit more from classroom instruction only or from both classroom and reading resource instruction, several questions should be addressed:

☐ How will the student respond to being taken from the classroom to go to a special teacher?
☐ Can the classroom teacher provide the student with the special help and attention needed?
☐ Does the classroom teacher have the resources best suited to the student's needs?
☐ Does the classroom teacher have the skills necessary to promote reading improvement, given the needs of the student?
☐ Will the classroom and reading resource teacher communicate often with each other about the instructional features most appropriate to support each other's reading instruction?

As discussed earlier, these questions relate to the development of an individualized reading program. The importance of such questions is apparent in most public-school reading programs today. In the majority of public schools, the reading resource teacher works with a large number of students for approximately 45 to 60 minutes daily. As a result of this large number of students, there is the possibility that communication between a given student's classroom teacher and his or her reading resource teacher will not occur as frequently as it should. Therefore, it is extremely important for both the classroom teacher and the reading resource teacher to talk with each other about a given student's progress and the instructional features that are successful in improving that student's reading development. The following example illustrates the importance of both teachers working cooperatively to enhance a student's reading growth.

The Importance of Cooperation

Marie was a first grader who was considerably behind her peers in reading development. She did not know letter names, had limited writing abilities for her level of development, was reluctant to participate in language-experience activities, showed little progress in her development of word-recognition strategies, knew very few high-frequency sight words, and was difficult to keep on task.

Marie's teacher had the results of the school-administered reading-assessment test and also had examples of Marie's classroom work to substantiate her concerns about the student's lack of progress in reading. Marie's teacher met with the reading resource teacher to discuss her findings and to seek recommendations for developing a more effective instructional program for Marie. They cooperatively reviewed the information regarding Marie's reading development and the reading resource teacher felt that additional information about Marie's reading would be beneficial in identifying her reading strengths and weaknesses.

Marie went to the reading resource teacher for 60 minutes daily for a week. During this time the reading resource teacher formally and informally gathered additional diagnostic data about Marie's reading. Although the results indicated that Marie lagged considerably behind her peers in reading development, several pieces of additional information were noted. Marie worked really well in the individual situation with the reading resource teacher. Furthermore, she was able to learn several sight words that stood for concrete objects (e.g., *dog, cat, big, little, Mother, Dad,* etc.) when the teacher used a picture to represent the word. Also, Marie was able to read short phrases that were used to label objects in the classroom, such as "This is the light switch," "Marie sits here," "This is a chair," and so forth. The reading resource teacher discovered that although Marie was reluctant to dictate stories for language-experience activities, Marie would dictate endings for stories that the teacher read to her.

More formal types of diagnostic tests revealed that Marie appeared confused about sounds represented by letters and letter names. However, by using the sight words and the phrases she knew, Marie was successful in naming letters and in recognizing sounds represented by letters in these words. With closely supervised practice, Marie was able to consistently name several letters and associate sounds represented by these letters both in isolation, in combination (*at, et, ap,* and so forth), and in her sight words.

The reading resource teacher concluded that Marie learned best in situations that were highly concrete and that built on her existing knowledge. She also responded well to highly structured teaching that progressed in small, incremental steps. Furthermore, the teacher noted that much practice and review was needed for Marie to reach a level of **automaticity** (rapidly performing the task without devoting much thinking to it), and such practice should be closely supervised. Several practice activities with teacher supervision were needed to ensure that Marie understood what she was to do in independent activities.

The reading resource teacher met with Marie's classroom teacher to review and discuss his findings. Specific instructional recommendations were discussed in terms of how they could be implemented in classroom instruction. The reading resource teacher emphasized the importance of making instruction meaningful by building on Marie's experiential background and by relating her reading to concrete experiences as much as possible. Both teachers felt that Marie would benefit from attending the reading resource class regularly. They planned to cooperatively share with each other the features of instruction each was using so they would be consistent in their teaching. In addition, it was decided that Marie's parents should be contacted and a meeting arranged to share with them their recommendations for her reading program.

The incident presented in the case study illustrates how the classroom and reading resource teachers worked together to provide the most effective instruction available. Both teachers shared their findings about Marie's reading with the intent of developing a quality reading-instruction program. The reading resource teacher used diagnostic strategies that, although available to the classroom teacher, were used on a one-to-one basis that classroom demands often make impossible for a classroom teacher. The decision for the reading resource teacher to provide instruction for Marie came about because Marie's classroom teacher realized that additional help was needed. The direct result of this cooperative effort was the development of a reading program for Marie that would ensure her reading growth.

RESPONSIBILITIES OF THE READING RESOURCE TEACHER

The reading resource teacher's responsibilities are essentially threefold. First, the resource teacher assists in the interpretation of diagnostic data gathered by the classroom teacher and makes instructional recommendations to enhance students' reading development. The reading teacher may review the classroom teacher's data on students' reading, gather additional diagnostic data through the use of both formal and informal means, and/or observe the students' reading in the classroom. Second, the reading resource teacher should provide remedial instruction in either a resource room setting, a classroom setting, or both. Third, the resource teacher should assist the classroom teacher with all phases of developmental and corrective reading programs. The reading resource teacher may recommend and help the classroom teacher to select and use diagnostic instruments and strategies, materials, or instructional strategies for the classroom.

The reading resource teacher fills an extremely important role in facilitating changes in classroom reading instruction that enhance the quality of teaching. Teachers are often enthusiastic about recommendations from

An important responsibility of the reading resource teacher is to assist the classroom teacher in meeting students' reading needs. (Andy Brunk/Merrill)

the reading resource teacher that can improve the quality of their reading instruction, but they can also be threatened by recommended changes. It is the reading resource teacher's responsibility to "get these changes into classrooms without damaging the esteem of the teachers" (Horn, 1982, p. 411). Getting teachers involved, appreciating what they are already doing, and encouraging them to continue—these attitudes guarantee that the classroom teacher's prestige is reinforced.

All of these responsibilities are equally important; overlooking any of them may jeopardize the efficiency of a school's total reading program. The ultimate goal of both the reading resource teacher and the classroom teacher is to help all students read at their highest potential. To accomplish this, both teachers must work cooperatively—the skills of each complementing the skills of the other.

☐ SUMMARY

This chapter emphasized the importance of meeting students' individual needs in corrective and remedial reading instruction. The discussion focused on individualized reading instruction in relation to the teacher and the instructional responsibilities. Briefly stated, both the classroom teacher and the reading resource teacher must strive to implement individualized corrective and remedial reading instruction.

The model of individualized reading instruction focuses on a logical analysis of the instructional variables—learner style, task conditions, resource attributes, and teacher style. Information from the individualized instructional plan is then used as the basis for developing direct-instruction lessons that meet the reading needs of the students. The model for individualizing reading instruction is a process that recognizes reading as an integrated act that involves the reader, the text, and the conditions for reading.

☐ IN-TEXT ASSIGNMENTS

FIELD-BASED ACTIVITY

Visit an elementary or reading resource teacher's classroom to observe how the teacher individualizes corrective or remedial reading instruction. Focus your observation on whether or not the teacher appears to build on students' strengths, provides purposes for learning, uses written examples, motivates students' active participation in the lesson, and employs ongoing diagnosis. Evaluate what you observe by classifying the information under learner style, task conditions, resource attributes, and teacher style.

SHARING AND BRAINSTORMING

Reread the sections of this chapter that present the examples of the individualized instructional plan and the direct-instruction lesson. Either individually or in small groups, identify features of subsequent direct-instruction lessons for the students' data presented in the individualized instructional plan. The first step could be to identify follow-up and reinforcement instruction to increase students' understanding of making inferences in reading narrative text. Carefully consider what resource attributes you would use, how to maximize students' attention to task (motivation), how to build on students' past learning and experiential backgrounds, what instructional strategies should be emphasized, and what ongoing diagnosis procedures you would use. Share your information with classmates and discuss the basic features of this follow-up lesson.

RESOURCE ACTIVITY

Invite a reading resource teacher to visit your class to discuss how to diagnose and teach students who are experiencing reading problems. Questions to guide your discussion could focus on:

☐ How are students placed in the reading resource program?
☐ What diagnostic procedures are used to identify students' reading strengths and weaknesses?
☐ What role does the reading resource teacher play in relation to classroom reading instruction?
☐ How do students react to being placed in a resource classroom?
☐ What role do students' attitudes and motivation play in their reading development?
☐ How does the resource teacher work with parents of students in the resource program?

☐ REFERENCES

Harris, T. L. & Hodges, R. E. (Eds.). (1981). *A dictionary of reading and related terms.* Newark, DE: International Reading Association.

Horn, J. L. (1982). The reading specialist as an effective change agent. *The Reading Teacher, 35,* 408–411.

Lipson, M. Y. & Wixson, K. (1986). Reading disability research: An interactionist perspective. *Review of Educational Research, 56,* 111–136.

Samuels, S. J. (1984). Resolving some theoretical and instructional conflicts in the 1980s. *Reading Research Quarterly, 19,* 390–392.

Wixson, K. K. & Lipson, M.Y. (1986). Reading (dis)abilities: An interactionist perspective. In T. E. Raphael (Ed.), *Contexts of school-based literacy* (pp. 131–148). New York: Random House.

4

Correlates of Reading Problems: Considering Causes and Symptoms

☐ OVERVIEW

There are many possible causes and interactions of causes that contribute to students' reading problems. Knowledge of these many causes can help teachers determine which students might develop reading problems; teachers can then provide reading instruction to minimize the effects of such causes on students' reading development. Many causes associated with reading problems—for example, psychological and neurological problems— are outside the domain of a teacher's direct influence. Causes such as these are not only difficult to identify, but are usually beyond the teacher's area of expertise.

A note of caution is warranted here: When considering the relationship between reading ability and other variables, remember that a strong relationship between reading ability and other variables does not mean that these variables explain reading ability. Remediating the suspected cause of a reading problem, such as visual problems or hearing impairments, does not guarantee that reading growth will automatically occur. After the potential or suspected cause is identified, the teacher must provide quality reading instruction that focuses on identifying reading conditions that will promote students' reading development.

Today's educators realize that many factors contribute to reading development; they know that reading is an interactive process that varies in terms of students' capabilities, the learning task, the text being read, and the purposes for reading. Causality cannot be assumed just because a variable or a combination of variables correlates highly with reading skills and abilities. As noted by Lipson and Wixson (1986):

> . . . we can expect readers' performance in different reading situations to vary as a function of the interaction among many factors. . . . There is no doubt that the decades of research using isolated word recognition, oral reading, comprehension questions, and free recall measures have demonstrated that there are differences in the performance of able and disabled readers. . . . Performance on these measures varies for both able *and* disabled readers as a function of the conditions of the reading situation. This calls into question any model of (dis)ability that seeks to identify only causal factors within the reader. (pp. 115–116)

Decades of reading research have failed to identify a *single* cause that explains why some students have reading problems (Samuels, 1984). Among the many possible causes and combinations of causes that receive diagnostic and instructional attention are (1) physical deficiencies, (2) language deficiencies, (3) social and emotional problems, (4) intellectual and cognitive deficiencies, and (5) educational deficiencies. Each of these factors will be explored in the following sections.

After reading this chapter, the teacher should be able to

□ identify major factors that could contribute to students' reading problems.
□ consider analytically the probability of specific deficiencies affecting students' reading development.
□ determine whether the suspected cause(s), if identifiable, can be treated and how to adjust instruction to promote students' reading growth.
□ recognize and use classroom screening procedures to pinpoint possible causes that might be contributing to students' reading problems.

PHYSICAL IMPAIRMENTS

Areas of physical impairment that could be linked to students' reading problems involve vision, hearing, neurology, and general health. Research findings support the relationship of these variables to reading achievement.

Visual Impairments

Investigations of visual impairments and their relationship to reading are numerous. Their conclusions vary considerably. Ruth Strang's explanation for the variability of research evidence, although given more than 20 years ago, is still applicable today: "Some children with certain visual defects can be successful in reading, while others in whom visual defects are barely recognized may be severely retarded in reading" (Strang, 1968, p. 18).

Lack of clear-cut support for a relationship between vision problems and reading problems presents a dilemma for both classroom teachers and reading diagnosticians. Visual impairments (1) may be the direct cause of a reading problem in some students, (2) may contribute to, but not be the direct cause of, a reading problem in other students, and (3) may be only coincidental in other students. Nevertheless, even though the relationship between visual impairments and reading difficulties is tenuous, any student having a reading problem should be screened for possible visual impairments as a first step in diagnosis.

Visual Impairments That Can Impede Reading Growth

Visual acuity. The clearness of the image transmitted to the brain

Near-point acuity. The clearness of the image at reading distance

Far-point acuity. The clearness of the image at a distance of 20 feet

Binocular vision. The use of both eyes together to see clearly without **diplopia** (seeing single objects as double); also referred to as **fusion**, which is the coordination of the separate images of the same object in the two eyes into one

Monocular vision. Vision with only one eye, which may be congenital, injury related, or self-induced

Amblyopia or suppressed vision. Monocular vision apparently caused by suppression of the image coming from the less effective eye; over time information from the less effective eye is not interpreted and the eye ceases to function. A binocular defect may result in only one of the eyes transmitting an image to the brain.

Achromatic vision. Total color blindness resulting in a complete loss of color sense; less severe color blindness may result in loss of color sense for only some colors, such as red-green. Color blindness is, 99 percent of the time, evidenced only in males.

Hyperopia or farsightedness. A lack of refracting power sufficient to focus parallel rays on the retina

Myopia or nearsightedness. The focusing of rays coming from an object beyond a certain distance in front of the retina

Astigmatism. Blurring of vision due to a defect in the curvature of the refractive surfaces of the eye; light rays form a diffuse area rather than focusing to a single point. An astigmatism may affect vertical, horizontal, or oblique vision.

Strabismus. A squint deviation of one of the eyes from a proper direction. **Absolute strabismus** occurs at all distances for the fixation point. **Relative strabismus** occurs for some and not for other distances. In **convergent strabismus** the eye or eyes cross inward in focusing on an object. In **divergent strabismus** the eye or eyes turn outward when focusing.

Normal Eye Movements During Reading Movement of the eyes along a line of print during the act of reading is said to be **saccadic**. Although it appears to the mature reader that the eyes are moving in a fluid fashion, the eyes make a number of stops to see a word or a group of words. These stops are **fixations**, and exterior muscles shift the eyes to the right for subsequent fixations. **Interfixations** occur when the eyes are moving from one fixation to the next. **Regressions** result when the eyes shift to the right and then back to the left to return to a word or words to get meaning. **Return sweep** is the diagonal sweep of the eyes at the end of a line of print to begin reading on the next line.

Symptoms of Visual Impairments It is not our intent that teachers should become classroom optometrists or ophthalmologists, nor do we encourage teachers to believe that they can accurately diagnose or treat students' visual problems. Many of the symptoms of visual problems overlap; students who have problems reading from the chalkboard, for example, may suffer from myopia, astigmatism, or both.

Some symptoms of visual problems are more overt than others and can be diagnosed through observation. Persistent symptoms that may indicate a visual defect or defects include the following:

☐ Covering one eye to read at a near point or a far point
☐ Squinting when looking at an object or reading
☐ Turning both eyes or one eye inward
☐ Holding books too close or too far away
☐ Watering or inflammation of the eyes
☐ Complaining of frequent headaches during visual tasks

Awareness of visual behavior that deviates consistently from the norm helps in the identification of students with possible visual problems; however, some symptoms are more significant than others. Referring students to an eye specialist is warranted if symptoms such as the following persist:

☐ Loses place frequently while reading
☐ Holds book too close to face
☐ Distorts facial expressions
☐ Shows rigid body postures during far-point visual tasks
☐ Moves head excessively when reading
☐ Rubs eyes frequently
☐ Avoids near-point visual tasks
☐ Assumes poor sitting posture
☐ Thrusts head forward
☐ Tenses during near-point tasks
☐ Tilts head to side (Wilson & Cleland, 1985)

Visual problems are not always exhibited in an overt fashion. Suppressed vision, for example, may be an impairment that even the reader is

Visual impairments may be the direct cause of reading problems. (Phillips Photo Illustrators)

unaware of—slight astigmatism can impede reading progress without observable symptoms being present; and far-point vision screening frequently does not screen for binocular vision defects. Because overt symptoms do not necessarily accompany visual impairments, the following informal visual screening procedures are recommended for students who exhibit reading problems.

Screening Procedures to Identify Visual Impairments Research suggests that faulty saccadic eye movement in reading is a symptom of a reading problem rather than a cause. Less capable readers have a longer fixation time span, make more regressions, and are less efficient in their return sweep than more capable readers. Screening of saccadic eye movements may help to identify possible visual impairments.

One simple procedure can be used easily by teachers. As the student reads, stand behind him or her and hold a pocket mirror at book level in front of the student. This way the eye movements can be observed. Note whether the student moves the eyes or head, if both eyes appear to focus together on a line of print, if both pupils are approximately the same size, if the eyelids flutter excessively, and if both eyes are coordinated in their movement. If the student is distracted by the placement of the mirror, the teacher may sit on the floor in front of him or her and watch for the identical symptoms.

A simple screening procedure for fusional defects can be conducted by the classroom teacher. The student should hold one end of an 18-inch piece of string at the bridge of his or her nose. The teacher should hold the other end directly in front of the student's eyes. The teacher then asks the student to tell how many strings are seen, where the strings begin, and where the strings end. The student should respond by noting a V-shaped pattern consisting of two strings—the point of the V beginning at the bridge of the nose and each side of the V ending on either side of the head. If only one string is seen, this could indicate monocular vision. If the point of the V is seen in front of the thumb at the far point of the string, this suggests divergent strabismus.

Coordinated eye movement can be screened informally by holding a pencil or penlight 12 to 18 inches in front of the student's eyes. Ask the student to follow the object with only his or her eyes as it is moved horizontally to the right and left and up and down vertically. The student should be able to focus both eyes on the object and follow it without moving the head. Eye movement should appear smooth rather than jerky.

In summary, these informal screening devices are not intended to yield an exact diagnosis of visual problems, but information from these kinds of screening procedures combined with observation and vision test results help to identify students who should be referred to an eye specialist. (See Chapter 15 for additional visual screening information.)

Hearing Impairments

As with visual impairments, the relationship between hearing impairments and reading problems is not well-defined. Hearing impairments may be the direct cause of a reading problem or they may only be a contributing factor. Students who are hearing impaired are at a disadvantage in most reading instructional settings and experience difficulty with both whole-word and code-breaking reading approaches. Students experiencing auditory problems in the high-frequency range may not be able to hear such consonant sounds as *p, s, t, b, v, c, fl, ch,* and *th* (Spache, 1963). Whole-word approaches can also cause problems if students cannot hear the pronunciation of words or if they hear distorted pronunciations.

Students with reading problems should be tested with an audiometer. This is especially true for primary-grade students since hearing loss tends to have a cumulative effect on reading problems as students progress through school. Many reading problems could possibly be prevented if all children were administered a hearing test upon entering school and were then tested at regular intervals thereafter.

Symptoms of Hearing Problems Teachers who notice signs of hearing problems can make a referral to the school nurse, a physician, or a hearing specialist. Persistent symptoms that warrant such a referral include the following:

□ Inattentiveness
□ Turning one ear in the direction of the speaker
□ Failure to follow simple oral directions
□ Facial distortions when listening
□ Consistently speaking too loudly
□ Speech difficulties
□ Cupping a hand behind an ear
□ Speaking in a monotone
□ Frequent earaches or drainage from an ear
□ Frequent rubbing of ears

Informal Screening The following whisper test is an informal screening procedure that teachers can use with students who have possible hearing problems. It is recommended that first- and second-grade teachers routinely administer this test to *all students* at the beginning of the school year. This test can be administered to an individual or to a small group.

The teacher stands four to five feet behind the students and whispers simple directions. For example, students could be directed: "Raise your right arm. Take one step forward. Raise both arms. Take three steps forward. Lower your left arm," and so forth. This procedure can be modified by having students cover first one ear and then the other with a hand while following the whispered directions. Students who hesitate or who look around to see how others are responding may have hearing problems. Students who exhibit such behaviors should be referred for further auditory screening; such a referral is necessary since the whisper test will identify only students with a possible difficulty.

Neurological Impairments

Neurological impairments can also be contributing causes of students' reading difficulties. The terms **specific reading disability, learning disability**, and **dyslexia** are often used when describing children who have neurological impairments. The term *dyslexia* has no widely accepted definition, and interpretations of it range from individuals who have "severe reading problems" to those who have a "disorder of constitutional origin manifested in a difficulty in learning to read, write, or spell, despite conventional instruction, adequate intelligence, and socio-cultural opportunity" (Texas State Board of Education, 1986, §21.924). In the *Dictionary of Reading and Related Terms* (Harris & Hodges, 1981), the difficulty in identifying an acceptable definition of dyslexia is discussed.

> Due to all the differing assumptions about the process and nature of possible reading problems, dyslexia has come to have so many incompatible connotations that it has lost any real value for educators except as a fancy word for a reading problem. Consequently, its use may create damaging cause and effect assumptions for students, family, and teachers. Thus, in referring to a specific student, it is probably better that the teacher describe the actual reading difficulties and make suggestions for teaching related to the specific difficulties, not apply a label which may create misleading assumptions by all involved. (p. 95)

The implication of this definition is that labeling a student as being dyslexic serves no real purpose in terms of providing appropriate reading instruction.

Although *dyslexia* is not clearly defined, it is still important for the teacher to be aware of the symptoms or indicators of neurological impairments or dysfunctions. As noted by Dishner and Olson (1986–87) ". . . medical evidence of neurological dysfunction as a causative factor in reading and related disorders is rarely, if ever, available. What is available to educators are symptoms or indicators of a problem" (p. 13).

Characteristics of Neurological Impairments Recent research investigations have focused on several aspects of neurological functioning (Lyon & Watson, 1981) in terms of developmental reading disorders. Conclusions from this research have led to the belief that there are numerous subtypes of neurological impairments. These subtypes and their characteristics have been described by Hynd (1986–87) and are presented in the following list. Although each type contains the word *dyslexia*, this word has a distinct meaning that is related specifically to neurological functioning.

1. Developmental surface dyslexia (phonetic reading and poor use of context)

Readers demonstrate an ability to read regular words (words that are spelled as they sound—*big, dad*) but experience difficulty or an inability to read irregular words (words that are not spelled as they sound—*was, are*). Whole-word recognition is difficult and readers have no route from visual analysis of the word to whole-word recognition. Difficulty with comprehension is evident; comprehension occurs only after decoding each word by using phonics. Text that adheres to phonic generalizations is often read better orally than silently, and these readers better comprehend text after reading it orally.

2. Developmental direct dyslexia (good word calling, poor comprehension)

Readers can recognize print by using phonics or whole-word strategies, but are deficient in linguistic analysis of words (syntactic and semantic) and comprehension. They are characterized as being fluent oral readers with poor comprehension and can read aloud much better than they can comprehend. Both nonwords and complex irregular words are identified by these readers extremely well; however, this ability to identify words is much better than the ability to use language. It appears that the lexical semantic system is bypassed.

3. Developmental phonological dyslexia (whole-word recognition, good use of context, good comprehension)

Readers have difficulty applying phonic generalization (using grapheme-phoneme correspondence) even though they can easily read familiar words (especially nouns). Some of these individuals also have problems with multimorphemic words, often adding, dropping, or substituting prefixes and suffixes. Difficulties with function words (*is*, *are*, *those*, *and*, etc.) are also noted. Problems with semantics (meanings) are not evident; a reader with this problem has an average oral vocabulary. Errors made when reading orally are either words that are visually similar to the text word or that are derivational forms of the text word (e.g., *running* for *run*, *happier* for *happy*).

4. Developmental deep dyslexia (concrete word recognition, good use of context)

This neurological problem is characterized by difficulty with grapheme-phoneme correspondence (letter-sound relationships) similar to phonological dyslexia. However, it differs from phonological dyslexia because derivational errors (derived words) are more common and word substitutions that are semantically correct do occur. Concrete nouns are often read better than are adjectives, verbs, or abstract nouns. Errors that are visually similar to the text word (mitten-mutton) are noted and there is a reliance by the reader on imaginability, concreteness, and word frequency. There is also a context affect in that readers can often use context clues as an aid to word identification.

The primary symptoms distinguishing phonological and deep dyslexia are "(1) the occurrence of semantic paralexias (e.g., seeing 'mutton' and saying 'sheep'); and (2) the concrete/abstract dimension with deep dyslexia. It has been argued that readers with this problem, however, are reading by a completely different system" (Hynd, 1986–87, p. 20).

Students who exhibit symptoms associated with the previously noted reading problems may not have neurological impairments. All children can, at points in their reading development, exhibit some of these behaviors. It is when such behaviors persist over a period of time, setting a child apart from his or her peers, that the possibility of a neurological impairment should be considered and referral to a physician recommended.

Students with neurological impairments have a learning deficiency rather than a developmental learning problem; therefore, *reteaching* the skills they appear to lack will not usually result in improved reading. The reading needs of students who have neurological impairments should be based on their strengths in reading. They will need instruction that provides them with successful reading experiences to enhance their motivation and attitudes toward reading. Also, in many instances these students will benefit from specialized methods of teaching reading, such as VAKT (Visual, Auditory, Kinesthetic, Tactile Approach), Cunningham Method, and Rebus Readers. (See chapter 16 for specialized methods.)

General Health Problems

Whether one is teaching reading at the developmental, corrective, or remedial level, students' progress is enhanced if they are alert and are participating actively in instructional activities. Students who are tired, malnourished, or chronically ill can seldom give their full attention to learning. As a result, their reading progress is jeopardized or completely halted. Persistent health problems can lead to reading problems as the lack of learning begins to have a cumulative effect.

Teachers who are aware of a student's general health problems can refer the student to the school nurse and/or inform the parents. Experience indicates that in many cases parents are not aware of a health problem. For example, parents who leave for work before their children leave for school may assume that their children are fixing their own breakfast when, in fact, they are not. Many parents are willing to follow the teachers' recommendations—for example, that their children get more sleep because they are too tired to participate actively in class.

Recommendations to parents for improving their child's general health need to be handled with tact. Because some parents are unwilling to accept or to follow a teacher's recommendations, practical alternatives must be explored. Demands that parents make certain changes at home are beyond the teacher's domain of influence.

SOCIAL AND EMOTIONAL MALADJUSTMENT

Symptoms of social and emotional maladjustment are displayed frequently by students experiencing reading problems. The causes of such problems are difficult to isolate; they can be due to a combination of deeply rooted educational, environmental, psychological, and/or physical factors. Social and emotional maladjustments that accompany reading difficulties can, as noted by Challman (1939), be considered in three possible ways. First, emotional factors can cause maladjustment that contributes to or causes the reading problems. Second, reading difficulties can cause emotional and social adjustment problems. Third, reading difficulties and maladjustment can exist independently, with neither contributing to the severity of the other.

If maladjustments contribute to or cause reading difficulties, reading growth is likely to be inhibited until the cause of the maladjustment is identified and treated. However, causes beyond the teacher's domain of influence require outside assistance. Although reading instruction can be adjusted to minimize the educational effect of a student's problem, assistance from social workers, physicians, or psychologists is required to identify and treat the problem.

If reading difficulties cause the maladjustments, then improving the student's reading abilities should have a positive affect on the maladjustments as well. Research (Rupley, 1971) and classroom experiences suggest that emotional and social adjustment does improve with reading growth. Students who exhibited excessive withdrawal, poor ego strength, poor social conformity, and excessive aggressiveness showed marked improvement when reading instruction accommodated their particular problem.

If maladjustments and reading problems exist independently, corrective or remedial instruction could proceed without interference from the social or emotional problem. Recent research suggests, however, that the incidence of maladjustments for students experiencing reading difficulties is great enough to warrant consideration in both diagnostic and prescriptive instruction.

Observation alone is insufficient for diagnosing students who have social and emotional maladjustments. Rating scales, which do not require extensive training to administer and interpret, help one focus on particular social and emotional behaviors. An example of such rating scales is *Burks' Behavior Rating Scales* (1968), which allow the administrator to evaluate potential problem behaviors in 20 categories (see chapter 16). After each category is defined, possible causes and classroom intervention techniques are suggested. Such scales should be viewed as screening devices. Students who exhibit serious personality and adjustment problems should be recommended for a more complete diagnosis by specially trained professionals.

ORAL LANGUAGE

The relationship of oral language to reading was discussed in chapter 1. Oral language is a facilitative reading factor that does not ensure reading growth but does facilitate the development of functional reading. As noted by Anderson, Hiebert, Scott, and Wilkinson (1985):

> Reading instruction builds especially on oral language. If this foundation is weak, progress in reading will be slow and uncertain. Children must have at

Before children can learn to read, they must have a basic vocabulary and knowledge of the world, and the ability to communicate their knowledge. (Phillips Photo Illustrators)

least a basic vocabulary, a reasonable range of knowledge about the world around them, and ability to talk about their knowledge. These abilities form the basis for comprehending text. (p. 30)

Development of Oral Language and Reading

Evidence suggests a strong relationship between oral language development and reading achievement (Ruddell & Haggard, 1985); however, reading problems cannot be linked solely to deficiencies in language acquisition. Some basic language factors could certainly contribute to a student's reading difficulties. Some contributing factors could include developmental, dialectal, and/or pathological language variations. These three language factors and their relationship to reading difficulties are described by Hodges (1976):

> *Developmental variation* suggests that many so-called reading difficulties may represent a mismatch between the level of a child's developing linguistic sophistication and that of reading material with which he is confronted. *Dialectal variation*, on the other hand, may pose another kind of possible mismatch, that which results from differences between the formal features of the language of instruction and the formal features of language which the child has learned in his particularly linguistic community. *Pathological variation*, in turn, poses the possibility that, in addition to whatever developmental or dialectal differences might exist, special instructional techniques may be needed that are not ordinarily encompassed in a reading program; as, for example, the techniques that may be used in working with the visually or auditorily handicapped child. (pp. 40–41)

Developmental, dialectal, and pathological variations are not the only possible language variations that could contribute to reading problems and could require instruction to be adjusted to the language needs of the students. However, students with reading problems may well exhibit one or all of these variations. Reading growth can often be improved if instruction is designed to improve language facility. Chapter 14 focuses on dialectal variations that warrant consideration in corrective and remedial diagnosis and instruction.

Developmental Oral Language Stages

The developmental aspects of language acquisition for elementary-age children are presented in table 4–1 and are referred to in chapter 14. The age chart of language sequence and stages is based on Loban's research conclusions (1976). His stages of language development incorporate the findings of several longitudinal investigations conducted in England, Florida, and Tennessee. Although variation in language abilities may be found at any given age level, considerable deviation warrants further investigation to determine its effect on reading performance.

WRITTEN LANGUAGE

Although the oral language capabilities of students and their experiential backgrounds provide a strong facilitative base for reading, the facilitative factor of direct experience with written language is extremely important for reading success. Knowledge that children gain in their early years about the relationship between oral and written language and their use of that

TABLE 4–1 Major Stages of Language Development

Approximate Age	Major Oral Language Accomplishments
5–6 years	Settles the use of pronouns and verbs, in present and past tense, using the inflections of their family. Complex sentences appear more frequently.
6–7 years	Additional progress occurs in speaking complex sentences, particularly those using adjectival clauses. Conditional dependent clauses, such as those beginning with *if* appear.
7–8 years	Use of relative pronouns as objects in subordinate adjectival clauses. ("I have a cat which I feed every day.") Subordinate clauses beginning with *when, if*, and *because* appear frequently. Gerund phrase as object of the verb appears. ("I like washing myself.")
8–10 years	Connectors—*meanwhile, unless, even, if*—are used to relate concepts to general ideas. Use of present participle active begins to appear. ("Sitting up in bed, I looked around.") Use of the perfect participle appears. ("Having read *Tom Sawyer*, I returned it to the library.") Also, the gerund as object of preposition begins to be used. ("By seeing the movie, I didn't have to read the book.")
11–13 years	Complex sentences with subordinate clauses of concession introduced by connectives—*provided that, nevertheless, in spite of, unless*—are used to frame hypotheses and envision their consequences. Auxillary verbs such as *might, could*, and *should* appear more often than at earlier stages. The state of thinking "if this, then (probably) that" is emerging in speech. Advanced in using longer communication units and subordinate adjectival clauses. Nouns modified by participle or participle phrases appear more frequently. Also appearing more frequently are gerund phrases, adverbial infinitives, and compound predicates.

Source: Walter Loban, *Language Development: Kindergarten Through Grade Twelve* (Urbana, Ill.: National Council of Teachers of English, 1976), pp. 81–84. Copyright © 1976 by the National Council of Teachers of English. Reprinted by permission of the publisher and the author.

knowledge when they read contributes significantly to their reading development (Wells, 1983). This early stage of literacy, therefore, lays the foundation for ongoing success in reading and has important implications for considering whether or not students with reading problems lack such understandings (Teale, Hiebert, & Chittenden, 1987).

Basic understandings about written features of language that facilitate reading development are presented in the following section. Children who lack such understandings may experience difficulty in reading development. Again, some children will possess more of the following characteristics than other children will; it is when a child lags *considerably* behind his or her peers that the teacher might suspect this as contributing to a reading difficulty.

Understandings About Written Language and Reading

The following characteristics associated with understanding the relationships between oral and written language are important for students' reading development. They are particularly important in terms of helping students understand that the purpose of reading is comprehension. These basic concepts are:

1. Knows that the basic functions of written language are to provide enjoyment, information, and directions
2. Understands that oral language can be represented by print and that the purpose of both speaking and writing is to communicate meaning
3. Recognizes common environmental print, such as labels, signs, brand names, and so forth
4. Retells parts or all of stories read aloud and associates what is heard with the book used
5. Can point to specified words, phrases, or sentences on the page while being read to or while reading by him- or herself
6. Has favorite story books and can "play read" or retell the story from the book(s)
7. Reads stories or books to parents, classmates, or teachers by using familiar stories or pictures before the child is actually able to read
8. Moves from left to right when reading, "play reading," or telling a story using a series of pictures
9. Creates written types of text that may contain only scribbles or a combination of scribbles, letters, and some words; child can "read," that is, tell a story about this writing, or can "write" using a combination of drawings, scribbles, or letters to tell a story
10. Provides additional events and endings for stories read aloud or created by him- or herself
11. Has some knowledge of the alphabetic principle—written letters represent speech sounds
12. Understands the basic syntax (word order in English language) of language and its representation in print

Students will vary in their understanding about the relationships between oral and written language, and for those who experience difficulty understanding these relationships, reading instruction that builds a strong connection between oral and written language is necessary. Noting the presence or absence of such understandings is best determined by the use of informal diagnosis that provides many reading-writing opportunities for the students.

INTELLIGENCE AND COGNITION

Intelligence and cognition are not the same, nor should they be treated as such. **Intelligence** (mental capacity) facilitates **cognition** (reasoning ability), but high intelligence does not ensure that a child will be able to reason about and understand the act of reading. Less-than-normal intelligence, on the other hand, may impede the reasoning process and result in reading difficulties. In this instance, instructional methods that fail to make adjustments for the needs of a student are contributing to his or her reading problems.

Although researchers have found a relationship between intelligence and reading success, the relationship is only moderate (Stanovich, Cunningham, & Feeman, 1984). Typically, the relationship is positive—high intelligence results in getting off to a successful start in reading. It is important to note, however, that the relationship between intelligence (as conventionally measured) and reading achievement may be due to the heavy language bias of such measures.

Students who have difficulty in learning to read are often administered an intelligence test. Such an assessment can give teachers information about the likelihood of students' success in reading and can provide information about how to adjust reading instruction. It is important, though, that teachers understand the limitations of different types of intelligence tests. Standardized group measures of intelligence typically penalize students who have reading problems because in order to respond to the test items, students must be able to read silently and comprehend at an efficient rate. Group intelligence measures may result in an intelligence quotient that is inaccurately low as a result of the reading abilities needed to take the test. Chapter 14 discusses this possibility in terms of intelligence testing and culturally different children.

Individually administered intelligence tests that do not require reading may provide better estimates of intellectual functioning to compare with reading performance than would group-administered tests. The two most-often-used instruments are the *Wechsler Intelligence Scales for Children-Revised* (WISC-R) and the *Stanford-Binet Intelligence Scales.* As mentioned, these are individually administered, nonreading tests. Both must be administered by trained and certified personnel, and both yield a global intelligence quotient of intellectual functioning.

The decision to administer either the WISC-R or the *Stanford-Binet* depends on the training and preference of the administrator, who is usually the school psychologist or psychometrist. Global IQ scores from either test provide an indication of mental abilities, which help to identify the expected level of reading achievement. While scores in the average range suggest that a student has the necessary abilities to learn to read, scores below average indicate that instruction must be adjusted to a lower learning ability.

Cognitive Abilities and Reading

Cognition and its relationship to reading development has been investigated extensively (Downing & Leong, 1982; Stanovich, 1986). Research results indicate that children's growth in understanding the purpose and nature of reading depends on

1. understanding the communication purpose of written language,
2. conceptualizing the symbolic function of writing,
3. understanding the concepts of **decoding** (figuring out the word) and **encoding** (making sense of the message),
4. learning the linguistic concepts, and
5. developing the corresponding technical terminology for abstract units of language.

Reading problems may result from the student's inability to realize and to understand the purpose and nature of reading. Before coming to school, few children have been asked to think about words in either their oral language or in the context of print. Students who cannot reason about print or understand the language that the teacher uses to teach reading (terms such as *words, letters, sounds, sentences,* etc.) may become cognitively confused about what it means to read. This state of cognitive confusion, if it exists at the beginning reading levels, has a cumulative effect as the student advances to higher grade levels. Such confusion about what it means to "read" can be a contributing factor to many students' reading problems.

Greenslade (1980) noted that students must acquire several concepts that enable them to better understand that reading is a meaningful process. First, they need to become aware of the relationship between oral language and print. Second, students need to understand that printed language is made up of words that represent units of meaning. Third, they must recognize that reading is a thinking process that enables them to make varied interpretations of text. All of these concepts are related to how students think about reading and are directly affected by the teacher's reading instruction. When students are not helped to develop the cognitive abilities needed to understand such concepts, they may become cognitively confused.

The relationship of reading difficulties to cognition may be that some readers do not understand that reading is a problem-solving task requiring getting information from a variety of sources: letters; words; existing knowledge about people, places, and things; and understandings about language (Anderson, Hiebert, Scott, & Wilkinson, 1985). All of these contribute to understanding the linguistic relationships between oral language and written language. Failure to develop such understanding can contribute to reading problems. Hence, helping students who have reading problems to understand the process and purpose of reading could result in improved reading abilities. Teachers cannot assume that they are providing students with an understanding of the reading process when they are teaching reading. Helping students become cognitively clear about reading requires instruction that promotes an understanding of reading as a meaning-getting process and not as an acquisition of a set of skills.

EDUCATIONAL DEFICIENCIES

Chapter 2 emphasized that teachers do make a difference in students' reading achievement. From a logical viewpoint, teachers must assume much of the responsibility for students' success or failure in reading, yet their reading difficulties are more often explained in terms of other factors, such as poor home background, lack of motivation, and uninterested parents. As mentioned earlier, such variables can contribute to reading problems, but teachers are responsible for adjusting their instruction to take these factors into account in light of diagnostic findings.

Educational deficiencies contribute to or are the cause of reading problems for many students. Our experiences in the University Reading Clinic of Texas A & M suggest that educational deficiencies contribute to almost half of the reading problems of students encountered there. These deficiencies contribute to difficulties either directly (that is, poor instructional practices caused the reading problem) or indirectly (that is, instruction was not adjusted to accommodate specific reading strengths). For example, it has been found that many comprehension problems often exhibited by fifth and sixth graders can be traced to faulty word instruction in the lower grades. Likewise, researchers have identified reading problems among primary-age students that resulted from a lack of sequence in the instructional program.

The teacher's knowledge of educational deficiencies that can result in reading difficulties serves two purposes. First, many reading problems can be prevented if such deficiencies are identified and corrected before they contribute to or cause a reading problem. Second, a student's reading growth can be facilitated if suspected educational deficiencies, which contribute to reading difficulties, are identified and corrected through corrective or remedial instruction.

A number of poor teaching practices can result in reading problems. These can range from simple oversight to unsound instructional programs. Poor teaching practices can be minimized if both corrective and remedial reading teachers approach their instruction analytically. Durkin (1983) encourages all reading teachers to ask themselves questions about their instructional practices: "Is the skill I am teaching a necessary one for reading growth?" "Will my students become better readers as a result of learning this skill?" "Is my instruction aimed at the student's needs?" If a student is experiencing reading problems: "Are there materials and methods more appropriate for this student than those that I am using?" Such questions are representative of an analytical approach to reading instruction and help educators evaluate the quality of instruction offered.

EXAMPLES OF INSTRUCTIONAL DEFICIENCIES

From our own research, experiences, classroom observations, and discussions with fellow teachers, several examples of teaching practices have been accumulated that can interfere with learning to read. Many of these poor teaching practices could have been avoided if the teachers had approached the instructional practices analytically.

Lack of Attention to Instructional Details and Classroom Organization

Many of the following behaviors can occur in classroom reading instruction. It is when such instructional behaviors persist without the teacher attempting to correct them that reading problems can develop. (See chapter 2 for additional information about providing quality reading instruction.)

1. Failing to establish a purpose for reading that focuses on comprehension. This results in students who view reading as the correct identification of words, become cognitively confused about reading, or experience comprehension problems.
2. Seating students in such a position that not all of them can see the materials presented and so cannot relate these to the teacher's discussion.
3. Holding up flashcards and covering parts of words with one's fingers.
4. Writing that is illegible or too small for students to see.
5. Failing to demonstrate the application of learned skills and abilities for new learning.
6. Using reinforcement techniques with the assumption that all students will respond in an equally positive manner.
7. Failing to make sure that as a written word is presented, everyone is looking at the word and associating its pronunciation with its graphic representation.
8. Failing to take advantage of the fact that reading involves interaction with written text and devoting most of the instruction to verbal explanation of the lesson.
9. Failing to help students relate their past learning and background knowledge to stories that are read.
10. Failing to model a process or talk aloud about reading strategies to help students better conceptualize what they are being asked to do.
11. Failing to complete one or two practice examples of assigned independent work to ensure that all students fully understand the task.

12. Failing to develop independent activities that will enable students to experience a high success rate.
13. Failing to present and discuss new vocabulary words in meaningful written context to help students understand the meanings of new words.
14. Failing to use instructional time wisely, keeping students' attention focused on learning tasks.
15. Failing to take distractions into account—such as a sick child, distracting noises, or a fire drill—that can interfere with learning an important concept or skill and instead assuming that all students are attending to the instruction.

Failure to Provide for Individual Differences

The importance of providing for each student's reading strengths and weaknesses in instruction was stressed in chapters 1 and 2. Failure to provide for individual needs forces a student to *fit the curriculum* rather than making the curriculum *fit the student.* Reading difficulties are likely to occur for many students with unmet needs.

Lack of Instructional Balance

Too much or too little emphasis on isolated reading skills can lead to reading problems. Overemphasizing a code-breaking approach, for example, can lead to comprehension difficulties as students begin to view reading as the correct pronunciation of every word. Such emphasis makes it difficult for students to understand that developing word-recognition skills is a means to comprehension and not an end in itself. Likewise, overemphasizing a whole-word approach can stifle students' interest in reading, limit the development of word-recognition skills, and minimize the transfer of reading skills to reading materials other than a basal reader.

Placing considerable emphasis on reading skills through the use of meaningful drill activities may be necessary to promote automaticity and an ability to transfer to actual reading situations. However, reading problems can result when students are not provided opportunities to apply their skills and abilities in actual reading situations where the intent is to comprehend meaning.

Inappropriate Sequence of Skill Development

Proper sequencing of skills is necessary to ensure that new skills and abilities build on previous learning (Chall, 1983). Teaching some skills out of sequence or not at all can lead to reading difficulties. Failure to teach the application of phonic generalizations to polysyllabic words, for example, will limit the use of phonics for those students who do not intuitively recognize how to apply phonic generalizations to words of more than one syllable.

Inappropriate skill development, a major contributor to reading problems, occurs when skills that are not really reading skills are taught with the assumption that transfer to reading will result. An example noted frequently is teaching students to auditorily discriminate environmental sounds (e.g., a train whistle from a car horn) or visually discriminate shapes and objects with the idea that students will transfer these skills when attempting to discriminate the sounds and shapes of letters and words.

Instructional practices similar to the example given can result in reading problems. If teachers would ask themselves why they are teaching a particular skill, how the skill is related to past instruction, and whether or not it is an actual reading skill, many of these questionable practices could be avoided. Furthermore, the probability that students' reading difficulties are related to educational deficiencies should receive primary consideration. Students may have reading problems as a result of inadequate past instruction. Corrective or remedial reading programs must take this into account if improvement is to occur.

□ SUMMARY

Reading difficulties can, in many instances, result from a combination of causes. Many of these causes are outside the domain of teacher influences and competencies. In such cases the teacher must adjust the instruction to minimize the possible negative affects of the cause(s) on students' reading development.

Students' reading problems can result from a combination of physical impairments, language problems, social/emotional maladjustments, cognition problems, or instructional deficiencies. Each of these possibilities may warrant investigation for students with reading problems. Although deficiencies in any one area do not imply causality, the effect of suspected deficiencies on reading should be thoroughly explored through diagnosis and referral to qualified specialists.

Students' reading ability will vary in relation to the text, the task, and the purposes for reading. Therefore, it is the responsibility of the teacher to identify the instructional program that will best develop the students' reading abilities.

□ IN-TEXT ASSIGNMENTS

LIBRARY ACTIVITY

Read several articles on dyslexia and identify the different ways in which *dyslexia* is defined. In a short paper, compare and contrast the differing definitions. Summarize your paper by speculating about the difficulty of identifying one definition of dyslexia that will have a similar meaning for teachers, parents, reading specialists, and state legislatures.

FIELD-BASED ACTIVITY

Visit a reading resource teacher's classroom in a local school and discuss the various screening procedures he or she uses to identify possible correlates of reading problems. Areas of particular interest might include: (1) How are students screened for visual and hearing impairments? (2) What student behaviors are indicative of neurological impairments? What referral procedures are used for students suspected to have such problems? (3) How are suspected educational deficiencies identified? (4) How is information from parents obtained? Compile the information from your visit to share with your classmates.

SHARING AND BRAINSTORMING

Read the following excerpt and consider possible reasons for the behaviors exhibited by the student. Identify some important instructional features a teacher would have to consider in developing a reading program for this student.

Mark, a second grader, confuses the letters *b, d, p*, and *q*. For example, he reads *ball* as *dall, pen* as *den*, and *dug* as *pug*. He has difficulty with these letters more often in words than when he uses them individually. His problem could be visual, cognitive, or educational.

Discuss reasons for why you think his problem could be related to either a visual, a cognitive, or an educational cause. Identify some informal classroom procedures that you could use to gather diagnostic data about each possible cause. Discuss some instructional features that might be beneficial in correcting Mark's difficulty.

RESOURCE ACTIVITY

Invite a pediatrician to visit your class. Ask him or her to discuss the procedures that he or she follows when a child is referred for diagnosis of a suspected neurological impairment. Have the pediatrician specify how he or she reports to the child's teacher the results of the diagnosis and how this information could be used by the teacher in planning quality reading instruction.

□ *REFERENCES*

Anderson, R. C., Hiebert, E. H., Scott, J. A., & Wilkinson, I. A. (1985). *Becoming a nation of readers.* Washington, D.C.: The National Institute of Education.

Burks, H. (1968). *Burks' behavior rating scales.* El Monte, CA: Arden.

Chall, J. S. (1983). *Stages of reading development.* New York: McGraw-Hill.

Challman, R. (1939). Personality maladjustments and remedial reading. *Journal of Exceptional Children, 6,* 7–11, 35.

Dishner, E. K. & Olson, M. W. (1986–87, Fall/Winter). Dyslexia and the Texas mandate. *Teacher Education and Practice, 4,* 9–16.

Downing, J. & Leong, C. K. (1982). *Psychology of reading.* New York: Macmillan.

Durkin, D. (1983). *Teaching them to read.* Boston: Allyn & Bacon.

Greenslade, B. C. (1980, November). The basics in reading from the perspective of the learner. *The Reading Teacher, 34,* 192–195.

Harris, T. L. & Hodges, R. E. (Eds.). (1981). *Dictionary of reading and related terms.* Newark, DE: International Reading Association.

Hodges, R. E. (1976). Reactions to language acquisition and the reading process. In H. Singer & R. Ruddell (Eds.). *Theoretical models and the processes of reading.* (pp. 39–41). Newark, DE: International Reading Association.

Hynd, C. R. (1986–87, Fall/Winter). Instruction of reading disabled/dyslexia students. *Teacher Education and Practice, 3,* 17–36.

Lipson, M. Y. & Wixson, K. K. (1986, Spring). Reading disability research: An interactionist perspective. *Review of Educational Research, 56,* 111–136.

Loban, W. (1976). *Language development: Kindergarten through grade twelve.* Urbana, IL: National Council of Teachers of English.

Lyon R. & Watson, B. (1981). Empirically derived subgroups of learning disabled readers: Diagnostic characteristics. *Journal of Learning Disabilities, 14,* 256–261.

Ruddell, R. B. & Haggard, M. R. (1985). Oral and written language acquisition and the reading process. In R. B. Ruddell & H. Singer (Eds.). *Theoretical models and processes of reading* (3rd ed.) (pp. 63–80). Newark, DE: International Reading Association.

Rupley, W. H. (1971, January). Relationships between behavioral problems and reading retardation. *Indiana Reading Quarterly, 3,* 4–9.

Samuels, S. J. (1984). Resolving some theoretical and instructional conflicts in the 1980s. *Reading Research Quarterly, 19,* 390–392.

Spache, G. (1963). *Toward better reading.* Champaign, IL: Garrard.

Stanovich, K. E., Cunningham, A. E., & Feeman, D. J. (1984, Spring). Intelligence, cognitive skills, and early reading progress. *Reading Research Quarterly, 4,* 278–303.

Stanovich, K. E. (1986, Fall). Matthew effects in reading: Some consequences of individual differences in the acquisition of literacy. *Reading Research Quarterly, 4,* 360–406.

Strang, R. (1968). *Reading diagnosis and remediation.* Newark, DE: International Reading Association.

Teale, W. H., Hiebert, E. H., & Chittenden, E. A. (1987, April). Assessing young children's literacy development. *The Reading Teacher, 40,* 772–777.

Texas State Board of Education. (1986). Procedures concerning dyslexia (Section 21.924, Texas Education Code). Austin, TX: Texas Education Agency.

Wells, G. (1983). Language and learning in the early years. *Early Childhood Development and Care, 11,* 69–77.

Wilson, R. M. & Cleland, C. J. (1985). *Diagnostic and remedial reading for classroom and clinic* (5th ed.). Columbus, OH: Merrill.

5

Tools for Diagnosing Reading Levels and Abilities

☐ *OVERVIEW*

A variety of instruments and techniques are available for assessing students' reading. These diagnostic tools used to assess students' reading can be classified as either informal, norm-referenced, or criterion-referenced measures. Each tool has strengths and weaknesses; relying on only one type of measure as an indicator of reading performance would limit the scope of diagnosis. A single type of measure cannot provide accurate information about all students' reading development. Diagnostic tools only *sample* reading behaviors, and teachers may wish to employ a variety of measures—including informal, norm-referenced, and criterion-referenced instruments—to get an adequate sample of students' reading abilities.

As mentioned earlier, both facilitative and functional reading factors influence students' levels of reading performance in relation to the demands of instruction. Assessment in both facilitative and functional areas allows the classroom and reading resource teachers to better identify appropriate instruction for students that builds on their strengths. Assessment results are interpreted in terms of how well they will help the teacher in planning a quality reading program.

This chapter will discuss three types of assessment instruments and procedures—informal, norm-referenced, and criterion-referenced—and will suggest techniques for obtaining as much information as possible from each of them. Much of the discussion will be focused on individual students; however, most of the strategies can be used for group assessment as well.

As noted in chapter 4, the purpose of diagnosis is not to label students, but to gain insights into the reading strengths of individuals so that quality instruction can be provided (Johnston, 1984).

After reading this chapter, the teacher should be able to

☐ describe the strengths and limitations of informal, norm-referenced, and criterion-referenced assessment procedures.

☐ apply criteria to assist him or her in selecting the most appropriate instruments for a valid assessment of students' reading skills and abilities.

☐ develop informal assessment strategies that relate to specific instructional environments.

☐ analyze standardized test results to get more information about a student's reading ability than a single test score can provide.

☐ explain how assessment results can be used to identify instruction appropriate to a student's reading strengths.

☐ describe and develop procedures for analyzing measurement objectives as they relate to instructional objectives for corrective or remedial reading.

INFORMAL MEASURES OF READING

An **informal assessment instrument** or procedure is one that has not been standardized against certain performance norms or against a set of achievement objectives. Such an assessment of students' reading abilities and skills includes a wide range of procedures. Some are structured in a written format and can provide a permanent record of each student's reading strengths, weaknesses, and attitudes. Examples include informal reading inventories (IRIs), checklists, interest inventories, records of books read, cloze tests, and phonic surveys. Others are on-the-spot observations and procedures that provide insights into students' reading behaviors and attitudes. These observations of students' reading in various situations might include attitude and frequency of reading for enjoyment, use of the library, performance in reading instruction, and interviewing skills.

Informal Reading Inventory (IRI)

A widely used method of written informal assessment is the **informal reading inventory.** Inventories may be either commercially prepared or teacher prepared. Each type has advantages and disadvantages. Commercially prepared IRIs may be viewed as tests by both the teacher and the student, while teacher-prepared inventories may take too much time to construct. One advantage of commercially prepared IRIs is that the teacher does not have to spend time preparing materials. However, if the IRI is used to determine subsequent reading instruction, it is probably best to use a teacher-prepared inventory that samples the materials that will be used for reading instruction (Pikulski & Shanahan, 1982).

The format of the typical IRI, whether commercially or teacher prepared, generally consists of graded word lists, graded passages, and comprehension questions for each passage. **Graded word lists** are used for determining placement in the grade-level passage, assessing sight vocabulary for words in isolation, and getting some idea of how a student figures out unknown words. **Graded passages** provide clues about a student's use of context, attention to meaning, and strategies for coping with unfamiliar words. **Comprehension questions** enable one to sample comprehension outcomes at various levels for each passage.

Four different levels of reading are identified by applying criteria to the student's performance in both word recognition and comprehension. The first level, the **independent level**, is the level at which a student can read materials without any assistance. The second level is the **instructional level**, where the material is challenging, but neither too difficult nor too easy. The third level is the **frustration level**. As its name implies, this is the reading level at which students would be frustrated in their attempts to understand what they read. The fourth level is the **listening capacity** or **potential level**. This is the highest level at which students are able to understand material that is read aloud to them.

Oral reading of the inventory passages allows the teacher to identify independent, instructional, and frustration levels for word-recognition accuracy. The same levels are also identified for comprehension accuracy. Comprehension performance is determined by the student's response to the comprehension questions that accompany each passage. Silent reading of an IRI identifies the same reading levels but only for comprehension. Potential level is measured when the graded passages are read aloud to students and they are asked questions about their reading. Their responses are then used to identify their listening capacity.

Critieria for Determining Levels of Reading Competence   Different criteria for determining students' independent, instructional, frustration, and potential reading levels are available for teachers to use. Two examples of criteria for identifying reading competence levels are presented in table 5–1. Powell's (1977) criteria take into account word-recognition and comprehension accuracy in terms of passage-level difficulty. With easier materials, accuracy is not as necessary for comprehension as it is with more difficult materials. Powell has pointed out that with easier materials, students can make more word-recognition miscues and still understand the content than they can with more difficult materials. Betts's (1946) criteria do not consider passage-level reading difficulty for identifying reading competence levels and, therefore, can be applied to all passages regardless of difficulty level.

Recording Oral Reading Miscues   Most reading authorities agree that recording the miscues exactly as read provides a better understanding of students' word-recognition strategies (see table 5–2). However, omitting punctuation, making repetitions, and making spontaneous self-corrections

TABLE 5-1 Criteria for Identifying Reading Competency Levels on Informal Reading Inventories

| Levels of Reading Competence | Powell's Criteria | | | | | | Betts's Criteria | |
| | Word-Recognition Accuracy by Passage Levels | | | Comprehension Accuracy by Passage Levels | | | Word-Recognition Accuracy (All Passage Levels) | Comprehension Accuracy (All Passage Levels) |
	1–2	3–5	6+	1–2	3–5	6+		
Independent	98%+	98%+	98%+	81%+	86%+	91%+	99%+	90%+
Instructional	87%–97%	92%–97%	94%–97%	55%–80%	60%–85%	65%–90%	95%–98%	75%–89%
Frustration	86% or less	91% or less	93% or less	54% or less	59% or less	64% or less	90% or less	50% or less
Potential/Capacity							—	75%

TABLE 5–2 Recording Oral Reading Miscues

Miscue	Notation	Example
Insertion—inserted word or words that are not in the written text	∧	Mary has *long* ∧ brown hair.
Omission—word or words omitted from the written text	⬭	Sam bought a (shiny) new bicycle.
Mispronunciation—word or words pronounced incorrectly	Phonically spelled or diacritical marks	The thieves *thives* were *capitatled* captivated by the glow of the gold.
Substitutions—real word or words used in place of text words	Substitutions written above text word	The man put the money *box* in a bag.
Reversal—text word order reversed	∿	"Help is on the way," said Mark.
Unknown/Aided Words—words pronounced for the reader after a reasonable time period (usually 6–10 seconds)	——P——	A huge ⌐—P—⌐ locomotive stopped at the station.
Omission of Punctuation—no attention given to punctuation throughout the text	○	People wore hats made of feathers⌒ silk⌒ cotton⌒ and fur.
Repetition—part of a word, a word, or several words repeated	——R——	He ⌐ate a ⌐—R—bagel⌐ with cream cheese for lunch.
Self-corrections—a miscue or miscues corrected by the reader	✓	He wants a new coat for *went* ✓ his birthday.

are frequently referred to as recordable but not scoreable miscues. That is, these miscues are indicated but do not count in determining the reader's levels of reading competence.

Selecting an IRI Earlier, the pros and cons of a teacher-prepared versus a commercially prepared IRI were briefly presented. Essentially, the advantage of a teacher-prepared inventory was that it sampled a student's performance on material that would be used for instruction. The advantage of a commercially prepared IRI was that it did not require teacher time to construct. The final decision about which type of inventory to use must go beyond these considerations.

The purpose of any IRI is to help classroom and reading resource teachers make instructional decisions based on samples of students' oral reading behaviors. A student's performance helps answer questions such as the following:

What is the most appropriate basal level?

What trade books should be recommended?

What are specific word-recognition strengths and weaknesses?

What comprehension strategies does a reader attempt to use?

What is the student's knowledge of language structure (semantics and syntax)?

To provide accurate answers to such questions, an IRI must possess certain characteristics, regardless of whether it is commercially or teacher prepared.

Features of an informal inventory that facilitate administration and increase the probability that a student's oral reading behaviors and comprehension abilities are measured accurately include (1) graded word lists, (2) graded passages that cover several grade levels, (3) passage length that is sufficient to obtain a sampling of reading behavior, (4) passages that are cohesive, (5) comprehension questions that represent varying skills, (6) equivalent alternate passages for each grade level, and (7) motivation statements for each passage.

Graded word lists. Graded word lists typically accompany commercial reading inventories. The number of words on a list for each grade varies from 10 to 15 words. These words list usually range from preprimer through grade eight or higher. They serve to identify the passage level at which the student should begin reading in the inventory, provide some insights into a student's word-recognition strategies, and sample the student's sight vocabulary of words in isolation.

Those who develop their own IRI or select one that does not have a graded word list can construct or select an already developed list. This is a better option than is placing students in passages based on their current grade level or on their average reading grade determined from a recently administered standardized test, which can result in an entry level that may be too difficult or too easy. Instead, teachers who develop their own IRIs can select 10 to 15 words from each level of the basal series from which the passages are excerpted or can consult a compilation that lists word frequencies by grade level.

Graded passages. Grade-level ranges for the passages should begin at preprimer and then progress through grade eight or higher. Such a range ensures that the student can be placed at an appropriate entry level and progress through the passages until a frustration level is identified. If two IRIs are of equal quality, the one that covers more grade levels would be the better choice. Oral passages taken from basals are limited in their use by the grade or level range of the series. As a result, teachers constructing their own inventories may have to excerpt passages from reading materials beyond the highest basal level if a broader reading grade range is desired.

Passage length.   Passage length is another important consideration when selecting or preparing an informal reading inventory. Passages that are too short do not allow for an adequate sampling of students' reading behaviors. In addition, short passages restrict the number of comprehension questions that can be asked. These are serious limitations that can affect the identification of reading competence levels.

There is no ideal length for each level of an IRI; however, the best guideline to use in selecting an inventory is that passage length should increase as passage difficulty increases. The increase should range from 30 to 40 percent for primer through fourth grade and 10 to 20 percent for fifth grade through eighth grade. Thus, if a 100-word preprimer passage is the lowest level, the primer passage should contain 120 to 140 words; the first-grade passage, 166 to 196 words; and so forth.

Passage cohesiveness.   Not only is length an important consideration, but the cohesiveness of each passage and of the accompanying comprehension questions must also be evaluated. Passages that consist of unconnected paragraphs interfere with comprehension. When selecting or constructing an IRI, read each passage and the accompanying comprehension questions carefully. Passages should be cohesive and free standing, and comprehension questions should relate directly to the information presented in each passage. Chapter 9 should be helpful in writing and evaluating IRI comprehension questions.

Equivalent alternate passages.   The selection of equivalent alternate passages is encouraged for each level of an inventory. Alternate passages serve several purposes, and teacher-constructed or commercially prepared IRIs that have them are a better choice than those that do not. There are three basic reasons to select or construct a reading inventory with alternate forms. First, at the lower passage levels the number of student miscues needed to identify reading competence levels is less than at higher levels. Lower level passages contain fewer words, thus the number of miscues needed to identify each level is reduced. Limited miscues on lower passages may fail to identify any pattern of word-recognition strengths and weaknesses. However, when alternate passages are administered and the miscues analyzed and compared with those on the other IRI, specific word-recognition strengths and weaknesses can be better analyzed, resulting in more reliable information for instructional decision making.

Second, alternate forms provide a means to compare the student's comprehension on oral and silent reading. Discrepancies between these two comprehension responses may reveal more information than the data from oral reading alone could. Word-recognition difficulties noted during an oral reading may not interfere with students' comprehensions when they read silently. Since comprehension is the goal of all reading skill development, the word-recognition difficulties exhibited in oral reading may not require extensive instructional emphases if they do not interfere with comprehension when passages are read silently.

Third, pretesting and posttesting with alternate forms allows the teacher to assess the effectiveness of remedial or corrective reading instruction. Although it is possible to use the same form of an inventory for both pretesting and posttesting, there is a chance that posttest results will be contaminated; that is, a student's improved performance on the second administration is affected by having read those same pages during the pretest. The chance of this occurring is minimized by using equivalent alternate forms.

Motivation statements. For each IRI passage, it is important to include motivation statements, or a one- or two-sentence synopsis of each passage topic or theme. Such statements establish a purpose for reading and promote interest. It is easy to write and include such statements for passages in an IRI that do not have motivation statements.

Administering an IRI The following steps for administering an IRI are rather straightforward and help standardize the procedure, therefore maximizing the probability of getting accurate information. (A rationale is provided for those steps that are not readily apparent.)

1. Select a quiet area for administration and allow for an uninterrupted session of 30 to 45 minutes.
2. Tell the student why the inventory is being taken; for example, "I'm going to have you read aloud some words and some short stories. This is not a test, but I will be doing some writing as you read. The purpose of asking you to read for me is so I can help you become a better reader."
3. Use an audio recorder to record the student's reading and comprehension responses. The recording is used to facilitate an analysis of the student's reading when there is a question about whether or not miscues were recorded accurately. Also, parts of the recording can be played for the student to point out strengths and weaknesses, which may help the student realize the purpose for later reading instruction.
4. Administer the graded word list. Each list of words should be typed on separate cards (3″ × 5″ or 4″ × 6″). Begin with the list two years below the student's current grade level. Explain that the student is to read aloud each word on the list. Encourage the student to try to pronounce every word, even though a word may be unfamiliar. (This provides some analysis of the word-recognition strategies used for unfamiliar words.) If a miscue is made on the first list given to the student, drop to easier lists until there are no errors. Have the student read from increasingly difficult lists until the maximum number of words suggested in the

administration guide is missed. If a teacher-prepared list is used, three errors on any ten-word list would suggest that the student has reached the frustration level, and administration should end. The highest graded word list on which the student made no errors is the entry level for the passages.

5. Begin administration of the IRI passages and remind the student that this is not a test and that he or she should not worry about making mistakes; encourage the student just to do the best possible. Give the entry-level passage to the student and read the accompanying motivation statement. Tell the student that you would like him or her to read the story aloud. No silent prereading should be done on IRIs. Above all, tell the student that after the passage has been read, you will ask a few questions about it. Record the student's miscues as he or she reads. Allow five to ten seconds for the student to "figure out" a word before pronouncing it. After the entire passage has been read, remove it and ask the comprehension questions. When responses are too brief, help the student with casual questions, such as "Can you tell me more?" or "Is there another reason for that?" Avoid questions that may give away the correct answer by providing too many clues.

   As quickly as possible, count the number of miscues in the passage. Do not include titles, proper nouns, or dialect miscues. Whether or not teachers choose to count repetitions as miscues is their decision. Do, however, be consistent. (Note: Identification of the frustration level is much easier if the maximum miscues that a student can have on each passage is recorded at the bottom. For example, passage-level five consisting of 270 words allows for approximately 23 miscues before frustration level is reached.)

6. Next, determine the percentage of correct comprehension responses. It is advantageous to note at the bottom of each set of comprehension questions what percentage correct indicates the frustration level. For example, if there are 10 questions for passage five, then each question has a value of approximately 10 percent. If students answer less than five questions correctly, they are at the frustration level.

7. Continue administering subsequent passages until a frustration level is identified for either word recognition or comprehension or for both areas. It is possible that some students will reach the frustration level on one before they reach it on the other. In some instances, it is wise to continue with subsequent passages as long as the student is willing. Discrepant frustration levels on word recognition and comprehension can provide valuable information for formulating an instructional program.

Interpreting the Findings The guidelines and information on this section are intended to facilitate the selection and administration of an information reading inventory. As with many tasks, the tool selected often determines whether or not the task is accomplished successfully.

Using an IRI effectively requires more than just administering it. Interpreting the findings to help students who are having reading problems become better readers is its primary purpose.

A display, such as the one presented in table 5–3, provides a quantitative analysis of a student's reading performance. Levels of reading competence are identified and specific word-recognition miscues and comprehension errors are totaled. Although the information presented is hypothetical, this form is typical of those that accompany many commercially prepared inventories. The results shown in table 5–3 suggest that this student should use instructional materials at the fifth-grade level and library materials at the fourth-grade level. Material at grade level six and above would probably be too difficult.

The types of word-recognition miscues made in the oral reading passage indicate that the student may have problems attending to the content of the material. The number of insertions and omissions could reflect such a word-recognition problem. However, the information presented does not allow one to identify specifically what difficulties or incorrect strategies caused the mispronunciations.

The student's comprehension performance suggests that corrective or remedial reading instruction focusing on vocabulary development, sequence,

TABLE 5–3 Quantitative Analysis of a Sample IRI Performance

Passage Level	Word Recognition		Comprehension		Reading Potential
	Graded List	Passage	Oral	Silent	
PP					
P					
1					
2	100%				
3	100%	98% Ind	90% Ind	100% Ind	
4	90%	98% Ind	90% Ind	90% Ind	
5	80%	96% Inst	70% Inst	95% Ind	100%
6		94% Inst	50% Frus	85% Inst	95%
7		86% Frus	50% Frus	70% Inst	80%
8				50% Frus	80% Potential
9					60%

Reading Levels		Word Recognition Miscues		Comprehension Errors	
Independent	4	Insertions	6	Details	2
Instructional	5	Omissions	8	Main idea	1
Frustration	6–7	Mispronunciations	7	Vocabulary	4
Potential	8	Transportations	2	Sequence	5
		Teacher pronounced	3	Inference	7

and inference is warranted. However, the discrepancy of levels on the oral reading of a passage and on the silent reading of an alternate passage demands further investigation. Logically, this implies that the miscues recorded during oral reading are not interfering with the student's ability to get meaning when reading silently.

These interpretive decisions are basically quantitative. As such, they are based solely on the *number* of recorded miscues and the comprehension errors. Admittedly, such information is useful, because it answers questions about the most appropriate basal level and reading material level for instruction and recreational reading. However, minimal information is provided to answer questions that would allow for a better understanding of the student's word-recognition strengths and weaknesses, language competency, and the relationship between these and his or her comprehension abilities.

It appears as if many of this student's recorded miscues may not be interfering with comprehension when reading at higher passage levels than those where frustration occurred on the oral reading. There is a two-year difference between the frustration comprehension level on oral reading and the frustration comprehension level on silent reading. The quantitative information cannot explain why this phenomenon is present.

A more complete analysis of this student's performance can also result in more information about behavior. Qualitative information on reading behavior serves to better identify a more appropriate instructional program than can be provided by the quantitative data alone. Recalling that reading is comprehension, a qualitative analysis of miscues in relation to their effect on comprehension is helpful.

Qualitative analysis can be carried out by categorizing miscues and analyzing how they affect meaning. This kind of analysis gives the teacher a better understanding of the reader's strategies. Figure 5–1 presents a student's performance on a third-grade (level 10) passage.

Table 5–4 presents a model for recording miscues. Each miscue that is made on the oral reading of a passage is placed in the column labeled "Child" and then is compared with a text word. The comparisons are based on graphonic similarities (whether or not the miscue is similar to the sound/symbol relationship for the initial, medial, or final portion of the text word), syntax (whether or not the miscue is the same part of speech— noun, verb, adjective, and so on—as the text words), and meaning (whether or not the miscue changed or interfered with the meaning of the information conveyed in the sentence or phrase in which it occurred).

After all of the miscues have been categorized by using one or both of the categorization schemes, patterns of reading behavior can be analyzed by applying the following questions:

1. *Omissions*
   a. Did the omissions change the meaning of the text?

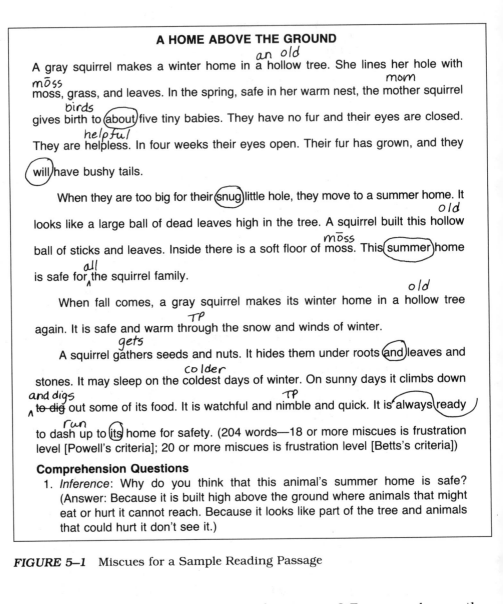

FIGURE 5–1 Miscues for a Sample Reading Passage

b. Is there a pattern in the type of omissions? For example, are they adjectives, adverbs, nouns, proper nouns, multisyllabic words, or word parts?

c. Did the omissions interfere with responding correctly to the comprehension questions?

d. Did the omissions result in comprehension responses different from the text, yet that still make sense in light of the word or words omitted?

2. *Literal*: Where does this animal make its winter home? (Answer: In a hollow tree.)

3. *Sequence*: What does this animal do with the seeds and nuts it finds? (Answer: Hides them and climbs down to eat them on sunny days.)

4. *Literal*: When do these animals move to their summer home? (Answer: When they are too big for their home in the hollow tree.)

5. *Vocabulary*: What does the word "watchful" mean in this story? (Answer: Always looking for or watching to see if there is danger.)

6. *Inference*: Why do you think that most baby animals are born in the spring? (Answer: So there will be plenty of food to eat. So they will be warm enough because they are born without fur. Accept any credible response.)

7. *Literal*: What does this animal line her nest with in the spring? (Answer: Moss, grass, and leaves.)

8. *Inference*: Why do you think that this animal and her babies have to move from their home in the hollow tree? (Answer: As the babies grow larger there is not enough room for all of them in the hollow tree.)

9. *Literal*: In what ways are this animal's winter and summer homes different? (Answer: The winter home is in a hollow tree that is smaller than the summer home. The winter home does not have to be built. The summer home is built by the squirrel in a tree. The summer home is made of leaves and sticks. Accept any combination of answers.)

10. *Inference*: Why do you think this animal hides food? (Answer: So that when the weather gets warm and the squirrel wakes up hungry it can find food to eat. It would be hard for the squirrel to find nuts and seeds with snow on the ground. The nuts and seeds would spoil because they got wet and the squirrel could not eat them. Accept any reasonable answer.)

Frustration Level = 5 errors or more

✔ = correct responses

DK = don't know; that is, no response is given or attempted

Incorrect responses are recorded beneath the question and the question number is circled.

Source: From "A Home Above the Ground" in *Animal Homes* by Sally Cartwright. New York: Putnam Publishing Group, 1973. Used with permission of The Evelyn Singer Literary Agency.

2. *Substitutions*
   a. Were the substitutions similar in shape to the text word?
   b. Did the substituted word begin with the same letter or letters as the text word?
   c. Were the substitutions correct syntactically; that is, did the reader substitute the same part of speech for the text word?
   d. Was the substitution semantically correct, such as *leap* for *jump*?
   e. Were the substitutions real words or nonsense words?

TABLE 5–4 A Scheme for Analyzing Word-Recognition Miscues

Text	Child	Graphonic Similarities Initial	Medial	Final	Syntax	Meaning
about	--	--	--	--	no	yes
will	--	--	--	--	no	no
snug	--	--	--	--	no	no
summer	--	--	--	--	no	no
and	--	--	--	--	no	no
its	--	--	--	--	no	no
a	an	yes	no	no	yes	no
hollow	old	no	yes	no	yes	yes
mother	mom	yes	no	no	yes	no
birth	birds	yes	yes	no	no	yes
helpless	helpful	yes	yes	no	yes	yes
gathers	gets	yes	no	no	no	no
coldest	colder	yes	yes	no	no	yes
dash	run	no	no	no	no	no
moss	mŏss	yes	no	yes	--	yes
for the	for ⋀ the (all)	--	--	--	no	no
to dig	⋀ digs (and)	--	--	--	yes	no
always ready	ready always				yes	no
through	TP					
nimble	TP					

3. *Insertions*
    a. Did the insertions change the meaning of the text?
    b. Was there a pattern to the insertions, such as inserting adjectives or adverbs to possibly aid comprehension?
    c. Did the insertions make sense when earlier miscues were taken into account? For example, if the student read an earlier phrase as "The lady was ⋀(not) (hot and) tired" and a subsequent phrase as "She took a ⋀(short) nap," the earlier miscue could account for the later insertion.
4. *Mispronunciations*
    a. Did the mispronunciations indicate an attempt to use a word-recognition skill, such as phonics or structural analysis?
    b. Were the mispronunciations of a particular type, such as proper names, multisyllabic words, or irregular words?
    c. Were portions of a word pronounced correctly and was there an evident pattern, such as mispronunciation of initial, medial, or ending parts of words?

5. *Meaning*
   a. Did any of the miscues change the meaning of the text material?
   b. Was there a pattern to the meaning change, such as tense, action, setting, sequence, etc.?
   c. Did the miscues interfere with correctly answering the comprehension questions?
   d. Were the miscues a result of earlier miscues? For example, if the reader read "Mark and Mary ate ⓐ̶cookie. They really liked it̶.", then the miscue in the second sentence agrees with the miscue that occurred in the preceding sentence.

      (handwritten above: cookies ... them)
   e. Did the reader attend to meaning as he or she read, such as by using words that were syntactically and semantically correct and did not result in a meaning change?
   f. Were any of the miscues the result of dialect differences? If so, they are not miscues, but their affect on comprehension should be evaluated.

Answering these questions enables the teacher to begin looking at miscues in order to gain insight into a student's reading strengths and weaknesses. Although the miscues in table 5–4 are for only one passage, answering the questions helps one to better understand this student's reading behavior.

Looking back at table 5–4, it appears that only one of the student's six omissions changed the meaning of the text (*no* indicates that there was not any change or little change in text meaning). The omission of the word *about* changed the author's intent to convey to the reader that there may be more than or fewer than five babies born to the mother squirrel. The substitutions of *old* for *hollow*, *birds* for *birth*, *helpful* for *helpless*, and *colder* for *coldest* did change the meaning of the text. However, substituting *mom* for *mother* did not change the meaning, nor did *gets* for *gathers* and *run* for *dash*. The mispronunciation of *moss* did cause a meaning change, but this word may not have been in the student's language background. (That is, if he or she has never heard the word before, it is difficult to know when it is recognized correctly and when meaning is associated with it.) The insertions and the transposition, also, had no influence on the meaning of the passage. Overall, this student made approximately 23 scoreable miscues, which would have suggested that this is his or her frustration level. However, in looking at his or her performance qualitatively, there were only approximately eight miscues that had any meaning change relationship.

While such information alone is insufficient as an accurate indicator of a student's comprehension, it provides insights into some of his or her reading behaviors and strategies. Qualitative analysis of miscues also highlights the student's strengths and weaknesses with specific word-recognition strategies. Even though the previous categorization of miscues only dealt with one passage, it appears that this reader has well-developed word-recognition skills and was focusing on meaning as the passage was read.

A note of caution is appropriate when interpreting students' reading comprehension from their performance on an IRI. Although the majority of commercially published informal reading inventories identify the level of each comprehension question (literal, inferential, critical, and the like), evidence is accumulating to suggest that students' comprehension subskill strengths and weaknesses are not revealed by their performance (Drahozal & Hanna, 1978; Schell & Hanna, 1981). For example, even though a published IRI categorizes comprehension questions as literal, inferential, or critical, it may be inappropriate to conclude that a student's performance actually reveals strengths and weaknesses in those comprehension subskills.

Because of the role that informal reading inventories can play in corrective and remedial reading, considerable time has been devoted to the discussion and the interpretation of IRIs. Many reading authorities view reading inventories as one of the most important tools for diagnosing reading levels and skills. To use them to their fullest, one must be able to analyze both the features of the instrument and the results obtained from its administration. A list of commercially available IRIs follows:

> *Analytical Reading Inventory (ARI)*, 4th ed., by Mary L. Woods and Alden J. Moe. Columbus, OH: Merrill, 1989.

> *Classroom Reading Inventory (CRI)*, 5th ed., by Nicholas J. Silvaroli. Dubuque, IA: W.C. Brown, 1986.

> *Informal Reading Assessment (IRA)*, by Paul C. Burns and Betty D. Roe. Boston, MA: Houghton-Mifflin, 1986.

> *Ekwall Reading Inventory*, by Eldon E. Ekwall. Boston, MA: Allyn & Bacon, 1985.

Alternative Procedures for Administering an IRI   The previous sections presented a method of administering and interpreting an IRI by having students read it orally. However, the IRI can also be administered in a variety of ways that will often yield additional information for teachers to use in planning their instruction. Several of these alternatives for administering an IRI are discussed in the following list.

1. Administer one form of the IRI orally and the equivalent form silently. This will provide information about students' word-recognition strategies and comprehension when reading orally and comprehension when reading silently.
2. Administer a silent IRI only. Using the graded word list to determine initial placement in the passages, have students read each passage silently, respond to the comprehension questions for the passage, and continue reading passages until the frustration level for comprehension is reached.
3. Administer alternate passages silently and orally. That is, students read

the entry-level passage silently and respond to the comprehension questions for that passage, then they read the next level passage orally and respond to the questions for that passage. This procedure continues until the frustration level is reached for both the oral and the silent reading. The teacher records students' miscues for their oral reading and can then compare oral reading comprehension with silent reading comprehension.

4. Administer the IRI orally after students have had an opportunity to first read each passage silently. This provides information about whether or not practice will facilitate their word-recognition and comprehension performance. This procedure can be modified to allow students to read one passage orally on sight, then read the next passage orally after first reading it silently.

5. Administer one passage (it does not matter if this is done orally or silently), remove the passage from the student and ask the comprehension questions, then administer the next passage level and allow the student to keep the passage to refer back to as he or she responds to the comprehension questions. Continue alternating the administration in this fashion until the student reaches his or her frustration level. Comprehension performance on the passages can then be compared to evaluate the effects of having and not having the text to refer to.

Using these alternative strategies will still require the teacher to qualitatively analyze students' performances to better understand the reading processes used, and to plan instruction to build on students' reading strengths.

Modification of the IRI to Enhance Its Usefulness   Although IRIs are often used to identify students' reading levels (independent, instructional, frustration, or potential) it is our belief that their real value lies in the qualitative analyses of students' reading behaviors. For many teachers, such analyses may seem like quite a time-consuming task; however, the benefits in terms of providing quality corrective and remedial reading instruction are well worth the time invested. Because interpretation of students' performances on an IRI should go beyond specifying reading levels, there are several important concerns about IRIs that must be addressed. Several recommendations adapted from recent reading research literature are presented in the following sections to enhance the value of using an IRI.

Students' performance on any given passage could be a reflection of their prior knowledge.   Since most commercial IRIs represent a wide range of topics, a student who is extremely familiar with the passage topic may do well in reading it, but may do poorly for a passage about a topic for which he or she has no background knowledge. This problem can be addressed by having a student read both familiar and unfamiliar passages. The student's performance in word recognition and comprehension could then be compared for the familiar and the unfamiliar text (Caldwell, 1985).

Such a comparison could reveal different reading levels—one for familiar materials and one for unfamiliar materials.

Determining students' familiarity with an IRI passage can be done by giving them the passage title as well as a capsule overview, and then asking them to say whether or not they are familiar with the topic and having them predict what kind of information will be found in the passage. Information gained about students' interests from interest inventories and from discussions with them can also be used to predict students' familiarity with a passage's content.

It is important that IRI passages are cohesive and free standing. This feature is important because it provides a uniform text for the reader. Passages should possess many of the features associated with story structure—starter events, character goals, and goal achievement. IRI passages that are poorly written make it difficult for students to read them, and such passages provide no real insight into students' reading processes.

In addition to making sure that passages are coherent and free standing, a distinction needs to be made between narrative text (story-type text) and expository text (content-area text, such as science or social studies). Teachers cannot assume that students' performances on one type of passage will transfer directly to other types of passages. Caldwell (1985) recommends that students should be exposed to only one form of text (either narrative or expository). She recommends that for primary-age students, narrative-type text is more reflective of their reading demands. For students in grades four and above, expository test is probably more useful given the content expectations for these classrooms.

Most IRIs use predetermined questions to assess students' comprehension. Predetermined questions are typically based on literal information and little emphasis is placed on unaided recall (asking students to recall information without the aid of a question). Differences in students' reading comprehension could exist between aided and unaided recall, and knowing these differences could be important in instructional planning. For example, a student may comprehend more information in unaided recall than questions alone would indicate, may have an interpretation of text that is novel in terms of his or her experiential background, may have difficulty with sequence of events, or may have only a limited idea of what the story was about. By using both aided and unaided comprehension assessment, the teacher can compare comprehension performance for familiar versus unfamiliar text, narrative versus expository text, and aided versus unaided recall.

Example of Using an IRI with Groups An informal reading inventory used with either a group of students or with the whole class can help identify students' levels of reading competence and can serve as a survey to identify students for whom additional reading diagnosis is warranted. An IRI administered in this fashion focuses on students' comprehension by

TABLE 5–5 Comprehension Performance Based on Administering an IRI to a Group of Third-Grade Students

Student	IRI Comprehension Levels and Percentage of Questions Answered Correctly by Students							
	1	2	3	4	5	6	7	8
Lisa	90%	90%	80%	90%	80%	70%	60%	40%
Billy	100%	90%	90%	90%	80%	80%	70%	70%
Jerry	80%	70%	70%	60%	60%	40%		
Becca	80%	80%	60%	50%				
Julie	80%	70%	50%					
Jeff	60%	60%	40%					

using questions for which students must provide written answers, providing written summaries of passages and having students select the one that best summarizes each passage, using passages that are familiar or unfamiliar, and using texts that are narrative or expository.

An example of using a silent IRI with questions for hypothetical third-grade students to answer is presented in table 5–5. The third-grade students began reading the level-one passage silently, then wrote their responses to 10 comprehension questions that accompanied the passages. They were instructed to read each passage in this manner, looking back at the passage if necessary to help them identify an answer for each question. Also, students were instructed to continue reading each passage until they had difficulty answering at least five of the questions correctly; then they were asked to stop. The teacher circulated among the students to monitor their responses and to answer any questions. After all the students had finished, he collected their answer sheets and scored the percentage of comprehension questions correctly answered.

The results of the silent administration of the IRI are presented in table 5–5. Using Powell's criteria for comprehension, Lisa's independent level is 4, instructional level is 6, and frustration level is 7; Billy's independent level is 4, instructional level is 8, and because 8 is the highest level read, there is no frustration level identified; Jerry's instructional level is 3 and frustration level is 6; Becca's instructional level is 3 and frustration level is 4; Julie's and Jeff's instructional levels and frustration levels are 2 and 3, respectively. Based on this group administration, the teacher could gather additional diagnositic information for the following students:

1. Billy—identify an IRI or construct passages that go beyond level 8 since there was no frustration level identified.
2. Jerry and Becca—administer an equivalent form of the IRI to each of these students in a similar manner to identify independent reading levels.
3. Julie and Jeff—administer an oral IRI to each student to identify strengths and weaknesses in word recognition and to gather additional information about their reading comprehension.

Reading Miscue Inventory (RMI)

The *Reading Miscue Inventory: An Updated Version* (Goodman, Watson, & Burke, 1987) is another informal tool that teachers can use to diagnose and evaluate students' reading. Five basic steps for administering the inventory are outlined in the *RMI* manual. A general overview of each step is presented here.

1. A student orally reads an unfamiliar story selected from either a trade book or a textbook. The story content should be familiar to the student, cohesive, and long enough to take about 15 to 20 minutes to read. Teachers are advised to have available two or three stories at differing difficulty levels. The selection chosen should be of sufficient difficulty that the student will make a minimum of 25 miscues. Goodman and Burke suggest that the first story be one grade level above that which is usually given to the student in class.

   The student's oral reading of the story is recorded on audiotape for later analysis. The teacher must sit with the reader as he or she reads, but no help should be given during the reading. A marking system similar to the one used with an IRI is used to record as many of the reader's miscues as possible on a "worksheet," which is a verbatim copy of the story. After reading the entire selection, the student retells the story. The teacher does not ask any leading questions, but does probe the student to recall as much information about the plot, characters, and description as he or she can.

2. The teacher checks and confirms miscues noted on the worksheet by listening to the tape recording of the student's oral reading. The teacher also replays the student's retelling of the story and calculates a retelling score, using an outline of the story as a guide. Procedures for calculating the retelling score are based on the story format (fictional, biographical, or informational) as well as on how many of the story features the student provided.

3. Each oral reading miscue noted on the worksheet is recorded on the *RMI* coding sheet, which is found in the manual. For each miscue recorded, the teacher determines whether or not it was (a) a dialectal variation, (b) a shift in intonation, (c) graphically similar to the text word(s), (d) similar in sound to the text word(s), (e) a grammatical function of the text word(s), (f) a correction, (g) grammatically acceptable, (h) semantically acceptable, and (i) a change in meaning from the text. Information about these nine areas on the *RMI* coding sheet enables the teacher to determine comprehension relationships. ("Comprehension Pattern") and grammar-meaning relationships ("Grammatical Relationship Patterns"). Results are then modified through simple arithmetic computations for transfer to the *RMI* reader profile.

4. The *RMI* reader profile displays a student's reading strengths and weaknesses graphically. Profiles can be prepared in an ongoing fashion

to provide insights into students' reading progress. Each profile does, however, require the administration of a different and unfamiliar story selection.

Strengths and Weaknesses of the* RMI *Compared with an IRI As with any diagnositic tool, the *Reading Miscue Inventory* has strengths and weaknesses. Its strengths include the following:

1. It uses a complete and coherent story for sampling oral reading. This feature is a major strength of the *RMI*. Because most IRIs use short passages and often not well-developed stories, they do not reflect real reading tasks.
2. It focuses on the analysis of the quality, rather than the quantity, of miscues. Although qualitative analysis of miscues can be conducted for IRIs, this is an additional procedure that the teacher must employ. The *RMI* is based on such a qualitative analysis of miscues.
3. It allows for the interpretations of students' language effects on their oral reading miscues from evidence provided by the analysis of miscues. A teacher may elect to perform such an analysis for an IRI, but it entails an extra step.
4. It focuses on the comprehension of printed language in terms of features that are associated with story structure (characters, events, plot, and theme). Informal reading inventories assess comprehension in terms of students' responses to identified questions, which are often literal in nature.
5. It provides an accompanying comprehensive set of strategy lessons intended to support the identified reading strategies that students are developing. Few IRIs provide comprehensive recommendations for enhancing students' reading development.

Among the potential weaknesses of the *Reading Miscue Inventory* are the following:

1. Administration is lengthy, time consuming, and requires special training.
2. Interpretation and scoring of students' performances is time consuming. Furthermore, interpretation of the students' retelling is highly subjective. Decisions about students' comprehension strengths and weaknesses in relation to their miscues should be considered tentative.
3. Provisions are not made for assessing students' comprehension when they are reading silently so that a comparison can be made with their oral reading comprehension performance.
4. Information to assist the teacher in identifying students' reading competence levels is not provided. Because the story selected for oral reading must be at a difficulty level to produce a minimum of 25 miscues, insights about possible independent and instructional reading levels are difficult to obtain.

One of the major disadvantages of the *RMI* noted in the previous list is the amount of time required to score and interpret a student's performance. This problem, however, can be minimized by using the *Reading Miscue Inventory System Disk* available from Literacy Plus Software, P.O. Box 2872, Denton, TX 76202. This program is intended to complete a miscue analysis with greater accuracy and in less time than if completed by hand. This "user-friendly" program is to be used on the Apple II computer with 64K Random Access Memory. It provides a reader profile for percentages of meaning construction, grammatical relations, and graphic/sound relations.

Although the *RMI* has disadvantages, it can provide important diagnostic information about students' reading. It is compatible with an IRI in corrective and remedial diagnosis, and there may be students for whom administration of both instruments will be beneficial in planning an effective instructional program.

Cloze Procedure

Since its inception, **cloze** has been widely used primarily in the area of reading for diagnostic purposes. The accepted definition of the cloze procedure consists of a transmitter (written passage), mutilation of the transmitter's language (deleting every *n*th word), and administering the mutilated patterned passages to the reader who attempts to make the passage whole again.

Passages are generally 250 to 300 words of free-standing prose with every fifth or tenth word deleted. Teachers may discover that an every fifth word deletion is too difficult for students below the fourth grade. A tenth word deletion may be more appropriate for those students. Deletion of the first word begins well into the first sentence or with the *n*th word in the second sentence.

Administering a cloze test, computing the percentage of correct replacement, and identifying the reading level is a quantitative procedure similar to identifying reading competence levels with an IRI. The levels identified with the cloze procedure, however, provide information about the reader's ability to deal with the content structure of the information presented. As such, it is essentially a means for determining readability. Student performance on a cloze test assists the teacher in assessing the students' ability to deal with contextual features, such as organization, language structure, and concepts. This information is useful in determining which students are capable of reading specific textbooks. Insightful information about students' reading abilities can be further gleaned through the use of qualitative procedures.

The percentage of correct cloze items is determined by dividing the number of correct cloze items by the total number of cloze items on the test. The percentage of cloze items completed correctly can then be compared with a criterion scale, such as the one developed by Rankin and Culhane (1969). Correct replacement of 61 percent or more of the deleted

A HOME ABOVE THE GROUND

A gray squirrel makes a winter home in a hollow tree. She lines her hole with moss, grass, and leaves. In the spring, safe *in* her warm nest, the *gray* squirrel gives birth to *her* five tiny babies. They *have* no fur and their *eyes* are closed. They are *little*. In four weeks their *eyes* open. Their fur has *grown* and they will have *big* tails.

When they are *real* big for their snug *home* hole, they move to *a* summer home. It looks *like* a large ball of *dead* leaves high in the *tree*. A squirrel built this *big* ball of sticks and *leaves*. Inside there is a *soft* floor of moss. This *new* home is safe for *all* the squirrel family.

When fall *comes* a gray squirrel makes *its* winter home in a *big* tree again. It is *nice* and warm through the *cold* and winds of winter.

Mom squirrel gathers seeds and *nuts*. It hides them under *sticks* and leaves and stones. *Mom* may sleep on the *cold* days of winter. On *other* days it climbs down *and* dig out some of *its* food. It is watchful *and* nimble and quick. It *is* always ready to dash *in* to its home for *food*.

FIGURE 5-2 Sample Cloze Passage

words is the independent level. The instructional level would be determined by the correct replacement of 41 percent of the deleted words, and less than 40 percent correct replacement would be the frustration level.

The passage introduced in figure 5–1 is now presented in figure 5–2 as a cloze passage. Every fifth word was deleted, resulting in 37 deletions. The reader's responses are given for each of the deletions. The number of exact replacements of deleted words (research indicates that scoring only exact replacements is the most efficient way of determining levels) is 17 out of 37. Dividing 17 by 37 equals a correct replacement percentage of approximately 46, which is the instructional level. Using this information as a determinant of readability for narrative text would suggest that the material from which this passage was taken would be appropriate for instruction. Categorization of the types of errors, however, offers insight that level identification overlooks.

Evaluating incorrect word choices leads to a better understanding of the reader's use of syntax (word order and tense), semantics (meaning), and reasoning as the material is read. If many of the errors are correct syntactically, this suggests that a reader is using the words preceding and following the deletion in an attempt to supply the missing word. Errors that are semantically correct indicate meaning is occurring. If errors are related to continuity of material, that is, where previous textual material implies replacement of the missing word or there appears to be reasoning on the part of the reader in supplying the missing word, this could reflect that the student is synthesizing information and recognizes its continuity.

TABLE 5–6 Summarizing Cloze Errors

Syntax	Semantics	Continuity
gray (mother) ----------gray (mother)		
her (about)		
little (helpless) --little		
big (bushy) ------------big (bushy)		
real (too) ----------------real (too)		
home (little)		
big (hollow)-------------big (hollow)		
new (summer) --new		
all (the)		
big (hollow) --big		
nice (safe) --------------nice (safe)		
cold (snow) --cold		
mom (a) --mom		
sticks (roots) ----------sticks (roots)		
mom (it) --mom		
cold (coldest)---cold		
other (sunny)---other		
and (to)		
in (up)--------------------in (up)		
food (safety) --food		

The summary of cloze errors in table 5–6 reflects an ability to understand the structure of written English. Many of the words that were substituted did not interfere with the intended meaning. Continuity errors, as well as correct responses, indicate an attention to context and synthesis of the information. For example, *little* was a good choice for a reader who has background knowledge about the size of baby squirrels; also, the word *tiny* would lead a reader who can synthesize text information to predict that they are little. Other examples of continuity, such as *new, big,* and *mom* also indicate that the reader has given attention to meaning as he or she reads the text. The other continuity errors add further support to the idea that this reader focuses on getting meaning as he or she reads.

Error categorization provides more information for instructional decision making. Not only can the reader handle this material at an instructional level, but specific reading strengths and weaknesses come to light. Such information combined with other diagnostic findings enables the teacher to identify the most appropriate corrective or remedial reading instruction.

Modifications of the Cloze Procedures In addition to administering a cloze test such as the method noted previously, there are modifications that teachers can consider that will provide additional diagnostic information to use in planning reading instruction.

1. Develop cloze tests for both familiar and unfamiliar materials. Note whether or not students' performances vary in their use of syntax, semantics, and continuity. If, for example, there is no variation in syntactic errors, this could indicate that the students have understandings about the structure of written language. If their performances for semantics and continuity are better on familiar passages, this indicates that they are able to synthesize information as they read and focus on comprehending text.
2. Delete selected words in a passage, such as nouns, verbs, adjectives, pronouns, and so forth. Note students' areas of strengths and weaknesses related to understanding language structure of written materials.
3. Provide students written choices for each of the words deleted. Depending on their ability to complete cloze tasks, these choices can be very similar (for more capable students) or very different (for less capable students), which will influence their ability to select a word for each deletion. Selective deletion of words as noted in number 2 can be used to get an idea of students' attention to both language structure and context as they read.
4. Delete every other sentence from a free-standing passage and have students either write a sentence that makes sense or select from choices providing sentences that make sense for each sentence deleted. The responses can be analyzed to better understand if students integrate text as they read and if they understand how story information is related.

Teacher Observation, Interviews, and Teacher-Made Tests

Observation, interviewing students, and teacher-made instruments are three of the more powerful reading diagnostic tools. They enable the teacher to use ongoing diagnosis that focuses on both students' reading development and on the quality of reading instruction. Observation, interviews, and teacher-made tests can focus directly on the content of classroom instruction for all phases of the reading program, not just the basic skill development that is reflected in standardized tests (see the section "Norm-Referenced Measures of Reading Strengths and Weaknesses").

Observation and Interviews Teacher observation includes a variety of techniques. Group and individual instruction, worksheets, library reading, and daily reading assignments are areas for which observation is a powerful tool. One of the more difficult teacher tasks for each area is knowing what to look for. Several procedures enable the teacher to collect valuable observation data about students' reading.

A first step in systematic observation is identifying the goals and subgoals of reading instruction for students. Goals and subgoals can be referred to as the objectives of instruction—the task conditions (see chapter 3) that identify the reading behaviors students are supposed to acquire. Without such information to guide the observation of students' reading, gradual improvement may be inaccurately interpreted as no improvement.

Observation can also focus on the organizational and instructional features of corrective remedial reading programs. In the situations, the focus is not only on students' reading improvement, but also on how students react to oral tasks, written tasks, structure, motivational strategies, and the like. For example, some students may need more structure, longer time periods to complete tasks, more teacher feedback, frequent teacher attention, and so forth. Again, it is important for the teacher to identify precisely the organizational and instructional characteristics that will be assessed through observation.

Examples describing the use of observation in reading diagnosis are presented throughout the text (see chapters 4, 7, 9, and 15). These examples include collecting observational data through the use of checklists, worksheets, and daily reading assignments for the areas of word recognition, comprehension, interest and attitudes toward reading, language development, motivation, group instruction, and individual instruction. Examples also illustrate the purposes for making such observations and the procedures for interpreting the information that is gathered for the reading area under consideration. The key point for teachers to remember is that observation is one of their most powerful diagnostic tools. It provides information that cannot be gathered by written means.

Interviewing students about different features of reading can be a valuable source of diagnostic information. Too often, teachers fail to talk to their students about "why" they are doing something a certain way and then assume that students do poorly because they lack skill development. However, taking the time to talk to and interview students in a relaxed and informal manner will provide insights into their reading development. Interviews can either be structured with predetermined questions or on the spot. Regardless of the type of interview, valuable information for use in planning reading instruction can be gained. Examples of questions that teachers can use when interviewing students include:

1. When you come to a word you do not know, how do you figure it out? Show me in this story how you would figure out this word if you did not know it. (Provide student with an example.)
2. What do you think makes a good reader? (Provide encouragement and prompts if necessary.)
3. If you were to read a story about horses (or any chosen topic), what kinds of information do you think you would find in the story?
4. If we had a new student entering our class who did not know what it meant to read, how would you describe reading to him or her?
5. When I ask you to read a story so we can later discuss it, what do you think I mean? Tell me how you would read that story and prepare for the discussion.
6. What makes understanding some stories hard or easy for you?
7. What does a story title tell you?

Valuable information that can be used when planning reading instruction is often gained from interviewing children about different features of reading. (David Strickler)

8. What makes a story fun or interesting to read?
9. What makes a story hard or uninteresting to read?
10. If I asked you to retell a story to our class, how would you read it so you could do this?

These questions are examples of those teachers could use to interview their students. If students experience difficulty in responding to certain questions, examples or prompts might be necessary to help them in their responses. Students who have difficulty in responding or give brief responses may have reading difficulties associated with the questions asked.

As with observation, talking with students about their reading can give teachers insights that are not available through any other means.

Teacher-Made Tests   Most teachers construct and use teacher-made tests in their corrective and remedial reading programs. The cloze test discussed earlier is one example of a teacher-made reading test. Such tests require careful planning and call for considerable time, knowledge, and effort in their construction. Before teachers attempt to construct their own reading tests, they must consider whether or not a quality commercial test is available that meets their needs. If such a test is unavailable, then the following questions should be answered before preparing a teacher-made test.

What is the intended purpose of the test?   If the test is to be diagnostic, then it should point out reading strengths and weaknesses. If the results are to be used to compare what students in the class have learned, then the test is more appropriate for program evaluation.

A test that is diagnostic in nature would assist the teacher in determining individual students' strengths and weaknesses in contextual analysis. It would not focus on how one student compares with others in the classroom, but on his or her capabilities in using context clues. A test designed to evaluate the contextual analysis skills of an entire class would most likely be broader in its content. Test results would be used to compare each student's performance with that of the whole class. Often, teacher-made tests can be either diagnostic or evaluative depending on how performance is interpreted. Interpretations that focus on specifying strengths and weaknesses for individuals—or for the class as a whole—are diagnostic; those that focus on comparing performances are concerned with evaluation.

What reading behaviors are to be measured?   The test can measure performance in terms of either specific instructional objectives or of general program objectives. Instructional objectives are intended to assist teachers in analyzing students' progress in terms of their direct instruction. Program objectives are usually global in nature and are based on the long-term goals of a grade level, school, or school district.

Regardless of the reading behaviors to be tested, it is important to specify accurately the behavior that the test is to measure. Reading behaviors should be specified in a behavioral objective format that clearly identifies an observable behavior—for example, "Students will read four given passages containing a series of major events, and for each passage, they will identify four of the events by writing them in their proper sequential order"; "Students will read ten short passages and select from a list of five titles the one passage title that best fits each passage." These examples do not identify an acceptable criterion level, such as 80 percent accuracy. We believe that it is important for the teacher to judge an individual student's performance not in terms of mastery, but in terms of (1) whether or not the student is showing growth, and (2) what level of performance is necessary for maximizing the student's success in subsequent instruction.

Each objective identified for testing should be measured by a single test. If the test includes more than one instructional or program behavior, it may confuse students and, therefore, provide an inaccurate sampling of their reading behavior. Also, it is easier to write and analyze test items that focus on a single behavior; thus the quality of the test items and the analysis of students' performances are enhanced.

What kinds of test formats and test items are most appropriate for the identified objectives and intended use of the results? Because teacher-made tests are intended to provide a written record of students' reading that can be analyzed to assist in planning effective corrective or remedial reading instruction, test items will be either objective or essay. Objective test formats present information to the students, who select or write a response. Multiple-choice, matching, and true/false questions are examples of items for which students select a response. Items that require students to write one or two sentences or to fill in a blank are examples of items where students write a response. Essay items can require students to write short or lengthy answers, depending on the reading behavior that is being tested.

When deciding which test format and test items to use in constructing a test, it is important that teachers select the most appropriate format or item for the behavioral objective being tested. Basic reading skills such as phonics, contextual analysis, and syllabication lend themselves well to objective test formats. Tests intended to diagnose or evaluate comprehension of actual reading materials may be limited by reliance on an objective format alone. Therefore, an essay format is recommended for the evaluation of comprehension behaviors, such as making inferences about an unfinished story, describing a story setting, detailing character traits, and evaluating plot. When writing either type of test item, pay careful attention to providing clear and understandable directions for taking the test, using vocabulary and reading materials familiar to the students, making sure that each item is independent, and providing only one correct response for each item. Procedures for evaluating each of these concerns include: (1) take the test and ask yourself whether directions are clear, vocabulary is appropriate, items are independent, and only one correct response has been listed for each item; (2) ask other teachers to take the test and evaluate it; and (3) administer the test to a group of students who are at a similar reading level but are not in the class or group for whom the results will be analyzed. Revise or eliminate those items identified as ambiguous or inappropriate in the evaluation procedures.

Constructing diagnostic reading tests is a time-consuming and demanding task. Teacher-made tests are, however, important diagnostic tools. Well-made tests can provide important information that may be unavailable from other sources.

Independent Practice/Application Activities

An important source of diagnostic information about students' reading is their performance on independent practice and application activities. Teacher-made worksheets and quality workbook activities can be analyzed to identify students' reading strengths and weaknesses. Important areas of consideration in analyzing students' performances in such activities are discussed here:

□ When several students miss identical items on an assigned activity sheet, it could suggest that these were not within their experiential/conceptual background. That is, the concepts or the format of the items were ones that the students were not familiar with. Therefore, the students may possess the skill or ability, but could not apply it because they lacked the necessary background knowledge. In such a situation, the teacher could talk with the students about why they responded as they did, or could identify similar activities containing familiar formats or information. A comparison of students' performance on the familiar activity with the one suspected of being unfamiliar will help the teacher determine if the students are in need of additional instruction or if the activity was of questionable quality.

□ If the content is familiar and a quality activity is used, students who have difficulty may need more teacher-supervised instruction before they can independently transfer their learning to seat work tasks.

□ Students who have problems with independent tasks may need more practice examples on activity sheets to better understand the task. Completing one or two examples with students before they are to complete an activity on their own will help them to better understand what they are to do.

□ If students have difficulties with a particular worksheet, it may be due to the fact that it does not relate directly to the teacher's instruction. The students, therefore, have not been provided the opportunity to learn the skills and abilities necessary to successfully complete the task. This is often the case when basal reader workbooks are used with a basal reader lesson. Students may need to be reintroduced to the focus of the worksheet if its content deals with past instruction, instead of the lesson at hand.

□ Worksheets that focus on isolated skills, such as learning lists of words without knowing any contextual information, do not reflect reading as an act of getting meaning. Students who do poorly on such activities may not exhibit problems if they are provided contextual clues that more accurately reflect reading. Rather than assuming that the students need reteaching when they do poorly on isolated skill activities, teachers can compare their performances on the same skill when it is presented during an actual reading task.

□ Qualitative analysis of students' worksheet performances can help the teacher gather diagnostic data about whether or not the students were focusing on meaning, even though their responses were incorrect. For example, if the student was to select the word *silk* from a given list of words to complete the sentence, "Daddy has a new _____ tie," but then writes *blue* in the blank, this indicates that the written response makes sense and that meaning was a focus of the student's response.

□ Observation can also be used to determine if a student just guessed at the answers or had difficulty applying the skill or ability. If a student hurriedly completes an activity and is finished before the other students, this could indicate that he or she was simply guessing and did not concentrate on responding correctly. Teachers who suspect this can work individually with the student as he or she completes the examples on the worksheet. This will help in determining if his or her performance was due to a lack of understanding or a lack of concentration on the task. If the student tends to rush through activity sheets, the teacher might want to give him or her less to do or supervise the student more closely while he or she is completing independent activities.

Word-Recognition Assessment Tools

Many commercial informal word-recognition tests and surveys are available. They are informal because there are no specific norms for comparing a reader's performance with a national sample. There are, of course, guidelines for administering the instrument and for interpreting the results. Many of these diagnostic instruments are intended for group or individual administration. One instrument, the *Botel Reading Inventory*, has two equivalent forms for assessing word recognition, word opposites—listening, word opposites—reading, and phonics mastery. Others are to be administered individually. One example is the *Diagnostic Reading Scales*, which consists of three word-recognition lists, two reading selections for primer to eighth-grade reading levels, and eight phonics tests.

It is not our intent to list and discuss the commercially available diagnostic instruments here. Many of them are discussed in the following chapters and are listed in the appendix. The focus of this section is to help teachers approach the selection and interpretation of such instruments in an analytical fashion.

There are several points to consider when selecting a commercially published word-recognition diagnostic instrument. The most important include:

How are the results to be used?

Does the instrument relate to current and past instruction?

Does the instrument assess actual reading skills?

How Are Results to Be Used? One of the four variables important for an individualized instructional program is learner style. Selection of a word-recognition instrument should facilitate decision making in this area.

A group diagnostic instrument can be a valuable survey technique. Administering it to a group of students facilitates identification of those who need specific word-recognition instructions and those who do not. Once students who exhibit weaknesses are identified, individually administered instruments can be given. Individual diagnostic tests can be used to point out specific areas of reading strengths as well as weaknesses needing remedial or corrective instruction.

If the results are to be used to ensure that corrective or remedial instruction is aimed at specific reading strengths and weaknesses, individually administered instruments should be used. Findings, however, should be substantiated through the use of other diagnostic tools. Student performance on any diagnostic assessment represents only a sampling of reading behavior, and decisions based on the results of one instrument could be unreliable.

Does the Instrument Relate to Current and Past Instruction? This question appears to contradict the concern that remedial and corrective reading be individualized; however, it is unwise to administer a group instrument to assess phonic skills, for example, if previous reading instruction concentrated on a whole-word approach. The results would reflect a deficiency in phonics for the majority of students. The correct tack would be to administer a group survey instrument that determines competency with recognition of words in relation to instructional emphases. The teacher can use the results from the survey test to determine those students who are having problems and then administer individual instruments. Also, by focusing on what has been taught, teachers can identify students who are not learning with a specific approach and method. This information may indicate that the previous approaches and methods were not the best for a particular student or that there were gaps in past instruction.

Does the Instrument Assess Actual Reading Skills? It is important to analyze the items on word-recognition instruments or subtests to determine if actual reading skills are being measured. Items should deal with reading skills as they relate to actual reading situations. Such a characteristic ensures that the instrument is valid. For example, test items that require the students to listen to the teacher's pronunciation of words or letters, interpret likenesses or differences in pictures, or match rhyming words may, in fact, be assessing skills that are not actual reading skills. Listening to sounds represented by letters, groups of letters, or words is different from reading them in print. Picture or object discrimination is not the same as letter and word discrimination. Likewise, poor performance with rhyming words does not mean that a reader has difficulty auditorily discriminating words with the same last sounds; some readers may not know what *rhyme* means. Furthermore, even if students do well on a rhyming test, it may not mean that they attended to auditory discrimination of ending sounds. Rhyming words tend to have similar spelling patterns, and the readers may have focused on this feature, rather than on the sounds represented by the letters.

The more closely the test items approximate student performance in actual reading situations, the more valid are the results. A good first step in evaluating instrument validity is to ask, "Are these items assessing word-recognition skills as they are applied in actual reading situations?" If the answer is no, then a different instrument should be found or constructed.

Whether teachers construct their own informal word-recognition instrument or select a commercially published version, they should take an analytical approach. Considering how the results are to be used, if the test items are related to previous instruction and experiences, and if actual reading skills are measured enhances such an analysis. Remedial and corrective reading instruction cannot meet students' reading needs if those needs, as well as strengths, are not determined as accurately as possible.

NORM-REFERENCED MEASURES OF READING STRENGTHS AND WEAKNESSES

Standardized norm-referenced reading measures sample reading behavior in a controlled, systematic fashion. Such features as administration, scoring, and interpretation are prescribed. The test items, reliability, validity, and norms have been experimentally determined.

There are two basic types of norm-referenced measures for evaluating students' reading behaviors. General achievement tests include subtests that measure reading skills. For example, the *SRA Achievement Series* identifies a reading comprehension score, a vocabulary score, and a total reading score, which is an average of comprehension and vocabulary. Diagnostic standardized reading tests differ from general achievement tests in that they sample only reading behavior. Their interpretation focuses on identifying strengths and weaknesses. Both types of tests may be appropriate for either group or individual administration, and such information is stated in the administrator's manual.

For the novice tester or diagnostician, the number of available tests and subtests could be overwhelming. Additional test information can be found in Buros's compilation of reading tests. Because so many tests are available, teachers will have to decide what they need and select the test that will best meet those needs. The teacher must first decide what classification—that is, group, individual, oral, mastery, or reading skills—he or she desires. The next step would be to look at validity, reliability, ease of administration, and cost.

The value of norm-referenced tests has long been debated in educational circles. Some of the most-often-cited shortcomings of such tests are that they are biased, are used only for purposes of labeling the student, are irrelevant for today's curriculum, and do not help the learner learn. These may indeed be shortcomings if the individual using the test does not concentrate on minimizing such factors through careful selection and interpretation.

Selecting a Norm-Referenced Test

We cannot overemphasize the importance of selecting an instrument, whether it is informal or standardized, by giving major consideration to how the results will be used. If the results are used to survey a class's or an individual's reading ability, then selection of an improper instrument is not too damaging. However, if a student's test performance will be evaluated to determine candidacy for a remedial reading program, then improper test selection can have a damaging effect. Ideally, the teacher will always attempt to select the most appropriate assessment instruments available in relation to how the results will be used. For norm-referenced test selection, teachers should focus on such test features as validity, reliability, and normative population.

Validity Test **validity** implies the appropriateness of a measure in view of its instructional results. Teachers often complain that a test is not valid. Even though the validity of the instrument is substantiated in the administrator's guide, these teachers are often correct in their concerns for test validity.

For example, imagine an achievement test had been administered in the spring to four classes of third-grade students. The reading subtests were to be used to evaluate students' reading growth by comparing the present results with test results taken in the spring of the second grade. Student performance on the third-grade assessment showed minimal growth. As a result, the teachers questioned whether their instruction was ineffective or whether the test was invalid. A review of the reading subtests item by item, classifying each item in terms of the skill it was measuring, resulted in a unanimous conclusion by the teachers that the subtests focused primarily on comprehension. Some interesting points can be illuminated by reviewing the teachers' reading-instruction emphases for the school year and by matching what was taught with what the test measured. As a result of student performance on the second-grade test, the teachers had identified several word-recognition skills that needed continued emphasis in the third grade. These word-recognition areas became the focus of their instruction, and they placed minimal emphasis on comprehension. The reading subtest administered in the spring to the third graders devoted a considerable number of test items to comprehension, which accounted for the poor performance by the majority of students.

Thus, the test was not valid in terms of the content measured. However, this procedure made the teachers realize the importance of developing a more balanced reading program that focused on both word recognition and comprehension.

This example illustrates the importance of considering content validity when selecting a standardized norm-referenced reading test. Even when a test is called a reading test and a check of the items indicates that reading skills are measured, the test may still not "fit." For a test to fit, the test items must measure reading skills and abilities in relation to past instruction. **Content validity** means that the reading skills and abilities measured by the test are those that were taught in the instructional program.

A basic reason for testing is to determine student progress in the instructional program. Those who are having reading problems can be identified, and instruction can be planned to better meet their needs. Tests that do not have content validity do not provide the information necessary for that kind of decision making. Such an instrument, in fact, measures student knowledge of a subject prior to its even being taught.

A good procedure for determining the content validity of a test is to review each test item, categorize the items into reading skill areas, and determine if the items and skill areas measure learnings taught in past instruction. A review and classification of each item enables teachers to determine more objectively how the skills are measured and if there are enough items to assess each skill accurately. The majority of items, and especially the skill areas, should relate to previous instruction; however, the wording of test items need not be identical to previous reading instruction. Identical items would, most likely, be too easy and would not reliably discriminate; thus, the test's validity would be lowered. The important point is that test items should sample students' reading behaviors based on previous instruction.

If test scores are to be used to predict future reading performances or to provide an estimate of present performances on a related task, the teacher must then be concerned with **criterion-related validity**, which is how well a test predicts a student's future performance in an area other than that which the test covered. For example, a reading survey test could be used to predict student performance in future instructional programs. An individual phonics test might be administered to estimate a student's present skill in identifying new words. The former example predicts performance over time; the latter example evaluates the relationship between a measure and current performance.

How well a test predicts a student's future performance in instruction is important for early identification of students who may have reading problems. For example, if performance on test *ABC* has a high correlation with reading test *LMN*, expressed as a correlation coefficient, then performance on *ABC* should predict those students who will do well and those who will do poorly on test *LMN*. A reading readiness test, for example, is one piece of information about students' performances that is used to predict success in beginning reading instruction. Most standardized readiness tests provide information about the correlation of the test with the tests that are typically used to assess later beginning reading performances. The higher the validity coefficient (correlation between two instruments), the more accurate is the prediction from one test to the other. A perfect positive relationship would be expressed as 1.0. As a validity coefficient approaches 1.0, the accuracy of prediction increases.

Another example in which criterion-related validity could be a useful factor is an instance in which a teacher who uses record keeping, observation, and teacher-made tests to determine students' phonic skills in attacking new words may wish to adopt a less time-consuming procedure. A phonics test or a word-recognition test might be less time consuming but just as accurate. To find out if this is the case, an appropriate test is identified and administered to the students, and the test scores are correlated with the teacher's evaluation scores. A high correlation of 0.70 or greater indicates that the test could serve as a valid measure of word recognition; a low correlation would indicate that the test is not assessing those skills deemed important by the teacher.

Another important test validity is **construct validity.** This is the extent to which test performance can be interpreted in terms of certain psychological constructs (Gronlund, 1976). A psychological construct is an assumed quality that explains some behavior; for example, reading comprehension is a construct. People who comprehend what they read possess certain behaviors, and these behaviors form the theory for reading comprehension. Construct validity is important in test selection because it affects test interpretation. Construct validity, like content validity, can be evaluated by reviewing the recommended interpretations and then determining the strength of the evidence supporting such interpretations.

Careful examination of the test items and the examiner's manual helps ensure that the test is valid for its intended use. However, Gronlund has identified other factors that can lower the validity of test results. Unclear directions to the student, test items that are too easy or too difficult, ambiguous statements, improper arrangement of items (items should be arranged in order of difficulty), unauthorized assistance, test length that is too short, and items inappropriate for the outcomes being measured are defects that jeopardize the validity of an instrument and limit its usefulness when making instructional decisions.

Reliability **Reliability** is the feature of a measurement instrument that deals with consistency of results. When a reliable instrument is administered to the same group on two different occasions, similar test scores are obtained. Reliability is important because it means that the findings are consistent. Unreliable tests place the teacher in a weak position when interpreting the results. If a student's score on test X is 20 on one administration and 100 on another, interpretation is almost impossible. Which of these scores most accurately reflects performance?

Reliability for norm-referenced tests is presented as a coefficient. Test *X*, mentioned earlier, would have a low coefficient in comparison to a test having a 0.90 or greater reliability coefficient. A reliability coefficient above 0.85 is acceptable. There may be times when the most appropriate instrument for a specific reading skill has less than the desired coefficient. In such a situation the instrument's validity is of primary importance. However, if a less reliable instrument is the only one available, it is still better to use that test than to concede that a particular skill is not worth assessing.

High reliability is one feature to consider when selecting an assessment instrument. However, it does not ensure that the instrument is valid. A test can be consistent in measuring a reading skill, but if the skill is unimportant, such information is of little value.

Normative Population   A norm-referenced test allows the teacher to compare a student's reading performance with that of a representative sample, called the **normative population**. The population on which the test was normed is usually described in detail in the administrator's guide. If the norming group is not representative of the students taking the test, then comparing the student's performance with the national norming group is of little value. Suppose, for example, that test *EFG*'s norming population was composed of only rural males. Administering test *EFG* to female students living in the city and comparing their performance on test *EFG* with the norming population would be of little value, unless, perhaps, the teacher was interested in seeing how these female students' scores on *EFG* compared with the males' scores.

Interpreting Norm-Referenced Test Results

Standardized measures, like informal measures, can be interpreted both quantitatively and qualitatively. Quantitative interpretation, while inherently valuable, can be much more valuable when it is combined with qualitative interpretation.

Quantitative Interpretation   Student performance on standardized norm-referenced reading tests is reported in several ways. Grade-equivalent scores, percentile ranks, and stanines are typical norm-referenced scores. However, such scores do little to help the teacher identify a student's particular reading strengths and weaknesses. Students who score considerably below their present age or grade level may or may not have reading problems. Conversely, students who score considerably above their present age or grade level may, in fact, have a reading problem. Students can score above their present age or grade level and still not be reading at a level appropriate to their expected reading level. Also, norm-referenced reading test scores often indicate a student's frustration level. The instructional level is usually at a lower level than the score on the test indicates.

Grade-Level Equivalents. **Grade-level equivalents** have been used frequently in the past to report a student's performance on a standardized norm-referenced test. The International Reading Association passed a resolution in 1981 urging users to abandon the use of grade equivalents to report students' reading performances. Furthermore, the resolution urged test publishers to eliminate grade equivalents from their tests. While publishers may not heed the advice of the resolution, users should consider discontinuing the use of grade equivalents in reporting students' reading performances.

There are a number of major disadvantages associated with grade-level equivalents. Grade-level norms do not indicate where a student should be reading or where he or she is actually reading. For example, a grade equivalent of 8.3 for a third grader does not mean that he or she has mastered skills equal to the eighth-grade third-month level. Likewise, a grade equivalent of 3.2 for an eighth grader does not mean that he or she reads at a third-grade second-month level. Grade-level equivalents can be interpreted in such instances to mean that these students' raw scores on the test were equivalent to the raw scores obtained by the *average* students in the eighth year, third month of school and in the third year, second month of school, respectively.

Grade-level scores should be interpreted cautiously. They have limited value both in assessing students' progress and in identifying their reading strengths and weaknesses. You should not use grade-level scores to compare students' progress over time, primarily because they do not represent equal units at different parts of the distribution and between different tests.

Stanines. **Stanines** are also used to report students' reading test performance. Stanines range from 1 through 9 and divide the distribution of raw scores into nine parts. Unlike grade and age levels, they are not fixed scores but a range. Stanine 5 is the mean or average score and includes from one-fourth of a standard deviation on both sides of the mean. The other stanines are distributed evenly above and below stanine 5. Stanines 4 through 6 are considered average, 3 through 1 below average, and 7 through 9 above average. Because stanines do not specify levels, they do not place the student at a fixed grade or age level. Also, the interpretation of reading growth based on pretest-posttest results is significant if a difference of two or more stanines is found.

Percentile Ranks. Another popular means for reporting performance, **percentile rank**, refers to an individual's rank in some particular group. Thus, a percentile of 75 means that 75 percent of the individuals in the norming group scored at or below this score. The percentile unit, however, is not equal as it ranges from 1 through 99. Test differences in the middle ranges (for example, 40 to 60) are smaller differences in test performance than at the extremes. When interpreting a percentile gain, a smaller gain at either extreme can represent greater growth than a larger percentile gain in the middle range.

A final note about quantitative test interpretation is appropriate before we move on to qualitative analysis. Standardized norm-referenced tests contain a margin of error, which is reported in the administrator's guide as the **standard error of measurement**. Because of this margin of error, a score should be viewed as a band rather than as a fixed value. For example, if the standard error of measurement for reading test *ABC* is 0.5 grade levels, and a student's score on the test was equivalent to a 3.2 grade level, then the performance should be interpreted as plus or minus 0.5. Thus, the score is not 3.2, but between 2.7 and 3.7. This is a one-year range and points out the absurdity of treating a single test score as an accurate assessment of reading ability.

A severe limitation of relying solely on quantitative test results is the assumption that students who have identical scores also have similar reading strengths and weaknesses. Assume that eight fourth-grade students are administered a norm-referenced reading test and each of them scores at the sixth stanine. Regardless of whether the test is administered as a group test or individually, one cannot assume that each student has the same reading ability. One student could have answered correctly each item on the first half of the test and missed every item on the second half. Another student may have reversed the process. Still others may have answered every other item correctly. A more analytical approach for identifying the reading needs of students is to use some techniques to analyze their test performance qualitatively.

Qualitative Interpretation Qualitative analysis enables teachers to gather data that can help them determine students' reading strengths and weaknesses. Even if the test is not intended to be diagnostic, valuable information for instructional planning can be gained by looking at patterns of performance and conducting an item analysis. Several qualitative procedures for analyzing norm-referenced test results have been identified by Ladd (1971). Each of these is presented in the following sections with a brief description of the procedure and its purpose.

Item Analysis. Each item of the test is analyzed and categorized as to what it is measuring. Recalling that content validity is important in test selection, this procedure helps to determine whether or not it exists. The categories may differ from those identified by the test publisher, but in relation to past instruction the difference may be warranted. The correct responses and errors of each student are recorded for each of the categorized items. This information serves to identify mastery of reading skills for the class as a whole, as well as for individual students.

Patterns of Performance. As mentioned earlier, test items are arranged in order of difficulty. The pattern of correct responses often indicates when a student has ceased to answer items based on knowledge and has started to guess. A high number of correct items in relation to those answered is a good indication that skills and abilities are being tested. When this pattern becomes less noticeable (that is, there are more incorrect responses in relation to items attempted), this suggests that the student has begun to guess. Students should be discouraged from guessing. Ladd says, "Guessing contributes nothing to anyone, neither pupil nor teacher, which is helpful in improving instruction" (p. 307).

Untimed Score. Those students who have not completed the test within the specified time limit are allowed to finish using a marking instrument of a different color. Optically scanned answer sheets can be marked with a color that is not picked up by the scanner. As a result of removing time restrictions, two scores are obtained. One is the score for the test time limits, the other is the untimed score. If a sizable difference between the two is noted, students may need instruction in developing more efficient reading habits.

Reinforced-by-Hearing Technique. The reinforced-by-hearing technique results in a measure of reading potential or capacity for comparison with a reading measure obtained on the standardized administration. Following the administration of the test under standard conditions, the same test or an alternate form is read aloud to the student. The student follows along reading silently while the teacher reads each item and its possible answers. After both tests are scored, a three-stanine difference in favor of the version read aloud probably means that the student has a higher ability in understanding the material than indicated by a standard assessment of reading achievement. Further individual diagnosis is warranted to identify areas that need corrective or remedial instruction.

Norm-referenced reading tests for evaluating and identifying reading strengths and weaknesses are neither inherently good nor bad. How such tests are selected and how their results are interpreted determine whether or not they benefit students. Teachers who are aware of the features on which to focus when evaluating standardized tests for possible use—such as what reading skills and abilities are assessed, how the results should be interpreted, and what logical decisions about student reading can be made—limit the possibility that the instruments will be used improperly.

CRITERION-REFERENCED MEASURES OF READING STRENGTHS AND WEAKNESSES

Varying definitions of what constitutes a criterion-referenced test (CRT) appear in the literature. Popham and Husek (1969) define criterion-referenced measures as those which are used to ascertain an individual's status with respect to some criterion, i.e., performance standard. It is because the individual is compared with some established criterion, rather than other individuals, that these measures are described as criterion-referenced. (p. 2)

A criterion-referenced test is defined by Livingston (1972) as any test for which the test user wants to compare each student's score not with the mean of some group, but with a specified criterion score that does not depend on the scores that students actually obtained on the test. Similar to this definition is Otto's (1973), which indicates that criterion-referenced measurement relates test performance to absolute standards, usually stated in terms of behavioral objectives. Jackson (1970) emphasizes that the method of construction is the defining factor of criterion-referenced tests and applies to "a test designed and constructed in a manner that defines explicit rules linking patterns of test performances to behavioral referents" (p. 3).

Differences Between Criterion-Referenced and Norm-Referenced Tests

As reflected in these definitions of criterion-referenced tests, differences exist between CRTs and norm-referenced tests. Klein (1972) states that the essential difference between the two is not an intrinsic measurement, but a question of the interpretation of the measurement's results. One major difference cited by Otto (1973) is that there is a low degree of overlap among the instruction objectives of norm-referenced tests; however, the overlap for criterion-referenced tests is "absolute"—the objectives of instruction are the referents. One of the basic differences between norm-referenced measures and criterion-referenced measures in Randall's (1972) opinion is that their designs have to do with the different purposes that underlie each measure. He clarifies this point by saying:

> Norm-referenced measures design assumes a trait or ability is present in varying degrees in different individuals. The attempt is to design a measure that will separate these individuals in terms of scores on the test which measure that trait or ability. Thus, the test items must constitute a homogeneous set of items; the concern is to measure some defined level of development or mastery on some specified class of problems or tasks. (p. 2)

Thus the major difference is that, unlike norm-referenced measures that are designed to compare individuals or to identify an individual's relative standing with respect to a defined variable, criterion-referenced measures are designed to measure specified behaviors performed by individuals and to indicate those individuals' mastery of a specific skill.

Construction of Criterion-Referenced Standardized Tests

It is important to note that different types of measurement instruments are required for different purposes. This same principle holds true for criterion-referenced measures. Differences among criterion-referenced tests address the purposes for testing. Randall (1972) has identified three cases of criterion-referenced tests. In case 1 items are sampled from a known universe, for example, recognition of three words beginning with the letter *n*; in case 2 one item constitutes the set in question, for example, bouncing a ball off a wall 10 times without stopping; and in case 3 examples of a class of problems or tasks cannot be well-defined but can be rather accurately described, for example, discriminating size, color, or shape.

Klein and Kosecoff (1973) review the basic steps in the development of criterion-referenced tests and the major issues associated with these steps. They point out that criterion-referenced tests used for making decisions about an individual's level of performance have to be longer than tests used for group assessment. If they are not long enough, they do not ensure an adequate level of test reliability.

Once the purpose or purposes and the objectives for a criterion-referenced test have been identified, the focus shifts to the identification of test items to measure the objectives. Several factors influence the number of items to be constructed for each objective. Some of the factors include the amount of testing time available, the proposed use of the test (individual or group), and the cost of making an interpretation (for example, incorrectly judging that a student has attained mastery when this has not occurred).

Identifying test items requires specification of objectives and construction of items to assess mastery of those objectives. In the area of word recognition, Johnson (1973) recommends that teachers state their instructional objectives and evaluate them by using synthetic words, constructing group tests, testing decoding—not encoding—abilities, and evaluating frequently. In relation to establishing objectives, Johnson indicates that the tests of word recognition should relate directly to the skills that are taught. Thus, the objectives would reflect the instruction. The student's score on the test would indicate the level of mastery the student has attained in relation to the skills taught.

Shortcomings of Criterion-Referenced Tests

A large number of states have legislated mastery competence tests. For example, in 1980 38 states had Mastery Competence Tests. These tests are administered at identified grade levels throughout a student's educational program and are often administered as certification of a high-school diploma (Resneck, 1982). The format of such tests is typically criterion-referenced; they are used not only to certify a high-school diploma, but also as a standard of promotion for students in elementary schools. Students' performance is evaluated by their attainment of **mastery**, which is generally established at 80 percent or greater as a minimum performance level. The problem with such mastery criterion for reading is the assumption that reading is based on the acquisition of a hierarchical set of subskills.

Diagnostic tools for reading only sample students' reading abilities; they are not conclusive in and of themselves. (Gale Zucker)

Reading, as noted throughout this book, is an interactive process that is related to the text, the reader, the task, and the context in which it occurs. CRTs, however, often break the act of reading into many subskills and measures students' "mastery" of these with four to six items for each objective. As noted by Rupley and Blair (1988):

> Mastery is not an all-or-nothing proposition. In some instances a student may exhibit lack of mastery in a particular reading skills area but still not exhibit any major problems in reading for comprehension. . . . Just because a student's score is at or above mastery does not mean that the student needs no further instruction in that area. As the structural and contextual difficulty of reading tasks increases, students are likely to exhibit a lack of mastery and to need additional instruction in a reading skill. (p. 8)

It seems reasonable that the concept of mastery is questionable in attempting to apply it to reading comprehension. Has a third grader "mastered" cause-effect relationships, main idea, or inference when he or she reaches an 80 percent level of performance? Hardly; readers never master such abilities because such abilities are lifelong learnings.

The basic disadvantages and shortcomings to using CRTs include the following:

1. Reading may be broken down into so many distinct skill areas that each skill becomes an end in itself. Students' capabilities in reading for meaning may, therefore, never be assessed and reading instruction becomes skill-focused.
2. As noted previously, there may not be enough items for each objective to adequately sample students' reading. When only four to six items are used to determine mastery, students can miss one or two of them and fall below a mastery level.
3. Many CRTs do not list the objectives for each of the subtests that make up the whole test. Teachers are then left to answer the question: "Mastery of what?" Without knowing what is being assessed, little usable information is available for developing an instructional program based on students' needs.
4. Commercially published CRTs that have identified levels of mastery may not be appropriate for a given classroom or student. Furthermore, their objectives may not deal with valued reading skills and abilities. For example, identifying the *schwa* sound or knowing 44 phonic generalizations contribute very little to a student's reading development. Teachers can determine the value of an objective by asking themselves: "Is it a reading skill that contributes to getting meaning?" and "How will my students become better readers as a result of learning the skill?" Asking such questions will force the CRT to serve the teacher's instructional needs, rather than the teacher serving the CRT and feeling obligated to teach that which will be tested.
5. Many commercially published CRTs provide information for the interpretation of students' performance in relation to national samples or norms. As a result these tests are no longer criterion-referenced in their interpretation, but are norm-referenced achievement tests.

Criterion-referenced tests are not inherently good or bad, just as norm-referenced tests are not inherently good or bad. They are intended to complement, not to replace, norm-referenced measures in the assessment of a student's skills. The decision to use either a norm-referenced test or a criterion-referenced test hinges on the purpose of the testing. The shortcomings and advantages of both measures should always be taken into account when interpreting the results.

□ *SUMMARY*

The large number of instruments available for assessing a student's reading strengths and weaknesses need not complicate the process of selecting those to fit specific needs. If anything, the number of assessment instruments available should facilitate selection rather than make it more difficult.

The decision of which test or combination of tests—informal, norm-referenced, or criterion-referenced—to use must be approached analytically: What reading behavior does the test sample? How will the results be used? What interpretation procedures will provide the most information? These are all important considerations in test selection and use.

Informal assessment received considerable attention because informal reading inventories; Goodman, Watson, and Burke's *Reading Miscue Inventory* (1987); observation; and teacher-made tests are versatile instruments that provide considerable insight into a student's reading behavior. The selection and interpretation of each, however, is of paramount importance, and procedures for guiding selection were offered.

Other informal assessment measures, such as word-recognition tests, are also important diagnostic tools of reading skills levels. These too must be selected and interpreted in an analytical fashion. The instruments that are more commonly used were intentionally not listed so as to avoid endorsement of particular instruments. Only teachers can decide what is best for their situations and select the most appropriate instruments to meet their needs.

Selection and interpretation of norm-referenced tests must also be done logically. Knowing how reliability, validity, and normative data affect interpretation of the results influences this selection. Suggestions for qualitative analysis of norm-referenced tests were included because qualitative analysis provides additional information on reading behavior.

Finally, a discussion of criterion-referenced tests was presented. This discussion was less extensive than the discussion of informal measures and standardized measures. Criterion-referenced tests can be advantageous; however, as is often the case, they tend to fragment reading instruction by breaking reading into too many skill areas. As a result, instruction tends to focus on facilitative rather than functional reading factors.

In addition to the information presented in this chapter, the appendix provides a selected bibliography of various types of reading assessment measures and other measures used in reading diagnosis. This bibliography should prove useful for an initial screening of tests. More detailed test information can be found in publications that review tests more thoroughly.

☐ IN-TEXT ASSIGNMENT

FIELD-BASED ACTIVITY

Obtain a copy of a commercially published informal reading inventory (see the listing of IRIs earlier in the chapter) and administer it to an elementary-school student. Use an administration procedure of alternating each passage read—oral, silent, oral, and so on—until the frustration level is reached.

Analyze the student's oral reading miscues and comprehension both quantitatively and qualitatively. Compare the student's comprehension performance on the passages read orally with those read silently. Identify the student's strengths for both word recognition and comprehension.

SHARING AND BRAINSTORMING

Select a basal reader series and identify several levels from which you can construct informal reading inventory passages. For example, you may wish to select two levels: one for third grade and one for sixth grade. Identify a story from each level appropriate for use as an IRI passage. Construct two IRIs for the passages—one using a whole, coherent story and one where you delete important text features from the story. Administer each of the IRI passages to a student or a friend. Analyze the reader's miscues and comprehension for each passage and then compare the reader's performance on the coherent text and the less coherent text. Discuss with your class the differences noted in the reading performance. (If you plan to administer the IRI to a friend, use a college-level textbook to identify IRI passages.)

DISCUSS AND DEBATE

Obtain copies of the third- and sixth-grade state minimum competency test to give to everyone in the class. (If none is available, obtain copies of a CRT for reading from your reading lab, local school, or educational psychology department.) Divide the class into two groups; one group is pro competency testing and the other group is con competency testing. Debate the advantages, disadvantages, strengths, and weaknesses of the competency tests obtained.

□ REFERENCES

Betts, E. A. (1946). *Foundations of reading instruction.* New York: American Book Co.

Caldwell, J. (1985, November). A new look at the old informal reading inventory. *The Reading Teacher, 39,* 168–173.

Drahozal, E. C. & Hanna, G. S. (1978, February). Reading comprehension subscores: Pretty bottles for ordinary wine. *Journal of Reading, 21,* 416–420.

Goodman, Y., Watson, D., & Burke, C. (1987). *Reading Miscue Inventory: Alternative procedures.* New York, NY: Richard C. Owen.

Gronlund, N. (1976). *Measurement and evaluation in teaching.* New York: Macmillan.

Jackson, R. (1970). *Developing criterion-referenced tests.* Princeton, NJ: ERIC Clearinghouse on Tests, Measurement, and Evaluation.

Johnson, D. (1973). Guidelines for evaluating word attack skills in the primary grades. In W. MacGinitie (Ed.), *Assessment problems in reading* (pp. 21–26). Newark, DE: International Reading Association.

Johnston, P. H. (1984). Assessment problems in reading. In P. D. Pearson (Ed.), *Handbook of reading research* (pp. 147–182). New York: Longman.

Klein, S. P. (1972). *Ongoing evaluation of educational programs.* Paper presented at the meeting of the American Psychological Association, Honolulu, Hawaii.

Klein, S. P. & Kosecoff, J. (1973). *Issues and procedures on the development of criterion-referenced tests.* Princeton, NJ: ERIC Clearinghouse on Tests, Measurement, and Evaluation.

Ladd, E. (1971, January). More than scores from tests. *The Reading Teacher, 24,* 305–311.

Livingston, S. (1972). *A classical test-theory approach to criterion-referenced testing.* Paper presented at the meeting of the American Educational Research Association, Chicago.

Otto, W. (1973). Evaluating instruments for assessing needs and growth in reading. In W. MacGinitie (Ed.), *Assessment problems in reading* (pp. 14–20). Newark, DE: International Reading Association.

Pikulski, J. & Shanahan, T. (1982). *Approaches to informal evaluation of reading.* Newark, DE: International Reading Association.

Popham, J. & Husek, T. R. (1969). Implications of criterion-referenced measurement. *Journal of Educational Measurement, 6,* 1–9.

Powell, W. R. (1977). *Informal reading inventory scoring criteria.* Mimeographed. Gainsville, FL: University of Florida.

Randall, R. (1972). *Contrasting norm-referenced and criterion-referenced measures.* Paper presented at the meeting of the American Educational Research Association, Chicago.

Rankin, E. & Culhane, J. (1969, December). Comparable cloze and multiple choice comprehension test scores. *Journal of Reading, 13,* 193–198.

Resnick, D. P. (1982). History of educational testing. In A. K. Wigdor & W. R. Garner (Eds.), *Ability testing: Uses, consequences, and controversies* (part 2) (pp. 33–67). Washington, DC: National Academy Press.

Rupley, W. H. & Blair, T. R. (1988). *Teaching reading: Diagnosis, direct instruction, and practice* (2nd ed.). Columbus, OH: Merrill.

Schell, L. M. & Hanna, G. S. (1981). Can informal reading inventories reveal strengths and weaknesses in comprehension subskills? *The Reading Teacher, 35,* 263–268.

6

The Process of
Diagnostic Instruction

☐ *OVERVIEW*

Diagnosis is at the heart of all good teaching. It respects the student and
the teacher as well as their environment. The overall purpose of this
chapter is to provide a process or framework that all reading teachers
(classroom or clinic) can use as a guide in the diagnostic teaching of
reading.

After reading this chapter, the teacher should be able to

☐ discuss the nature and role of diagnosis.
☐ evaluate his or her diagnostic attitude toward students and toward the
reading program.
☐ differentiate between classroom and clinical diagnoses.
☐ design and implement workable schemes for synthesizing data on students' reading abilities.
☐ distinguish between diagnostic and corrective hypotheses.
☐ plan appropriate classroom strategies in harmony with diagnostic
decisions.

THE NATURE AND ROLE OF DIAGNOSIS

It has been stressed that teachers need to be able to prescribe appropriate
instruction for their students. Underlying this capability is the teachers'
understanding of the nature of diagnosis. Knowledge of the reading process,

The correct blend of teaching methods, materials, and grouping plans depends on diagnostic thinking. (Kevin Fitzsimons, Merrill)

reading abilities, and teaching techniques are useful only if teachers are guided by an efficient diagnostic process. Simply stated, an effective teacher must be a highly skilled diagnostician.

Diagnosis is the process of determining a student's present level of achievement and of ascertaining those factors that are impeding further learning. This process seeks to determine not only a student's weaknesses, but also a student's strengths in learning. A diagnostic mind-set is a necessary prerequisite whenever a teacher plans learning experiences for an individual student or for a group of students. Furthermore, any time a teacher provides feedback to an individual student or to a group of students regarding an aspect of learning to read, it is based on some type of diagnosis. The diagnosis may be formal or informal; it may be based on the use of tests and other measurements, or it may grow out of teacher observation. The following section presents a comprehensive view of the diagnostic process, highlighting the importance of quality instruction.

DIAGNOSTIC TEACHING

Teachers expend a great deal of energy in the teaching of reading. Whether it is teaching a comprehension lesson, previewing map skills, or developing basic sight vocabulary, teachers are caught up with "doing." This instruction should, nevertheless, be preceded by and predicated on diagnostic considerations. Without this diagnostic thinking, instruction becomes mindless drudgery for all concerned. The "doing" must fit into a conscious framework of diagnostic teaching. The process shown in figure 6–1 represents one possible conceptualization of the diagnostic teaching of reading.

Knowledge of the Reading Process

Chapter 1 discussed the facilitative and functional aspects of the reading process. It offered a rationale for each area along with its implications for instruction. It was assumed there that teachers knew the basic content of facilitative and functional skills. In fact, other chapters will review the content of reading skills and recommend corrective measures for teaching these skills. Beyond understanding the processes in the teaching of reading and the correlation of instructional practices, knowledge of the skills themselves is a top priority in discussing any diagnostic model in teaching reading. While other factors are important, success or failure in responding to students' needs hinges on a teacher's knowledge of those skills. In order to act in an appropriate manner, teachers need to know the full range of word-recognition, comprehension, and study skills. If a student is

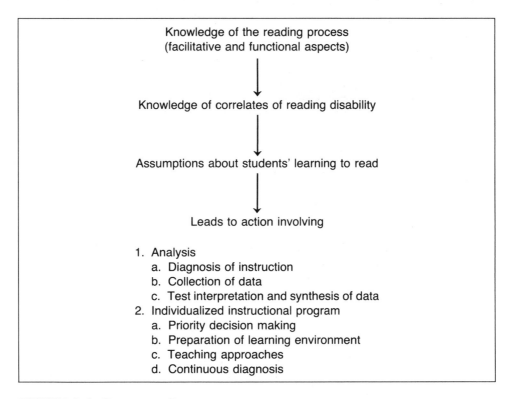

FIGURE 6–1 Diagnostic Process

experiencing difficulty with certain vowel principles in phonics instruction, for example, the teacher must know the principles, what learnings are essential to success in mastering vowel principles, and several different methods of teaching them depending on the student's strengths and weaknesses. Teachers who do not know phonics content will be unable to respond to the student's need.

Knowledge of Correlates of Reading Disability

In addition to possessing knowledge of the various skills in teaching reading, all teachers need a basic understanding of the many possible causes of reading failure. This step in the process of diagnostic teaching is the second knowledge component.

Knowledge of the many possible causes of reading failure will aid the teacher in collecting necessary data on a student and will aid him or her in making decisions for instruction. While many of the possible causes of reading problems are within the domain of teacher influence, many others are outside this domain. In viewing the possible problem areas, it is helpful for teachers to differentiate those optimistic areas from those that are negative in nature. Such explanations of a student's failure to learn to read, such as poor family background, do not help teachers, since the variable itself is outside the teacher's domain of responsibility. On the other hand, knowing that a student not making progress in reading because he or she has an inability to learn by a phonics approach is extremely helpful to a teacher and falls within his or her domain of influence.

Optimistic causes of reading failure are those that are under the influence of the teacher. These are areas in which corrective measures can be taken; a poor family background is not open to amelioration by teachers. This is not to suggest that teachers should ignore those problem areas over which they have little control. Knowledge of these areas can help the teacher to understand, if not to correct, the problem.

Assumptions About Students Learning to Read

It is widely accepted that teachers' attitudes influence the learning situation. Most communities expect that teachers will "individualize" instruction based on students' needs, promote a healthy environment, be accepting and trusting in the classroom, promote healthy self-concepts, and so on. We hold the view that knowledge of the reading process, skills, diagnosis, techniques, and strategies are not enough in working with students. Teachers need the right attitude to turn their knowledge and skills into meaningful instruction. In order to be an effective diagnostic teacher, teachers must think through their assumptions regarding students learning to read. We are not concerned with "what are you, as the teacher, trying to do" (that is educational jargon), but what assumptions teachers are operating under and how they manifest themselves in their day-to-day teaching. Teachers should review their assumptions about students learning to read and then compare those assumptions with their actual practices. The principles in figure 6–2 are offered as a vehicle for such an evaluation.

Once a teacher's assumptions are brought out into the open, we feel that discrepancies between beliefs and actual practices can be reconciled. It is one thing to hold certain beliefs and another to make them operational with students. Teachers' beliefs and attitudes are the key, however, for techniques cannot change unless attitudes are changed. Look at the scale in figure 6–2. If a teacher agrees with most of these principles, his or her classroom should not be organized so that everyone is learning the same thing at the same time. Likewise, a teacher would not spend 30 minutes on a phonics lesson and then not promote a favorable student attitude toward what has been learned. Attitude and ability go hand in hand in the diagnostic teaching of reading, and this linkage must be continually reevaluated.

Diagnosis of Instruction The detection and correction of reading problems do not depend only on noting a student's reading strengths and weaknesses but also on examining the type and quality of instruction utilized by the reading teacher to meet the individual student's needs within the classroom or clinic. Traditional diagnostic-remedial thinking focuses mainly on the student; very little attention is paid to the teachers and to their programs. It is our contention that the most important area of scrutiny in the diagnostic-remedial process should be instructional practices. Teachers are encouraged first to examine their programs, and then to collect, interpret, and synthesize test data on their students. As discussed in chapter 2, recent research has revealed several important characteristics of effective teaching. These characteristics can be grouped broadly under the areas of instructional concerns (for example, basic skill emphasis, direct-instruction format, teacher expectations, and interactive strategies) and management concerns (provision of time for direct instruction, class organization that leads to increased student time-on-task, and level of classroom control). The importance of these characteristics to the reading achievement of students should remind teachers to look at themselves and their programs before looking at individual students. The diagnosis of one's own instructional program (or delivery system) and the diagnosis of a student's reading abilities are interrelated and interdependent. The Teacher Effort Scale in Reading (see figure 6–3 on pages 136–137) devised by Blair (1975) can be used to evaluate a teacher's instructional program, whether it is in a classroom or clinic-type situation. Chapter 2 contained a summary of an investigation in which this instrument was used, the results of which were published in *The Reading Teacher* (Blair, 1976). The study showed that teachers who exerted more effort when teaching reading in the areas evaluated by the instrument had significantly higher reading achievement

1. Students bring different interests and background experiences to the reading task.

Agree	No strong feeling	Disagree

2. Students learn to read at varying rates.

Agree	No strong feeling	Disagree

3. Some students learn best through one mode of instruction, while others need more than one.

Agree	No strong feeling	Disagree

4. A healthy self-concept is related to success in reading.

Agree	No strong feeling	Disagree

5. Students have a right to share in making decisions regarding their own learning.

Agree	No strong feeling	Disagree

6. At times, students learn best from other students.

Agree	No strong feeling	Disagree

7. Students should be active in the learning process.

Agree	No strong feeling	Disagree

FIGURE 6–2 A Sample Scale of Assumptions About Students Learning to Read

scores in their classes than did teachers who exerted less effort. The components of the Teacher Effort Scale in Reading—variety of materials, differentiated instruction, record keeping, and teacher-initiated conferences—can be viewed as four action steps needed for effective instruction. Teachers are encouraged to rate themselves on the effort scale and to determine what changes are warranted. This process is a nonevaluative way to obtain reasonable information about the reading program. Rating themselves or other reading teachers will make teachers become more conscious of what is or is not being done; what areas need to be improved and what areas are satisfactory; and what emphases in the present program need to be omitted, retained, modified, or expanded.

Collection of Data   The data-collection phase of the process concentrates on decisions regarding assessment instruments for use in diagnosing the strengths and weaknesses of students learning to read. To illustrate this point and the remaining steps that should affect a teacher's actions, two hypothetical case studies will be presented side by side. One will be a classroom situation, and the other a clinical situation. However, each illustration is to be interpreted as one possible means for implementing effective instruction. Where feasible, alternatives will be mentioned. It is also expected that the reader will find additional possible ways to achieve similar goals.

Situation 1: Classroom

Mr. Brown is teaching a fourth-grade self-contained class of 25 students. The school uses a basal approach as its main program. Since it is the beginning of the school year, he has a standardized reading score on each student as well as the levels of the basal books each was in at the end of last year.

Purpose: Collect data to aid in decision making regarding instructional levels of students, grouping information, strengths, and weaknesses in word analysis and comprehension.

Recommendations: (1) List the name of each student along with his or her standardized test score and the level of the last book used. (2) Divide the class into three or four groups based on available information for now. (3) Focus the program on individual reading and sharing, rather than on group work. Groups will change after more information is gathered. Read informally with each student. Encourage students to talk about themselves, school, interests, and their attitudes toward reading. (4) Administer a group word-analysis test to all students. (5) Administer individual IRIs to those students who you feel were initially misplaced or whose standardized test scores exceed their last year's basal placement by two years or more.

Variety of Materials

1. Teacher seeks out and uses supplemental materials, textbooks, and games during the reading period in order to teach the skills needed for learning.

	Rarely		Sometimes		Frequently	
1	2	3	4	5	6	7

2. Teacher produces teacher-made materials in reading to assist in providing instruction for the specific skill needs of students.

	Rarely		Sometimes		Frequently	
1	2	3	4	5	6	7

3. Teacher uses audiovisual materials (records, films, overhead projectors, filmstrips, tape recorders, language masters, controlled readers, television) when appropriate to the students' needs.

	Rarely		Sometimes		Frequently	
1	2	3	4	5	6	7

Differentiated Instruction

1. Teacher strives to match instruction to students' learning needs through flexible grouping for all students in reading.

	Rarely		Sometimes		Frequently	
1	2	3	4	5	6	7

2. Teacher utilizes results from standardized tests and administers informal teacher tests, such as the informal reading inventory, to provide instruction suited to the student's needs.

	Rarely		Sometimes		Frequently	
1	2	3	4	5	6	7

3. When needed, the teacher provides a student with one-to-one instruction before school, during school, or after school.

	Rarely		Sometimes		Frequently	
1	2	3	4	5	6	7

Figure 6–3 Teacher Effort Scale in Reading

Situation 2: Clinic

Ms. Fram has just been hired as a reading specialist. Her duties include working with small groups of students who require special help in reading. She has her own reading room and a teacher aide. It is the beginning of the school year, and Ms. Fram has two weeks to individually test students who have been referred for special help.

Purpose: Collect relevant data to verify each student's placement in the program and to make instructional decisions.

Recommendations: (1) Administer an interest inventory to each student. (2) Collect standardized test results and IQ scores from each student's cumulative folder. If IQ scores are too old or not available, administer a nonverbal intelligence test (*The Quick Test, Peabody Picture Vocabulary Test*, and so on) or a listening comprehension test to aid in

Record Keeping

1. Teacher keeps a record of each student's strengths and weaknesses in the areas of word recognition and comprehension in order to pattern instruction after the needs of the students.

	Rarely		Sometimes		Frequently	
1	2	3	4	5	6	7

2. Teacher keeps a record of the number and the types of books independently read by students in the reading class.

	Rarely		Sometimes		Frequently	
1	2	3	4	5	6	7

3. Teacher retains a folder on each student with samples of their work in reading for evaluation and parent-teacher conferences.

	Rarely		Sometimes		Frequently	
1	2	3	4	5	6	7

Teachers-Initiated Conference

1. Teacher holds conferences with other teachers regarding individual student's strengths and weaknesses in reading.

	Rarely		Sometimes		Frequently	
1	2	3	4	5	6	7

2. Teacher actively seeks help if it is needed from various specialists (reading consultant, elementary supervisor, psychologist, principal, social worker, speech teacher) regarding individual student's progress or lack of progress in reading.

	Rarely		Sometimes		Frequently	
1	2	3	4	5	6	7

3. Teacher makes a special effort to contact parents concerning an individual student's progress in reading.

	Rarely		Sometimes		Frequently	
1	2	3	4	5	6	7

Source: Adapted from Timothy R. Blair, *Relationship of Teacher Effort and Student Achievement in Reading.* Unpublished doctoral dissertation, University of Illinois, 1975.

determining reading expectancy. (3) Administer both silent and oral parts of an IRI. (4) Administer a word-analysis test. (5) Except for using supporting tests in the previously mentioned areas, refrain from further testing until it is determined whether or not a significant discrepancy exists between performance and potential.

Data collection in each of the case studies was determined by three factors: (1) time, (2) environment, and (3) purpose. Both classroom and clinic situations required information on interests, instructional levels, and strengths and weaknesses in word analysis. While the classroom situation demanded information for grouping purposes, the clinical situation did not. On the other hand, the clinical situation allows the teacher to individualize the diagnostic process to a much greater degree. A comparison of performance and potential will initially verify that a student should be in the program and will suggest corrective measures to substantiate or disprove the initial decision. Yet, in both classroom and clinic the same framework or guide is followed; alternative means are utilized to accomplish the same goal.

Notice, however, that the depth of data collection depends not on the number of instruments administered, but on the expertise of the teacher to react correctly to students' responses. Efficiency and knowledge are the keys. The adage "more is better" does not apply in the diagnostic process.

Test Interpretation and Synthesis of Data In the interpretation and synthesis phase of the diagnostic process, the teacher analyzes the data and pulls it together in order to make decisions. Besides being dependent on all previous steps in the model, the accuracy of interpretation is directly related to the teacher's knowledge of the data-collection instruments. This analysis and synthesis will help the classroom teacher answer the following questions:

☐ What is the range of instruction levels in my class?
☐ What are students' strengths and weaknesses in the areas of word recognition and comprehension?
☐ Which students are in need of adaptive instruction?

The clinician will be able to answer those questions as well as the following:

☐ What discrepancy, if any, is there between the student's potential and actual reading ability?
☐ What further diagnostic testing (if any) is warranted?

Situation 1: Classroom

At the end of two weeks of school, Mr. Brown has collected the information shown in figures 6–4 and 6–5. With the data arranged in this fashion, he can decide on the number of groups he can effectively handle and the number of students to place in each group. This is the important step—placing students at a level of instruction that ensures a level of success for them. Other decisions can be made by examining the data, and these will be discussed under priority decision making.

Situation 2: Clinic

Ms. Fram had the advantage of devoting 100 percent of her time to individual assessment during the first two weeks of school. Figure 6–6 shows one record-keeping system that Ms. Fram used to synthesize data. The word-analysis and comprehension checklist used by

Mr. Brown can also be utilized in the clinical setting. The same synthesizing process occurs for Ms. Fram except that she does not have to worry about grouping assignments for the moment. For each student, she should be able to decide the following:

- □ Interest and attitude toward reading
- □ Degree of reading problem—determined by comparing performance and potential
- □ Instructional and independent levels—oral and silent
- □ Strengths and weaknesses in word recognition and comprehension
- □ Preferred modality
- □ Amount of further testing necessary

This synthesis of various bits of information leads to the next step of the process: The development of an individualized instructional program for students that incorporates learner style, task conditions, resource attributes, and teacher style.

	Names of Students		
	1.	2.	3.
Standardized reading test results			
Last book in basal (level)			
IRI independent and instructional levels			
Initial level placement			
Corrected placement level			
Observations and comments			

FIGURE 6–4 Basic Data on Class

	Names of Students		
	1.	2.	3.
Consonants			
Vowels—long			
Vowels—short			
Vowel principles			
Syllabication			
Consonant digraphs			
Vowel digraphs			
Prefixes and suffixes			
Contextual clues			
Endings			
Basic sight vocabulary			
Literal comprehension			
Interpretative comprehension			
Critical comprehension			
+ mastery √ adequate – weak			

FIGURE 6–5 Word-Recognition and Comprehension Checklist

	Names of Students		
	1.	2.	3.
Standardized test score			
IQ			
Discrepancy between performance and potential			
IRI instructional and independent levels			
Modality preference			
Observations and comments			
Further testing			

FIGURE 6–6 Clinical Synthesis of Data

Individualized Instructional Program

In this final phase of the process, teachers make diagnostic decisions and provide instruction to students. Prior analysis, in which teachers examined their own instructional programs in light of research findings on teacher effectiveness and assessed students' needs, provides a sound basis for designing an effective instructional program.

Priority Decision Making The "action" that takes place every day in a classroom or clinic should follow directly from a teacher doing "first things first." The action is the next step in the diagnostic process. After interpreting and synthesizing relevant data, teachers must decide on priorities for instruction. They must evaluate a student's learning style and determine areas where discrepancies exist. Once they have come to a decision regarding the potency of the areas of discrepancy, these priority areas become the immediate goals of instruction (task conditions). It must be remembered that learning to read is being ready for one step after another. A parallel can be drawn to the construction of a house. The foundation of a house must be poured before the frame is started. The same concept holds true for many reading skills. For example, mastery of vowel sounds is a necessary prerequisite to learning vowel principles. The factors that affect teachers' decisions are the strengths and weaknesses of their programs, the environment, the range of individual differences, the maturity of their students, the availability of outside help, and the potency of known weaknesses in relation to students' progress in reading. Knowledge of the reading process and of each student's strengths and weaknesses is necessary to discover those areas that need attention first. These judgments, which are tentative in nature, are labeled **diagnostic hypotheses** or hunches. These diagnostic hypotheses are then translated into **corrective hypotheses**, which deal with the techniques, strategies, and materials needed to correct the problem. Whether classroom or clinic, the closer the relationship between diagnostic and corrective hypotheses is, the more confidence the teacher can have in achieving success.

Situation 1: Classroom

After synthesizing his data, Mr. Brown decided on the reading levels of each student and placed them in groups. By examining the results of the IRI and the word-analysis test, he further delineated each student's strengths and weaknesses in word recognition and comprehension. Now he is turning his diagnosis from global to specific concerns. This synthesis will enable him to group students according to their skill needs across instructional basal levels, which will ensure that he is meeting the specific needs of each student. Observation provides information on attitudes and interests that can be converted into interest groupings for independent reading or related activities such as art projects in connection with a story. This whole process is one of (1) making judgments regarding areas of discrepancy as shown in the synthesis of the data and (2) deciding which one of these areas requires immediate attention over the rest. For example, some students might have difficulty in summarizing the main idea of a story, and at the same time their basic vocabulary is weak. While not ignoring the students' need to know how to summarize the main idea of a selection, emphasis should first concentrate on improving the students' basic sight vocabulary.

Situation 2: Clinic

Having synthesized the data on each student, Ms. Fram can now analyze it and prescribe a specialized plan for each student. The process is the same as Mr. Brown's, except that the constraints of the classroom environment will not inhibit Ms. Fram's decisions. For each student, she must first compare performance with potential to determine if the student has a reading problem. While labels can be dangerous, this label indicates only that a particular student needs further diagnosis and consideration. Further inspection may disprove this initial diagnosis. If a significant discrepancy does exist between performance and potential, an analysis of the student's test scores may indicate those areas that are causing the discrepancy. These areas of discrepancy will convert into diagnostic hypotheses, which will then be translated into a corrective program. Further testing may be required to discern specific problem areas. If performance and potential are the same, the student is performing as well as possible and is not a candidate for a reading clinic situation. Such a student would require a good sequential reading program based on individual needs in the regular classroom. Regardless of whether a discrepancy is significant or minimal, the first step is to locate specific strengths and weaknesses; then those skills that would bring about the greatest student improvement should be identified. Ms. Fram can then formulate diagnostic hypotheses and prescribe an individual corrective program.

Preparation of Learning Environment Providing instruction based on students' needs requires thoughtful planning with respect to materials.

Corrective hypotheses are turned into action through the use of selected materials. Proper material selection is crucial. Two important guidelines to consider when preparing the teaching environment are the number of materials and the type of materials needed. First, a large quantity of materials are needed simply because of the number of students in a class and because of their diverse abilities, interests, and backgrounds. The teacher will also need reading materials that span several readability levels to ensure that students will be able to find material that is appropriate for them. Second, the teacher will need many different types of materials in his or her specific situation. To achieve instructional goals and to capitalize on students' interests and abilities, a classroom should have an assortment of basal texts, workbooks, trade books, paperbacks, supplemental kits, audiovisual equipment, and commercial and homemade games and activities. While these guidelines apply to classroom and clinic, differences in their application do exist.

Situation 1: Classroom

Mr. Brown has now decided on his groups, skill groups, and students who will perhaps require some individual attention. In order to put his corrective hypotheses in action, he must make sure that he has a sufficient supply of books at appropriate grade levels to carry through his basic reading program. He also needs a variety of materials for adaptive instruction and independent reading. The key to material use in the classroom is not so much quantity as utilizing the materials effectively to teach students the skills needed for improvement. There must be a one-to-one correspondence between the goals set for certain students and the materials or vehicles used to achieve those ends.

Situation 2: Clinic

Decisions concerning materials are similar to those of a classroom for a clinic or small-group situation. The same guidelines apply regarding the number and types of materials. The major differences Ms. Fram has to allow for are fitting material usage to the preferred mode of learning and not using materials the students have worked in before. Without the pressure of handling a whole class of students, Ms. Fram can attempt to match modality preference with materials for correction. For example, if a student learns well through the auditory mode, Ms. Fram might use a language master and/or listening module to help teach phonics. Also, in a clinic situation Ms. Fram must make sure she is not using materials that are "old" to the student. New and exciting materials should be the rule whether they are commerical or homemade.

Teaching Approaches It has been emphasized that there are many ways of achieving goals. Knowledge of a variety of approaches is essential to good teaching. If teachers truly believe that students are different in a multitude of ways, each classroom should incorporate a variety of teaching approaches. By using only one teaching approach in reading instruction rather than adjusting the program to meet the needs of the students, many schools really demand that students adapt to the program. In such a situation, the school is operating under the assumption that all students are alike and can learn to read by the same approach. In reality, some students respond positively to certain approaches and negatively to others. Thus, all teachers need to know a variety of approaches (auditory, visual, individualized, basal, linguistic, multimedia, language experience, and so forth). Along with using various teaching approaches, teachers must know and use a variety of organizational plans to achieve their goals. Students' performances will vary under certain grouping conditions, such as individual tutoring, small-group, large-group, teaming, structured, or unstructured instruction. Some learnings are more effectively taught using a particular grouping situation. A phonic lesson, for example, would probably be more successful in a small-group setting, and a presentation of a textbook study method might best be handled in a whole-class situation. The correct mixture of teaching methods and grouping plans is different for all teachers and all classes. The right blend depends on teacher knowledge, teacher style, and goals of instruction that are based on students' strengths and weaknesses. The key is knowing students thoroughly; then, and only then, can the teacher implement corrective hypotheses successfully.

Situation 1: Classroom

Mr. Brown's reading program is centered on the basal reader system, however, he must be familiar with many other approaches if he is to capitalize on the strengths of individual students. Besides utilizing a variety of approaches to meet the needs of each student, he can also vary grouping procedures depending on instructional goals. These alternative approaches and grouping plans must lend themselves directly to accomplishing his corrective hypotheses. Utilizing a variety of approaches and grouping patterns also helps ensure the student interest will be high and that boredom resulting from an unchanging classroom routine will not occur.

Situation 2: Clinic

Ms. Fram also manipulates teaching approaches and grouping plans to accomplish her goals (corrective hypotheses). However, in her case, she sees only a small group of students at one time. This enables her program to be more "individualized" with respect to teaching approaches. Based on her informal appraisal, Ms. Fram can tailor-make her corrective lessons, capitalizing on the strengths of each student. She can select from the same approaches as Mr. Brown to reach her goals. She also has available various specialized techniques (for example, the Fernald technique,* specialized phonics approaches, and mechanical reading devices). Many of these require one teacher to work with one student for a period of time. In addition, Ms. Fram should try to select a different reading approach than the one used in the regular classroom. A clinic setting demands innovative approaches since the student has seemingly already experienced much difficulty with traditional classroom approaches. Fresh approaches also help gain student interest.

*See chapter 16 for a discussion of the Fernald and other special techniques.

Continuous Diagnosis The effective teacher of reading continually diagnoses each student every day, either formally or informally. Without this step in a diagnostic framework, inadequate instruction will always follow. Initial diagnostic decisions on students must be continually evaluated and reshaped if necessary, and appropriate changes made in the corrective procedures. Initial diagnostic hypotheses reflect the teacher's "best guesses" regarding a student's lack of progress. If the prescribed instruction verifies the initial diagnosis, changes will occur when a deficiency is corrected. If the teacher's instruction disproves his or her initial decisions, the teacher can then prescribe a different plan of action immediately. Classroom or clinic, the same principle is paramount.

Directly related to continuous diagnosis is the teacher's ability to keep accurate records on each student's strengths and weaknesses. One possible method, besides keeping charts on all students as suggested earlier, is to maintain a folder on each student that includes teacher comments and samples of the student's work. This is one way of accurately monitoring student progress in such areas as word recognition and comprehension. As the teacher reads individually with students each week, he or she can evaluate their word-recognition skills and comprehension abilities. After a few weeks, the teacher will have in essence administered an IRI and can note improvements or areas of concern in their folders. Record keeping is an individual matter. The only important point is that it must be done in some way. Continuous diagnosis holds no meaning without it.

□ SUMMARY

A process of diagnostic instruction was presented for the teaching of reading in a classroom or clinic. The process reflects the belief that effective instruction results only from knowing why the teacher is following a certain course of action with the students. Emphasis is first on teacher knowledge, program characteristics, and teacher assumptions about students learning to read. Diagnostic thinking then shifts to collecting relevant data, making effective decisions, and planning appropriate instruction for students. Further chapters in this book will explain each step of the diagnostic process and discuss specific tests, corrective measures, approaches, and materials.

□ IN-TEXT ASSIGNMENTS

LIBRARY ACTIVITY

Visit the library and examine several issues, spanning the last five years, of the journal *The Reading Teacher.* Select and read two articles dealing with the topic of diagnosis. On a 3″ × 5″ card, prepare a short summary of each article and be prepared to discuss whether the thesis is aimed at diagnosis of the student or of instructional practices.

FIELD-BASED ACTIVITY

Interview a public school teacher regarding various reasons for the lack of reading progress among students performing below grade-level expectations. Afterward, classify the reasons for reading disabilities in that particular class as being optimistic (teacher has some control over it) or negative (teacher has little or no control over it).

SHARING AND BRAINSTORMING

A very important relationship should exist between a teacher's diagnostic and corrective hypotheses. Why does there need to be a close relationship between them? How is this accomplished?

DISCUSS AND DEBATE

Examine the Teacher Effort Scale in Reading found in the chapter. Form groups of three to five based on interest in the primary grades (1–3) and intermediate grades (4–6). For each item in the scale, write how it is actually operationalized in a classroom setting. In addition, list any items under the subscales that could be added. As a total class, compare and contrast your group findings with others for both the primary and intermediate grades.

□ REFERENCES

Blair, T. R. (1975). *Relationship of teacher effort and student achievement in reading.* Unpublished doctoral dissertation, University of Illinois.

Blair, T. R. (1976). Where to expend your teaching effort (it does count!). *The Reading Teacher, 30,* 293–296.

PART TWO

Diagnosis and Correction of Specific Reading Problems

7

Word Recognition: Sight Vocabulary

☐ OVERVIEW

Instant recognition of words on sight is an important word-recognition strategy. Although this ability cannot be considered reading as we have defined it, a large sight vocabulary allows the reader to focus on getting meaning rather than on puzzling over each word as if it had never been seen before. The sight method is also referred to as a whole-word or look-say method of word recognition. All of these labels describe the ability to recognize a whole word quickly and assign meaning to it rather than focusing on its parts.

Not only will the apprehension of meaning be limited for students with limited sight vocabularies, but the development of other word-recognition strategies may also be delayed. Students are more likely to be successful learning other recognition strategies—structural analysis, context, and phonics—when instruction is related to their sight vocabularies. Without an adequate sight vocabulary, students may have difficulty forming the concept of reading to get meaning. They may view reading as simply the correct pronunciation of every word; they may never understand fully that decoding words is a means to comprehension.

If reading ability is to develop and grow, students must quickly recognize words found in reading materials. Recognition of basic sight words (e.g., *to, this, and, my,* and so forth) that are function words helps students to better understand the features of written language as well as the idea that language has a definite structure (Heilman, Blair, & Rupley,

147

1986). One of the major problems encountered by teachers when teaching corrective and remedial reading is students who have a small and unreliable sight vocabulary. This chapter, which is devoted to sight vocabulary (chapter 9 discusses the role of vocabulary in comprehension), discusses assessment procedures, instructional strategies and practice materials, and principles for effective retention.

After reading this chapter, the teacher should be able to

☐ select and administer several assessment instruments to determine a student's sight vocabulary strengths and weaknesses.
☐ identify instructional strategies and practices aimed at correcting and/or remediating sight vocabulary problems.
☐ arrive analytically at an individualized corrective or remedial reading program that meets the individual needs of students.
☐ incorporate in his or her instruction several principles for ensuring effective retention of sight vocabulary.

IMPORTANT AREAS OF SIGHT VOCABULARY

When measuring a student's sight vocabulary, the focus should be on identifying words that can and cannot be recognized quickly. The teacher's instructional practices can then build on the student's strengths and accommodate weaknesses. Assessment should, therefore, include a measurement of sight vocabulary in the following areas: (1) service words, (2) high-frequency content-areas words, and (3) high-frequency words found in instructional reading materials.

Service Words

Words that appear with a high degree of frequency in written materials are classified as **service words.** There are several listings of service words available, including *The Dolch Basic Sight Word Test* (Dolch, 1942), "A Basic Vocabulary for Beginning Readers" (Johnson, 1971), and "The New Instant Word List" (Fry, 1980). The service words found in basic sight-word lists can be categorized as either irregular words or regular words.

Irregular words are those that are not spelled as they sound. Examples on the Dolch list include *know, they,* and *two.* Students need to recognize these and other irregular high-frequency words on sight. Students cannot rely on sound-symbol relationships to attack such words. Attempting to identify such words through analysis alone will not yield even an approximation of the words' pronunciations or, ultimately, what they mean in context. Furthermore, *many of the irregular service words are important in sentence construction and must be recognized on sight because of their frequency of use and meaning in context.*

Sight recognition of regular words appearing on lists of service words is also important for reading development. **Regular words** are sounded as they are spelled. Examples of regular words found on the Dolch list are *hot, big, can,* and *cut.* This direct correspondence between pronunciation and spelling emphasizes major spelling patterns of the English language. If students possess a sight vocabulary of regular words, the teacher can use these words to teach word-recognition skills that enable students to identify other words that have similar spelling patterns.

High-Frequency Content-Area Words

Recalling chapter 1's discussion of reading as a learning tool, it is impossible to overlook the assessment of students' sight vocabularies in the content area. Many words found in content-area texts appear so frequently that students need to recognize them on sight. Examples of such words include:

- □ mathematics—*add, more, less, divide*
- □ social studies—*farm, city, home, school*
- □ science—*sun, earth, rain, heat*

These words are only examples; a list of high-frequency sight words can be compiled for each content area. Such a list would focus on high-frequency words and/or words whose meanings are essential to understanding basic concepts.

High-Frequency Words in Instructional Reading Materials

Students may have difficulty reading instructional materials when they cannot quickly recognize words that appear frequently. Most instructional materials for reading control the vocabulary. This control allows readers to encounter the same words frequently throughout much of their reading. Repeated use of selected words increases the likelihood that students will begin to recognize these words on sight. When students cannot recognize such high-frequency words on sight, they often have a difficult time progressing through the materials.

ASSESSMENT OF SIGHT VOCABULARY

There are two important considerations when assessing students' sight vocabulary. First, words must be presented in a manner that measures the reader's ability to recognize the word instantly. Second, the procedure should also determine whether or not the reader knows what the word means.

Many assessment procedures and sources of diagnostic information provide insights into students' sight vocabulary strengths and weaknesses.

Among these are graded word lists, cloze passages, standardized tests, tachistoscopic devices, service word lists, informal reading inventories, and teacher observation. Some of these procedures will be discussed in the following sections.

Graded Word Lists

"The New Instant Word List" developed by Edward Fry (1980) is presented in figures 7–1, 7–2, and 7–3. The 300 words and their common variants (created by the addition of the most common suffixes, such as *run—runs*, *ask—asked*, *old—older*, *kind—kindly*, and *high—highest*) represent 65 percent of the words found in textbooks and newspapers. Fry says that "it

First 25 Group 1a	Second 25 Group 1b	Third 25 Group 1c	Fourth 25 Group 1d
the	or	will	number
of	one	up	no
and	had	other	way
a	by	about	could
to	word	out	people
in	but	many	my
is	not	then	than
you	what	them	first
that	all	these	water
it	were	so	been
he	we	some	call
was	when	her	who
for	your	would	oil
on	can	make	now
are	said	like	find
as	there	him	long
with	use	into	down
his	an	time	day
they	each	has	did
I	which	look	get
at	she	two	come
be	do	more	made
this	how	write	may
have	their	go	part
from	if	see	over

Common suffixes: *s, ing, ed*

FIGURE 7–1 The Instant Word First Hundred

Source: Edward B. Fry, "The New Instant Word List." *The Reading Teacher, 34*, (December 1980): 284–289. Reprinted with permission from Edward B. Fry and the International Reading Association.

is impossible to achieve fluency in reading or writing unless the words are known 'instantly' " (p. 287).

These words can be administered to students in several sittings to determine the students' knowledge of a core of common sight words. To diagnose students' recognition of common variations, selected suffixes plus appropriate root words can be chosen and administered to students over a period of time. Qualitative analysis of their performance can be accomplished by looking for patterns in order to categorize students' responses. For example, if a student does not recognize service words such as *the, of, a,* and *is,* then the teacher can develop instructional strategies and procedures that teach such words in isolation and in context.

First 25 Group 2a	Second 25 Group 2b	Third 25 Group 2c	Fourth 25 Group 2d
new	great	put	kind
sound	where	end	hand
take	help	does	picture
only	through	another	again
little	much	well	change
work	before	large	off
know	line	must	play
place	right	big	spell
year	too	even	air
live	mean	such	away
me	old	because	animal
back	any	turn	house
give	same	here	point
most	tell	why	page
very	boy	ask	letter
after	follow	went	mother
thing	came	men	answer
our	want	read	found
just	show	need	study
name	also	land	still
good	around	different	learn
sentence	form	home	should
man	three	us	America
think	small	move	world
say	set	try	high

Common suffixes: *s, ing, ed, er, ly, est*

FIGURE 7–2 The Instant Word Second Hundred

Source: Edward B. Fry, "The New Instant Word List," *The Reading Teacher, 34* (December 1980): 248–289. Reprinted with permission from Edward B. Fry and the International Reading Association.

Tachistoscopic Devices

Tachistoscopic devices are apparatus that briefly expose visual stimuli to students. Commercial tachistoscopes for assessing vocabulary words are available for use with both groups and individuals. The Tach-X (Educational Developmental Laboratories) is a 35-mm filmstrip projector that can be used with groups or individual students. A library of specially developed verbal filmstrips, ranging from kindergarten through grade-level 13, is designed for use with the projector. Materials contained in this library are classified as word recognition, spelling, and vocabulary. Words can be flashed on a projection screen at rates ranging from 1/100 second through 1½ seconds.

First 25 Group 3a	Second 25 Group 3b	Third 25 Group 3c	Fourth 25 Group 3d
every	left	until	idea
near	don't	children	enough
add	few	side	eat
food	while	feet	face
between	along	car	watch
own	might	mile	far
below	close	night	Indian
country	something	walk	real
plant	seem	white	almost
last	next	sea	let
school	hard	began	above
father	open	grow	girl
keep	example	took	sometimes
tree	begin	river	mountain
never	life	four	cut
start	always	carry	young
city	those	state	talk
earth	both	once	soon
eye	paper	book	list
light	together	hear	song
thought	got	stop	leave
head	group	without	family
under	often	second	body
story	run	late	music
saw	important	miss	color

Common suffixes: *s, ing, ed, er, ly, est*

FIGURE 7–3 The Instant Word Third Hundred

Source: Edward B. Fry, "The New Instant Word List," *The Reading Teacher, 34* (December 1980): 284–289. Reprinted with permission from Edward B. Fry and the International Reading Association.

A hand-held tachistoscope, the Flash-X, is also available from Educational Developmental Laboratories. Designed to be used individually, the Flash-X comes with both prepared word cards and blank cards. The blank cards can be used for assessing and teaching sight words appropriate to individual students' needs. The Flash-X is simple to operate and exposes a word at a set rate of 1/25 of a second. It has been found that most primary-level students have little difficulty operating this machine. As an alternative, the teacher can always construct a tachistoscope. This has the advantages of limited expense and, even more important, using word lists that meet individual students' needs.

Flash Cards

Another assessment device for use in both diagnosing and teaching sight words is flash cards. Each of the sight words that is being assessed or taught is carefully printed on a card of uniform size (3″ × 5″ or 4″ × 6″). It is important to use cards that are all the same size and to replace cards as they become worn and dirty, or students may focus on a feature of the card, such as a torn corner, as a cue for identifying the word. Each card should be flashed quickly for the student to identify the word. Cards can be separated into two piles—those that are instantly identified and those that are not—for quick determination of known and unknown words. Such cards can also be used for instruction and review of words.

Reading Behaviors That Suggest Sight Vocabulary Problems

Each of the following reading behaviors could indicate a sight vocabulary problem:

- ☐ Common single-syllable irregular words are misread, but their pronunciation is phonically correct.
- ☐ The amount of time taken to pronounce high-frequency sight words, such as those on a graded word list, is exceedingly lengthy (greater than the number of words times 10 seconds, for example, 3 words × 10 seconds = 30 seconds).
- ☐ Words are quickly identified on sight, but meaning for them is lacking or limited.
- ☐ A greater or equal number of single-syllable common words are misread than polysyllabic less common words.
- ☐ A pattern of using only initial letter cues to identify words similar to ones that are recognized on sight is apparent.
- ☐ High-frequency words with abstract meanings are misread.
- ☐ Mispronunciations of words when reading orally is small, but there are a disproportionate number of real-word substitutions that are meaningless in context.
- ☐ There is a difference of two years or more between word-recognition competency and comprehension competency in favor of word recognition.

□ Poor phrasing is used when reading orally; however, each word is read as if correct pronunciation is the purpose for reading.

□ Oral reading rate on IRI passages is approximately the same rate as when equivalent passages are read silently.

Students who exhibit such reading behaviors may need corrective or remedial reading instruction that focuses on sight vocabulary development. Although many of these behaviors will occur together on diagnostic instruments, even a single one might warrant further assessment of sight vocabulary, and the time required to construct a tachistoscope and present a list of words to a student is minimal. In addition, some students can fool teachers into thinking that they have a sight vocabulary, when, in fact, they are overrelying on word-analysis skills to identify every word.

ISSUES RELATED TO SIGHT-WORD INSTRUCTION

Research findings that suggest instructional strategies and practices for teaching sight vocabulary vary considerably. Conflicting evidence exists as to the desirability of teaching words in isolation, in combination with a picture depicting the word, or in context (Ceprano, 1981). Durkin (1983) suggests that some new words be introduced in context to ensure that students have meaning associated with the word. She emphasizes that function words (*as, to, and,* etc.) should always appear in context because they derive their meaning from other words. Three other types of words also require some context, in her opinion: homonyms (*can* do—*can* of pears), homographs (*wind* the clock—strong *wind*), and homophones (grocery *aisle*— *I'll* be there). Samuels (1985) notes that beginning readers use component letters in a word for recognition, selecting the easiest cue for recognizing the word. By using words that are similar in their spelling patterns, students are forced to look at the whole word, rather than just its initial or final letter, for identification.

Frequently teachers point out incidental features of a word, such as its shape or length, to help students recognize it. Although students may exhibit rapid learning when taught to focus on such cues, this learning can occur at the expense of learning to transfer to functional reading, and students are left to guess at the identification of words that have similar shapes. Configuration cues have been found to be of little use to beginning readers in word identification (Feitelson & Razel, 1984). Even though there is some research support that adult, capable readers use letters, configurations, and length cues for recognition of words (Haber, Haber, & Furlin, 1983), use of all these features in working with beginning readers and readers who experience word-recognition problems may impede reading progress and cause cognitive confusion.

Selecting words that have a high associability to each other has been found to increase the response availability or hook-up of the appropriate response with the cue (Samuels, 1985). Examples of response availability words are *butter—bread, rain—cloud, dog—bark, blue—sky, green—grass,* and *ice—cold.* Each of these pairs has an associate connection between them. If a student recognizes one of the words, this connection should assist with rapid recognition of the new word.

Whether or not it is more effective to teach sight words in isolation or in context was investigated by Ceprano (1980). She found that how students are tested to determine their recognition of sight words may affect whether teaching words in context or words in isolation is more effective. If students are taught sight words in context but are tested with words in isolation, they may not perform as well as those students taught to recognize words in isolation. The clear implication of this finding is that the test should match the instruction; that is, if sight-word instruction is focusing on application of words in context, then students should be tested within a contextual format.

Several studies (Ehri & Roberts, 1979; and Ehri & Wilce, 1979–80) support the idea that teaching sight words in context may result in slower learning of the graphic and phonic features of sight words. Both investigations reported that students who were taught sight words with flash cards could identify the graphic and phonic features of words more readily than students who were taught words in context. However, students who learned sight words in sentence context also enhanced their learning of written language features, such as syntax and semantics.

In light of the conflicting evidence about how best to teach sight words, teachers should guard against relying on a single instructional strategy or procedure. Identification of new words, homographs, homophones, and homonyms would appear to be enhanced by teaching them in minimal context (*the* door; *I'll* do it, *can* of, and *wind* blew). Identification of known words (words in students' language background) would appear to be enhanced by presenting them in isolation; however, such learning may not transfer to functional reading tasks unless the teacher provides for such transfer. Pictures may facilitate the learning of some sight words as long as the teacher directs such learning to ensure that students focus on the word and not just the picture. Finally, one cannot assume that identification of words in isolation will transfer to reading in a contextual situation. Instruction must focus on helping students make that transfer.

Although there is a lack of agreement about how best to teach sight vocabulary, two features of such instruction are extremely important. First, considerable rehearsal and recitation are often necessary for students to be able to immediately recognize words on sight. Second, a teacher-directed approach is strongly recommended for teaching sight words (Groff, 1981). Such instruction should be presented in small, well-demonstrated and illustrated steps that are repetitively and briskly paced to ensure mastery and success in students' learning of sight words (McNinch, 1981).

INSTRUCTIONAL STRATEGIES FOR THE CORRECTION/REMEDIATION OF SIGHT VOCABULARY PROBLEMS

McNinch (1981) has recommended an instructional strategy for teaching sight words to students who have reading problems. Its essential features are based on many of the findings of the teacher-effectiveness research presented in chapter 2. The steps of the strategy are presented in the following list and are illustrated in figure 7–4 (pages 162–165), a teacher-directed instructional lesson along with practice activities for sight vocabulary development. The steps of the strategy include:

1. *Demonstration*—The teacher selects a word of value for the students, which means that the word is in their oral-listening background. The word is presented in oral context in a normal language manner.
2. *Continued demonstration*—The orally presented word is presented in a written sentence or phrase context where all other words are in the students' sight vocabulary.
3. *Interaction*—The new word is written in isolation from the sentence, and the teacher directs the students to note features of the word, such as beginning letter, ending letter, and number of letters, and to see if it is the same as the identified word in the written sentence or phrase.
4. *Clarification*—Students read the word in sentences or phrases where all other words are sight words. The focus is on students' oral reading of the context in which the word appears. If errors are made, they should be corrected immediately by the teacher and then reread by the students.
5. Application—Students read, with teacher direction, a meaningful context in which the word appears. The text should be familiar to students and may include parts of a book, portions of a basal reader story, or excerpts from their language-experience stories. The word under study should appear several times throughout the text to provide meaningful practice.
6. *Practice for mastery*—The teacher selects activities, such as games, flash cards, word banks, and so forth, that can be kept short and briskly paced and where competition is between students of similar abilities. Such practice activities should be structured to ensure a high student success level (85–100 percent), so that correct responses are being practiced.

The instructional strategy that McNinch recommends maximizes students' chances of being successful in learning new sight words. Also, it is teacher-directed instruction and highly intensive; therefore, its affect on students' learning sight words should be monitored closely. However, students who have problems learning sight words will most likely benefit from such an approach, which is adaptable to many other instructional strategies and procedures.

Students' comprehension of new words is influenced by their experiential/conceptual backgrounds. (Sandra Anselmo)

Research has found McNinch's strategy and the following instructional strategies and procedures to be effective. However, all instructional games, materials, and approaches for correcting and remediating sight vocabulary problems should be evaluated analytically. For this reason, the following discussion provides a means for evaluating any activity aimed at sight vocabulary instruction, rather than presenting specific examples of games materials, methods, and so forth.

□ Select words that are similar in their initial spelling patterns. This forces students to focus on more than beginning or ending letters as cues for word identification. For example, if students use only the beginning letter to identify a word, this method works well until they encounter other similarly shaped words beginning with the same letter as the known word. If an unknown word begins with the same letter as a known word, students overgeneralize and identify it as the known word.

When words with similar spellings are used, the initial letter cue will not work. Teachers could then use direct instruction, games, and worksheets to help students focus on all the letters or several letters in a word to reach rapid identification. If students begin to focus on final letters as cues for identification when two words begin with the same letter, then instruction could emphasize words that begin and end with similar letters. This forces students to focus on beginning, middle, and ending letters for quick recognition of the word. Examples of practice words are

can	does	and
cat	down	any
call	dawn	are
car	done	ate

□ If students depend on word shape to quickly identify words, instruction should aim at getting them to focus on a letter or letters as cues to instant recognition. Instruction should include words that are similar in their configurations, which increases the need to focus on cues other than shape.

there	fall	gave	sit	mark	must	pour
these	full	give	sat	make	much	pawn
those	fell	gone	six	made	most	pout

Using a tachistoscope or flash cards to present such words can help show the student that relying on word shape for identification is difficult when words with similar shapes have to be recognized quickly. A pair of similarly shaped words could be presented one at a time and the graphic differences between the words discussed. The student can then be taught to focus on these differences for rapid identification. After the student can rapidly identify two words of similar shape, another word would be introduced. The graphic differences of this third word could be illustrated by comparing it with the other two. When the student can quickly identify these three words, another similarly shaped word would be introduced, and so on. Allow students to transfer to functional reading tasks the words they can identify on sight. Above all, do not delay transfer. If, after an instructional session, the student can only recognize one or two words on sight, transfer this skill to applying it in context.

☐ Games and worksheets that require the student to discriminate visually between similarly shaped words can provide practice and reinforcement of what cues should be focused on. Appropriate for this purpose are bingo-type games in which the student is asked to match a flashed word with an identical word on the bingo card. Word banks (see chapter 13) can be used to enable the student to keep a record of words recognized quickly. Sight words can then serve as examples in discussions about the cues used to identify similarly shaped words. Instruction should then focus on helping the student transfer this knowledge of cues to those words not in the word bank.

☐ If student is having problems associating meaning with words, associability can be developed between known words and problem words. We have found the following modification of Samuels's (1985) recommendation to be highly successful with students who have difficulties with word meaning. Teachers select words that have high associability and construct sentences such as the following:

> He put *butter* on the *bread.*
>
> Fire is *hot* and ice is *cold.*
>
> The *grass* is *green.*
>
> The *dog* began to *bark.*

When this procedure is followed, the meaning of the words as they are used in context is better learned and transferred to actual reading. Furthermore, this intermediate step builds learning in small, highly related steps that are based on students' past learning.

☐ Response availability of known words with unknown words can also be used to teach instant recognition of both regular and irregular high-frequency words. Pairing the known word with the new word increases the likelihood the student will more quickly learn the new word; for example, *funny—laugh, start—stop, word—write,* and *it—is* can be paired.

Instruction should focus on the relationship between the two words and why the words go together. Continual focus on the graphic representation of the unknown word helps the student begin to associate its pronunciation with how it is written. Each word can be printed on a card. Give the student half the cards. Present a word card quickly to the student and ask the student to look quickly through the cards and find the words that should be "hooked-up" with it. Note the time it takes for the student to locate the word, if he or she appears to use initial or terminal letter cues for words with the same beginning and ending letters, and if the student can pronounce both words correctly. When both words are pronounced correctly, the student may keep them; when the responses are incorrect, the teacher keeps the words. This makes an instructional game of this activity, which may serve to motivate the student. However, this activity can also provide ongoing diagnostic information. If the student is selecting a word that begins or ends with the letters of the correct associate word but the choice is incorrect, it could indicate that the student is relying on letter cues that do not enable rapid identification of the word. Instruction based on similar spelling patterns can force the student to focus on more than initial or terminal letters as cues to word recognition.

☐ Meanings associated with sight words having concrete referents can be further developed by using an illustration for the story. After the material has been read, discuss and reread with the student those portions that contain problem words. Focus the discussion on the meanings of the words as they are used in the story and direct the student's attention to getting word meanings from the illustrations.

☐ Worksheet activities can be constructed for teaching sight words through response availability. On the same sheet, present the known words in one list and the new words in another list. The student must write the new word beside the appropriate known word associate. Another activity would present a known word and a list of three similarly spelled and shaped words, one of which is the associate word. The student must identify the associate word correctly by writing it next to the known word.

start _____   funny _____
        step   cough
        stop   laura
        crop   laugh

This activity can then be extended to larger written units, such as sentences and paragraphs, that focus on context clues and comprehension. "Norma thought the dog looked *funny*, and she began to *laugh*."

☐ Words can be grouped according to **higher order spelling units**—spelling patterns that have invariant spelling-to-sound correspondence. For example, *sh* and *st* are higher order spelling units for

fish   stop
mesh   first
rush   list
dish   start
wish   step
shake   stand

Teaching the student to focus on how the higher order unit combines with recognized other letters in the word can facilitate rapid recognition of words.

To introduce other words with the same higher order spelling units, build on known words. Instructional games and worksheets can be used to maximize the probability that the spelling unit is recognized instantly. This facilitates rapid identification of new words in which the higher order spelling unit is combined with other letters. Additional instruction similar to that used to teach spelling patterns and configurations can be used to develop sight vocabulary and provide transfer to functional reading tasks.

☐ Two strategies for the application and reinforcement of sight words in context are the say-and-write method and directed sentence reading (Gold, 1981). The say-and-write method is used with a language-experience approach and involves the following steps:

1. Students watch and listen as the teacher writes the sentences they dictate.
2. The teacher says each word with normal pronunciation and tone as he or she writes it.
3. The teacher reads each sentence that is written with natural speed and inflection.
4. The teacher reads the entire story as students watch and listen. Students may make changes by using the say-and-write method in step 1.
5. Students state an appropriate title or titles for the completed story.

Gold suggests that the students must be directed to read and reread their stories. To ensure that students do in fact recognize the words, random sentences are used for directed sentence reading.

During directed sentence reading, the teacher guides the student to locate and read sentences that contain specific information. A key feature of this procedure is that sentences are selected randomly rather than in the dictated story sequence. Repeated verbatim reading of the story can result in memorization of the content—students may not actually recognize the words.

Students are directed to read the selected sentences in order to locate specific facts. These facts can be based on *who, what, when, where, how,* and *why* questions. Thus, students' attention is directed to using their sight vocabularies in each of the sentences.

Figure 7–4, as mentioned previously, is a teacher-directed instruction lesson with practice activities for the area of basic sight vocabulary. This lesson is representative of the instructional strategies teachers could develop from individualized instructional plans for students needing basic sight-word instruction.

FIGURE 7–4 Teacher-directed lesson and practice for basic sight vocabulary

□ **AREA OF NEEDED READING INSTRUCTION**

Practice and reinforcement of basic sight vocabulary.

□ **INTENDED LEARNING OUTCOME**

Given a variety of activities focusing on sight-word development, students will select the sight words to complete each activity correctly.

□ **PAST LEARNING**

Students can recognize some words on sight.

Students can work cooperatively in small groups and attend to the task at hand.

Students understand each activity and the teacher monitors their performance closely during the activity.

□ **BUILDING BACKGROUND**

Depending on the activity selected, review its basic features and purpose. Focus on both the purpose of the activity and how it is to be completed.

□ **INDEPENDENT STUDENT PRACTICE**

There are several small-group and individual activities you can use for the practice and reinforcement of basic sight vocabulary. Again, it is extremely important to prepare students for each activity by reviewing its basic features and purpose through the use of examples. You should be readily available to students as they work on the activity to make sure they are not confused and that they are experiencing success.

One such activity involves the use of word banks. **Word banks** are files of words that students encounter when reading in a contextual setting. Words for inclusion in a student's word bank can come from teacher-directed group and individual instruction, recreational reading, content-area reading, and individuals and groups. The students or the teacher can identify words for inclusion in a word bank. Words selected for a word bank are written on index cards by the students or by the teacher. Word banks can be used for individual and small-group activities, such as classification (nouns, verbs, adjectives, action, and so forth); completion of sentences; and logical extension of sentences. A few examples follow:

1. A group of students can be directed to use words from their word banks to play a game in which each student selects a word from his or her word bank to construct sentences. For example, the first student might begin a sentence with the word *the*, the next student might continue the sentence with the word *big*, the third student might add the word *dog*, and so forth. Students can keep score by counting the number of words he or she uses from his or her word bank for each sentence constructed.

2. Teachers can give students two or three categories (*animals* and *action*, for

example). Students take turns selecting words from their word banks that fit in the proper category.

3. You can prepare several short phrases that students can logically extend using words selected from their word banks. Each student takes a turn adding a word to extend the phrase. Students can keep score on the number of words each of them adds to each phrase.

a. Bob and Sam_____

b. Today is a_____

Students could complete the previous phrases in the following manner:

a. student #1: *are*; student #2: *going*; student #3: *to*; student #1: *play*; student #2: *ball*.

b. student #3: *good*; student #1: *day*; student #2: *to*; student #3: *play*.

Three other activities for the practice and reinforcement of basic sight vocabulary follow:

Sight-Word Match

Directions: On oak tag or cardboard, print sight-word phrases that you want students to practice. Print at least three copies of each word. Cut the words apart to form a deck of sight-word phrase cards. A small group of students can deal out all of the cards equally to each person in the group. The first person places a sight-word phrase card in the middle of the table; the person to the left of the first player takes this card if he or she can match it. If this student does not have a match, he or she places a card next to the first player's. The next person to the left can take both cards if he or she has matching cards in his or her hand. Teach students to play their cards by placing the matching card from their hand next to the card on the table, pronouncing the word phrase, and stacking the played cards in front of them face down. The game ends as soon as a player has played all of his or her cards.

Sight-Word Puzzles

Directions: On a sheet of oak tag or cardboard, print several sentences or short phrases that students can read. On the back of the sheet, paste a picture of something with which students are familiar. This picture should be large enough to cover the back of the sheet completely. Using a razor blade, carefully cut out the selected sight words from each sentence or short phrase. Give the student the puzzle with these pieces removed. Instruct the student to read each sentence or phrase carefully, select the puzzle piece that makes sense in the sentence or phrase, and place the piece in its proper location. Once the puzzle is completed, students can turn it over and look at the picture on the back to find out if they assembled it correctly. If the picture is correct, then they selected the right words.

The level of difficulty of the puzzle can be changed by making all puzzle pieces exactly the same size (increases difficulty level) or by making each piece a distinctly different size (decreases difficulty).

Example of sight-word puzzle

Puzzle pieces

Bob and Bill ▇▇▇▇▇ to the farm.

| are going |

The dog ▇▇▇▇ in the woods.

| was lost |

▇▇▇▇ play a game.

| We will |

My ▇▇▇▇ is at school.

| mother |

There ▇▇▇▇ fish in our room.

| are two |

We have art ▇▇▇▇▇.

| on Monday |

Name It

Directions: Divide two 24″ × 24″ pieces of cardboard into 4″-square grids. Paste pictures of objects into each space on one piece of cardboard. On the other piece of cardboard, print the naming word phrases for the pictures. Cut out each grid. Teach students to distribute an equal number of naming word cards to each other. (If four students are engaged in this activity, each student could be given five naming word/phrase cards; if three students, then each student could be given six naming cards.) The remaining naming cards are placed next to the picture grid, which is put in the middle of the table. Students take turns playing a naming card from their hand by placing it on the appropriate picture on the playing grid. A student who cannot play a card puts it on the bottom of the cards

Picture Grid   **Word Cards**

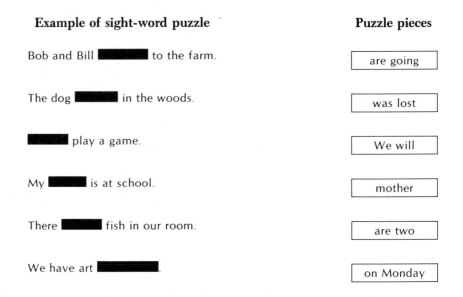

A dog	A house	Some toys
A bed	A ball	Some food
The bat	A doll	A cat

in the middle of the table and takes the top card as a replacement. The next student plays. The game continues until all cards have been played.

☐ ONGOING DIAGNOSIS

It is extremely important that students experience a high degree of success during practice and reinforcement activities. Monitor performance closely as students engage in these activities. If some students are having difficulty, gather data to answer the following questions: Do they understand how to participate in this activity? Do they lack the basic skills necessary to participate in the activity? Do they not get along well with other members of the group? Do they not perform well if they do not win? Answers to these questions will help you determine if you need to review some basic sight words with the students, regroup the students, teach them how to participate in the activity, provide activities that minimize competition, or provide more structure and teacher supervision.

☐ MODIFYING INSTRUCTION

Students who are successful with a particular game can be placed with those students having difficulty. This will help the students who are having difficulty to better understand the game and experience success in playing the game. The student who is successful could be designated the "game-show host," which means that he or she does not play the game, but explains to the other students how to play and helps them with the game when necessary. The activities can be simplified by decreasing the number of choices, such as in the "Sight-Word Puzzle"; pairing students together for playing "Sight-Word Match"; and printing on the pictures the same phrases appearing on the word cards in the "Name It" activity.

Source: From *Teaching Reading: Diagnosis, Direct Instruction, and Practice,* 2nd ed. (pp. 104–108) by W.H. Rupley and T.R. Blair, 1988, Columbus, OH: Merrill. Copyright 1988 by Merrill Publishing Company.

USING MICROCOMPUTERS TO CORRECT/REMEDIATE BASIC SIGHT-WORD PROBLEMS

A number of software packages are available for providing students with drill and practice in the area of basic sight-word development. There are essentially two types of formats available. In one type of program format, a word is presented which the student is to match to a given definition; in the other type of format, the student is to identify a word with a similar or different meaning to the given word, in the context of a short passage. In comparing these programs, teachers would probably wish to use those programs that present the word in meaningful context, because the focus is on both recognition of the word and on assigning meaning to it within its context.

Two software programs that provide students with meaningful practice in learning basic sight words found on the Dolch List of 220 Basic Sight

Words as well as in learning basic words selected by the teacher are available from Hartley Publishing Company, P.O. Box 431, Dimondale, MI 48821. The first program, *Vocabulary—Dolch*, is a program that drills students, using a cassette-control device, on the 220 basic sight words. A word is presented on the monitor to the student, the student says the word, then the cassette recorder plays the correct pronunciation of the word. The student responds by indicating on the keyboard whether he or she knows the word. Each student's responses are stored on the program diskette for later evaluation by the teacher (Rude, 1986). The second software program that both classroom and reading resource teachers might find very useful is named *Create—Vocabulary*. This program allows teachers to develop their own lists of sight words for students to practice. Words can be selected from basal stories, language-experience stories, sight-word lists (such as Dolch's *Basic Sight Word Tests* and Fry's *New Instant Word List*), and content-area texts for inclusion in the computer program. This program is beneficial to teachers who want to provide individual practice related to students' needs after having introduced new words to students and having supervised their learning of these words.

☐ SUMMARY

A meager sight vocabulary leads to many reading problems. Students who rely only on word analysis or irrelevant cues to identify every word they read will be impeded in their functional reading development. Sight vocabulary problems inhibit students' understanding that the purpose of reading is to get meaning; as a result, students are limited in their comprehension.

Assessment of students' sight vocabulary strengths and weaknesses should include the areas of service words, high-frequency content words, and high-frequency words in instructional reading materials. Tachistoscopes, graded word lists, IRIs, cloze procedures, and teacher observations can be used to assess sight vocabulary in these areas.

Diagnostic information is used to develop an individualized corrective or remedial reading program. Information gathered on learner style, task conditions, resource attributes, and teacher style form the basis for instruction. Ongoing diagnosis during instruction allows the teacher to evaluate students' progress and make necessary changes in instruction.

Selection of materials, methods, and approaches for correction or remediation of sight vocabulary problems should be done analytically. Instruction must focus on the use of relevant cues that are transferable to actual reading situations. Although instruction that focuses on cues such as initial letters, word shapes, word lengths, colors, and pictures may result in rapid learning, this can occur at the expense of transfer to functional reading tasks. Analysis of the instruction that the teacher offers the student enhances the likelihood of success. The guidelines presented allow teachers to select instructional strategies that are effective and that transfer to functional reading, enabling the student to become a competent reader.

☐ *IN-TEXT ASSIGNMENT*

LIBRARY ACTIVITY

Obtain several examples of elementary science, social studies, or math textbooks from your curriculum library or other available source. Select a passage from each book and conduct a frequency count of content-area words that appear with high frequency. (For example, science words such as *rain, water, cycle, clouds,* and *wet* might occur frequently in a unit on the water cycle.) From your frequency count, compile a list of high-frequency words that students would need to learn as sight words. Evaluate the teacher's edition of the textbook chosen to determine if any provisions are made for teaching these high-frequency words. Prepare a brief lesson or activity that could be used for diagnosing and teaching the basic content-area sight words that you identified.

DISCUSSION AND DEBATE

Form small groups and analyze the following scenario about a hypothetical student who has sight-word recognition problems. Review the teaching recommendations found in this chapter and identify two or three activities that could be used with this student. Modify the activities to maximize the student's chance of success, establish a meaningful purpose for learning the words, and provide for application of the sight words in meaningful context.

Mary is a first grader who depends primarily on word shape and initial letter cues to identify words. She does have a limited sight vocabulary that includes such words as *the, fall, fun, six, must, pet, mom, dad, Mary,* and *I.* Mary is motivated by game-type activities, verbal praise, and structured learning situations, and she works well in small groups.

RESOURCE ACTIVITY

Invite a representative from a publisher of reading series to speak to your class about how vocabulary is controlled in their beginning reading texts. (Most publishing companies of elementary-school basal-reader programs have area representatives that will come and speak on request about their reading series.) Focus your questions for the representative on what the basic sight words are in his or her series, whether instructional provisions are included for developing basic sight words, how sight words are identified for inclusion in a basal, what the philosophy is of the reading program, and so forth.

□ *REFERENCES*

Ceprano, M. A. (1981, December). A review of selected research on methods of teaching sight words. *The Reading Teacher, 35,* 314–322.

Dolch, E. W. (1942). *The basic sight word tests parts 1 and 2.* Champaign, IL: Garrard.

Durkin, D. (1983). *Teaching them to read* (4th ed.). Boston, MA: Allyn & Bacon.

Ehri, L. C. & Roberts, K. T. (1979, September). Do beginners learn printed words in context or in isolation? *Child Development, 50 ,* 675–685.

Ehri, L. C. & Wilce, L. S. (1979–80). Do beginners learn to read function words better in context or in lists? *Reading Research Quarterly, 15,* 451–476.

Feitelson, D. & Razel, M. (1984). Word superiority and word shape effects in beginning readers. *International Journal of Behavioral Development, 7,* 359–370.

Fry, E. B. (1980, December). The new instant word list. *The Reading Teacher, 34,* 284–289.

Gold, P. C. (1981, November). Two strategies for reinforcing sight vocabulary of language experience stories. *The Reading Teacher, 35,* 141–143.

Groff, P. (1981, Summer). Direct instruction versus incidental learning of reading vocabulary. *Reading Horizons, 21,* 262–265.

Haber, L. R., Haber, R. N., & Furlin, K. R. (1983). Word length and word shape as sources of information in reading. *Reading Research Quarterly, 18,* 165–189.

Heilman, A. J., Blair, T. R., & Rupley, W. H. (1986). *Principles and practices of teaching reading* (6th ed.). Columbus, OH: Merrill.

Johnson, D. D. (1971, October). A basic vocabulary for beginning readers. *Elementary School Journal, 72,* 31–33.

McNinch, G. H. (1981, December). A model for teaching sight words to disabled readers. *The Reading Teacher, 35,* 269–272.

Rude, R. T. (1986). *Teaching reading using microcomputers.* Englewood Cliffs, NJ: Prentice-Hall.

Rupley, W. H. & Blair, T. R. (1988). *Teaching reading: Diagnosis, direct instruction, and practice* (2nd ed.). Columbus, OH: Merrill.

Samuels, S. J. (1985). Word recognition. In R. Ruddell & H. Singer (Eds.), *Theoretical models and processes of reading* (3rd ed.) (pp. 256–275). Newark, DE: International Reading Association.

8

Word Recognition: Phonics, Structural Analysis, and Context

□ *OVERVIEW*

A multitude of investigations of word recognition have led to the common-sense conclusion that using a combination of word-recognition strategies to teach reading is the most beneficial means of promoting reading development. With what is presently known about reading, this eclectic position is the only defensible one given the belief that children are truly different. Reading programs that line up students and "pound into them" a single word-recognition technique to the exclusion of others are built on quicksand. The central question today is not which approach is better, but which emphasis or particular combination of approaches is best for each particular student. Chapter 7 dealt with the word-recognition strategy of sight vocabulary. This chapter focuses on the other major word-recognition strategies—phonics, structural analysis, and context—each of which fosters independent identification of unknown words. Within this chapter, all references to *word recognition* are to these three strategies.

After reading this chapter, the teacher should be able to

□ discuss the importance of phonics, structural analysis, and context in relationship to the model of the reading process presented in chapter 1.
□ identify formal and informal ways of assessing a student's strengths and weaknesses in word recognition.
□ describe the influence of linguistic thinking on present word-recognition instruction.

169

☐ critically evaluate and select materials intended for the application of word-recognition skills.
☐ list guidelines for providing effective instruction.
☐ know how to teach a word-recognition skill through the direct-instruction method.

COMPONENTS OF WORD RECOGNITION

Research has supported the relationship between word-recognition facility and total reading performance (Weaver, 1978; Anderson, Heibert, Scott, & Wilkinson, 1985). This relationship is directly related to overall comprehension. As reviewed in chapter 4, once a student's word recognition or decoding becomes automatic, the more a student can pay attention to comprehension. Early emphasis in the primary grades on word-recognition techniques will thus pave the way for greater reading growth. This emphasis on word recognition or decoding can, at the same time, be made more meaningful by using words in students' listening and speaking vocabularies and by asking students to explain the meanings in the text they are reading.

A basic premise in interpreting the reading process is that the underlying building block of learning is the child's spoken language. It is the teacher's responsibility to narrow the gap between a student's oral language vocabulary and his or her reading vocabulary. The overall goal of this expansion is increasing the student's reading vocabulary. Chapter 7 dealt with the development of a sight vocabulary; one method that might be used to increase a student's *reading* vocabulary is the whole-word, look-say, or sight-word method. This is especially appropriate for words that do not have a stable sound-symbol relationship. Yet, the goal in word recognition is to enhance individual students' abilities to enlarge their vocabularies on their own using the techniques of phonics, structural analysis, and context.

The linguistic influence on reading methodology has been minimal, although publishers have hopped on the bandwagon, calling just about everything "linguistic" (even when it is not). Although the majority of English words can be decoded by using generalizations, many words are irregular in nature—for example, *the* and *to.* Linguistic basal readers try to eliminate such confusion by minimizing the number of irregular words and emphasizing instead regular grapheme-phoneme patterned words. Other beginning reading texts have incorporated, to various degrees, this aspect of controlling the amount of irregular words in their stories. These texts recommend a methodology that involves comparing minimal pairs of words that differ by one phoneme, for example, *lick—like* or *ball—tall.* Many new reading materials have incorporated this technique to teach new words.

Also included in descriptive linguistics are the areas of **morphology**, the study of minimal units of meaning (morphemes) in a language, that is, roots, affixes, and inflectional endings; and **syntax**, or word order—patterns of words and sentences. The examination of word-recognition errors in relation to these two areas and their effects on comprehension provides a teacher with information about students' strengths and weaknesses and offers direction in developing corrective strategies.

The rest of this chapter deals with the word-recognition techniques of phonics, structural analysis, and context. While each will be treated separately, it must be remembered that students rarely use just one technique; rather, they employ a combination strategy utilizing all three techniques. It has been stated that the ultimate aim of word-recognition training is to provide students independence in their learning. A crucial addition to this statement is the flexible, problem-solving attitude that should be fostered in the learning environment. The English language, as those who speak it know, is not even close to perfect in the relationship between sounds (phonemes) and letters (graphemes) that constitute a word. Because of this, flexibility of word-recognition strategies is imperative and should be viewed as a means to comprehension.

Phonics

English is alphabetic in that written words represent a collection of speech sounds. This fact allows speakers to use **phonics**, a method used to relate letters to the speech sounds that they represent. Data indicating the importance of instruction in the area of phonics have been accumulating in the professional literature (Johnson & Baumann, 1984; Stanovich, 1986). Stanovich reports that facility in phonological awareness, the "conscience access to the phonemic level of the speech stream and some ability to cognitively manipulate representations at this level" (p. 362), is linked directly to early reading success. Summarizing the importance of phonological awareness to early reading acquisition, Stanovich states:

> A beginning reader must at some point discover the alphabetic principle: that units of print map onto units of sound. This principle may be induced; it may be acquired through direct instruction; it may be acquired along with or after the build-up of a visually-based sight vocabulary—but it must be acquired if a child is to progress successfully in reading. Children must be able to decode independently the many unknown words that will be encountered in the early stages of reading. By acquiring some knowledge of spelling-to-sound mappings, the child will gain the reading independence that eventually leads to the levels of practice that are prerequisites to fluent reading. (p. 363)

Reading programs must be concerned with phonics and the teaching of its **content** (connections that exist between letters and the sounds they record in syllables) to students. It is an unfortunate reality that a lawful, one-to-one correspondence does not exist between sound and symbol. In fact, of

Basic reading skills such as phonics mastery are best taught through the direct-instruction approach. (Kevin Fitzsimons/Merrill)

all alphabetic languages, English is perhaps one of the worst in this regard. The English language has many more speech sounds than letters (26 letters, but anywhere from 42 to 46 speech sounds). Nevertheless, there is sufficient agreement that the content of phonics (letter-sound generalizations and factors affecting letter-sound correspondences) deserves direct instruction to make phonics one major avenue for students to utilize in identifying unknown words on their own (Anderson et al., 1985).

The following is a summary of the consonant letter-sound relationships and vowel generalizations by Heilman (1985), a noted authority in this area.

Consonants In general, consonant letters are quite consistent in the sounds they represent. Letters which represent only one sound include *b, d, f, h, j, k, l, m, n, p, r, w,* and initial *y*.

Consonants which combine are:

1. *Consonant blends* (clusters)—two or more letters which are blended so that sounded elements of each letter are heard: *bl, black; str, string; spl, splash; gl, glide.*

2. *Consonant digraphs*—two-letter combinations which result in one speech sound that is not a blend of the letters involved: *sh*all; *wh*ite; *th*is (voiced *th*); *th*ink (unvoiced *th*); *ch*air; *ch*orus (*ch* = *k*); *ch*ef (*ch* = *sh*).

Some consonants and consonant combinations have irregular spellings:

1. Nonsounded consonants in specific combinations:
   a. The *k* is not sounded in *kn* (ᴋnew, ᴋnee).
   b. Double consonants—only one is sounded (sum̸mer).
   c. When vowel *i* precedes *gh*, the latter is not sounded (li̸g̸ht).
   d. The *w* is not sounded in *wr* at the beginning of words (ᴡ̸ring).
   e. When a word ends with the syllable *ten*, the *t* is often not sounded (of̸ten, fas̸ten).
   f. The *ck* combination is pronounced *k* (sac̸k, cloc̸k).
   g. The *b* is not sounded in *mb* at the end of words (com̸b, lam̸b).

There are two sounds for consonant *c*:

1. *c* = *k* in *cake, corn, curl*.
2. *c* = *s* when followed by *i, e, y* (city, cent, cycle).

There are two sounds for consonant *g*:

1. regular sound in *go, game, gum*.
2. *g* = *j* when followed by *e, i* (gem, giant).

Other irregularities are:

1. *ph* = *f* (photo = foto; graph = graf).
2. *qu* = *kw* (quack = kwack). The letter *q* has no sound of its own. In English spellings, *q* is always followed by the letter *u*.
3. The letter *s* may be sounded in a number of ways.
   a. *s* = *s* (most common) (sell, soft, said).
   b. *s* = *z* (his = hiz; runs = runz).
   c. *s* = *sh, zh* (sugar, treasure). (Heilman, 1985, p. 64)

Vowels

1. A single vowel in medial position in a word or syllable usually has its short sound (man, bed, fit).

   EXCEPTIONS:

   a. The vowel *o* followed by *ld* usually has its long sound: *sōld, cōld, ōld, gōld*.
   b. The vowel *i* followed by *nd, gh, ld* often has its long sound: *fīnd, līght, chīld*.
   c. The vowel *a* = *aw* when it is followed by *l, ll, w, u*: *walk, fall, draw, because*.
   d. A vowel followed by the letter *r* results in a blended sound which is neither the short nor long sound of the vowel: *car, her, for*.

   e. The spelling *ir* is usually pronounced *ur* (*bird* = *burd*) except when followed by a final *e* (*fire*).

These exceptions are usually treated as separate generalizations.

2. When there are two vowels together, the first usually represents its long sound, and the second is not sounded. (This generalization applies most frequently to *ee, oa, ea, ai: fēed, bōat, bēat, māil.*)
3. In words with two vowels, one of which is final *e*, the *e* is usually not sounded and the first vowel is usually long (*tāke, tūbe*).
4. *Ay* at the end of a word has the long sound of *ā* (*may, pay, play*).
5. When the only vowel in a word (or accented syllable) comes at the end of the word (or syllable), it usually has its long sound.
6. When *y* concludes a word of two or more syllables, it has the long sound of *ē* heard in *lucky, badly.*
   Y functions as a vowel when it:
   a. concludes a word which has no other vowel;
   b. concludes words of more than one syllable (*happy*);
   c. follows another vowel (*may*).
7. Diphthongs are two adjacent vowels, each of which contributes to the sound heard (house, plow, oil, boy).
8. The combination *ow* is sometimes pronounced as long *ō*. (Snow, show—context provides major clue to pronunciation.) (Heilman, 1985, pp. 82–83)

   It should be remembered that the previous listings are only recommended phonic generalizations to be taught to students. Naturally, the amount of phonic instruction necessary for each student will vary depending on a host of factors, including the student's instructional level, the extent of the student's listening-speaking vocabulary, his or her knowledge of other word-recognition techniques, and the student's overall comprehension ability. Three sources containing a more complete coverage of the whole content of phonics are texts by Schell (1979); Heilman (1985); and Logan, Rupley, and Erickson (1988).

   Before the decoding process can begin in earnest, students should have an adequate background in the recognition and differentiation of written symbols and the sounds they represent; however, of the two, the former is the more important. Pure knowledge of letter names is no guarantee to success in phonics, while knowledge of letter names combined with sounds has been shown to facilitate reading acquisition (Ohnmacht, 1969).

   Other skills besides an adequate background knowledge are needed for the decoding process. Important visual skills include **visual memory span**, which is the ability to recall letters and words in their proper order immediately after seeing them presented, and **visual discrimination**, which is the ability to note likenesses and differences in letters and whole words.

Auditory skills include **auditory memory span**, or the ability to recall related sounds after hearing them presented; **auditory discrimination**, or the ability to note likenesses and differences between sounds represented by letters; and **auditory blending**, or the ability to analyze and blend parts or words together to form known words. These visual and auditory skills are usually covered in most reading readiness programs, but their application should extend to all instruction in phonic analysis. Too often students are assumed to have acquired these abilities in kindergarten and first grade, and instruction encompassing these skills is neglected when teaching various phonic generalizations in later grades. In addition, the following are possible explanations for students' difficulties with phonics:

lack of mastery of phonics skills taught

lack of blending ability although individual sounds are known

use of phonics exclusively to decode unknown words

inability to distinguish one sound from another in words

inability to pronounce individual sounds after seeing the letter(s) in isolation or within words

insufficient listening-speaking vocabulary (Lass & Davis, 1985)

After initial training in visual and auditory skills and in using letters and the sounds they represent, the content of phonics should be taught. It should be emphasized that every student will not need the same amount of instruction in each area, and the order of teaching the skills depends on the strengths and weaknesses of the student and on the reading series the teacher is using. The crucial point is that all students need a basic foundation in phonics to attack unknown words on their own.

Teaching Methods. There are a multitude of teaching techniques in the area of phonics. Basically, instruction can be termed analytic or synthetic.

Analytic phonics begins by having students learn a certain number of words by the whole-word approach, after which they examine the relationships that exist between the phonic elements. Using this approach, there are two basic ways of teaching a skill lesson: *inductive*, in which the teacher begins by giving examples illustrating a generalization and then guides the students to a conclusion; and *deductive*, in which students are told the generalization and then asked for examples to verify it.

An example of the inductive approach includes the following:

☐ It is assumed that students know the words *ball, bat,* and *bundle* or the words are taught through the whole-word approach.
☐ The teacher asks students what is alike about the three words and leads students to discover that the words contain the letter *b*, which represents the /b/ sound.
☐ Other words are solicited with the sound of /b/.

□ The words given are presented in written context.
□ Practice exercises are given using the words in context.

An example of the deductive approach includes the following:

□ The words *ball, bat,* and *bundle* are listed on the board (words that are in the students' listening-speaking vocabulary).
□ The teacher tells students that all the words begin with the letter *b* and represent the /*b*/ sound, as in *big.*
□ Other words are solicited with the sound of /*b*/.
□ These words are presented in written context.
□ Practice exercises are given using the words in context.

Most educators prefer the inductive approach over the deductive approach, although this decision rests with the teacher, since some students respond better to the deductive method.

Synthetic phonics begins with direct instruction of phonic elements, beginning with letters of the alphabet, followed with syllables, then with monosyllabic words through polysyllabic words, then phrases, and finally with whole sentences. Once students learn the sounds represented by the letters, they blend the parts of the words together to form a known word. Synthetic phonics includes the following three variations of sound blending: (1) sounding letter-by-letter (*b-a-t*), (2), the initial consonant is sounded and the rest of the word is added as a word family (*b-at*), and (3) the initial consonant with a vowel is sounded together and then the final consonant is added (*ba-t*).

The analytic approach to phonics is more widely used today. Keep in mind, however, that the difference between analytic and synthetic is one of initial emphasis (whole word versus letter). Emphasis must be evaluated in terms of both successful teacher implementation and learner preference. Auditory blending is a crucial skill in the analytic approach, as well as in the synthetic approach, because a student must be able to divide an unknown word into syllables or structural elements, must attempt pronunciation of the smaller units, and then finally must blend the units together. Many students can pronounce syllables but have problems blending all the parts together. Since we decode syllables, not individual letters or words, it is recommended that a student identify the first vowel or vowels in a word. Vowels affect the sounds represented by surrounding letters and are the key to success in blending. Once the basic phonic elements are taught (initial consonants, final consonants, short vowels, long vowels, basic vowel principles), students should learn to follow a pattern of unlocking the pronunciation of a word. It is important to note at this point that a combined word-recognition strategy using phonics, structural analysis, and the context is recommended; however, the following procedure is recommended for *initial* instruction in phonics. With the teaching of vowel principles, students can

1. find the first vowel or vowels in a word or syllable.
2. determine if the vowel represents a long, short, or silent sound.
3. pronounce the vowel.
4. blend the vowel sound with the sound represented by the initial consonant.
5. blend the final sounds.

For example, the application of these five steps for blending the word *hat* is:

1. a
2. short vowel, cvc (consonant, vowel, consonant)
3. ă
4. hă
5. hat

Another application is pronouncing the word *gate:*

1. a
2. long vowel, consonant-final *e*
3. ā
4. gā
5. gate

Once the basic phonic syllabication generalizations are introduced, the auditory blending pattern would be:

1. Find the first vowel or vowels in a word or a syllable.
2. Attempt to divide the word into the first syllable.
3. Determine if the vowel represents a long, short, or silent sound.
4. Find the next vowel or vowels.
5. Determine if the vowel represents a long, short, or silent sound. (Repeat steps 4 and 5 for words with more than two syllables.)
6. Blend the first vowel sound with the sound represented by the initial consonant.
7. Blend the second vowel sound with the sound represented by the surrounding consonants.
8. Blend all sounds together.

For example, the application of these eight steps for blending the word *music* is as follows:

1. u
2. mu
3. long vowel at end of syllable
4. i
5. short vowel, cvc (consonant, vowel, consonant)
6. mū
7. sĭc
8. music

Once again, visual and auditory discrimination and auditory blending exercises must accompany all phonic instruction, whether it be inductive or deductive, analytic or synthetic. Students in a corrective or remedial program often need more than the normal repetition and practice to ensure that their skills become automatic.

Structural Analysis

Another word-recognition technique that leads to independent word recognition is the use of structural analysis. While phonics deals with the sounds of language (phonemes), structural analysis is a process of arriving at the meaning or pronunciation of words by identifying their meaning units (morphemes). **Morphemes** are meaningful linguistic units that contain no smaller meaningful parts. A morpheme may be either a prefix, suffix, inflectional ending, or root word. For example, *talked* is composed of two morphemes—*talk* and *ed.*

The use of structural analysis allows students to rapidly decode larger units of words in the sense that they learn to not react to each letter or grapheme. In reality, both structural analysis and phonics are combined in word identification. A discussion of a combination strategy is presented later in this chapter.

As in phonics, students need direct instruction in the skill content of structural analysis. Most reading programs include step-by-step procedures for teaching the following:

Root word: Element of the word remaining after all affixes have been removed.

Prefix: Meaningful element attached to the beginning of a root word

Suffix: Meaningful element attached to the end of a root word

Inflectional endings: Suffixes added to words to change the grammatical intentions of words, such as case, gender, number, person, mood, or voice

Contraction: Shortening of a word or words by omitting one or more sounds or letters within a word or between words

Compound word: A word consisting of two or more independent words that combine their meanings to make a new word

Syllabication principles: Determining basic units of pronunciation

Helping students determine the basic units of pronunciation (syllables) is an aid to effective word learning. Traditionally, syllabication is included under structural analysis because it is strictly the division of a word into its basic units of pronunciation; only after this division are phonic generalizations applied to letters. The following is a list of syllabication generalizations by Heilman (1985).

Generalizations Relating to Syllabication There are as many syllables as there are vowel sounds. Syllables are determined by the vowel sounds heard—not by the number of vowels seen.

Number of vowels seen		Number of vowels seen		Number of vowels seen		Number of vowels heard	
measure	(4)	mezh'er	(2)	moment	(2)	mo'ment	(2)
phonics	(2)	fon iks	(2)	cheese	(3)	chēz	(1)

Syllables divide between double consonants—or between two consonants.

hap·pen	can·non	sud·den	ves·sel	vol·ley	com·mand
bas·ket	tar·get	cin·der	har·bor	tim·ber	wig·wam

A single consonant between vowels usually goes with the second vowel(s).

fa mous	ho tel	di rect	ti ger	ce ment	pu pil
ea ger	wa ter	po lice	lo cate	va cant	spi der

As a general rule, do not divide consonant digraphs (*ch, th,* etc.) and consonant blends.

tea*ch* er	wea*th* er	ma *ch*ine	se *c*ret	a *g*ree

The word endings *-ble, -cle, -dle, -gle, -kle, -ple, -tle, -zle* constitute the final syllable.

mar ble	mus cle	han dle	sin gle	an kle	tem ple

In general, prefixes and a number of suffixes form separate syllables.

re load ing   un fair   dis agree ment   pre heat ed
(Heilman, 1985, pp. 101–102)

Materials abound for teaching structural analysis, but they must be chosen in relation to the needs of students. As stated before, direct instruction is recommended; the inductive approach described under "Teaching Methods" is appropriate for structural analysis when it is combined with interesting and varied practice. Auditory and visual discrimination and blending practice should also accompany structural analysis instruction to ensure mastery. Structural analysis, used in conjunction with phonics and context, is an extremely useful word-recognition technique that allows for independent word learning by students. Adequate time and attention should be given to it by teachers of reading.

Context

Another major word-recognition technique that students use for identifying an unknown word is the application of context clues. Of the major word-identification skills, the use of context is probably the most valuable to adult teachers. This realization should compel teachers, at all stages, to give proper attention to developing students' use of context clues as they learn to read. Developing students' ability to determine the meaning of a word from the other words in a passage should come about through both direct and informal instruction along with the use of other word-recognition strategies. As stated earlier, word learning is related to comprehension. Whether students are developing sight vocabularies or using phonics or structural analysis, they must have interesting, varied, and realistic practice with words in context. The use of context not only reflects the natural reading process, but also allows each student to focus on meaning to aid him or her in determining if the word(s) make sense in context.

The two broad kinds of context clues are syntactic and semantic. **Syntactic clues** involve the characteristics of word order, and the English language is very much influenced by these. For example, in the sentence "The _____ in the pool is bright blue," it is known just from the syntax that (1) the word is a noun because of the word *the* (*the* is a marker that signals information about a word or a letter just as the word *an* signals a noun beginning with *a, e, i, o, u*); and (2) the word is singular because of the word *is*. In another example, "They _____to the store just as fast they could," it is known from the syntax that the word is a verb, and it is in past tense because of *could*. Students need direct instruction to be able to use syntax in an automatic fashion.

Semantic clues help the reader to figure out a difficult word from the other words in the sentence. In the first example, *gelatin* would not make sense semantically. Based on the reader's experiences, gelatin is seldom found in a swimming pool. The words *bright, blue,* and *pool* signal that *water* is the sensible choice. Of course, here we are hoping that students can make sense of what they are reading.

Interest in context clues is on the rise. Writers are delineating several different types of context clues, which we feel need not be taught directly to all students. They are, however, helpful for informal diagnostic teaching purposes. Artley's list (1943) of specific contextual aids is an excellent compilation for all teachers:

- ☐ Typographical (quotation marks, italics, boldface type)
- ☐ Structural (appositive clause, signal words)
- ☐ Synonyms and antonyms
- ☐ Roots, prefixes, suffixes
- ☐ Figures of speech
- ☐ Pictorial aids
- ☐ Inference
- ☐ Direct explanation
- ☐ Subjective aids (tone, mood, intent)
- ☐ Background experiences

The value of context clues lies in their easy application to whole-word learning, phonics, and structural analysis. While direct instruction is recommended to expose students to the power of this technique, it can be applied in all areas of the curriculum. From readiness training to advanced instruction in high school and college, context can and should receive its share in the instructional program.

Combination Strategy

Except for the beginning stages of learning to read, a flexible approach to word recognition combining phonics, structural analysis, and context to figure out an unknown word is recommended. Early in the reading process, students are learning the basic rudiments of these word-recognition techniques, and it is perhaps unrealistic to expect them to employ a flexible combination approach. However, once mastery of basic techniques in each area has been achieved, students should be encouraged to use all the aids or "prompts" available to identify unknown words in actual reading situations. There is no one best method of combining techniques; yet, combining techniques is necessary to illustrate the problem-solving approach that students must take when figuring out an unknown word. The overriding factor is the existence of many English words that are irregular in nature (lacking a one-to-one correspondence between letters and sounds they represent). The following is one recommended strategy for students to employ when identifying an unknown word:

1. Use context clues (syntactic and semantic clues).
2. Examine the word for familiar structural units—that is, prefixes, suffixes, or root words.
3. Find the first vowel.
4. Divide the word into syllables, looking for familiar patterns of letters.
5. Look for special letter combinations—that is, *oo, oi, oy, eu, aw,* and so on.

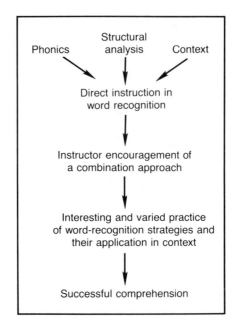

FIGURE 8–1   Flexible Word-Recognition Strategy

6. Pronounce the word.
7. Be sure it makes sense in the sentence.

Since comprehension is the end product of word recognition, it must be stressed to students that they should use a flexible trial-and-error approach. Overreliance on one technique may interfere with student's ability to achieve the final goal of comprehension. Good readers make simultaneous use of all three techniques to identify words on their own. Figure 8–1 summarizes this flexible word-recognition approach.

ASSESSMENT

Effective instruction in word recognition can best stem from a diagnosis of a student's strengths and weaknesses. Recalling the diagnostic process of instruction, the teaching or action in the classroom or clinic is affected by several factors. An economical assessment is necessary to teach students the skills they need to become independent readers. It must be remembered that not all students need the same amount or type of instruction in word-recognition strategies. The practice of giving worksheet after worksheet to everyone in a reading group or class is ineffectual and inevitably leads to boredom and nonlearning on the part of many students. Before "instructing," it is necessary to first determine a student's instructional level to be able to select materials of the appropriate level of difficulty for instruction in word recognition. For example, two students might both need instruction in the same vowel principles, but one student might be performing on the 3^1 level and the other on the 1^2 level. The teacher will have to work on vowel principles using different materials that suit each student's instructional or independent reading levels.

Keeping these guidelines in mind, teachers can operate on three levels in assessing their students' word-recognition needs:

1. informal observation and assessment,
2. administration of a criterion-referenced test, or
3. administration of a standardized analytic skills test.

The decision as to which level is most appropriate will depend on the needs of the students, the purposes of the assessment, and the teaching environment (classroom or clinic).

Teacher Observation and Informal Assessment

Teacher observation is an important vehicle for assessment. Remember it is the teacher who is the key ingredient in the classroom, and judgments made there are more than likely to be valid. Caution at this point is warranted, however, because teacher observation must be keen and accurate, and a record must be made as soon as possible of each student's strengths and weaknesses.

With continual diagnosis throughout instruction, a teacher can maintain a daily or weekly progress chart on each student. Taking advantage of the multitude of opportunities to read with students in both formal and informal situations strengthens the power of such an observational recording system. Such observation can lead to an awareness of discrepancies in a student's growth in word-recognition skills and thus pinpoint areas to work on in a corrective or remedial situation. In analyzing patterns of reading behavior obtained from an IRI, it is recommended that the questions listed in chapter 5 be used to determine those miscues that are interfering with comprehension. Needless instruction can be avoided if the focus of evaluation is on each student's strengths and weaknesses in relation to comprehension abilities.

Criterion-Referenced Tests

Criterion-referenced tests are one means for determining students' word-recognition needs (see chapter 5). Criterion-referenced tests on the market today are easily adaptable to various classroom or clinic needs in assessing a student's mastery of specific skill areas. Teachers can administer several subtests as a prelude to instruction or can administer selected subtests to verify teacher observation. A list of some criterion-referenced reading tests assessing word-recognition abilities can be found in the appendix.

Formal Assessment

Norm-referenced instruments assessing word-recognition skills are in great supply. Such tests are called analytical or specific because they attempt to assess several aspects, including phonics, structural analysis, and context. Formal measures are most effective when a causal relationship exists between the results and subsequent skill instruction. It is important to realize that while the items are carefully constructed, reliable, and valid, the instrument must provide the teacher with the information wanted for his or her class. If the test fits the instructional goals for the teacher's particular group, then he or she should seriously consider using it. It is always a good procedure to analyze the test before administration to decide if the test content is appropriate, if the test measures what it purports to measure, and whether or not it is a fair test for a particular class. Most analytical tests provide a systematic synthesis of the results in the form of an individual and/or class profile of strengths and weaknesses. This data facilitates the planning of corrective instruction; however, qualitative analysis can reveal more specific strengths and weaknesses and should also be used. An annotated list of some analytical or specific word-recognition tests for use in a classroom or clinic are included in the appendix.

CORRECTIVE TEACHING GUIDELINES

Deciding what word-recognition skills to teach is a very real problem for teachers. Effective diagnostic procedures can help pinpoint student strengths and weaknesses. We have not offered long lists presenting an optimal sequence of word-recognition skills because research has not yet revealed a universal list acceptable to the profession. Although most reading programs offer both scope and sequence, it is essential to remember that there is no one right sequence. Decisions must be based on each student's needs. Beyond questions of the *what* and *when* of word-recognition skills is the concern of how they should be taught.

Teach to Strengths

Remembering that students in a corrective or remedial situation have failed to master essential skills, there are basically three avenues open for instruction. The first is the begin-over approach using the same reading method with different materials, the assumption being that with more intense instruction, the student will be able to correct difficulties. The second is the begin-over approach in conjunction with a preferred method of instruction. This avenue of instruction depends on the teacher's expertise in assessing each learner's strengths. The third avenue is not to begin over, but to fill in gaps. This approach can combine the use of different materials with a preferred method of instruction.

Examples of methods for teaching necessary word-recognition skills include using programmed materials, linguistic readers, a language-experience approach, or a multisensory approach. The important point is that if a student has failed using a particular method and set of materials, using a different method with different materials to which a student responds positively may increase the chances for success.

Instruction at the Proper Level

Aside from assessing the strengths and weaknesses of word-recognition skills and following an appropriate sequence of instruction for a particular student, instruction in word-recognition skills must be offered at the student's instructional level. For example, a teacher might have two students who need work on vowel principles. One student might be on the fourth-grade instructional level and the other on the second-grade instructional level. In terms of vocabulary used to teach the skills and appropriate follow-up activities, each student should be operating on a different level. Failure to take this fact into account could result in poor transfer to reading situations or no transfer at all.

Direct Teaching

A third overriding factor in corrective and remedial instruction is that students need direct instruction in whatever reading method is successful for them. Most readers in corrective and remedial programs have received instruction in the skills they are lacking. While there are many possible explanations for their initial failures, one prominent explanation is that the word-recognition skills were only "half learned" and complete transfer was not made. As a result, there are gaps that interfere with their reading comprehension. It is our contention that many problems in the word-recognition area are the result of "half learnings", accumulated through the primary grades. Missing skills must be retaught in a direct manner and students given sufficient practice to make the skills automatic. We recommend that such direct instruction be short and to the point. Only one skill should be taught per lesson unless the lesson is a review of several elements (all consonant clusters, vowel principles, and so on). In terms of phonics, structural analysis, and context, lessons can be 5 to 10 minutes long excluding time for applying the skill in actual reading material. In essence, the direct-instruction approach includes three stages: readiness, teaching, and practice. Figures 8–2, 8–3, and 8–4 contain direct-instruction lessons in each of the following areas: phonics, structural analysis, and context. Many times worksheets are given to students with the pretense that the worksheet will teach the skill. This is nonsense! Direct teaching must precede *any* worksheet or game used to reinforce a skill. Both teaching and appropriate practice are needed to ensure a maximum degree of success. Such direct teaching demands that teachers given an appropriate rationale for a lesson and identify in their own minds prerequisites that are essential for students to be successful in that lesson. These important considerations must be attended to before any instruction is given. Even if a student requires an unusual amount of reteaching in a basic skill area as a result of years of half learnings, the teacher must not give in to the temptation to cover too much at once. McCullough (1962) spoke of this very point by noting, "Rabbits don't become kangaroos by eating carrots faster."

FIGURE 8–2   Sample direct-instruction lesson for phonics

☐ AREA OF NEEDED READING INSTRUCTION

Understanding of the vowel diphthongs *oi* and *oy*.

☐ INTENDED LEARNING OUTCOME

Given a series of words containing the vowel combinations *oi* and *oy*, students will be able to pronounce the words correctly.

☐ PAST LEARNING

Students know the vowel sounds (long and short).
   Students know vowel principles.

☐ BUILDING BACKGROUND

Review with students the vowel principle that helps them pronounce the words *heat* and *boat*. Remind students that when you discussed this principle, you reminded them that it did not hold true all of the time. Tell them that today they will learn two vowel combinations that do not follow the double vowel principle.

☐ TEACHER-DIRECTED INSTRUCTION

On the board write two lists of known words that contain the *oi* and *oy* vowel combination. For example:

oil	toy
soil	boy
boil	joy

Ask students to pronounce the words. Next ask: How many vowels are there in each word? What usually happens when there are two vowels together in a word? Do you hear the sound of the first vowel in *oil* and *toy*? Tell students that *oi* and *oy* are special vowel combinations that usually stand for the sound heard at the beginning of *oil*. Isolate the sound of *oi* for students. Solicit other words that have this sound. Lead students to the conclusion that *oi* and *oy* represent the vowel sound found in the word *oil*. Present a new list of real and nonsense words containing the vowel combinations *oi* and *oy*. Make sure they can pronounce the words correctly.

☐ INDEPENDENT STUDENT PRACTICE

Write the following words on the chalkboard and ask students to fill in the sentence blanks with the correct words. After they finish, read the sentences aloud to check mastery of *oi* and *oy* combinations.

soil	enjoy
boy	moisture
coin	toy
noise	poison

The plastic airplane was his favorite _____.

The _____ is dry and needs to be watered.

The insects were killed with _____.

That 1923 dime is a rare _____.

I hope you will _____ the picnic.

The _____ in the air caused rain.

The _____ in the yellow shirt threw the ball.

The neighbors next door make a lot of _____.

☐ ONGOING DIAGNOSIS

Read with each student individually during the silent reading section of a directed reading activity. Note the student's application of the vowel combination of *oy* and *oi* and decide if further direct instruction and/or practice is necessary.

☐ MODIFYING INSTRUCTION

The independent student practice can be simplified by using pictures representing the words that students are to select to complete the sentences. Write the naming words beneath each picture to emphasize the written text that represents the pictures. Another modification is to write a choice of words beneath the blank and have students select the one that makes sense to complete the sentence. For example:

The plastic airplane was his favorite _____.

                                                             toy   enjoy   soil

This can be made easier by giving the students only two words from which to select.

The difficulty level can be increased by providing several choices that make sense in each sentence; have students identify all words that would meaningfully complete the sentences.

□□□

Source: From *Teaching Reading: Diagnosis, Direct Instruction, and Practice*, 2nd ed. (pp. 124–125) by W.H. Rupley and T.R. Blair, 1988, Columbus, OH: Merrill. Copyright 1988 by Merrill Publishing Company.

FIGURE 8–3 Sample direct-instruction lesson for structural analysis

□ AREA OF NEEDED READING INSTRUCTION

Use and understanding of the function of prefixes (for example, the use of *re* when it means again).

□ INTENDED LEARNING OUTCOME

Given several words containing prefixes (*re*), students will write sentences using the words correctly.

□ PAST LEARNING

Students can recognize and associate meaning with several root words for which the prefix *re* forms a new word.
> Students can construct and write short meaningful sentences.
> Students have a basic understanding of what a prefix is.

□ BUILDING BACKGROUND

Review the concept of prefix with students. Remind them that a prefix is a meaningful unit of language that helps them to identify words and to understand what they read, it is placed at the beginning of a root word, and it affects the meaning of the root word. Assuming, for purposes of this example, that students have been taught the prefix *un*, list the following words on the chalkboard:

> *un* + root word means *not* + root word
>
> unsafe
>
> unable
>
> unsure
>
> untied
>
> unhappy

Remind students that they learned the prefix *un* means "not." Explain that the word *unsafe* means "not safe." Using the words in the list, ask individual students to pronounce a word and to define it highlighting the prefix.

□ TEACHER-DIRECTED INSTRUCTION

Write selected root words on the chalkboard for which the prefix *re* forms a new word meaning "to do again."

> play
>
> paint

> test
>
> write
>
> learn

Remind students that these are words they know. Call on individuals to give sentences using one of the words. Assist anyone who is having difficulty by using prompts and cues. Direct students to look at the list of root words again, then introduce the prefix *re* by writing it in front of the root word, emphasizing each time that *re* means to do again.

> replay
>
> repaint
>
> retest
>
> rewrite
>
> relearn

Call on individuals to read a selected word from the list and to define it—*repaint* means "to paint again." Point out to students that the prefix *re* tells them that something has been done at least once and now will be done *again.* Use *rewrite* to illustrate this by writing an example on the chalkboard such as *I am hoppy.* Point out that you will have to *rewrite* the sentence because you misspelled *happy.* Ask students if you should just *rewrite* the misspelled word or *rewrite* the entire sentence. Direct them to tell how you should *rewrite* the misspelling.

Write several sentences such as the following on the chalkboard.

1. Bobby and Sally are going to *play* the game again.
   Bobby and Sally are going to _____ the game.
2. The *paint* on the house is the wrong color.
   They are going to _____ the house.

Call on individuals to select a word from the list that means "to do again" for the underlined word in the first sentence; ask the student to use it in the blank of the second sentence. Check students' understanding of the prefix *re* by listing additional words on the chalkboard (*repack, refold, redo,* and so forth) and asking them to use these words in sentences.

☐ INDEPENDENT STUDENT PRACTICE

Distribute a worksheet similar to the following example and complete one or two items with students before they complete the activity on their own.

reread	1. Will you _____ the barn this year?
redo	2. I had to _____ the story so I could understand it.
repaint	3. Sara had to _____ the paper because it would not
replay	fit in the envelope.
rebuild	4. Mr. Smith has an old car that he is going to _____.
rewrite	
repack	
refold	

Students are to complete each sentence by selecting a word from the list that makes sense. Explain that they will not use all of the words in the sentences. Have them write their own sentences for the words they do not use. Do one example with them to make sure they all understand. If you suspect that some of the students will have difficulty identifying words for which they are to write sentences, you can mark these words for them.

☐ ONGOING DIAGNOSIS

Observation of students during group instruction to evaluate their learning of both the function and meaning of prefixes.

Teacher-made tests can be developed after several prefixes have been taught. Items such as the following can be written to assess your students' learning.

Underline the prefix in each of the following words listed and write the meaning for each word.

1. repack _____
2. unsafe _____
3. reglue _____
4. precook _____
5. inactive _____

You can also give students a list of words containing such prefixes and direct them to write a sentence or phrase using each word correctly.

☐ MODIFYING INSTRUCTION

The difficulty level of independent student practice activities can be lowered by listing two possible word choices beneath the blank and having students identify the one that is correct. The sentence can also be replaced with such phrases as the following:

to paint again _____
to build again _____
to write again _____

Ask students to select the word that means the same as the phrase.

☐☐☐

Source: From *Teaching Reading: Diagnosis, Direct Instruction, and Practice,* 2nd ed. (pp. 128–131) by W.H. Rupley and T.R. Blair, 1988, Columbus, OH: Merrill. Copyright 1988 by Merrill Publishing Company.

FIGURE 8–4 Sample direct-instruction lesson for context

☐ AREA OF NEEDED READING INSTRUCTION

Ability to understand sentence structure (syntax)—noun markers, nouns, verb markers, and verbs.
Ability to understand language structure in written text.

☐ INTENDED LEARNING OUTCOME

Students will identify nouns and verbs in sentences on a teacher-made worksheet by correctly circling the noun phrases and underscoring the verb phrases.

☐ PAST LEARNING

Students understand that a noun is a word that represents a person, place, or thing and that a verb represents the action of a sentence.

Students are familiar with the objects and actions represented by noun and verb phrases used for instruction.

☐ BUILDING BACKGROUND

Review the concepts of noun and verb phrases with students by providing a list of mixed examples of each on the chalkboard. Also write the definitions of *noun* and *verb* on the chalkboard for reference purposes.

Discuss the definitions of *noun* and *verb* and help students to identify the nouns and verbs in the list by circling the nouns and underscoring the verbs. Call on individuals to state whether or not a word on the list is a noun or verb. Ask them to explain their answers.

a dog

a cat

will walk

the car

can hike

☐ TEACHER-DIRECTED INSTRUCTION

Remind students of the meanings of a noun and a verb by using written examples on the chalkboard of sentences that contain a single subject and verb, such as: *A girl plays. The dog barks at the girl.*

Assist students in identifying and distinguishing the noun and verb phrases in each sentence by relating the meaning of a noun and a verb with specific words contained in the sentence examples. Circle the noun and underline the verb in the examples.

Write additional sentences and tell students to identify the noun and verb in a specific sentence by quickly telling you which words you are to circle and which words you are to underline.

(The boys) can jump

(A cow) is eating in the field

(Some men) are working hard.

(John) is playing ball.

☐ INDEPENDENT STUDENT PRACTICE

Hand out a teacher-made worksheet of sentences containing noun and verb phrases similar to those used for teacher-directed instruction. Instruct students to identify each noun and verb in the sentences by underlining the verb and circling the noun. Check students' understanding of the activity by completing the first sentence on the worksheet with them.

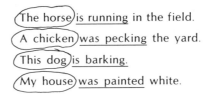

☐ ONGOING DIAGNOSIS

Teacher evaluation of students' written responses to the teacher-made worksheet concerning nouns and verbs in sentence structure.

☐ MODIFYING INSTRUCTION

This activity can be extended to include sentences that contain multiple nouns and action verbs in each. Have students circle and underscore the correct words.

Two boys and a girl are eating the apples and drinking the milk.

Students can also be given short phrases and directed to combine the phrases in as many ways as possible that still make sense using the multiple nouns and action verbs that are provided.

Source: From *Teaching Reading: Diagnosis, Direct Instruction, and Practice*, 2nd ed. (pp. 133–135) by W.H. Rupley and T.R. Blair, 1988, Columbus, OH: Merrill. Copyright 1988 by Merrill Publishing Company.

Distinction Between Goals and Means of Accomplishment

Following the direct instruction of needed skills, application is usually given in the form of a worksheet or two. In this instance there is a one-to-one correspondence between the goals of the lesson and ensuing worksheet(s). Such a practice is fine, but the skills must be practiced in varied reading situations if students are to achieve mastery and independence. Each skill formally taught should be repeatedly illustrated and practiced in as many reading situations as possible. In reinforcing a skill, the teacher can teach it several times in the classroom in different situations—the point being that the same skill is being reinforced, but in varied situations. For example, if direct instruction was given in prefixes, further and varied practice can be obtained not only on a worksheet following the lesson but also in reading orally with a student individually during a directed reading activity (DRA), in a content area while reviewing vocabulary, or in learning stations involving independent activities.

Examples and counterexamples must be given in a variety of situations from different vantage points. Important learnings are thus sustained without students getting bored doing worksheet after worksheet. An analogy can be drawn to any popular television detective show that uses basically the same plot week after week. Why have many detective shows been so popular? One possible explanation is that even though the charac-

A reading skill formally taught must be practiced in varied situations. (Gale Zucker)

ters are the same and the purpose is the same each week, one week the detective is in Germany, the next time in the mountains of California, and the next in Washington, DC. The sample plot was used but the scenery changed. So, too, in teaching word-recognition skills—you might be teaching prefixes, but you can shift the substance to all curriculum areas and still get at the same generalization. The more varied, interesting, and meaningful the practice the better the chance of success.

Correct Use of Supplemental Materials

Students learning the various word-recognition skills may need additional practice materials to ensure mastery. The importance of applying such skills in a variety of contexts cannot be overemphasized. Commercial materials for such purposes are coming off the press at an ever-increasing rate (see figure 8–5). Teachers need to have a variety of such practice materials on hand in the classroom or clinic for several reading levels. Besides commercial skill books, kits, activities, and games, many teachers construct their own materials to provide students with the necessary practice. Paramount to using any supplemental material is the diagnostic thinking that precedes its use. First, goals of instruction should be based on what students need. The indiscriminate use of supplemental materials just because they are convenient and easy to use is not teaching. Second, the

FIGURE 8–5 Practice activity for decoding

Name _____ 32

If <u>st</u> comes at the beginning of the word, write the word under the picture of the stick. If <u>st</u> comes at the end, write the word under the picture of the nest.

best step stop fast list stack steep cast stale mist

1. step 2. best

3. stop 4. fast

5. stack 6. list

7. steep 8. cast

9. stale 10. mist

Source: From Skillpack for Level 5, *Birds Fly, Bears Don't,* of the GINN READING PROGRAM by Theodore Clymer and others, © Copyright 1982 by Ginn and Company. Used by permission of Silver, Burdett & Ginn, Inc.

teacher *must* have a correct relationship to the materials. Teachers must view all materials as something that might or might not assist students in acquiring mastery of a particular skill. It is very easy to fall into a rigid pace where each student is working on the same page in the same book. Teachers should view materials as an aid instead of becoming assistants to the materials.

Next, any independent work done by students should be closely monitored to prevent students from going through materials only to achieve another series of half learnings. Supplemental materials, if used correctly, have an important place in the reading program. Commercial and teacher-made games are very popular for providing repetition and skill review; however, the games must be monitored carefully by teachers or they will defeat their original purposes.

SPECIFIC INSTRUCTIONAL STRATEGIES AND TECHNIQUES

Realizing that some students require further instruction in word-recognition skills, Schell (1978) recommends a method of direct instruction, named the PPARR (presentation, practice, application, review, re-review) cycle, to ensure student mastery. The PPARR cycle can be applied to the teaching of any word-identification ability. This strategy follows the teaching guideline offered in the previous section in which an outline for a phonics lesson was presented. With the PPARR cycle, "one element or principle is presented, practiced, applied, reviewed, and re-reviewed in a systematic, structured sequence" (Schell, 1978, p. 877). In the first step to the method, teachers are encouraged to take the necessary time to provide a complete introduction of the principle or skill under consideration. Students should pay close attention to this initial presentation of the skill, and teachers should make the introduction as meaningful to students as possible. In the initial practice step, teachers provide exercises for students to complete that are not difficult. Easy material ensures student success. Also required in this step is immediate teacher feedback regarding the student's understanding of the task at hand. Next, many opportunities should be provided to students to help transfer the new skill to actual reading. This integration must take place if the student is to use the skill in various reading situations. The need for additional practice for corrective and remedial readers is emphasized in the review step. It is here that large amounts of interesting and varied practice are provided until mastery is achieved. The last step, re-reviewing, points out a necessary quality in any teaching situation—that is, the provision of periodic practice in various reading situations to ensure automaticity of a skill or ability.

A technique that may be used as part of the PPARR cycle was reviewed by Hopkins (1979). The technique calls for the use of every-pupil response cards popularized by Donald Durrell (1956). This procedure can be used in group instruction for many skills and abilities, including word identification. Hopkins states, "The every-pupil response technique requires each child in a classroom or small group to respond simultaneously to the teacher's oral questions by displaying the appropriate response, selected from a set of manipulative materials" (p. 173). Depending on the goal of the lesson, each student would have cards printed with *yes, no,* or various letters, numbers, or words. Students then display the appropriate card to answer questions posed by the teacher. In this manner, the teacher can ascertain if students understand the lesson objective.

The advantages, according to Hopkins, are many. Students become active in each lesson and improve their listening habits, and the technique allows for a greater number of student responses in a given period of time. Also, students are no longer singled out for their responses in front of the class, and the technique cuts down on paperwork. In addition to these advantages, this technique helps to foster many of the components of the direct-instruction format (see chapter 2), notably, increased student time-on-task and immediate feedback.

A common occurrence among students in corrective and remedial programs is word-identification fluency. In order to improve both word-identification fluency and comprehension simultaneously, Cunningham (1979) reviewed the following four techniques that were found successful in a classroom and a clinic setting:

Imitative method (Huey, 1908/1968; Chomsky, 1976)

Impress method (Heckelman, 1969)

Repeated readings (Dahl, 1974; Samuels, 1979)

Modified cloze (Cunningham, 1979)

The **imitative method** requires the teacher to tape a story that is on the student's instructional level. The student then follows along in the text while listening to the story on tape. This process is repeated until the student can easily read the story fluently with expression.

The **impress method** attempts to increase oral reading fluency by requiring unison reading aloud by the teacher and by the student. The reading material should be on the student's instructional level and should be first read silently by him or her. Next, the teacher sits slightly behind the student and to the right. As the teacher and student read the material aloud, the teacher's hand is used as a guide as his or her voice is directed at the student's ear. Keeping up a smooth pace, the teacher can expect to be a little ahead of the student. As the student improves, the teacher can allow the student to take the lead. This method is repeated on one passage until fluency is achieved; then another passage can be chosen.

The technique of **repeated readings** is a third way to help students achieve automaticity in word identification and fluency in oral reading. Samuels (1979) states that a repeated reading "consists of rereading a short, meaningful passage several times until a satisfactory level of fluency is reached with a new passage" (p. 404). As with the other two techniques, the passage should be on the student's instructional level. The student first is asked to silently read the passage (no more than 100 words) and second to read the passage aloud to the teacher. The teacher records on a graph the oral reading errors and the reading rate. The student practices the same passage silently to improve fluency and again reads the passage to the teacher. Using the same passage, this procedure is repeated three or four times assuming there is an increase in fluency and rate.

Cunningham's **modified cloze** technique has as its purpose "to teach students to integrate the use of sound-symbol relationships with syntactic and semantic context clues so that they will not have to completely process all words visually" (1979, p. 423). The procedure entails selecting a passage on the student's independent level and modifying approximately every 20th word to show only the initial consonant or the consonant cluster. The remaining letters of every 20th word should be covered in the same manner. First, the student reads the passage silently with an accompanying comprehension check. Second, the student reads it aloud. When the student can read the modified cloze passage fluently, it is a sign that the technique is beginning to work.

□ SUMMARY

This chapter presented a balanced instructional program in word-recognition techniques, highlighting their overall contribution to comprehension. Realizing that word recognition is a means to comprehension, each technique that fosters independent word learning (phonics, structural analysis, and context) was reviewed. Several assessment techniques were presented for consideration in determining student strengths and weaknesses. Besides encouraging a trial-and-error approach to word recognition by students, an analytical approach for teacher instruction was recommended in which the multitude of materials on the market was suggested as a resource for practice. Teaching guidelines and strategies were presented that emphasize the teacher's role in giving proper instruction.

□ IN-TEXT ASSIGNMENTS

LIBRARY ACTIVITY

Professional publications in reading are excellent sources for new and varied ideas for teaching word recognition. Spend some time in your library consulting the ERIC system (examine several copies of the ERIC publication *NIE*), and the reading journals *The Reading Teacher, Read-*

ing Psychology, Reading Research and Instruction, and *Reading Horizons.* Select five articles dealing with word recognition and summarize them using a 3 × 5 card for each article. Share your article summaries with the class.

FIELD-BASED ACTIVITY

Either in a public school classroom or in your university class, plan a word-recognition lesson and teach it to a small group of children or a small group of your peers. Follow the steps contained in the direct-instruction lessons in this chapter. After your lesson is completed, respond to the following questions:

1. Was your motivation technique successful in beginning your lesson?
2. Was your step-by-step explanation complete enough for your students?
3. Was any reteaching necessary?
4. Did you recap main points?
5. What would you do differently next time?

SHARING AND BRAINSTORMING

It is important to know a variety of techniques and activities when teaching a particular word-recognition skill. Remember, automaticity is the goal you want students to reach. Brainstorm about various ways to teach the same concept in different situations. Use the following format:

Goal	*Means*
short *e*	
root words	
syntactic cue	
vowel diagraph	

□ REFERENCES

Anderson, R.C., Heibert, E.H., Scott, J.A., & Wilkinson, I.G. (1985). *Becoming a nation of readers.* Washington, DC: National Institute of Education.

Artley, A.S. (1943). Teaching word meaning through context. *Elementary English Review, 20,* 68–74.

Chomsky, C. (1976). After decoding: What? *Language Arts, 53,* 288–296.

Cunningham, J.W. (1979). An automatic pilot for decoding. *The Reading Teacher, 32,* 420–424.

Dahl, P.A. (1974). An experimental program for teaching high speed word recognition and comprehension. *University of Minnesota Final Report* (Project No. 3–1154). Washington DC: U.S. Department of Health, Education, and Welfare.

Durrell, D.D. (1956). *Improving reading instruction.* Yonkers, NY: World Book.

Heckelman, R.G. (1969). A neurological impress method of remedical reading instruction. *Academic Therapy, 5,* 277–282.

Heilman, W. W. (1985). *Phonics in proper perspective* (5th ed.) Columbus, OH: Merrill.

Hopkins, C.J. (1979). Using every-pupil response techniques in reading instruction. *The Reading Teacher, 33,* 173–174.

Huey, E.B. (1968). *The psychology and pedagogy of reading.* Cambridge, MA: The M.I.T. Press. (Originally published in 1908 by MacMillan)

Johnson, D.D. & Baumann, J.F. (1984). Word identification. In P.D. Pearson (Ed.), *Handbook of reading research* (pp. 583–608). New York: Longman.

Lass, B. & Davis B. (1985). *The remedial reading handbook.* Englewood, NJ: Prentice-Hall.

Logan, J.W., Rupley, W.H., & Erickson, L.G. (1988). *Phonics competencies for reading teachers.* Dubuque, IA: Kendall/Hunt.

McCullough, C. (1962). *Meeting individual needs by group for reading.* [Monograph]. *Contributions in Reading, 19.* Boston: Ginn.

Ohnmacht, D.C. (1969). *The effects of letter knowledge on achievement in reading in the first grade.* Paper presented at American Educational Research Association, Los Angeles, 1969.

Rupley, W.H. & Blair, T.R. (1988). *Teaching reading: Diagnosis, direct instruction, and practice* (2nd ed.) Columbus, OH: Merrill.

Samuels, S.J. (1979). The method of repeated readings. *The Reading Teacher, 32,* 403–408.

Schell, L.M. (1978). Teaching decoding to remedial readers. *The Reading Teacher, 31,* 877–882.

Schell, L.M. (1979). *Fundamentals of decoding for teachers.* Boston: Houghton Mifflin.

Stanovich, K.E. (1986). Matthew effects in reading: Some consequences of individual differences in the acquisition of literacy. *Reading Research Quarterly, XXI,* 360–407.

Weaver, P. (1978). *Research within reach: A research-guided response to concerns of reading educators.* St. Louis, MO: Research and Development Interpretation Service—CEMREL, Inc.

9

Comprehension of Narrative Materials

☐ OVERVIEW

The goal of corrective and remedial reading instruction is improved comprehension. Facilitative factors (see chapter 1) are a means toward accomplishing this goal; however, as pointed out in chapters 7 and 8, these skills must first transfer to meaningful reading tasks where they can be used to comprehend what is read.

The discussion of comprehension has so far focused on the idea that meaning is obtained from written materials. We have emphasized that students' comprehension is influenced by their word-recognition capabilities, their purposes for reading, their experiential/conceptual backgrounds, the content and language structure of the text, and the setting in which reading occurs. It is now time to look at various views of the reading comprehension process and to explore some of the variables that affect it. Such information will help in the selection, administration, and interpretation of diagnostic strategies; but more important, it will increase the teacher's ability to use instructional strategies that meet the reading comprehension needs of students.

After reading this chapter, the teacher should be able to

☐ understand the comprehension process of narrative text as it has been identified by research findings.
☐ select diagnostic strategies for assessing comprehension strengths and weaknesses.
☐ interpret analytically diagnostic findings through the use of quantitative and qualitative procedures.

☐ select instructional materials and strategies that transfer facilitative reading skills to the comprehension of narrative text.

☐ use appropriate corrective and remedial strategies for enhancing students' reading comprehension.

ELEMENTS OF THE READING COMPREHENSION PROCESS

Older research investigations of reading comprehension focused on how much a person could remember after reading. If the person correctly answered questions or restated parts of what was read, then it was assumed comprehension had occurred. Today the concept of reading comprehension has been expanded to include not only how much is remembered, but also a person's understanding of what is read and how one learns from reading. This implies more than remembering words or ideas. Understanding the text in relation to the reader's experiential/conceptual background is essential to comprehension. How a reader goes beyond simply remembering information to understanding it is a complex mental process that today is recognized as a major feature of reading comprehension.

It is known that facilitative factors (word recognition, vocabulary knowledge, language skills, and so forth) are important in reading comprehension. However, pronouncing words, knowing the meaning of words, adding the meanings together, and combining the meanings of sentences is only a partial feature of reading. In addition to getting meaning from the letters and words, reading includes the process of choosing and using one's knowledge of texts, people, places, and things to comprehend (Anderson, Heibert, Scott, & Wilkinson, 1985). Therefore, students can be competent in pronouncing words and recalling text information but still have comprehension difficulties. Why these students have problems can be better understood by looking at researchers' conceptualizations of the reading process.

CONCEPTUALIZATIONS OF READING COMPREHENSION

Three theoretical views or concepts of reading are prevalent in the recent research literature. These views of reading are labeled *bottom-up*, *top-down*, and *interactive.*

The text-based or **bottom-up view** is based on the idea that the page is the major source of information for the reader. In other words, readers begin reading without much information about the content; then word parts and words are processed sequentially, and meaning is gotten directly from them. Comprehension of the author's message continues in this sequential manner as readers focus their attention on words. Readers who are text-based separate their experiential/conceptual backgrounds from what they are reading. They may read as if reading meant a word-perfect representation of a text and the purpose for reading was detached from their own experiences (Tierney & Pearson, 1985).

A concept-driven or **top-down view** is based on the idea that the reader brings more information to the written text than the text brings to the reader (Strange, 1980). Essentially, reading is perceived as an "inside out" process. Readers are involved in hypothesis testing as they proceed through written text. Their prior knowledge of the world and language is used to make informed predictions about what is being read. As readers continue reading, they either conform or modify their predictions as these relate to prior knowledge. This model has also been referred to as "reader-based" and students whose interpretations of text are too reader-based can result in understandings that are too global for the text and its interpretation. To illustrate potential comprehension problems, Tierney and Pearson (1985) compare the reading behaviors of a reader-based student to the example of reading a description of an experiment in a science text:

> To explain or perform the experiment adequately, the science student cannot take liberties lest he or she err in the performance of the experiment. Unfortunately, readers with tendencies toward being too reader-based do not know *that* or *what* they do not know. They presume they know the material better than they actually do or need to . . . they often fail to recognize subtle but important text signals. They fail to monitor their interactions with a text. In the context of many classrooms, these students escape identification, for they might be successful readers in most situations and, furthermore, can "bluff their way through" most teachers' questions. (p. 872)

The **interactive view** of reading assumes that what readers bring to the page and what is written on the page are both important in getting meaning. According to this view, readers are using decoding and language skills along with information about their world to get at the meaning of print. The text stimulates readers to use their decoding strategies; as words are processed, readers use their knowledge of the world and the print to accept or reject hypotheses about meaning. Essentially, comprehension is based on readers filling in the gaps about the topic they are reading and then integrating the information as they read. As a result, various interpretations of the same text are possible because of the differences in readers' world knowledge.

The interactive view of reading seems to be the most helpful in terms of understanding how meaning is derived from print. If reading were top-down, how could anyone learn new information? How could individuals reading an identical text reach any agreement about what they read? If reading were a bottom-up process, then individuals reading the same text would be in total agreement about meaning—the possibility of individual interpretations in light of experiences, interests, occupations, and so forth would not exist (Rystrom, 1977).

We feel that the interactive conceptualization of reading is the most applicable and beneficial for teachers of reading. It recognizes the need for readers to use both their word-recognition strategies and their world knowledge to comprehend. With this view in mind, instruction to enhance reading comprehension can be thought of as teaching students the minimum word-recognition strategies necessary for them to use print effectively to activate their world knowledge for comprehension and learning.

INTERACTIVE CONCEPTUALIZATIONS OF READING

A major theory that looks at reading as an interactive process is called the **schema theory**, in which reading is considered to involve analysis of the text through the use of several processes that occur at the same time. These processes include the graphophonemic (letter-sound relationships), morphemic (meaning units), semantic (meanings represented by words in context), syntactic (word order), pragmatic, and interpretive processes (Anderson, 1985). The schema theory has been described by Rumelhart (1981) as:

> a theory about how knowledge is represented and about how that representation facilitates the *use* of the knowledge in particular ways. According to "schema theories" all knowledge is packaged into units. These units are schemata. Embedded in these packets of knowledge is, in addition to knowledge itself, information about how this knowledge is to be used. (p. 4)

Relating this description to reading comprehension, readers have schemata for such things as story structures, reading concepts, words, language structures, and life experiences. Such existing knowledge is what enables readers to comprehend print. Students' schemata influence their comprehension, learning, and remembering of text information. Anderson (1985) has identified several functions of schemata:

□ A schema helps readers determine what text features are important. A schema enables a skilled reader to know where to pay close attention when reading for meaning.
□ A schema assists readers in elaborating on text information to fill in the gaps since no text is totally explicit; readers must go beyond literal information to comprehend.
□ A schema helps readers edit and summarize text information.
□ A schema serves to help readers reconstruct the text through inference, which means that if there are memory gaps, these can be filled in by recalling specific text information and making hypotheses about the missing information.

The role of inference in the reading comprehension process is a major feature of the schema theory. Literal information serves to activate schemata that lead the reader to hypothesize (infer) about features of the text (story structure, words, language features, and meaning). Schemata may be changed, elaborated on, or discarded as the reader proceeds through the text. The reader comprehends by using existing knowledge, which can change when new information is encountered. Changes in schemata can be considered new learning that may result from modifying an existing schema or from creating a new one.

Schema theory is an attempt to explain reading comprehension as an interactive process in which readers use their world knowledge to arrive at a consistent understanding of text. Rumelhart (1984) offers several possible reasons for a reader's failure to comprehend:

☐ The reader may lack the appropriate schemata. For example, students may have no schema for world politics, death, farm life, and so forth, and, therefore, have no way to hypothesize about story content. Likewise, the text may be written in a manner that goes beyond the reader's understanding of written language structures; thus, the reader has no way to access shemata for understanding the content. In such cases, the reader simply cannot understand the concepts being communicated.

☐ The reader may have appropriate schemata for both the language structure and the content, but the author may not have provided enough clues to suggest them. Comprehension is difficult in such instances and students will need assistance in the form of additional information to fill in the gaps to understand the text.

☐ The reader may find a consistent interpretation of the passage, but not the one intended by the author. In such cases, the reader's schemata are activated and he or she perceives that comprehension has occurred; however, the understanding gained is different from that the author was attempting to communicate. This problem in comprehension is often related to readers who are too top-down (reader-based) in their reading of text.

Each of these reasons for failure to comprehend has direct implications for diagnosing reading comprehension. Students who lack the world knowledge for story content may lack the schemata to facilitate comprehension. The failure to comprehend is not due to a reading problem; the students simply lack the past experiences necessary to get meaning. Problems in comprehension can also be related to the quality of the text students are reading. If a poorly written text or one that lacks story structure is used to diagnose comprehension, students may exhibit problems that are not indicative of their capabilities. Finally, if comprehension is assessed by how accurately students understand text content, it may be inaccurate to say that they did not comprehend. A more correct interpretation would be that they comprehended but did not understand the author's intended message.

Another interactive conceptualization of reading has been developed by Miller and others (1975). Their theory of the comprehension process has three basic features:

Identifying important text elements.

Constructing representations of important text information.

Matching representations of text to existing concepts.

Identifying Important Text Elements

Important elements of a text provide cues that help focus the reader's attention. Elements can be specific text information, such as dates or names in a history text, experimental procedures or results in a science text, or character relationships and events in a language arts text. Other important text elements could be those that appear frequently or those connected by story events or grammatical relationships.

It seems that when teachers guide students in a discussion of a story's content and set specific purposes for reading, they are helping students focus on important text elements and relate these elements to their experiential/conceptual backgrounds. For example, asking students to read a story about a wild pony because they would enjoy it does not provide any cues for focusing on important information. In contrast, discussing ponies and the differences between tame and wild ponies can activate students' prior knowledge, which in turn can enable them to match their experiences to important features of text elements. Furthermore, asking them to read the story for the purpose of discussing why it was difficult to tame the wild pony provides students with additional cues to the important text elements. In the latter case, students would be more attentive to what makes a pony wild and why these characteristics make the pony hard to tame.

Constructing Representations of Text Information

After important elements are identified, they are then represented internally. The process of internal representation may be visual, verbal, haptic (touch), or a combination of the three. Four subprocesses make up the internal representation process.

First, information is retrieved from long-term memory to form representations for the content read. This long-term memory information could have been stored through visual processing (pictures, objects, films, and so forth); verbal processing (hearing, reading, or both); haptic processing (touching); or a combination of these. A breadth of long-term memory information allows the reader to form appropriate representations of what is read.

Comprehension of the wild pony story would be enhanced for the student who knows that a wild pony is larger than a dog, and will buck, kick, bite, and resist being ridden. Such information is of even greater importance if it is not mentioned in the story. The more information about ponies that is stored in long-term memory, the better the reader can draw

Students' comprehension is influenced by their experiential/conceptual backgrounds. (Northshore Publishing)

on it to form representations. Again, it is extremely important that teachers help students match their own experiences to story events by guiding them in a discussion of their prior knowledge before they begin to read.

A wide background of experiences aids comprehension because it helps students form representations of story ideas. For example, a seven-year-old was told that the neighbors had their camper opened up in the driveway to air out; it was evident that the child understood all the words but not the idea when she asked, "Will it go flat like my swimming pool?" Her representation of what it meant to "air out" something was limited to letting the air out of her plastic pool.

Elaborating on the text information or abstracting it to remove unnecessary details is the second subprocess. The wild pony story may only describe the pony as having black-and-white spots. A student reading the story might elaborate on this information and perceive the pony as having large black spots, a long white tail, a white face, and so forth. Thus, the representation of the pony may take on those features of pony information stored in long-term memory. Through such elaborations, readers may be able to better comprehend what they read and integrate such information with later story information.

In other instances a reader may remove all unnecessary details to form a representation. This behavior suggests that too many details either interfere with constructing and understanding internal representations or that the content is so familiar in light of experiences that details are unnecessary for comprehension. For example, if the setting for the wild pony story was highly detailed in describing the terrain, the weather, the vegetation, and so forth, a reader familiar with such a setting may abstract it by referring to it as a desert. Another reader less familiar with such a setting might abstract this information and refer to it only as "the place where the pony lived," because the details interfered with comprehension.

A third subprocess of forming representations of ideas is integrating important text information. Integration may involve making inferences about a representation and its relationship to new text information or identifying and adjusting inconsistencies among representations. If, as the research suggests, readers comprehend in terms of how they form representations of ideas, then integration of ideas is one of the major comprehension factors.

Many students with comprehension problems exhibit difficulties with integrating the ideas presented in a story. Often, they can discuss the story information but do not understand the relationships among the pieces of story information. It may be that such students are unaware that their representations are inconsistent with each other or with story information. The former problem results in bits and pieces of unconnected information, and the latter results in total confusion.

Logic suggests that both problems could occur together, especially when representations are inconsistent with story information. For example, if the setting for the wild pony story is southeast Texas, and the information about Texas that is stored in the reader's long-term memory was acquired only through "Westerns," then inconsistent representations could result. Reading about the green rolling hills, the lakes, the pastures dotted with wild flowers, the tall pines, and the cool winters of southeast Texas would not fit well with the information stored about the southwestern setting of many cowboy movies. The reader's representation would probably include deserts, cacti, arid conditions, tumbleweeds, rattlesnakes, and so forth. An inconsistency then develops between the reader's representation of Texas and the author's information, which results in comprehension different from that intended by the author.

The fourth subprocess that helps a reader comprehend is assigning names to representations when story settings, topics, or characters are presented in a fashion that makes naming difficult. The importance of this process can be illustrated with the example of children learning to play a new game. Assume that the directions refer to the players as "first player," "second player," "third player," and "fourth player." One child reading these directions may not have any problem understanding the naming, but when four children get together to learn how to play the game, they may have problems understanding who plays when and how.

The directions may be better understood if each child's name is associated with the numbered players in the directions text. This results in a better representation of the directions and, consequently, improved comprehension.

Matching Representations to Existing Concepts

The third major stage takes place when the reader's representations are matched with something already known. Representations can be thought about in a variety of ways, and the reader must search for the one that makes sense. Essentially, this is where readers bring together what is read and focus on comprehending large units of meaning in terms of their experiential/conceptual backgrounds—that is, readers' representations are used to construct meaning that makes sense to them, and the focus is on comprehending the total reading selection. This process recalls the earlier point that reading comprehension is more than just reconstructing the author's message. Information can be recombined in many ways; ideas are comprehended in terms of representations that make sense, and all this can result in new learning.

Both the schema theory and Miller's concept of reading comprehension present reading as an interactive process. What the reader brings to the text and what the text stimulates in the reader are important in comprehension. Interactive conceptualizations of reading comprehension have direct application to reading diagnosis and corrective/remedial instruction. The following sections present several procedures for comprehension diagnosis and instruction, which are based on an interactive concept of reading.

TEXTUAL FEATURES AND READING COMPREHENSION

Two recent areas of research related to an interactive conceptualization of reading are story grammar and story schema. **Story grammar** is the system of rules used for describing the consistent features found in a given text (Mandler, 1984). These rules describe the story parts, arrangement of the parts, and how the parts are related. **Story schema** is the mental representation that readers have of story parts and their relationships (Lehr, 1987). Thus, the basic difference between story grammar and story schema is that story grammar deals with the text that is read and story schema deals with what readers have in their heads about how stories are organized.

Although there are several different conceptualizations of story grammar, all of them basically include a setting, a plot (problem, goal, or attempts of the main characters), and a resolution (Schmidt & O'Brien, 1986). **Story setting** includes both major and minor settings. Major settings are such things as time, place, and characters. Each of these may be either stated directly or implied. For example, "Sam looked out his bedroom window and saw the sun rising over the tops of the trees.", is more of a direct statement of time, place, and characters than is "Long, long ago in a little kingdom lived a happy king." Minor settings include features similar to major settings but serve to develop the story. For example, in the major setting, time may be a two-week summer vacation; in the minor setting, time could be a day during the vacation. Place could be at a hotel in the major setting and at the beach in the minor setting. Major characters could be family members and minor characters represented by cab drivers, lifeguards, and so forth.

Story plots are composed of subparts that include (1) starter events, which get the story started and may be a character action or an event; (2) inner responses, which relate to the characters' feelings, thoughts, subgoals, or plans; (3) action, which is the characters' attempts to achieve their goals or subgoals; (4) outcomes, which are the characters' actions; and (5) reaction, which is a response to the outcome of the characters' actions (Gordon & Braun, 1983).

Finally, **story resolution** is when the character or characters achieve their goal(s). Resolutions can also include morals, such as "If a person works hard, he will achieve his goal(s)."

Another description of simple story structure from the perspective of the reader is offered by Stein and Trabasso (1981). They point out that readers have an internal organization of story knowledge. **Setting** is an introduction of the main time period of the story. **Episode** has five different categories: the **initiating event** begins the episode and initiates the story line, which is the goal of the main character. This goal is included in the second category, **internal response**. Here the main character is motivated to carry out a plan of action. **Attempt** is the action carried out by the main character toward achievement of the goal. Whether or not such a goal is achieved constitutes the fourth category, **consequence**. Finally, **reaction** may include the character's response to reaching the goal, what happened as a result of attaining the goal, or a moral about achieving the goal.

Not all stories follow the story grammars just presented. The majority of the research in this area has been conducted with folk tales and fables; therefore, story grammar research does not generalize directly to a variety of stories and readers. Stories that have complex structures and several connected episodes do not fit existing story grammars very well (Carnine & Kinder, 1985). There are, however, some features of story grammar that have been recommended for instructional use that can enhance students' interactions with stories (Schmitt & O'Brien, 1986; Morrow, 1985; Pearson, 1982):

☐ The story grammar can be used for both prereading and postreading discussion to emphasize important aspects of the story.

☐ The story's organizational framework can be used as a guide for identifying questions to enable students to predict story information both prior to and after reading the story. For example, "How do you think the character felt when he learned that his new bicycle was stolen?" (inner or internal response).

☐ Story grammar can be used to identify questions to help students recognize important relationships and synthesize information. "Why did the king have to travel to a new country?" "What did the king do when he found someone who could help him?" "How did the people of the new country and the king's new friend feel when the king could return to his kingdom?" These questions are examples of how teachers can use story grammar to help students synthesize information about inner or internal responses, plans or actions, and reactions or consequences.

☐ Story grammar can be used as a guide for teachers to assist students in activating their experiential/conceptual backgrounds to relate personal experiences to character motives, problems, goals, actions, outcomes, and reactions.

☐ Diagnosis of students' story comprehension abilities or assessment of their overall understanding of a story can be based on story grammar framework where students are prompted to retell a story. For example, students could be directed to retell or summarize a story by asking them to tell about what got the story started, how the character felt, what the character did, what the character's actions were, and what happened as a result of the character's actions.

The previously mentioned uses of story grammar are intended to help teachers diagnose students' understanding of story structure and its possible influence on their reading comprehension. Furthermore, knowledge of story grammar can assist teachers in motivating students' interactions with story content both prior to and after reading. None of the recommendations advocate the direct teaching of story grammar to students; teaching students to analyze stories by using story grammar could result in their giving too much focus to the structure rather than the content.

VOCABULARY AND READING COMPREHENSION

The role of vocabulary in reading comprehension is recognized as being of major significance. Stanovich (1986) notes that "there is a growing body of data indicating that variation in vocabulary knowledge is a casual determinant of differences in reading comprehension" (p. 379). The importance of word knowledge (vocabulary) is viewed by Devine (1986) as one of the most important capabilities for reading comprehension. Students' knowledge of words can be thought of as hooks or labels for their schemata; thus the broader their vocabulary, the better able they are to select appropriate schemata to understand text.

Although vocabulary is recognized as a major factor in reading comprehension, there is some disagreement about whether or not direct instruction can enhance vocabulary growth. Nagy and Anderson (1984) believe that in about third grade and beyond, vocabulary growth is related to the amount of students' free reading. A similar view is proposed by Stanovich (1986) that direct instruction in vocabulary may not enhance students' vocabulary backgrounds. He argues that vocabulary growth is directly related to the "rich-get-richer" phenomenon—that is, students who are good readers will read more, learn more word meanings, and become even better readers. In addition, vocabulary is affected by students' home backgrounds. If students grow up in homes where they are exposed to words and encouraged to increase their vocabularies, then their vocabularies will be greater and will facilitate learning in other tasks that require vocabulary (Sternberg, 1985).

Although the previous researchers question the effectiveness of direct instruction in increasing students' vocabularies, a review of the effects of vocabulary instruction by Stahl and Fairbanks (1986) provides support for teaching vocabulary. They conclude that vocabulary instruction is a useful procedure in addition to learning from context. Methods of instruction that they found were most effective were those that provided both *contextual* and *definitional* information about the word to be learned. **Contextual knowledge** is knowledge of a core concept and activation of that knowledge in different contexts. **Definitional knowledge** is knowing the relationship between a word and other known words, such as in a dictionary definition (Stahl, 1985). It would appear that for vocabulary instruction to be beneficial for students, they must be provided with ways to define the new word by relating it to known words (definitional information) and be provided meaningful opportunities to learn the word in context.

READING COMPREHENSION OUTCOMES

It has long been thought that reading comprehension could be separated into at least three or four basic levels: literal, influential, critical, and affective. However, recent evidence suggests that these levels overlap each other and share many common features, which may not result in distinct categories of comprehension. Inferencing, for example, is considered crucial to the comprehension process (Johnston, 1981). Readers use inferences to associate meanings with words, connect sentences together, and relate authors' messages to their own experiences. The role of inference focuses on the reading process as individuals use their knowledge of language, world experiences, and authors' cues to get at meaning. Such meanings may not be a result of different comprehension processes, but they may be reflected as comprehension outcomes at a literal, inferential, critical, or affective level. This is not to suggest that there is a continuum of comprehension from literal to inferential to critical to affective. As noted by Tierney and Pearson (1985), "teachers may find that they are forcing a student to deal with the literal when it would be more appropriate to address the inferential or evaluative. We believe that every act of reading necessitates inferential and interpretive understandings. In fact, students may need to deal with inferential and evaluative prior to addressing the 'literal' " (pp. 877–878).

Literal Comprehension Outcomes

Literal comprehension outcomes involve the identification of factual, explicitly stated information. Recall or recognition of main ideas, details, sequences of events, character traits, comparisons, and cause-effect relationships explicitly stated in a story are examples of literal level comprehension tasks.

Recall requires a student to furnish an idea or ideas stated by the author. Recognition, on the other hand, requires the student to decide whether or not specific information was presented in the story. Naturally, teachers want students to be able to comprehend literal information found in text; however, teachers must distinguish simple recall or recognition of information from comprehension. If teachers only measured students' literal comprehension, it would not meet the definition of comprehension as understanding ideas. For example, if, after a student read, "Breggs raffled on the carbot squod," a teacher could ask the reader, "Who raffled?" "Where did Breggs raffle?" or "What did Breggs do?" and judge the correctness of the responses, even if the answers were correct, the reader has not comprehended the message.

Inferential Comprehension Outcomes

Inferential comprehension outcomes occur when the reader is directed to infer meanings that go beyond explicitly stated information. The major difference between a literal and an inferential outcome is that the information is not explicitly stated and readers have to "read between the lines." The following illustration should make this distinction apparent. Suppose a child read:

Sally ran home from school to see if her new bicycle had come. She ran into the house yelling, "Mother! Mother! Did my bike come?" "No," said mother, "but it may come tomorrow."

The teacher then could ask, "Is Sally excited in this story?" "Does Sally really want a new bike?" The answers cannot be gained from stated information. A student must infer that Sally was excited and that she really wants a new bike.

Inferential comprehension outcomes reflect the earlier discussion of the comprehension process. The reader's representation of ideas goes beyond recall of explicit information. In some instances of inferential comprehension, readers might have to elaborate on information; in others, they might have to abstract them. Also, it would seem necessary that these ideas must be integrated and then used as a basis for making inferences. For an example of an inferential comprehension worksheet, see figure 9–1.

Critical Comprehension Outcomes

When readers are asked to analyze, evaluate, and judge the merits of written text, they are primarily using their world knowledge to demonstrate such outcomes. Analysis could focus on accuracy of information, acceptability of conclusions, probability of events, evidence to support facts, and the like. The readers' experience of given criteria are then used to critically evaluate and judge the information.

It seems that critical comprehension outcomes require readers to compare their representations of ideas read with representations gained through past experiences. Analysis focuses on the match between these representations. The closer the match, the more likely the reader is to accept and agree with the ideas. A mismatch between representations could lead the reader to reject all or part of what the author said, which is also an outcome of critical reading.

When students are asked to make critical decisions about what they read, their performance has to be judged in relation to their experiences and capabilities. For example, asking first graders to demonstrate critical outcomes about solutions to world economic problems should be judged on the basis of what they bring to the task. This is not to suggest that first graders cannot critically comprehend such information; however, their performance should be evaluated in relation to their experiential/conceptual backgrounds.

Affective Comprehension Outcomes

Affective comprehension outcomes involve personal and emotional responses to the text. The reader's representations of what is read results in emotional involvement, identification with the story characters, appreciation of the author's style, and/or identification with a story theme. All teachers have heard or seen students comprehending a story at an affective level:

> "I cried at the end of *Old Yeller.*"
>
> "I know how Susan felt when her brother moved away."
>
> "I felt like I was in the mountains with Sam."
>
> "I like the way he writes."

Such reactions to a story are indicative of comprehension that requires affective involvement on the part of the reader.

Making Inferences
Guided Practice

Over and over, though he knew the number only too well, Matt counted his notched sticks. He kept hoping he had made a mistake. . . . Ten sticks. . . . . He couldn't remember exactly how many days belonged to each month, but any way he reckoned it the month of September must be almost over. . . . The maple trees circling the clearing flamed scarlet. The birches and aspens glowed yellow . . . the songbirds had disappeared. Twice he had heard a faraway trumpeting and had seen long straggles of wild geese like trailing smoke high in the air, moving south. In the morning, when he stepped out of the cabin, the frosty air nipped his nose. The noonday was warm as midsummer, but when he came inside at dusk, he hurried to stir up the fire. There was a chilliness inside him, as well, that neither the sun nor the fire ever quite reached. It seemed to him that day by day the shadow of the forest moved closer to the cabin. *Why was his family so late in coming?*

__X__ **1.** It is autumn.

__X__ **2.** Matt lives in a northern region.

__X__ **3.** Matt is using sticks as a calendar.

__X__ **4.** Each stick stands for one month.

_____ **5.** Matt cannot read.

6. Matt's home is in the woods. Sample answers:
Maple, birch, and aspen trees are around Matt's cabin.

7. Matt's family is away from home.
Matt wonders why his family is so late in coming.

8. Matt is worried about his family.
There is a chilliness of fear inside him.

9. The nights are cold.
The air is frosty in the morning. He stirs up the fire at dusk.

10. Matt is familiar with living in the countryside.
Matt knows the names of the trees. Matt knows how to build a fire.

Name _____ Date _____

Comprehension: Making Inferences from Narrative   Unit 13 • PAGEANTS

FIGURE 9–1 Comprehension worksheet: Inferences from narrative text

Source: From *Houghton Mifflin Reading*, Level N (practice workbook, teacher's ann. ed.) (p. 56) by W. Durr et al., 1986, Boston: Houghton Mifflin. Copyright 1986 by Houghton Mifflin. Used by permission.

DIAGNOSTIC ASSESSMENT MEASURES OF COMPREHENSION

Comprehension strengths and weaknesses can be identified with the use of norm-referenced, criterion-referenced, and informal measures. Each of these was discussed in chapter 5, and guidelines for their selection, use, and interpretation were offered. Other guidelines relate specifically to the assessment of comprehension. To help teachers analytically select and interpret comprehension assessment instruments and procedures, their major weaknesses are discussed in the following sections. Also presented are procedures that can be used to strengthen comprehension assessment. Since it is impossible to discuss every comprehension test available, our discussion focuses on features common to most of them.

Standardized norm-referenced and criterion-referenced tests are used often in public schools to assess students' reading comprehension. However, such tests have major weaknesses and shortcomings. One of these is the limited range of comprehension abilities that is assessed. Answers to comprehension questions are predetermined; that is, an answer is identified for each question in advance, and the student's answers are scored as either right or wrong. Question formats for comprehension tests may vary, but how well a student comprehends is usually determined by the total number of correct answers. Because most of these tests evaluate comprehension abilities based on the total number of correct items, many literal-level questions are asked. Inferential questions can be found occasionally, but the majority of questions are based on recall or recognition of specific story facts. Such tests assess only how well a student remembers or recognizes facts. Another major weakness is the fragmentation of reading into several isolated skills, which is often seen in criterion-referenced tests. This assessment of isolated skills fails to recognize that reading involves the simultaneous use of many skills and abilities to get at meaning. In addition to these major weaknesses, several additional limitations of how reading comprehension is currently assessed have been identified by Valencia and Pearson (1987) and are presented in figure 9–2.

Examples of Comprehension Tests' Formats

As noted earlier, the question format for comprehension tests may vary, but how well a student comprehends is usually determined by his or her total number of correct answers. The following examples of test question formats are similar to those found on most norm-referenced, criterion-referenced, or informal comprehension tests.

In a multiple-choice format, after reading a passage, the student is asked to select the best answer for each question about the story.

PASSAGE

Dot is a big yellow-and-black cat. She lives in a large house. Dot plays with string and yarn. She does not like to play outdoors.

New views of the reading process tell us that . . .	Yet when we assess reading comprehension, we . . .
Prior knowledge is an important determinant of reading comprehension.	Mask any relationship between prior knowledge and reading comprehension by using lots of short passages on lots of topics.
A complete story or text has structural and topical integrity.	Use short texts that seldom approximate the structural and topical integrity of an authentic text.
Inference is an essential part of the process of comprehending units as small as sentences.	Rely on literal comprehension test items.
The diversity in prior knowledge across individuals as well as the varied causal relations in human experiences invite many possible inferences to fit a text or question.	Use multiple choice items with only one correct answer, even when many of the responses might, under certain conditions, be plausible.
The ability to vary reading strategies to fit the text and the situation is one hallmark of an expert reader.	Seldom assess how and when students vary the strategies they use during normal reading, studying, or when the going gets tough.
The ability to synthesize information from various parts of the text and different texts is a hallmark of an expert reader.	Rarely go beyond finding the main idea of a paragraph or passage.
The ability to ask good questions of text, as well as to answer them, is a hallmark of an expert reader.	Seldom ask students to create or select questions about a selection they may have just read.
All aspects of a reader's experience, including habits that arise from school and home, influence reading comprehension.	Rarely view information on reading habits and attitudes as being as important as information about performance.
Reading involves the orchestration of many skills that complement one another in a variety of ways.	Use tests that fragment reading into isolated skills and report performance on each.
Skilled readers are fluent; their word identification is sufficiently automatic to allow most cognitive resources to be used for comprehension.	Rarely consider fluency as an index of skilled reading.
Learning from text involves the restructuring, application, and flexible use of knowledge in new situations.	Often ask readers to respond to the text's declarative knowledge rather than to apply it to near and far transfer tasks.

FIGURE 9–2 A set of contrasts between new views of reading and current practices in assessing reading

Source: Sheila Valencia & P. David Pearson. (1987). Reading assessment: Time for a change. *The Reading Teacher*, 40, p. 731. Reprinted with permission of Sheila Valencia and the International Reading Association.

TYPICAL QUESTIONS

Dot plays with
(a) string (b) balls (c) mice (d) cats

Other comprehension test formats are similar to the cloze procedure. The student selects from the choices the ones that best complete the sentences.

PASSAGE

Sam lives in an old bus. He took out all of the _____ and _____ the windows.
                                (1)   (2)

TYPICAL CHOICES

1. (a) seats (b) chairs (c) sofas

2. (a) climbed (b) painted (c) posted

In other formats, the student is asked to read a passage silently or orally and then answer the teacher's questions. This is similar to an informal reading inventory (see chapter 5) and the questions and acceptable answers are usually identified for the teacher.

PASSAGE

Sally picked two big red apples from the tree. She ate one of the apples and took one to Bob. Bob asked Sally where she got the apple. Sally told him that she picked it from the tree in her yard. Bob ate his apple. Sally was happy.

TYPICAL QUESTIONS AND ANSWERS

1. Who picked some apples?
   (Sally)

2. How many apples did Sally have?
   (two)

3. What did Sally do with the apples?
   (She ate one and gave one to Bob.)

A variation of this procedure is to have the student retell the story. The teacher notes what information was remembered and then asks for any information that was omitted. The responses are recorded on a question form such as in the following example, in which the teacher notes whether the student recalled the information with or without assistance.

PASSAGE

Joe and Mark rode on a train to the city. They were going to visit their grandmother. She lived in the city near a park. Joe and Mark liked going to the city. They would go to the park, zoo, and swimming pool.

TYPICAL QUESTION FORMAT

	Unaided Recall	Aided Recall
Joe and Mark	_____	_____
rode on a train	_____	_____
to the city.	_____	_____
They were going to visit their grandmother.	_____	_____

Modifying Comprehension Assessment Measures

Several procedures can be used to improve comprehension assessment measures. However, when norm-referenced tests are modified, a student's performance cannot be compared with that of the norming group. This is not a serious limitation, because the value of such modified tests as diagnostic tools is improved. Also, since many norm-referenced and criterion-referenced tests have equivalent forms for each level, a single form can be modified; the other form can be administered in the standardized manner and the student's performance compared with the norming group's.

The following suggestions (also see chapter 5) for modifying tests to better assess reading comprehension are only guidelines. There will be instances when teachers cannot modify existing tests to serve their needs; therefore, it is recommended that they develop their own tests, using the appropriate guidelines to better assess students' reading comprehension.

□ Teachers can write one or two purpose-setting questions for each reading comprehension passage. The intent of such questions is to help students activate appropriate schemata for comprehending the passage (Rowe & Rayford, 1987). (The 1986 edition of the Metropolitan Achievement Tests uses such questions in the assessment of reading comprehension). Purpose-setting questions that relate to students' experiential/conceptual backgrounds and are rich in information will better enable readers to activate appropriate schemata.

□ Teachers can write three or four summaries for each comprehension passage and have students select the one that they think best describes the selection (Valencia & Pearson, 1987). Teachers should discuss with students why they selected a particular summary. Students can also be encouraged to elaborate on the summaries, providing information they feel would be helpful for telling someone else about the passage.

□ Teachers can have students rate their familiarity with each passage after they have read it and answered the accompanying questions. A rating scale such as *I knew a lot, I knew something, I knew very little* for each passage can be developed. Students' comprehension for familiar topics versus unfamiliar topics can then be compared to ascertain their comprehension abilities in relation to their experiential/conceptual backgrounds. Teachers can also have students rate the difficulty of each passage in terms of word identification, vocabulary, and language structure to gain insights into how these influenced their comprehension. For example, teachers can ask their students if a selection was hard to read because the words were difficult to identify, the meanings of the words were difficult to figure out, or the sentences and how they were arranged made the passage difficult to read.

☐ In a small group or with the whole class, students can discuss with the teacher which multiple-choice answers for each question are either close to being correct, not close to being correct, or are correct. This will provide information about how students activate their experiential/ conceptual backgrounds in relation to their choices identified for each question. Students can be encouraged to discuss why each possible answer for a question is correct or partially correct. Students can also be directed to discuss with the teacher what information would have to be included in the passage for each of the possible answers to be correct. This will provide information about students' abilities to elaborate on text information by using inferences.

☐ Teachers can write additional questions for each comprehension passage and have students select those they think will help a classmate best understand the important ideas in the passage (Valencia & Pearson, 1987).

☐ Teachers can rewrite test questions to include some that are evaluative in nature. These can be administered to students and then students can discuss in groups their responses and how they arrived at their responses.

☐ Teachers can list information that might or might not be found in each comprehension test passage. Prior to reading the passage, students can predict whether or not the listed information would, would not, or would possibly appear in the passage. Their predictions will give the teacher insights into students' prior knowledge before reading the selection (Valencia & Pearson, 1987).

☐ Students can be directed to examine the titles of passages while the teacher assists them with predicting what kinds of information they are likely to find in each passage and with identifying questions they would like to answer about the content. This will help students establish purposes for reading.

The previous suggestions for modifying comprehension tests will provide the teacher with diagnostic information about students' comprehension when they (1) activate their background knowledge prior to reading, (2) read familiar versus unfamiliar text, (3) generate their own relationships among the ideas presented, (4) consider classmates' understanding of the text, and (5) elaborate on text information to make inferences. Through the use of such modification strategies, students' comprehension abilities can be examined in terms of their performance when tests are administered in both a standardized fashion and with teacher intervention (Paratore & Indrisano, 1987).

INSTRUCTIONAL STRATEGIES FOR THE CORRECTION/REMEDIATION OF READING COMPREHENSION PROBLEMS

Earlier chapters viewed facilitative reading factors as important components of reading comprehension; with this in mind, it is logical to assume that students who have major word-recognition problems will also have comprehension problems (Stanovich, 1986). Correction or remediation of word-recognition skills, however, does not ensure comprehension. There are some students who can identify words and their individual meanings, but who still cannot understand the ideas conveyed when the words are put together. Instruction for these students should focus on improving their comprehension abilities.

Research investigations and interpretations of these investigations by reading authorities offer some sound instructional guidelines for teaching reading comprehension. The following sections present some strategies and procedures for reading comprehension instruction that have been discussed in a number of these research investigations.

Enhancing Engagement with Text

Helping students maximize their engagement with the text is an important feature of comprehension instruction. Strategies for doing this both before and during students' reading have been suggested by Tierney and Pearson (1985) and are discussed in the following list.

□ If students appear uninterested in reading, the teacher can use highly motivating materials to which students can easily relate; that is, the content and language structure of these materials are within the students' schemata. In conjunction with motivating materials, teachers should require some type of student response, such as following directions, answering purpose-setting questions presented prior to reading, and summarizing key ideas.

□ Teachers should make students aware of what they are doing when they are reading successfully as well as when they are having problems. This can be done by discussing with students how they know when comprehension has occurred and how they know when comprehension has not occurred. Encouraging students in this way to discuss how they monitor their own comprehension is very helpful. Often students who have comprehension problems do not know how to adjust their reading strategies; when the teacher models the needed behavior, students have a concrete strategy illustrated for them.

□ If students experience difficulty in structuring information, teachers can provide them with maps or story diagrams that represent important text elements. They can also ask reporter-type questions (who, what, when, where) while students take notes and underline the answers as they read.

☐ For those students who appear to be too text-based or bottom-up in their reading, teachers can help them develop different strategies, such as skimming or scanning, to identify the basic ideas. Then teachers can model and discuss how to reread to understand relationships between text information and getting the meaning.

☐ Teachers can help students begin to develop their own purposes for reading in relation to their experiential/conceptual backgrounds. "What do I already know about the content of the text based on the title and other sources of text information?", "What do I want to learn?", "What story events could be the most important?", and so forth are examples of questions students can ask themselves to help activate appropriate schemata for improving their comprehension.

☐ Teachers can encourage and discuss varying interpretations of text to help students understand how their experiential/conceptual backgrounds influence their comprehension. Opportunities should be provided for students to interact and discuss with each other their comprehension of various texts as well.

As noted in the previous strategies, it is extremely important for students to activate their prior knowledge before reading to enhance their comprehension of what they will read. It has been recommended that for instruction, teachers consider not only the quantity of prior knowledge, but the quality of it as well. Students may activate their prior knowledge yet still experience comprehension difficulty if there are conflicts between their existing knowledge and their new learning. Students with comprehension problems may distort the text information to fit their prior knowledge if they have inaccurate notions or they use their knowledge inappropriately (Lipson, 1984). Therefore, when preparing students for reading, teachers should focus on activating important knowledge and on encouraging readers to check their comprehension with the information presented in the text.

Comprehension Monitoring

To assist students in becoming capable of monitoring their text comprehension, a procedure developed by Poindexter and Prescot (1986) can be used. Specific features of this technique are related to questions asked by the teacher about a story that students read; these features are presented in the following list:

Step 1: Students determine if the answer to a question is explicitly presented in the text. To do this, students identify key words in the question, then go back to the parts of the story in which the key words might be found. They then read this section of the text to try and find the answer. If the answer cannot be found, they go on to the next step.

Step 2: Students are directed to determine if the answer to the question is given indirectly. To do this, they first change the question into a statement; for example, if the question was "Why were the three little pigs afraid of the wolf?", students can convert this to: "The three little pigs where afraid of the wolf because . . .". Then, students read the portion of the story where information could be found to complete the statement. If they are unable to come up with a plausible answer, they proceed to the next step.

Step 3: The purpose of this step is to help students determine if the answer to the question could come from their own experiential/conceptual backgrounds. Students are directed to put "I think" in front of the statement they made in step 2: "I think that the three little pigs were afraid of the wolf because . . .". Students are then asked to think about any story information that would help them complete the statement as well as to think about what they already know about characters, events, and content related to the story; then, they are asked to combine the two and formulate an answer. For this step there is no right or wrong answer; however, students should be encouraged to share their reasons for their answers.

Teachers need to model and verbalize this technique for students to ensure that they understand it and can use it to answer either teacher- or student-identified story questions. During the teaching and modeling, teachers should also encourage *students* to verbalize how the technique is used to answer questions. Considerable teaching and practicing with students will be necessary to help them transfer this technique to their reading.

Story Grammar and Mapping

Research by Varnhagen and Goldman (1986) indicates that students who have reading comprehension problems will benefit from instruction that helps them understand causal relationships in stories. Two instructional areas that focus on such relationships are story grammar (see page 209) and mapping.

Although there is some debate about the effectiveness of teaching story grammar to students, several research investigations have found support for improved reading comprehension when students have knowledge of story structure (Tierney & Cunningham, 1984). Teaching story grammar can be done through the use of story maps (Reutzel, 1985). **Story maps** are visual representations of story information and are intended to help students both integrate the concepts and events found in stories and highlight relationships among story episodes. The major steps of constructing a story map are

1. Make a sequential summary list of the main ideas, characters, and events found in a given story.
2. Place the main idea in the center circle of the map.

3. Draw extensions from the circle to represent the main ideas and characters on the summary list.
4. Write the main ideas and characters in a sequential clockwise manner around the center circle.
5. Write the subevents and subconcepts in a sequential clockwise manner around the circles containing the main ideas and characters (Reutzel, 1985).

Story maps can be used to represent main ideas and events, character comparisons, and cause-effect relationships to help students understand story structure, represent important text elements, and integrate text information (see figure 9–3).

In addition to helping students understand the structure and relationships found in the stories that they read, story grammar can be used to help students summarize and report on books they have read. By providing students who have comprehension problems with guidelines for summarizing and reporting on books, teachers can improve and reinforce students' knowledge of story structure. Some general guidelines for teachers to help students summarize and write about books have been developed by Olson (1984).

☐ Help students understand that stories have common features. This can be done by using a story map (see figure 9–3) of a familiar story. Lead students to the understanding that stories have a basic structure (map), such as main characters, settings, events, goals, and so forth.

☐ Present the main categories of story grammar (see page 209 for identification of these categories) and use a familiar story to illustrate each category. Use the categories to identify questions to guide students in a discussion of each feature of the story: "Where did the story take place?" "Who is the main character?" "What is the main character wanting to do or accomplish?" "What major things happen to the main character?" "What happened to the main character at the end of the story?" "How did the main character feel at the end of the story?" Students may also complete a workbook activity such as the one in figure 9–4 on page 226 to further explore story grammar categories.

☐ Assist students in selecting a book to read after it has been determined through teacher-directed instruction that students can use the questions to guide both their reading and summarizing.

☐ To help students in writing their book reports, have them list the main characters and events and the relationships between them. This can be done by using a story map or by having students write responses to a list of questions similar to those presented in the previous guideline.

☐ Have students summarize information from either their story maps or their responses to the guiding questions; this results in their book

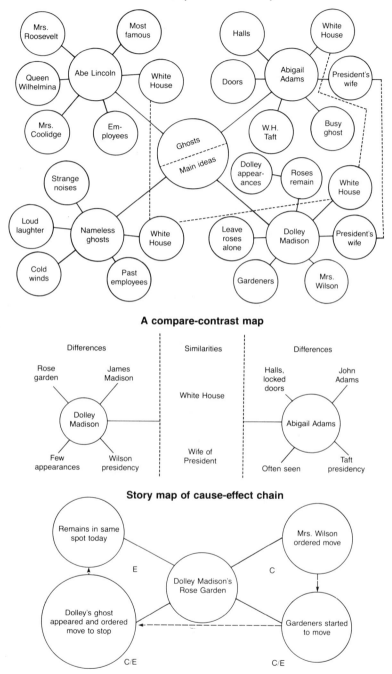

FIGURE 9–3 Examples of main idea-sequential detail, compare-contrast, and cause-effect story maps

Source: From "Story Maps Improve Comprehension" by D.R. Reutzel, 1985, *The Reading Teacher, 38,* pp. 401–403. Copyright 1985 by the International Reading Association. Reprinted with permission of D. Ray Reutzel and the International Reading Association.

Characters, Setting, and Plot

Guided Practice

It was a cold, windy November evening. Sarah shivered and pulled her jacket closer to her as she started on the long walk from the library to her home. "Perhaps I should have called Mom for a ride," she mused. Then she remembered that her mother was attending a school committee meeting and would not be home until later that evening. After battling the gusts of wind for half an hour, Sarah put her head down as if to butt against the blustering wind.

As she stepped from the curb to cross a seemingly empty street, a car suddenly careened around the corner, missing her by inches. She instinctively jumped backward to avoid being hit and slammed her ankle against the curb. The pain felt like a searing flame in contrast to the cold, whiplike wind.

The driver of the car sped away. Sarah was now faced with a decision. Should she brave the cold walk home and perhaps cause further injury to her ankle, or should she call a neighbor and ask for help?

1. Who is the main character? _____

2. Who is the minor character? _____

3. Describe the setting. _____

_____

4. What are the problem and the conflict facing the main character? _____

_____

_____

Name _____ **Date** _____

Literary Skill: Story Elements — Characters, Setting, and Plot

Unit 1   Triumphs, Notebook Section 5, Guided Practice   **1**

FIGURE 9–4 Workbook activity for story elements: Characters, setting, and plot

Source: From *Houghton Mifflin Reading,* "Triumphs" (teacher's notebook, sec. 5) (p. 1) by W. Durr et al., 1986, Boston: Houghton Mifflin. Copyright 1986 by Houghton Mifflin. Used by permission.

reports or summaries. For students who have difficulty writing a book report, consider having them draw a summary picture or a series of pictures that summarize the story.

This technique for helping students write book reports can provide them with opportunities to practice and develop an understanding of story structure. Also, the story maps and questions can be used for instruction prior to students' reading of a story to help them activate appropriate schemata for understanding story features as a means for improving their comprehension.

Vocabulary Development

Vocabulary development has been recognized as a major feature of reading comprehension. Improving reading vocabularies should be a major focus of instruction for those students who experience reading comprehension problems. Some principles of vocabulary instruction have been suggested by Blachowicz (1985) and parallel closely the recommendations found in the research literature. The basic features of her recommendations follow.

☐ Teachers should build a conceptual base or schema for learning a new word. This can be done through the use of analogies, where the new word is compared with known words in terms of meaning, such as comparing the vocabulary of a new game (soccer) to a known game (kick ball, basketball, etc.). The teacher can guide students in examining a word and how it relates to a larger set of words. For example, questions such as, "What is it made of?" "What are its parts?" "How is it used?" "What different kinds are there?" "What are other things related to it (the new word)?" "What are other words that mean the same thing?" Answers to questions such as these can be discussed and then illustrated with webs to help students build relationships between the new word and what they already know.

☐ Students should be actively involved in learning new words. Discussion should always be used; students should define new words in their *own* words as well as suggest sentences in which the new words can be used. The sentences should be written and elaborated upon by the students to ensure their understanding of the new words and these words' semantic relationships among other words.

☐ Words selected for teaching should be usable and should help students understand the meanings in the stories they are to read and get meaning from.

☐ Teachers should encourage and provide opportunities for students to use their new vocabularies to reinforce students' use of new words in their speaking and writing activities. Having a "word of the day" and recognizing students' use of the word encourages them to make the word a part of their language vocabulary.

☐ Vocabulary instruction should be a long-term goal. Provide students with many opportunities to encounter and use new vocabulary words.

In addition to these basic guidelines for teaching new vocabulary words, semantic mapping, which is similar to story mapping, is an effective way to teach vocabulary. **Semantic mapping** is "a categorical structuring of information in graphic form. It is an individualized content approach in that students are required to relate new words to their own experiences" (Johnson, Pittleman, & Heimlich, 1986, p. 779). Figure 9–5 is an example of a semantic map from a vocabulary lesson developed for the topic of Olympics. The instructional sequence for developing such a map includes:

☐ Choosing a word that is central to the topic or story.
☐ Writing the central word on the chalkboard and directing students to think of words related to the central word. These related words are written by category on the chalkboard.
☐ Guiding students in a discussion of the words listed under the categories. Focus the discussion on the relationships of new words to known words; using the new words in sentences; and determining the meanings of the new words in relationship to known words, and how the new word is used in the students' sentences.

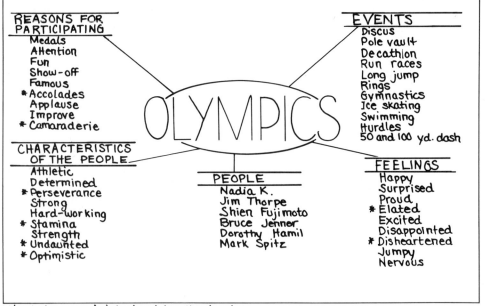

*Vocabulary word introduced by the teacher

FIGURE 9–5 Semantic map developed for the topic of Olympics

Source: From "Semantic Mapping" by D.D. Johnson, S.D. Pittleman, and J.E. Heimlich, 1986, *The Reading Teacher*, 39, p. 779. Copyright 1986 by the International Reading Association. Reprinted with permission of Dale D. Johnson and the International Reading Association.

Semantic maps can provide students with opportunities to (1) learn new words by relating them to known words and concepts, (2) understand relationships that exist between words, (3) develop and elaborate upon their existing schemata related to a topic, and (4) organize information presented in text that they read. In addition, teachers can use semantic maps as prereading activities to not only introduce new words, but also to activate students' background knowledge of the story content.

Language Features

Several variations of the cloze procedure can be used with students who have problems comprehending literal information and understanding syntax. Games and activities that progress from using sentences and lists of words to using longer passages prompt representations of the ideas presented and attention to syntax. For example,

the student recognizes a word: Joe put the fish back in the _____.
                                        water   fin   case

recalls a word: The boat skimmed across the _____.

recalls words for longer connected passages: The boat skimmed across the _____. Waves splashed on the _____. People stood on the beach and _____ at the driver of the boat. Soon, the boat was out of _____.

If the student recalls or selects words that make sense in the context of the sentence or passage, the teacher can safely assume that the student is representing and understanding the text and its structure.

An instructional activity similar to the cloze activity is to have students compose sentences that are meaningful continuations of given sentences. To construct logical continuations, readers must form a representation and understand the given sentence. For example, if students read the sentence, "Two boys dug up a dozen fishing worms," a logical continuation might be: "They went fishing in the afternoon." or "They sold them down by the lake." Constructing such logical continuations indicates both comprehension of the given sentence and attention to cause-effect relationships.

Worksheets and instructional activities can use various forms of this procedure. For example, students can select from a list of logical continuations the one(s) that make sense for given sentences.

Sentences	**Continuations**
1. Mary dove into the water.	a. He leaped high and caught it.
2. Tom hit the ball at Mark.	b. She bought two bags of candy.
3. Susan found five dollars.	c. Water splashed on her dog, Flo.

A similar activity can be used for improving comprehension abilities with longer passages. A connected story is presented with every other sentence deleted. The student must infer a sentence that logically continues the one deleted.

Ruth and Betty were going to meet their friends at the baseball game. 1._____
_____.
They all bought ice cream cones. 2._____
_____. Ruth said to Joe, "You better eat
fast or your ice cream will melt." 3._____
_____.

a. "Looks like we'll have to sit in the shade until Joe eats his ice cream," Ruth said laughingly.
b. Mark and Joe are waiting by the ice cream stand for them.
c. They all laughed when Joe got an ice cream cone with four different flavors.

Logical continuations of sentences can be meaningful as a procedure for introducing an assigned story and discussing it with students who have problems making inferences. Asking students to read key sentences or paragraphs and then to infer what will happen in the story provides for transfer of the skill to actual reading situations. After they have speculated about what will happen, ask students to read until they identify what actually did happen. Discussing their predictions in light of what they read promotes greater attention to story relationships and provides information about how students process text.

Introductory Activities

It is important to help readers relate their experiences to what they will be reading. If reading materials present concepts, facts, and topics too quickly, this heavy concept load can impair students' comprehension. Introductory and preparatory work done by the teacher can improve students' comprehension abilities in such cases. Introducing concepts and new ideas through demonstration, experimentation, and concrete illustration can prepare students for reading. During reading, the comprehension focus then becomes a reinforcement or confirmation of concepts rather than a learning of new ones. Through such an introductory procedure, students form ideas about what information is important, how it is related, and what it all means. They know the relevant features of the text; relationships among the text information and the text information itself are integrated.

The use of summary pictures and other concrete activities to depict main ideas and events of a story can prepare students for comprehension. Films, field trips, filmstrips, and concrete objects can supplement pictures to prepare students for comprehending a given story. Discussing how these represent ideas in the story and how the ideas are related to each other should facilitate comprehension.

Visual Imagery

Helping students with reading comprehension problems through introductory and preparatory work is similar to using visual imagery during reading; students are better prepared to visualize story information during their reading because they have concrete experiences to match with story information. Visual imagery and its potential use to improve reading comprehension has been the focus of several research investigations (Gambrell, 1982; Sadoski, 1982). These investigations have found that readers who visualize what they read comprehend better than readers who do not. Improving students' comprehension abilities by using visual imagery requires reading materials that are image-evoking, such as the worksheet in figure 9–6. Materials beyond students' experiential/conceptual backgrounds should not be selected if students are expected to use visual imagery.

Creative activities can play an important role in enhancing students' ability to form images of what they read. Activities such as reading a story and then drawing pictures of the important events, acting out a story, writing creative endings for unfinished stories, and discussing word pictures are all means toward developing the ability to visualize. These activities can be conducted in both individual and group settings. In a group setting, all students are encouraged to present and discuss their interpretations of the story events and each contribution is discussed by the group. What teachers ask students to visualize will be based on students' comprehension strengths and weaknesses. That is, students who have problems representing character traits could be encouraged to draw a picture or act out features of story characters. Students who experience difficulty inferring cause-effect relationships could be required to visualize such information through creative activities. Students who have problems integrating literal story information might be asked to recall as much information as they can to represent each piece of information with an individual drawing. As the information is being illustrated, a discussion of how each piece of information might be used to form one large picture would help the students integrate what they read. By incorporating each piece of story information into one summary picture, students should begin to understand how to visualize the relationships within the stories they read.

Materials used for corrective or remedial instruction are more effective if they use high-frequency oral language structures appropriate to the students' language. Furthermore, written activities that incorporate high-association words will better ensure attention to ideas and meaningful comprehension. One approach that accommodates the semantic abilities of the student is the language experience approach (LEA). The language experience approach (see chapter 12) also benefits students who have extreme difficulty representing ideas found in commercially published materials; it better prepares students for dealing with concepts they will encounter in their reading, since the concepts are ones with which they are familiar. The LEA, too, can benefit students who are having problems visualizing what they read and can introduce and model what is meant by using visual imagery.

*The new exercise in using imagery on this page is similar to previous ones except that students must select a picture for each part of a story (rather than for an entire, but shorter, story). Have the students complete this page independently. Then conduct a work check as usual.

Circle the picture that goes with *each part* of the story.

Do Cats Like Cheese?

PART ONE

Rosa taught her cat tricks. It was easy to teach her cat to grin. Whenever Rosa held up a piece of cheese, the cat would grin.

PART TWO

One day Rosa found out why the cat always grinned at cheese. She saw a mouse putting on a cat costume. The mouse had fooled Rosa for more than two years.

Using imagery: Selecting pictures to illustrate story parts

FIGURE 9–6 Workbook activity to develop visual imagery

Source: From *Catching On: Motivational Activities in Reading Comprehension,* 1987, Workbook III (teacher's ed.) (p. 18) by V. Anderson and C. Bereiter, LaSalle, IL: Open Court. Copyright 1987 by Open Court Publishing Company. Used by permission.

Direct Instruction

Although many of the previous suggestions allow for the application of corrective or remedial comprehension instruction in actual reading situations, different procedures may be necessary when reading commercially published basal readers. A technique developed by Schwartz and Sheff (1975) has proved to be successful with students who have reading comprehension problems. The technique consciously directs students through comprehending a story. The steps to this process are (1) posing a problem, (2) reasoning while reading, and (3) verifying.

Posing a problem is initiated and guided by the teacher. The title of a story or a representative picture may be used as the stimulus that encourages students to think about what they are going to read. After students have speculated about the title or picture (the first problem posed), they then read a short portion of the story. The teacher then asks literal questions about what they have read (the second problem), and the students answer. Following the discussion, another problem is posed that relates to the literal information discussed. The students then read another portion of the story to identify information that will solve the new problem. This procedure continues throughout the reading of the story, and new problems focus on inferential, critical, or affective comprehension outcomes. Such a technique activates students' experiential/conceptual backgrounds prior to reading and actively involves them in shifting from one piece of meaningful text to another as they progress through the story. The teacher helps students to focus on important cues, to represent their ideas, to understand the relationship of ideas, and to integrate story information.

A similar direct-instruction approach for use with commercial reading materials focuses on the integration of three types of knowledge shown to be associated with effective reading comprehension (Baumann & Schmitt, 1986). The three types of knowledge included in this approach are (1) **declarative knowledge**, which is the skill or strategy, (2) **procedural knowledge**, which is how the skill or strategy is used, and (3) **conditional knowledge**, which is why the skill or strategy is important and when it should or should not be used. The four steps (what-why-how-when) of this approach incorporate these three types of knowledge.

> *Step 1:* This is the *what* step. The teacher tells the students what comprehension skill they will learn and uses definitions, examples, and descriptions when appropriate.

> *Step 2:* This step is intended to help students understand *why* the comprehension skill or strategy is important and why it will help them become better readers. Again, examples of or modeling the skill or strategy in actual reading should help students better understand its importance in reading for meaning.

Step 3: In this step the teacher uses direct-instruction to ensure that students understand *how* the skill or strategy is used in reading for meaning. Demonstrating, modeling, and discussing are used by the teacher to help students understand the procedural knowledge of the skill or strategy. Bauman and Schmitt suggest using visual displays, think-aloud strategies (modeling), and so forth to demonstrate how the skill or strategy operates. Included in this step is guided practice and independent practice to gradually shift responsibility to the student.

Step 4: This last step is intended to help students understand *when* they should use the reading skill or strategy. The teacher should discuss and illustrate for the students under what conditions (types of written texts, purposes for reading, and so forth) the comprehension skill or strategy should be used.

Questioning Strategies

Asking students questions about their reading is important in comprehension instruction because these questions can help students interact with each other and share their interpretations of text. However, teachers often rely too heavily on literal questions in their comprehension instruction. Closer attention to carefully preparing questions and to asking questions that stimulate students' thinking can be facilitated by utilizing the following guidelines (Lange, 1982):

□ Identify a student by name, then ask the question. This ensures that the student heard the question and understands it. Avoid always calling on volunteers because this often eliminates some students from having an opportunity to respond to questions.

□ Wait four to eight seconds for a student to respond to a question. This gives the student time to think of a response.

□ Use probes and cues to help a student respond to a question. For example, if a student does not respond to the question, "Why was Hulk a good name for the dog?", the teacher can use cues such as, "What did the dog look like? What did he like to do?" Then, "What do you know about the word *Hulk* that makes you think that would be a good name for this dog?"

□ Identify and illustrate the steps students can use to find and verify answers. Provide opportunities for teacher-directed practice and application to ensure transfer to independent reading.

□ Ask both passage-dependent and passage-independent questions. Note whether or not students are having difficulty responding to either type of question.

□ Provide opportunities for students to practice answering questions for literal, inferential, and critical comprehension outcomes. Model the strategies they should use and provide them with many familiar and concrete reading selections for application.

☐ Prepare questions and strategies prior to teaching. Evaluate their effectiveness in relation to students' performance and modify or discard those that are ineffective.

☐ Respond to and direct students' processes of comprehending, but not just by telling students that an answer is correct or incorrect; help students reflect on the strategies they are using in order to enhance their awareness of those strategies.

USE OF COMPUTERS IN CORRECTING/REMEDIATING READING COMPREHENSION PROBLEMS

There is a limited number of quality microcomputer software programs available for teaching reading comprehension. Most of the microcomputer software designed for reading comprehension does not teach, but only assesses, students' abilities to answer workbook-type activities. There are, however, some microcomputer programs that can be used to improve students' reading comprehension.

Some of the commercially developed software, although not specifically designed to teach reading, requires students to read with understanding. Examples of such programs are games, computer magazines, and "participate stories" (Dudley-Marling, 1985). Programs such as these can be used to provide students with meaningful practice and application of comprehension skills taught earlier. Students are often highly motivated by such activities and will get continued practice and reinforcement through rereading each time they play the game.

Software programs specifically designed for teaching reading and for improving students' reading comprehension skills must be carefully evaluated to ensure that they engage students in reading activities that reflect what is known about the reading comprehension process.

Milliken Publishing Company, 1100 Research Boulevard, St. Louis, MO 63132 has several software programs that teachers might find useful in working with students who experience comprehension problems. For example, *Sentence Combining* is a program that presents a set of sentences for the student to combine by using words such as *and, but, before*, etc. Practice examples are provided and students can build new sentences by selecting words to be inserted. This activity could reinforce phrase grouping and help develop understandings about syntax.

Another program by Milliken uses a cloze procedure. Students are given a short passage with a word deleted and they must either select from a set of choices or type in a word that makes sense in the blank. This program also includes a manager program for the teacher to use in making individual assignments and reviewing students' performance. This program also focuses on syntax (antonyms, synonyms, pronoun referents, sequence, and time-order) and could be used for practice and application.

Two software programs that should be highly motivating for students are *Story Machine*, published by Spinnaker Software, 215 First Street, Cambridge, MA 02142, and *Story Maker*, available from Bolt, Beranek, and Newman, Inc., 50 Moulton Street, Cambridge, MA 02138. *Story Machine* appeals most to young children. It requires the student to type a simple sentence using the 40-word dictionary as a source, such as, "The dog hops." The sentence then appears on the lower part of the screen, and a dog appears hopping across the upper part of the screen. Such illustrated text can help communicate to students that language represents meaning.

Story Maker enables students to compose their own stories as they read. Story segments are presented to students and they select from three possibilities the one they want to use to continue or build the story. The story continues to build in this fashion and results in a complete story once students have made each selection. Students can reread each story and construct a different story by selecting alternatives that differ from their earlier choices. Their stories can then be printed out for them. Other programs are available that allow students to create their own stories. Such programs can help students understand story relationships and how events and characters in a story are related to each other.

As noted earlier, teachers should carefully evaluate microcomputer programs that are intended to teach comprehension. Many of these programs do not reflect quality reading comprehension instruction. Furthermore, many programs are no more than a different mode for presenting worksheets to students. As noted by Rude (1986), rather than using questionable programs for teaching comprehension, teachers would be better off having students read independently for 15 to 20 minutes a day.

□ SUMMARY

Improved comprehension is the goal of corrective and remedial reading instruction. Students' comprehension is influenced by their word-recognition capabilities, their purposes for reading, the content and language structure of what they read, their experiential/conceptual backgrounds, and the setting in which reading occurs. Therefore, comprehension is more than just remembering story facts and details, it is the interaction of reader and text for the purpose of getting meaning.

Several different conceptualizations of reading comprehension exist. The three most popular concepts are top-down, interactive, and bottom-up. We feel that the interactive concept, which recognizes the need for readers to use both their word-recognition strategies and their world knowledge to comprehend is the most applicable for teachers of reading. One interactive conceptualization of reading is Miller's (1975) model, which has three basic features: (1) identifying important text elements, (2) constructing representations of the important text information, and (3) matching the representations to the reader's existing concepts. Another interactive model of reading is based on the schema theory, which is a theory about how knowledge is represented and about how that representation facilitates using that knowledge in particular ways.

Assessment and interpretation of comprehension abilities can be accomplished with the use of several procedures, such as norm-referenced tests, criterion-referenced tests, informal tests, and teacher-developed strategies. Considerable emphasis was given to teacher-developed strategies that recognize the many factors that influence students' reading comprehension. Among the strategies suggested were (1) using purpose-setting questions, (2) writing summary statements for text read, (3) rating text familiarity, and (4) interviewing students.

Corrective and remedial instruction must be well-planned. Through careful evaluation of students' comprehension, an instructional program can be developed that meets students' reading needs. Observation of students' performance in various instructional settings serves as an ongoing diagnostic tool for determining the effectiveness of the program. As necessary changes are identified, the instructional program must be modified to accommodate them. Furthermore, reading comprehension should be treated as a process of understanding ideas and information from the reader's perspective as well as understanding the author's intent. Instruction should concentrate on activities that force and guide comprehension of story information. Application of these instructional guidelines will enable teachers to modify existing reading materials and to construct their own materials for corrective and remedial comprehension instruction.

☐ *IN-TEXT ASSIGNMENTS*

LIBRARY ACTIVITY

Obtain one or two examples of a norm-referenced test of reading comprehension from your reading lab, library, or other available source. Analyze the items of the test to determine what is required of the reader to respond to the comprehension items—simple recall or recognition of facts, inference about content, critical evaluation, and so on. Rewrite portions of the test to improve its quality of reading comprehension assessment. Give attention to those features that would enable students to: (1) activate their experiential/conceptual backgrounds prior to reading, (2) respond to inferential and critical types of comprehension questions, (3) respond to several different summaries for each passage, and (4) rate their familiarity with the content of the passage. Share your modifications with your classmates and discuss the rationale for your modifications.

FIELD-BASED ACTIVITY

Select a story from a basal reader to teach to an identified group of students, such as a public or private school classroom, a reading clinic program, or an individual student if unable to identify a group. Using the strategies discussed in this chapter, prepare a reading comprehension lesson. Teach your lesson to the students and evaluate its effectiveness by observing students' learning.

DISCUSS AND DEBATE

Form small groups and analyze a selected folk tale or fable by using one of the two story grammars presented in this chapter. After your group has completed the analysis, write a series of questions that could be used to guide students' prereading and postreading discussion of the story to help them understand story features. Also, identify three or four questions based on your analysis to use as a guide for helping students predict story information prior to reading.

RESOURCE ACTIVITY

Invite a textbook representative for a basal reading series to speak to your class about the comprehension features of the company's materials. Ask questions about how their materials are to be used and if the instructional recommendations reflect the recommended teaching strategies found in this chapter.

☐ REFERENCES

Anderson, R. C., Heibert, E. H., Scott, J. A., & Wilkinson, I.A.G. (1985). *Becoming a nation of readers: The report of the commission on reading.* Washington DC: National Institute of Education.

Anderson, R. C. (1985). Role of the reader's schema in comprehension, learning, and memory. In H. Singer & R. B. Ruddell (Eds.), *Theoretical models and processes of reading* (3rd. ed.) (pp. 372–384). Newark, DE: International Reading Association.

Baumann, J. F. & Schmitt, M. C. (1986). The what, why, how, and when of comprehension instruction. *The Reading Teacher, 39,* 640–647.

Blachowicz, C. L. Z. (1985). Vocabulary development and reading: From research to instruction. *The Reading Teacher, 38,* 876–881.

Carnine, D. & Kinder, D. (1985). Teaching low-performing students to apply generative and schema strategies to narrative and expository material. *Remedial and Special Education, 6,* 20–30.

Devine, T. G. (1986). *Teaching reading comprehension.* Boston, MA: Allyn & Bacon.

Dudley-Marling, C. C. (1985). Microcomputers, reading, and writing: Alternatives to drill and practice. *The Reading Teacher, 38,* 388–391.

Gambrell, L. B. (1982). Induced mental imagery and the text predictions performance of first and third graders. In J. A. Niles & L. A. Harris (Eds.), *New inquiries in reading research and instruction* (pp. 131–135). Rochester, NY: National Reading Conference.

Gordon, C. & Braun, C. (1983). Using story schema as an aid to reading and writing. *The Reading Teacher, 34,* 261–268.

Johnson, D. D., Pittleman, S. D., & Heimlich, J. E. (1986). Semantic mapping. *The Reading Teacher, 39,* 778–783.

Johnston, P. (1981). *Implications of basic research for the assessment of reading comprehension* (Technical Report No. 206). Urbana-Champaign, IL: University of Illinois.

Lange, B. (1982). Questioning techniques. *Language Arts, 59,* 180–185.

Lehr, F. (1987) Story grammar. *The Reading Teacher, 40,* 550–555.

Lipson, M. Y. (1984). Some unexpected issues in prior knowledge and comprehension. *The Reading Teacher, 37,* 760–765.

Mandler, J. M. (1984). *Stories, scripts, and scenes: Aspects of schema theory.* Hillsdale, NJ: Erlbaum.

Miller, G. A., et al. (1975). *Semantics, concepts, and culture: Conference on studies in reading* (Panel Report 1). Washington, DC: National Institute of Education.

Morrow, L. M. (1985) Reading and retelling stories: Strategies for emergent readers. *The Reading Teacher, 38,* 870–875.

Nagy, W. E. & Anderson, R. C. (1984). How many words are there in printed school English? *Reading Research Quarterly, 20,* 233–253.

Olson, M. W. (1984). A dash of story grammar and . . . Presto! A book report. *The Reading Teacher, 37,* 458–461.

Paratore, J. R. & Indrisano, R. (1987). Intervention assessment of reading comprehension. *The Reading Teacher, 40,* 778–783.

Pearson, P. D. (1982). Asking questions about stories. *Ginn Occasional Papers.* Columbus, OH: Ginn.

Poindexter, C. A. & Prescott, S. (1986). A technique for teaching students to draw inferences from text. *The Reading Teacher, 32,* 908–911.

Reutzel, R. D. (1985). Story maps improve comprehension. *The Reading Teacher, 38,* 400–405.

Rowe, D. W. & Rayford, L. (1987). Activating background knowledge in reading comprehension assessment. *Reading Research Quarterly, 22,* 160–176.

Rude, R. T. (1986). *Teaching reading using microcomputers.* Englewood Cliffs, NJ: Prentice-Hall.

Rumelhart, D. E. (1981). Schemata: The building blocks of cognition. In John Gutherie (Ed.), *Comprehension and teaching: Research reviews* (pp. 3–26). Newark, DE: International Reading Association.

Rumelhart, D. E. (1984). Understanding understanding. In J. Flood (Ed.), *Understanding reading comprehension* (pp. 86–94). Newark, DE: International Reading Association.

Rystrom, R. (1977). Reflections of meaning. *Journal of Reading, 9,* 193–200.

Sadoski, M. (1982). *An exploratory study of the relationship between reported imagery and the comprehension and recall of a story in fifth graders* (Technical Report No. R82007). College Station, TX: Texas A&M University.

Schmitt, M. C. & O'Brien, D. G. (1986). Story grammars: Some cautions about the translation of research into practice. *Reading Research and Instruction, 26,* 1–8.

Schwartz, E. & Sheff, A. (1975). Student involvement in questioning for comprehension. *The Reading Teacher, 29,* 150–154.

Stahl, S. A. (1985). To teach a word well: A framework for vocabulary instruction. *Reading World, 24,* 16–27.

Stahl, S. A. & Fairbanks, M. M. (1986). The effects of vocabulary instruction: A model based meta-analysis. *Review of Educational Research, 56,* 72–110.

Stanovich, K. E. (1985). Matthew effects in reading: Some consequences of individual differences in the acquisition of literacy. *Reading Research Quarterly, 21,* 360–406.

Stein, N. L. & Trabasso, T. (1981). *What's in a story: An approach to comprehension and instruction* (Technical Report No. 200). Urbana-Champaign, IL: University of Illinois.

Sternberg, R. (1985). *Beyond IQ: A triarchic theory of human intelligence.* New York: Cambridge University Press.

Strange, M. (1980). Instructional implications of a conceptual theory of reading comprehension. *The Reading Teacher, 33,* 391–397.

Tierney, R. J. & Cunningham, J. W. (1984). Research on teaching reading comprehension. In P. D. Pearson (Ed.), *Handbook of Reading Research* (pp. 609–656). New York: Longman.

Tierney, R. J. & Pearson, P. D. (1985). Learning to learn from text: A framework for improving classroom practice. In H. Singer & R. B. Ruddel (Eds.), *Theoretical models and processes of reading* (3rd. ed.) (pp. 860–878). Newark, DE: International Reading Association.

Valencia, S. & Pearson, P. D. (1987). Reading assessment: Time for a change. *The Reading Teacher, 40,* 726–733.

Varnhagen, C. K. & Goldman, S. R. (1986). Improving comprehension: Causal relations instruction for learning handicapped learners. *The Reading Teacher, 39,* 896–904.

10

Comprehension of Expository Materials

☐ OVERVIEW

Today's emphasis on learning "basic reading skills" has unfortunately led to a de-emphasis of instructional time devoted to important content reading abilities needed for lifelong learning. Research and practical experience indicate that good readers in the regular reading program are not necessarily able readers of particular materials for specific purposes; also, students who are having a difficult time with the regular reading program often have extreme difficulty with expository materials. These two points are readily noticeable in grades four and above, although most reading programs begin planned instruction in content reading skills and strategies in the primary grades (one, two, and three).

The cliché that every teacher should be a reading teacher has been repeated for years. In addition, most descriptions of a complete reading program encompass the instructional program, independent or enrichment program, and skill development in the content areas. Yet reading problems manifested by an inability to read expository materials effectively are on the rise. This chapter focuses on this crucial concern, the skills involved, and the corrective measures that can be used in the classroom or clinic.

After reading this chapter, the teacher should be able to

☐ understand the difficulties students encounter in content reading.
☐ know the elements of successfully reading expository text.
☐ apply a directed reading activity (DRA) to content readers.

241

□ teach an organized study method to students at different instructional levels.

□ know how to teach a study skill through the direct-instruction method.

DEMANDS OF CONTENT READING

Although content reading has as its foundation the skills and abilities taught in the instructional program (word recognition and comprehension), readers need to *apply* these reading skills and various expository reading strategies to be successful in content reading. Smith (1963) viewed study skills as those reading skills applied uniquely in reading content materials. She went on to define study skills as "skills used when there is intention to do something with the content read" (p. 307). Over 20 years later, Anderson and Armbruster (1984) similarly discussed studying by stating, "studying is a special form of reading. The way that studying differs from ordinary reading is that studying is associated with the requirement to perform identifiable cognitive and/or procedural tasks" (p. 657). A major difference today in viewing the requirements of successful content reading is the increased knowledge we have of the demands of content reading itself and the emphasis given to both developing and monitoring one's own reading strategies. Garner (1987) succinctly addresses the demands of content reading by stating,

> Reading and studying expository text is a cognitive task. To perform the task effectively, students must have (a) accessible conceptual knowledge in relevant domains, (b) a schema for expository text that specifies how ideas are related, and (c) text-processing strategies. (p. 299)

EXPOSITORY TEXT

While we believe a general reading ability exists in the primary grades, it is clear that beyond third grade, assessment of a student's general reading ability (for example, by using an IRI) does not predict the ability to read particular content materials for specific purposes. Text in the content areas is characterized by an **expository style** of structure (i.e., the text pattern is characterized by presenting new concepts and information in a compact fashion, usually in an organizational pattern such as sequence, cause and effect, enumeration, problem-solving, or comparison). Most elementary students are more used to the **narrative style** of text structure (elements of a story) used in basal readers. Unfortunately, students experiencing difficulty in learning to read are largely unaware of text structure and of ways to use text organization to comprehend what they read. In addition, content material is characterized by a high readability level due to a variety of factors, including higher vocabulary and concept levels. In synthesizing the research on helping students understand expository material, Anderson and Armbruster (1984) clustered the variables linked to successful reading in the areas of the students themselves, the text, and the processing variables. The following is a list of the major components under each heading.

Student
Background knowledge related to material to be read
Motivation

Text
Difficulty level
Type of content
Organization or structure of material

Processing Variables (i.e., "getting the information from the written page into the student's head" [p. 657])
Initial attention to intended purpose
Ability to fulfill one's purpose (understand what is read)
Ability to retrieve information when needed

Processing variables have received much attention in the comprehension and studying areas. These processing variables relate to what cognitive psychologists refer to as a student's **metacognitive status**, that is, "the knowledge and control the child has over his or her own thinking and learning activities, including reading" (Baker & Brown, 1984, p. 353). Metacognition or comprehension monitoring involves readers thinking about their reading while they read; in other words, appraising how well they are understanding and adjusting their reading strategies to meet the intended goal. Mier (1984) states that "most mature readers spontaneously monitor their comprehension, more or less consciously asking themselves: Do I understand? If not, why not? Should I reread a passage or look up a word to improve my comprehension?" (p. 771). Although the research is not conclusive, studies on teaching various processing strategies, such as summarizing, lookbacks, and self-questioning, through the direct-instruction approach shows an improved understanding of content material (Alvermann, 1987; Garner, 1987).

The problem of students' deficiencies in content reading and their resulting loss of reading growth is further compounded when we realize that students are not becoming independent learners. If we truly believe in the educational goal of independent learning, more than just an adequate amount of time must be given to teaching the skills needed for content reading. We feel that a lack of curriculum emphasis on teaching content reading skills and strategies explains many of the reading problems that suddenly come to light in the intermediate grades. For students to become independent readers, they must be taught the skills and abilities necessary to pursue the ever-increasing amount of knowledge in nearly all fields—that is, they must learn how to learn.

DIAGNOSIS

In order to determine a student's ability to be successful with expository materials and his or her ability to know and apply specific skills needed in the content areas, informal teacher-made tests are most effective. Standardized measures to assess strengths and weaknesses in content reading are not as plentiful as in other areas of reading development. While a few of the major achievement batteries assess some study skills, the information teachers need about student performance in expository text is best gathered through informal means.

Informal Content Reading Inventory

Since the readability and thus teachability of content reading materials depend to a large measure on a teacher's ability to provide differentiated instruction, it is essential to be able to determine students' varied abilities to read a particular content textbook. One way to aid in this group decision-making process in the content areas is for the teacher to construct and administer an informal inventory to the class at the beginning of the year. An **informal content reading inventory** is a teacher-made group exercise composed of a passage (approximately 1000–2000 words) from a content text the students will use in the classroom. Following the silent reading of a portion of a chapter, the students are asked to answer various teacher-designed questions about the passage. A group inventory has many advantages: the ease of design and scoring, the small time allotment required, the group versus one-on-one administration, and the efficient yet comprehensive coverage of important skills.

General Outline of Components for an Informal Content Reading Inventory

 I. Passage of approximately 1000–2000 words from the content text to be used for instruction
 II. Four to six questions on the literal comprehension level
 III. Four to six questions on the interpretive comprehension level
 IV. Two to four questions on the evaluative comprehension level
 V. Four to six vocabulary questions
 VI. Two to four questions on interpreting various graphic materials (maps, graphs, time lines, diagrams, charts, tables)
 VII. Additional questions depending on passage and instructional emphases (glossary, index, scanning, outlines, reading rate, following directions)

Test Interpretation and Decision Making Administering a group inventory using the textbook to be used in the classroom has the additional advantage of producing a probable one-to-one relationship between the results of the exercise and subsequent instruction. The results of the inventory should provide teachers with the following information to make instructional decisions:

students' general ability levels to read the text successfully

group and individual needs with respect to specific reading and study skills

Depending on the passing criterion used (usually 60 to 80 percent), results can indicate the number of students likely to experience some difficulty in reading the content textbook. These results will help teachers decide on the specific teaching strategies needed to help all students be successful in reading the text. Additionally, an item analysis of incorrect answers will indicate class response patterns. These results can provide teachers with specific information needed to design future skill lessons for groups of students. Most important, the results of this exercise can ensure that diagnostic teaching will occur in the content areas because the results are used to adjust future instruction.

INSTRUCTIONAL IMPLICATIONS

The underlying rationale for content reading instruction is promoting lifelong learning strategies. To effectively read in the content areas, readers must apply several reading skills successfully. These reading skills and abilities span the broad areas included in the developmental reading program, including emphasis on those skills needed by students for reading expository text. Reading skills applied in the content areas include (1) studying strategies to promote purposeful and analytic reading of expository text, (2) flexible reading skills in terms of reading rate and level of comprehension, and (3) specific skills in the areas of locating information and interpreting visual aids.

Studying Strategies

Directed Reading Activity   Successfully reading content chapters depends on the implementation of a directed reading activity (DRA). The DRA has long been an integral part of the regular reading program but has had little carry-over to content textbooks. "Open your science books to page 20; read the next eight pages and answer the questions on page 28" is not teaching. The same careful planning that goes into a basal story lesson should also go into every content chapter; however, the DRA in content areas should be modified to the demands of expository text. It is during the DRA that the teacher can teach and model studying strategies to promote comprehension monitoring on the part of students. An outline of a DRA for content chapters that includes important elements in each step follows:

I. Motivation and background
   A. Review past learning and relate this to new chapter
   B. Elicit student interest
II. Vocabulary and key concepts
III. Guidance
   A. Purpose(s)
   B. What organizational pattern is used
   C. Organizers and reading guides
IV. Active reading—silently
V. Comprehension check and meaningful oral reading
VI. Instruction on specific reading skills

The most important phase to be highlighted in a DRA is the prereading section. It is at this stage that the teacher can train students to monitor their own thinking about the material to be read and can create a mind-set in students for the upcoming material. As in any DRA, it is crucial to begin by reviewing past learnings and providing an overview of the upcoming chapter. Motivating students can be accomplished in a number of ways, including a discussion of the upcoming chapter and how it relates to their everyday lives, reviewing visual aids, examining real objects related to the chapter, or performing a short experiment. In addition to providing motivation and background, content vocabulary and key concepts should be identified and taught directly to students. At this point it is important to provide a preview of the material to be read and to inform students how they should read the selection. For example, students can

☐ read the story quickly
☐ read the story slowly
☐ skim the story before reading
☐ look for details and/or main ideas
☐ find out in what type of pattern the material is presented
☐ discover what main ideas will be developed
☐ find the author's outline
☐ discover their purposes in reading

Directed Reading-Thinking Activity   The Directed Reading-Thinking Activity (DR-TA) is another instructional format for teaching narrative or expository text. Similar to the DRA, the DR-TA emphasizes the prediction process in the readiness step, followed by guided silent reading focusing on reflective analysis, and then reaction to and review of text content (Stauffer, 1975). Haggard (1988) reports the major advantages of the DR-TA:

1. a focus on developing comprehension through making predictions, reading to confirm prior knowledge, and confirming or rejecting one's predictions;
2. the promotion of critical thinking; and
3. the establishment of a positive reading environment for discussing ideas.

Purposeful Reading   The importance of ensuring that students read with clear purposes in mind is crucial in content reading. Not only will comprehension of the subsequent material be positively affected by establishing purposes before reading, but also the reading rate will be improved.

Thomas (1978) devised such a method for establishing purposes, which he called the Directed Inquiry Activity (DIA). In the DIA, students preview the material to be read and then respond to "reporter" questions, which the teacher has written on the chalkboard. The responses—listed under each question—and their interrelationships are discussed with students. In this fashion, purposes for reading are established and students read to confirm or reject their predictions.

The DIA is one method of encouraging students to formulate their own questions about material to be read. Shifting the responsibility of question asking from teacher to student is at the heart of Singer and Donlan's (1980) "active comprehension." Singer and Donlan state that this process "consists of asking questions throughout the chapter or text, not only at the beginning. In general, it is a kind of dialogue between the student and the text with the student asking questions and the text 'answering' them" (p. 52). To foster active comprehension throughout the chapter or selection, students can be asked to turn each boldface heading into a question and then read to answer it.

Organizers and Reading Guides   One technique that aids comprehension is to provide students with an **organizer**—that is, a summary of major ideas—before the chapter is read. Aulls (1978) categorizes organizers as either textual or schematic in nature. Both types of organizers "focus the learner on the major topic ideas of relationships you want students to know about after completing a reading assignment" (p. 65). A **textual organizer** summarizes the main ideas in the passage, and can be written in an expository, comparative, or historical style. The teacher should read the passage, synthesize the main ideas in a 50- to 300-word passage, and have the students read and discuss the summary before they silently read the passage. A **schematic organizer** presents the main ideas and their relationships to students in the form of a flow chart, diagram, or table. Either type of organizer provides students with a welcome road map to guide them through the many details and main ideas in their reading assignment.

Reading guides are another type of comprehension aid meant to help students establish purposes for reading as well as to better understand the material they read. A reading guide is a set of questions and statements prepared by the teacher about the content of the text. This guide is presented to the students before reading to help them establish purposes for reading; students are asked to complete the reading guides as the text is read. One variation in using reading guides is the three-level guide. As described by Vacca and Vacca (1986), the three-level guide helps to systematically encourage students' thinking at the literal, interpretive, and applied levels. In constructing the guide, teachers first decide on the important ideas in a passage. Second, questions are written that reflect the literal, interpretive, and applied levels of thinking. Third, students discuss the questions prior to reading and answer the questions during their reading.

Concept Guide in Science

Topic: Food Chain

Part 1:
As you preview pages 444–450 in your text, complete these statements.

1. Organisms containing chlorophyll are _____.
2. Microorganisms that cause the decay of dead plants and animals are _____.

3. _____ are animals that eat other animals and plants.

Part 2:
Put the words in the list below into their proper group based on their method of obtaining food. (Use Appendix D to help identify any unfamiliar organisms.)

azalea bush	rabbit	grass
mushroom	man	bread mold
dandelion	eagle	seaweed
kangaroo	gardenia	spider
trout	fern	cedar tree
palm tree	roach	bacillus bacteria
horse	coccus bacteria	poinsettia
cactus	fly	bass
spirillum bacteria	slime mold	penicillium
tungus	mold	E. coli

Producer	Consumer	Decomposer
1. _____	_____	_____
2. _____	_____	_____
3. _____	_____	_____
4. _____	_____	_____
5. _____	_____	_____
6. _____	_____	_____
7. _____	_____	_____
8. _____	_____	_____
9. _____	_____	_____
10. _____	_____	_____

FIGURE 10–1 Example of a concept guide

Source: Adapted from a guide developed by Cliff McInturff, Ocoee Junior High School, Orange County Schools, Florida.

As an aid in teaching new concepts, vocabulary, and organizational structures, Cheek and Cheek (1983) recommend the formulation of a **concept guide**. Relating the underlying premise of the concept guide to the theory of "chunking" or rearranging new information in relation to existing knowledge for better comprehension, Cheek and Cheek feel the concept guide serves the following two purposes:

1. Students are helped in their recognition of major concepts within a selection, and
2. Students learn to associate the new information with ideas already known. (p. 219)

Steps in developing a concept guide include determining the main concepts within the material, reading the material and identifying statements that explain each concept, and writing a two-part worksheet, part one being sentences in which the concept is explained and the student is required to write in the concept, and part two being an application activity where students associate the major concept categories to new information. Figure 10–1 shows an example of a concept guide in science; figure 10–2 is an example of an application activity.

Organizational Structures   Being able to identify the organizational structure of the text passage to be read will help improve a student's comprehension of the material. McGee and Richgels (1985) synthesized research on content reading structures and reported on the following five expository text structures identified by Meyer and Freedle (1984): description, collection, causation, problem/solution, and comparison. Figure 10–3 describes each type of structure and includes a sample passage with clue words.

McGee and Richgels recommend a five-step approach to teaching expository text structures: (1) select appropriate passages of different structures; (2) prepare a graphic organizer for the passage; (3) explain, using the graphic organizer, one structure at a time to students; (4) write, along with students, a passage that mirrors the graphic organizer; and (5) compare the created passage with the actual passage. An example of a passage and graphic organizer for teaching the problem/solution structure is given in figure 10–4 on page 254.

Study Method   It is unfortunate that many students are not taught—and may not even be aware of—a systematic plan to approach content chapters in a meaningful fashion. The design of content textbooks requires the use of a study method for success. It is strongly recommended that beginning in the third grade, every teacher teach and reinforce a basic study method to all students (except those who are experiencing severe problems in learning to read). Too often students read a chapter in a textbook the same way they read a basal story. Reading a content chapter should be looked upon as following a road map: Students must be shown how to get from A to B in the shortest, most meaningful way. Many corrective problems in

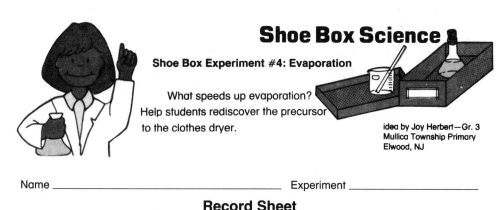

Shoe Box Science

Shoe Box Experiment #4: Evaporation

What speeds up evaporation?
Help students rediscover the precursor
to the clothes dryer.

idea by Joy Herbert—Gr. 3
Mullica Township Primary
Elwood, NJ

Name _____ Experiment _____

Record Sheet

Materials:
2 flat dishes	eyedropper
water	facial tissue
paper fan	clock
worksheet	meter stick

Procedure:

1. Label dish A and dish B. Place the dishes at least one meter apart.
2. Place a piece of facial tissue on each dish.
3. Put five drops of water on each tissue. Record the time now.
4. Use the paper fan. Make a gentle breeze over dish A. Do not fan dish B.
5. Observe how long it takes for the tissue in each dish to dry. Record the times when each tissue becomes dry. Answer the questions below.
6. Clean up!
   - Throw away the two tissues.
   - Dry the two flat dishes.
   - Put all materials except the meter stick in the box.
   - Give the completed record sheet to your teacher.

Observations:

1. Time at start of experiment _____

2. Time for drying tissue A _____

3. Time for drying tissue B _____

4. Which tissue dried first? _____

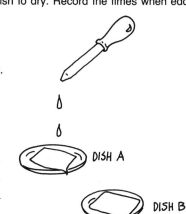

Conclusions:

1. Why did one tissue dry faster than the other?

2. How does wind affect the rate of evaporation?

Think! Do clothes dry faster on windy or calm days? What else would affect the rate of evaporation?

©The Education Center, Inc. • *THE MAILBOX* • *PRIMARY* • Aug/Sept 1988 Key p.56

FIGURE 10–2 Worksheet activity for conducting a science experiment

Source: From *The Mailbox* (primary ed.) (p. 20) by The Education Center, Inc., Aug./Sept. 1988, Greensboro, NC. Copyright 1988 by The Education Center, Inc. Used by permission.

FIGURE 10–3 Expository text structures with sample passages and clue words

Structure	Description*	Sample Passage	Clue Words
Description	Specifies something about a topic or presents an attribute or setting for a topic	The Summer Olympic Games are the biggest entertainment spectacles of modern times. Every four years they offer two weeks of non-stop pageantry and competition.	
Collection	A number of descriptions (specifics, attributes, or settings) presented together	The Summer Olympics have so many different things to offer. First, there are many kinds of events: big shows like the opening and closing ceremonies, pure competitions like the races and games, and events that are partly artistic and partly competitive like the subjectively scored diving and gymnastics contests. There are old things and new things, like the classic track and field events staged in 1984 in the same stadium where they were held in 1932, and the almost bizarre sport of synchronized swimming first presented in 1984.	*first, second, third, next, finally*
Causation	Elements grouped in time sequence (before and after) with a causative relationship (the earlier causes the later) specified	There are several reasons why so many people attend the Olympic Games or watch them on television. The first Olympics were held in Greece more than 2,000 years ago. As a result of hearing the name "Olympics," seeing the torch and flame, and being reminded in other ways of the ancient games, people feel that they are escaping the ordinariness of daily life. People like to identify with someone else's individual sacrifice and accomplishment, and thus an athlete's or even a team's hard-earned, well-deserved victory becomes a nation's	*so that, thus, because of, as a result of, since, and so, in order to*

FIGURE 10–3 Expository text structures with sample passages and clue words *(continued)*

Structure	Description*	Sample Passage	Clue Words
	victory. There are national medal counts and people watch so that they can see how their country is doing. Since the Olympics are staged only every four years and maybe only in a particular country once in a lifetime, people flock to even obscure events in order to be able to say "I was there."		
Problem/ solution	Includes a causative relation (between a problem and its causes) and a solution set, one element of which can break the link between the problem and its antecedent cause	One problem with the modern Olympics is that they have gotten so big and expensive to operate. A city or country often loses a lot of money by staging the games. A stadium, pools, and playing fields are built for the many events and housing is built for the athletes, but it is all used for only two weeks. In 1984, Los Angeles solved these problems by charging companies for permission to be official sponsors and by using many buildings that were already there. Companies like McDonald's paid a lot of money to be part of the Olympics. The Coliseum, where the 1932 Games were held, was used again and many colleges and universities in the area became playing and living sites.	*a problem is, a solution is, have solved this problem by*
Comparison	Contains no element of time sequence or causality; organizes elements on the basis of their similarities and differences	The modern Summer Olympics are really very unlike the ancient Olympic Games. Individual events are different. For example, there were no swimming races in the ancient Games, but there were chariot races. There were no women	*different from, same as, alike, similar to, resemble*

FIGURE 10–3 *(continued)*

Structure	Description*	Sample Passage	Clue Words
		contestants and everyone competed in the nude. Of course the ancient and modern Olympics are also alike in many ways. Some events are the same, like the javelin and discus throws. Some people say that cheating, professionalism, and nationalism in the modern Games are a disgrace to the ancient Olympic tradition. But according to ancient Greek writers, there were many cases of cheating, nationalism, and professionalism in their Olympics too.	

*Descriptions adapted from Meyer and Freedle, 1984, pp. 121–124.

Source: From "Teaching Expository Text Structure to Elementary Students" by L.M. McGee and D.J. Richgels, 1985, *The Reading Teacher, 38*, pp. 741, 742. Copyright 1985 by the International Reading Association. Reprinted with permission of Lea M. McGee and the International Reading Association.

the intermediate grades stem from students' lack of study methods, as well as their lack of specific study skills. The best-known study method is Robinson's (1961) SQ3R method. **SQ3R** stands for survey, question, read, recite, review. Students are taught to be analytical at each step—to ask questions that look past the details for key ideas.

We recommend modifications of the SQ3R method for use with corrective reading instruction in a classroom or clinic. But whatever approach is used, it is essential to remember that a study method is a general technique: Its success depends on specific content skills that must be directly taught. A basic study method should be introduced early in the year and then expanded throughout the year. Again, its application is mandatory to ensure its automatic use by students.

The following is a basic study method for reading a content chapter for grades three and four.

1. Read the introduction.
2. Examine each picture (chart, map, or graph).
3. Turn each boldfaced statement into a question and read to find the answer.

Forest Fires

An important problem for forest rangers is how to protect forests from being ruined by fire. Each year thousands of trees are destroyed by fire. Careless campers do not put their fires completely out. Cigarettes are left to burn on the dry ground. These small fires in dry forests can burn thousands of trees. One solution to the forest fire problem is to man lookout stations and use helicopters to spot fires. Fires that are spotted right away can be put out before they get too big to handle. Then fires will cause less damage to the forest. A second solution to the problem is to have experts and bulldozers ready to move in quickly to fight the fire. Bulldozers can throw huge amounts of dirt on a fire in a short time. The dirt helps put the fire out quicker. A third solution is to build fire lanes in the forests. Fire lanes are long breaks in the forest where there are no trees. These breaks prevent the fire from spreading and getting too large (McGee, 1982b, p. 66).

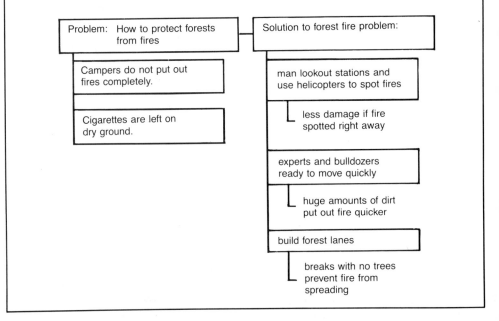

FIGURE 10–4 Sample problem/solution passage and graphic organizer

Source: From "Teaching Expository Text Structure to Elementary Students" by L.M. McGee and D.J. Richgels, 1985, *The Reading Teacher, 38*, p. 745. Copyright 1985 by the International Reading Association. Reprinted by permission of Lea M. McGee and the International Reading Association.

First, students should be told the meaning and value of an introduction in relation to the content to be covered as well as the value of the questions an introduction brings to mind. Next, students should be taught to analyze closely all pictures, charts, maps, or graphs. The old saying "A picture is worth a thousand words" is appropriate here. Authors do not include pictures just to fill up space; usually each picture is explained in the text. Students should be taught to ask questions concerning each picture (using the reporter questions—who, what, where, when, why, and how) and to read each caption to find some answers. The pictures, like the introduction, raise questions that can be answered by reading the text. This func-

Students need specific help in reading and learning expository text. (Bruce Johnson/Merrill)

tion is important; unanswered questions give students a good reason to read the chapter. The third step in the basic study method is to direct the students to read the chapter section by section, turning each boldface statement into a question and then reading to find the answer. Again, students need opportunities to practice turning such statements into questions by using the reporter questions. After sufficient practice, students will no longer open their books and start to read. When they use this study method, students at this level are aware of what the chapter is about, already know some of the content of the chapter, and have several questions to guide their reading. Success with this modified study method depends on the concurrent teaching of maps, graphs, charts, and main ideas.

Expanding on the previous steps, the following is a basic study method for grades five and above:

Previewing
□ Read the introductory paragraphs.
□ Examine each picture (chart, map, or graph).
□ Read all boldface statements.
□ Read the author's summary.
□ Read the author's questions.

Reading
□ Return to the beginning of the chapter and read through the chapter, turning each boldface statement into a question.

In this modification, students are again taken step by step through the reading process and are given much practice and review. Students are taught that the bold print in a chapter essentially makes up the author's outline. Not *all* boldface statements will be meaningful to students; they should know this. Statements that are not meaningful will still raise questions in the student's minds, yet the bold print will guide their thinking as they read.

The importance of a summary should also be discussed, and students should get practice in selecting the main ideas. The entire summary will not be understood by students, but reading the summary will help students raise more questions regarding the chapter.

Finally, studying the author's questions at the end of a chapter is just good common sense. In order to be able to pick out important ideas and facts, it will certainly help to know what the author feels is important. A positive effect of the other previewing steps is that many students will already be able to answer some of the questions.

The important point in both study methods is that students will be looking for answers to the questions they were not able to answer in the prereading steps, and thus their comprehension rates will be greatly increased when they do read the chapter. The specific skills needed for the study method for grades five and above are knowledge of topic sentences, outlining, main ideas, and recognizing an author's pattern. These skills, along with those needed for the study method given for grades three and four, need direct instruction concurrent with the teaching of the study method.

Commercial materials are plentiful in most classrooms and can be used as vehicles to teach parts of a study method. SRA (Science Research Associates) reading labs can be used to teach story selections, topic sentences, recognizing an author's pattern, and for practice in asking the reporter questions about pictures. Other materials with short selections can be used to sustain instruction of the different components of a study method.

Flexible Reading Skills Flexible readers vary their reading rates and depth of reading according to their original purpose. This ability to adjust the rate of reading to the type of material being read is the mark of an efficient reader. Successful reading in the content areas demands flexibility. Many students who are failing in the content subjects are unable to read material differently for special purposes. As a result, they read content material at a very slow rate; this slow rate can be attributed to word-by-word reading, vocalizing, and poor concentration. "Slow rate readers" do not adjust their rate to the level of comprehension desired and are totally helpless when faced with content books on their frustration level. These students must first be sensitized to the fact that not all material is read the same way. Systematic instruction and practice must be given using materials on an independent level so that these students can learn to vary their rate of and purpose for reading. Three types of reading are required in the content areas—skimming, scanning, and studying.

Skimming. Skimming is a quick method of covering a selection for the purpose of getting some of the main ideas and thus a general impression of the material without attending to details. Steps to go through in skimming a content selection in a text or reference book are (1) read the first paragraph line by line; (2) read the bold print as it occurs; (3) read the first sentence of every paragraph; (4) examine any pictures, charts, or maps; and (5) read the last paragraph. This procedure will fulfill the purpose of skimming and let the reader decide if further detailed reading is desired.

The following materials are useful for teaching skimming:

☐ Short stories
☐ Newspapers
☐ Content chapters
☐ SRA reading labs

Scanning. Scanning is a fast method of covering material for the purpose of locating a specific piece of information. The steps to follow are (1) use bold print to narrow the number of pages to scan; (2) use a zigzag eye pattern or a winding S eye pattern down the page—move the eyes down the page, not across, left to right; and (3) note capital letters if looking for a name, numbers for dates, and words in italics or boldface for vocabulary items; and (4) read only what is needed to verify the purpose.

Materials that might be useful in teaching scanning include the following:

☐ Tables of contents
☐ Dictionaries
☐ Telephone directories
☐ Stock market listings
☐ Reference books
☐ Content chapters
☐ SRA reading labs

Studying. Study-type reading in the content areas is deliberate and purposeful; its goal is total comprehension. Students should be given purposes to fulfill in their reading or should be able to generate their own purposes to guide reading. This type of reading can incorporate the prereading steps described under the basic study method.

These three types of reading can be taught to intermediate-grade students who are reading at least at the third- to fourth-grade instructional level. To become independent readers, students must have these three types of reading methods explained to them, must practice them under teacher supervision, and must have opportunities for independent practice.

SPECIFIC SKILL INSTRUCTION

Effective reading in the content areas requires readers to apply several reading skills successfully, including mastery of technical vocabulary and symbols, following directions, following ideas and events in sequence, classifying details and main ideas, summarizing major ideas, identifying differences as well as similarities, and evaluating ideas. Students need to learn and practice these and other specific study skills that are often applied in the content areas. While all reading skills are needed to be successful in content reading, students especially need to be able to locate and organize information about various topics and interpret various visual aids (i.e., graphs, maps, diagrams, charts, time lines, and other drawings).

The tasks of locating and collecting data requires students to be able to make effective use of a table of contents, index, card catalog, encyclopedia, atlas, almanac, *Reader's Guide to Periodical Literature*, and other sources of information. Having assembled several sources of information on a particular subject, students must learn to organize the essential information and discard that which is unimportant. Some of the specific skills needed to accomplish this include outlining, judging the validity of a source by consulting various references, and summarizing.

An ability to comprehend various visual aids is a specialized study skill needed in content areas. Success in using visual aids requires specific attention to the different types of a particular visual aid (for example, maps can show population, physical geography, political groupings, etc.), the purpose for the aid, the interpretation of the scale or key, and an understanding of the ideas presented. Graphs are increasingly being used to convey information in content reading. In figure 10–5, Fry (1985) presents an excellent taxonomy of the various types of graphs.

Learning the reading skills that are applied in the content areas as well as other specialized study skills requires teachers to design and teach lessons, such as the one shown in figure 10–6 on page 261, using the direct-instruction approach. Gentile (1981) concurs with this viewpoint, yet reports a lack of consistent and direct reading instruction in content

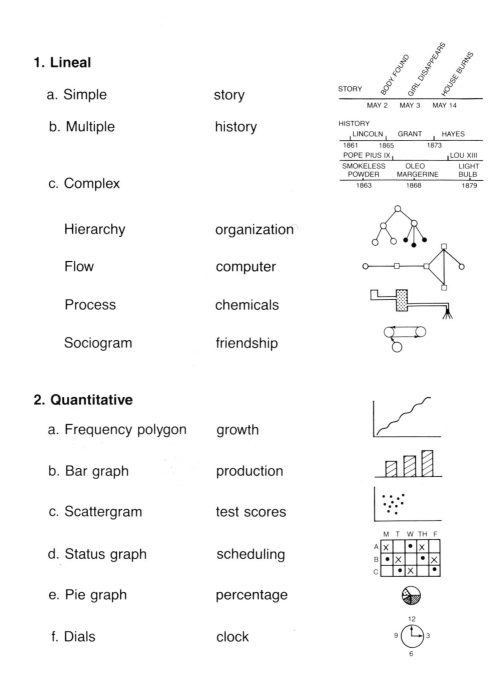

FIGURE 10–5 An illustrated version of a taxonomy of graphs

Source: From *The New Reading Teachers Book of Lists* (p. 177) by E.B. Fry, D. Fountoukidis, and J.K. Polk, 1985, Englewood Cliffs, NJ: Prentice-Hall.

3. Spatial

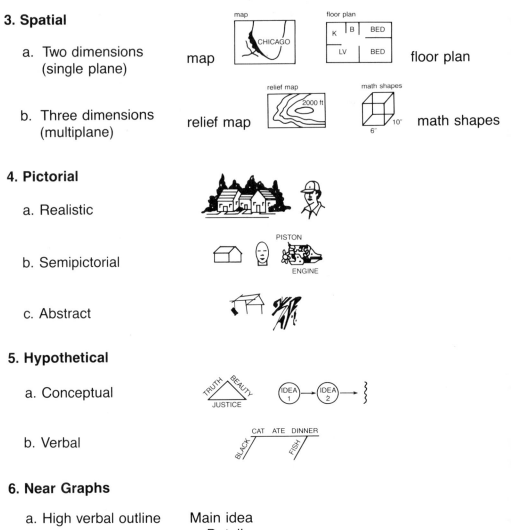

   a. Two dimensions   map   floor plan
      (single plane)

   b. Three dimensions   relief map   math shapes
      (multiplane)

4. Pictorial

   a. Realistic

   b. Semipictorial

   c. Abstract

5. Hypothetical

   a. Conceptual

   b. Verbal

6. Near Graphs

   a. High verbal outline   Main idea
                      a. Detail
                      b. Another detail

   b. High numerical

Table	
25	4.2
37	6.1
71	7.3

   c. Symbols

   d. Decorative design

FIGURE 10–5 *(continued)*

Source: From *The New Reading Teachers Book of Lists* (p. 177) by E.B. Fry, D. Fountoukidis, and J.K. Polk, 1985, Englewood Cliffs, NJ: Prentice-Hall.

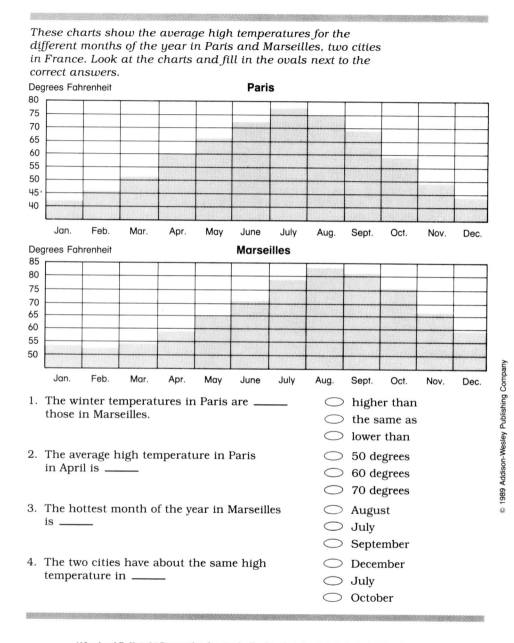

These charts show the average high temperatures for the different months of the year in Paris and Marseilles, two cities in France. Look at the charts and fill in the ovals next to the correct answers.

1. The winter temperatures in Paris are _____ those in Marseilles.

    ◯ higher than
    ◯ the same as
    ◯ lower than

2. The average high temperature in Paris in April is _____

    ◯ 50 degrees
    ◯ 60 degrees
    ◯ 70 degrees

3. The hottest month of the year in Marseilles is _____

    ◯ August
    ◯ July
    ◯ September

4. The two cities have about the same high temperature in _____

    ◯ December
    ◯ July
    ◯ October

80   (After Level E, Unit 6.) **Preparation for standardized testing.** Remind students to follow directions in tests carefully and to darken the ovals completely.

FIGURE 10–6 Activity to help students prepare for reading expository text in standardized tests

Source: From *Addison-Wesley ESL Activity Book E* (p. 80) by M. Walker, 1989, Reading, MA: Addison-Wesley. Copyright 1989 by Addison-Wesley Publishing Company. Used by permission.

reading. He states, "as a result students have few opportunities to practice and apply the specific skills that will aid them in 'reading to learn' using expository texts" (p. 13).

To give the teaching of specific skills in content reading a proper emphasis, then, we recommend a combination approach encompassing (1) the direct sequential instruction of content reading during the regular reading program and during the content periods, (2) the application of those skills during the content periods, (3) the inclusion of appropriate content skills in unit teaching in all areas, and (4) the teaching of all lessons in content areas incorporating steps in a directed reading activity. This approach balances needed systematic instruction with opportunities that promote content reading in an incidental manner.

Recommendations for Specific Skill Instruction

1. Teach only one skill per lesson unless it is a review lesson.
2. Provide interesting and varied practice.
3. Teach only those skills that are needed at the moment and that will be required for future assignments.
4. Teach skills in an appropriate sequence. For example, in the case of topic sentences, have separate lessons on the first sentence as the topic sentence, the middle sentence as the topic, the last sentence as the topic, and then paragraphs that have no topic sentence, requiring students to infer the main idea.
5. Follow this suggested outline when teaching a skill:

Planning
☐ Area of needed reading instruction
☐ Intended learning outcome
☐ Past learning

Teaching
☐ Building background
☐ Teacher-directed instruction
☐ Independent student practice
☐ Modifying instruction

Figures 10–7 and 10–8 contain sample direct-instruction lessons on specific skills.

FIGURE 10–7 Sample direct-instruction lesson—reference skills

---

☐ AREA OF NEEDED READING INSTRUCTION

Knowledge of the index and its use.

☐ INTENDED LEARNING OUTCOME

Given 5 to 10 questions on a teacher-made worksheet pertaining to the index of a familiar text, students will answer the questions presented using the index as their guide.

☐ PAST LEARNING

Students are able to distinguish the difference between author and subject indexes.
Students know that the numbers in the index represent page numbers.

☐ BUILDING BACKGROUND

Remind students of the purpose of an index and give an example on the chalkboard from an index. Instruct students to locate the index in their textbooks.

Discuss and present the concept of *key word* with the class. You can relate this concept to dictionary guide words and key words in sentences and paragraphs.

☐ TEACHER-DIRECTED INSTRUCTION

Write a question on the chalkboard that can be answered using the index of a particular text available to each student.

For example, write the following question on the chalkboard and help the class to locate information about it in their individual texts:

On what page could I read about pollution in this book?

Discuss and list all possible key words that could help locate information regarding pollution and write down respective page numbers as catalogued in the index:

pollution, 100–105
air pollution, 104–105
water pollution, 102–103

Direct students to locate the pages on pollution in their texts to ensure they understand the purpose of using an index.

Repeat the procedure using a second question pertaining to their textbook index to reinforce students' understanding of the activity:

Where could you locate information on great white sharks in this textbook?

List the information found in the textbook index, such as:

fishes, 585–600
sharks, 588–589
types of, 590–595
weights of, 595–596

☐ INDEPENDENT STUDENT PRACTICE

Ask students to complete 10 questions that pertain to using the index in their textbook. Example questions include the following:

1. In what chapter can information be found regarding the types of fruits that grow in Brazil?
2. List the states in America that produce cotton as an important economic product.
3. What page numbers and topics in this text tell about the vegetation prevalent in the Alaskan tundra?

Answer one or two questions with the students and provide ample time for them to complete the activity. Approximately 10–15 minutes are sufficient when 10 questions are to be answered. Time allocation really depends on the number of questions asked and the difficulty level of each question. For example, in the previous question 3, students might locate information about Alaska in their index but not be able to find anything about vegetation in that section of the text. They would then need additional time to locate information in their index about tundras.

☐ ONGOING DIAGNOSIS

By observing and monitoring students' completion of the independent activity, determine if any students had difficulty because (1) they misinterpreted the meaning of the question asked of them, (2) they were unable to locate key words from the index that related to the question presented on the worksheet, or (3) they had difficulty relating the key words from the question on the worksheet to practical application in the index of their text. Each of these areas could be retaught individually to ensure a student's success and decrease the difficulty level of the activity.

☐ MODIFYING INSTRUCTION

Allow students to work in pairs to design their own complex assignment for a different chapter in one of their content textbooks.

Source: From *Teaching Reading: Diagnosis, Direct Instruction, and Practice* (2nd ed.) (pp. 196–198) by W.H. Rupley and T.R. Blair, 1988, Columbus, OH: Merrill, Copyright 1988 by Merrill Publishing Company. Reprinted by permission.

FIGURE 10–8 Sample direct-instruction lesson—graph skills

☐ AREA OF NEEDED READING INSTRUCTION

Introduction to the ability to read graphs.

☐ INTENDED LEARNING OUTCOME

Students will identify picture, circle, bar, and line graphs on a teacher-made worksheet.

☐ PAST LEARNING

Students recognize that information can be represented in many different ways by being diagrammed pictorially as graphs and tables.

☐ BUILDING BACKGROUND

Use students' experiential backgrounds to show how information can be represented on a graph. Demonstrate how various types of flowers can be represented on a circle graph by drawing the following diagram on the chalkboard or an overhead transparency:

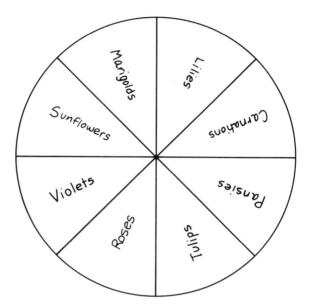

Discuss how each flower is represented in a particular section of the circle or pie graph. Have the class add other flowers to the graph. Stress to students that by graphing types of flowers they can record and read a great deal of information using a single diagram.

□ TEACHER-DIRECTED INSTRUCTION

Demonstrate different types of graphs and their functions by drawing an example of each kind on the chalkboard. Include a picture, circle, line, and bar graph. Explain the uses of each by graphing information about a particular topic. In using flowers as an example, you can use a pictograph to show the color variety of tulip blooms. On a bar graph, show when particular flowers are in bloom (see page 266).

A time line can be used to graph the best months of the year in which to sow seeds and plant different types of flowers (see page 266).

Ask questions about each graph; emphasize the amount of information that can be learned about flowers by reading the graphs. Ask students which graphs are easier to read and which ones are more difficult. Go back and clarify any difficulties that students are experiencing in reading a particular graph or graphs.

□ INDEPENDENT STUDENT PRACTICE

Distribute a teacher-made worksheet that contains picture, circle, bar, and line graphs. Have students write the appropriate title of each group in the space provided. Match the difficulty level of the graphs with students' reading capabilities. Help your students to complete the first example to ensure that they understand the activity.

□ ONGOING DIAGNOSIS

Teacher observation and monitoring of students' written responses on the teacher-made worksheet.

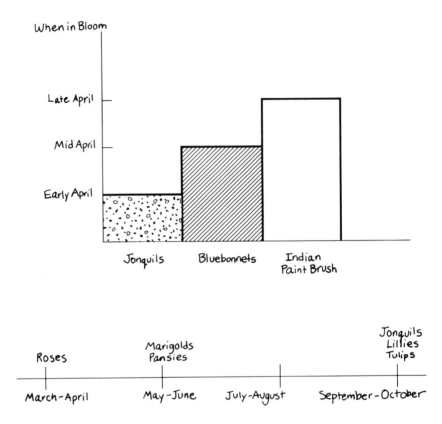

□ MODIFYING INSTRUCTION

This activity can be extended by having students construct their own picture, circle, bar, and line graphs for a specific set of information you provide them. For example, use any information pertaining to the class (hair color, number of members in the family, and so forth) to construct pictographs, circle or pie graphs, and bar or line graphs.

Students can also make graphs of different content areas. In science class students can graph temperature or amount of rainfall. In social studies they can graph population growth of a particular city or they can map current events on a large bulletin board display. Historical time lines can be graphed in history and government hierarchical systems can be graphed for a wall reference.

Source: From *Teaching Reading: Diagnosis, Direct Instruction, and Practice* (2nd ed.) (pp. 216–219) by W.H. Rupley and T.R. Blair, 1988, Columbus, OH: Merrill. Copyright 1988 by Merrill Publishing Company. Reprinted by permission.

□ *SUMMARY*

The pressing need to help students learn how to learn was the focus of this chapter. Success in content reading was related to students' knowledge of the subject, their ability to know the organization of expository text, their use of text-processing strategies, and their correct application of various reading and study skills. To correct deficiencies in content reading, an emphasis on direct instruction and teacher-guided student practice in a variety of situations were recommended. The chapter discussed the inherent difficulties in reading expository text and the importance of the concept of readability. Informal assessment procedures, guidelines for instruction, and suggested strategies to effect improvement were presented. The chapter stressed the key concept that the ability to read effectively in the regular basal text does not automatically mean the ability to read effectively in content materials. Realizing this difference, teachers should provide appropriate instruction to reduce corrective reading problems in this area and to promote independent learning habits.

☐ IN-TEXT ASSIGNMENTS

FIELD-BASED ACTIVITY

Interview a classroom teacher about how content reading responsibilities are carried out. Use the following questions as a guide. Share the results of your interview with the class.

1. Are there students in your class who are reading below grade level?
2. How do you handle this reality given that you must use content textbooks?
3. How do you provide instruction in specific reading and study skills in your classroom?

SHARING AND BRAINSTORMING

Divide into small groups and discuss the following hypothetical situation:

If you were teaching fifth grade and one-half of your students could not read effectively in the prescribed textbook, how would you differentiate your instruction? Be specific.

DISCUSS AND DEBATE

Take a stand for or against the following statement and give your reasons:

Students learn to read in the primary grades and read to learn in the intermediate grades.

☐ REFERENCES

Alvermann, D.E. (1987). Metacognition. In D.E. Alvermann, D.W. Moore, & M.W. Conley (Eds.), *Research within reach: Secondary school reading* (pp. 153–168). Newark, DE: International Reading Association.

Anderson, T.H. & Armbruster, B.B. (1984). Studying. In P.D. Pearson (Ed.), *Handbook of reading research* (pp. 657–680). New York: Longman.

Aulls, M.W. (1978). *Developmental and remedial reading in the middle grades.* (abridged ed.). Boston: Allyn & Bacon.

Baker, L. & Brown, A.L. (1984). Metacognitive skills and reading. In P.D. Pearson (Ed.), *Handbook of Reading Research* (pp. 353–394). New York: Longman.

Cheek, E.H., & Cheek, M.C. (1983). *Reading instruction through content teaching.* Columbus, OH: Merrill.

Fry, E.B., Fountoukidis, D., & Polk, J.K. (1985). *The new reading teachers book of lists.* Englewood Cliffs, NJ: Prentice-Hall.

Garner, R. (1987). Strategies for reading and studying expository text. *Educational Psychologist, 22,* 299–312.

Gentile, L.M. (1981). Subject-based reading skills in middle and secondary schools: Some issues and answers. In E.K. Dishner, T. Bean, & J.E. Readence (Eds.), *Reading in the content areas: Improving classroom instruction* (pp. 11–18). Dubuque, IA: Kendall/Hunt.

Haggard, M.R. (1988). Developing critical thinking with the Directed Reading-Thinking Activity, *The Reading Teacher, 41,* 526–535.

McGee, L.M., & Richgels, D.J. (1985). Teaching expository text structure to elementary students. *The Reading Teacher, 38,* 739–749.

Meyer, B.J.F., & Freedle, R.O. (1984). Effects of discourse type of recall. *American Educational Research Journal, 21,* 121–143.

Mier, M. (1984). ERIC/RCS: Comprehension monitoring in the elementary classroom. *The Reading Teacher, 37,* 770–775.

Robinson, F.P. (1961). *Effective study.* New York: Harper & Row.

Rupley, W.H. & Blair, T.R. (1988). *Teaching reading: Diagnosis, direct instruction, and practice* (2nd ed.). Columbus, OH: Merrill.

Singer, H. & Donlan, D. (1980). *Reading and learning from text.* Boston: Little, Brown.

Smith, N.B. (1963). *Reading instruction for today's children.* Englewood Cliffs, NJ: Prentice-Hall.

Stauffer, R. (1975). *Directing the reading-thinking process.* New York: Harper & Row.

Thomas, K.J. (1978). The directed inquiry activity: An instructional procedure for content reading. *Reading Improvement, 15,* 138–140.

Vacca, R.T. & Vacca, J.L. (1986). *Content area reading* (2nd ed.). Boston: Little, Brown.

PART THREE

Classroom Diagnosis and Correction/Remediation of Reading Problems

11

Classroom Implementation of Diagnostic Process

☐ OVERVIEW

The purpose of this chapter is to illustrate and recommend a high-effort commitment to teaching reading in the classroom. The process of diagnostic insruction presented in chapter 6 will be the basis for discussion.

After reading this chapter, the teacher should be able to

☐ apply the diagnostic process of instruction to a classroom setting.
☐ understand the differences in emphasis between primary and middle grades in relation to testing and planning for instruction.
☐ synthesize various sources of diagnostic information and plan whole-group, small-group, and individual insruction.
☐ list several alternative ways to implement each step of the diagnostic process.
☐ apply the variables for individualizing instruction (see chapter 3) to a whole-class setting.

ILLUSTRATION: HIGH-EFFORT TEACHERS VERSUS LOW-EFFORT TEACHERS

The following illustration points out how two different teachers might approach the teaching of reading in their classrooms. One example focuses on a teacher who is a low-effort teacher in planning reading instruction; the other example is that of a high-effort teacher's attention to reading instruction.

271

Time: Summer vacation has ended, and the teachers have returned to the local elementary school to start planning their school year. The students will begin school in one week.

Agenda: Besides attending a general meeting with the entire faculty and two meetings about the new social studies curriculum, the teachers are expected to prepare themselves and their programs in anticipation of the first official day of school.

Mr. Jones, a fourth-grade teacher, feels quite confident concerning the upcoming year because he has taught grade four in this school for the past three years. He is comfortable with the types of children he deals with in this grade. He has the reading program well-organized around a basal series and the grade-level curriculum guide; therefore, he knows just how and when he is going to teach each particular skill. He is equally confident in his goals for the year; his only remaining task is to obtain the records of his students to find out what reading book they finished last. Reading groups can then be set up, and his preplanning is done. Bring on the new year!

Ms. Turner, a second-grade teacher, also feels confident about the upcoming year. Although she has taught grade two for seven years and is comfortable with the reading program, her entire year's program is not, and will not be, planned this week. While her expectations are high concerning each student's growth in reading, she plans to wait to determine specific instructional goals until she learns what each student needs. As a prerequisite, she tries to collect as much information as she can about each class member's reading development in grade one by reviewing each student's file to gather information about his or her reading to help in planning the reading program. She reviews test performance, identifies the book each student was reading at the end of grade one, reads anecdotal comments made by the first-grade teacher, as well as reviews other available information. In addition, Ms. Turner begins to compile and plan the diagnostic strategies she will use with her students to gather information on which she will base her reading instruction program. She intends to use several informal strategies to gather information about learner style related to reading strengths and weaknesses, motivation, experiential background, concept of reading, and social/emotional adjustment. She has planned to administer a silent informal reading inventory to the whole class to survey students' reading comprehension and identify those for whom an oral inventory is needed. In addition, she plans to gather, through observation in small-group settings, information about the students' vocabulary knowledge, language capabilities, interests, word-recognition skills, and purposes for reading.

Although this example may oversimplify to achieve a point, you have certainly observed teachers who fit one of these descriptions. Mr. Jones's thinking and preparation for the new school year represents a narrow concept of reading that only reflects covering the skills and content of the materials; it fails to recognize that reading is an interactive process. Furthermore, his commitment to teaching reading along with recognizing students' individual differences is at a low level. Ms. Turner's thinking and preparation, on the other hand, represent an interactive view of reading; she recognizes that reading instruction is based on students' needs and that comprehension should be the focus of her instruction. She represents a high-effort commitment to teaching reading and is motivated by her understanding of the reading process and the needs of her students.

DIAGNOSTIC PROCESS

The heart of the diagnostic process of reading instruction is knowledge of (1) the reading process, (2) the correlates of reading problems, and (3) the identification of assumptions regarding reading instruction. The previous descriptions of the two teachers planning for the new year clearly indicated that Ms. Turner had a more sophisticated view of the reading process, had a better knowledge of the factors that influence students' reading, and had a more flexible attitude about how children learn to read than did Mr. Jones. Ms. Turner's actions illustrated her awareness that there are no "second-grade skills" as such—she must adapt her instruction to her students' learning needs. She realized that reading is a process that involves social, physical, emotional, intellectual, psychological, and cultural factors and their influence on students. On the other hand, Mr. Jones knew the "grade-four skills" and assumed that all his students could read and would meet the demands of his instruction. While the differences are grossly apparent here, even a small deficiency in a teacher's knowledge of the reading process, a slight lack of understanding of the factors affecting learning, or a slightly inflexible attitude can promote negative learning. These three factors are the foundation for the effective teaching of reading. The teacher's performance in the classroom is a direct result of his or her capabilities and attitudes in these three areas.

The remainder of the diagnostic process, the action based on the foundation just discussed, will be presented through two classroom teachers' eyes—one primary-grade teacher and one intermediate-level teacher. While Ms. Turner's second-grade class will be followed throughout the chapter, the sixth-grade class of another teacher, Mr. Harris, will be substituted for Mr. Jones's class. Mr. Harris, unlike Mr. Jones, has a concept of reading that is based on getting meaning, an awareness of the correlates of reading problems, and a positive attitude about meeting the needs of his students. In both Ms. Turner's and Mr. Harris's classrooms, effective instruction procedures will be presented. It must be underscored that this is only one possible way to organize a diagnostic teaching atmosphere in two classrooms; where appropriate, alternative means will be given. It is hoped that individual teachers will add or delete information depending on their particular situations.

Analysis

The first "action" steps of the diagnostic process involve analysis. Teachers must analyze and diagnose both their own instructional capabilities and their students' capabilities.

Diagnosis of Instruction Teachers must stand back and look at their own programs before the school year begins and should do so continuously throughout the year. It is essential to look at themselves before looking at their individual students in the classroom. The key difference between teachers who go through this process and those who do not is that by looking at their own programs first, they are identifying strong and weak points to help fit the curriculum to students' learning needs. The curriculum should be adapted to students at every grade level, not vice versa. Also, concerns for the curriculum differ depending on the grade level being taught. Ms. Turner (grade two) and Mr. Harris (grade six) are both teaching in the same school and are both using a basal reading series; yet, their concerns about their own programs will be slightly different. Some questions they may ask themselves include the following:

Variety of Materials

Ms. Turner

☐ Do I have supplemental reading programs—that is, language-experience approaches, phonic programs, computer-assisted instruction—ready to supplement the basal program or to use with students who are not successful in the basal series?

☐ Do I have varied activities, such as worksheets, games, and kits, for students to practice their reading skills in meaningful contexts?

☐ Do I know of any multimedia resources in my school and city to use in my program?

☐ Do I have a sufficient variety of library books and supplemental reading materials (newspapers, catalogs, travel brochures, plays, magazines, and so forth) for independent reading?

Mr. Harris

The questions cited for Ms. Turner plus the following would be appropriate:

☐ Do I have access to a variety of reference books, maps, and charts to enable students to apply reading as a tool for learning?

☐ Do I have books and materials for content-area topics on different levels of difficulty to meet students' reading needs?

☐ Do I have supplemental kits, materials, and activities to help students apply their reading in order to develop learning capabilities in a variety of meaningful situations?

Differentiated Instruction

Ms. Turner

☐ Do I have an informal reading inventory that will facilitate the placement of students in appropriate reading materials and will help identify their reading strengths and weaknesses?

☐ Do I have information about students' reading performances in last year's reading program?

☐ Do I have an informal word-analysis test to administer?

☐ Do I have checklists to facilitate the observation of students during reading instruction and to help gather informal information about areas

☐ related to reading development (vision, hearing, social/emotional status, interests, concepts of reading, and so forth)?

☐ Do I have information about the students' home backgrounds that will help identify appropriate features of reading instruction?

Mr. Harris

The questions cited for Ms. Turner plus the following would be appropriate:

☐ Do I have informal tests and strategies to help determine those students in need of corrective instruction in the content areas?

Record Keeping

Ms. Turner and Mr. Harris

☐ Do I have forms and checklists to keep track of students' progress in the various facilitative and functional reading abilities?

☐ Do I have a folder for each student to collect important papers?

Teacher-Initiated Conferences

Ms. Turner and Mr. Harris

☐ Do I have all pertinent information about my students from last year?

☐ Will I need to gather information from parents to aid in my planning of a reading program for particular students?

☐ Will I need an early conference with a specialist to aid in my planning for a particular student?

Collection, Interpretation, and Synthesis of Data   Certain initial analysis steps should be completed *before* students begin the school year.

☐ Record last year's norm-referenced reading test results for each student.

☐ Record last year's criterion-referenced test results for each student.

☐ Record the level or book that each student was reading in at the end of the last year.

☐ Record any significant information regarding a student's physical, emotional, psychological, social, or intellectual background.

Completing these steps enables the teacher to begin identifying students' reading strengths and weaknesses and planning additional diagnostic strategies. In addition, the teacher can begin to place students in reading groups. If a school program follows a plan of grouping for reading instruction, groups should be assigned flexibly and tentatively. A group's membership will most likely change for the following reasons: a different instructional program, a new teacher, new classmates, the growth or decline of reading capabilities over the summer months, or an instructional misplacement last year.

Because standardized test scores will most likely differ from a student's independent and instructional levels (see chapters 5 and 9), it is recommended that reading groups, if they are to be formed initially, be fairly

The classroom teacher needs to monitor individual student progress during reading instruction. (Rohn Engh)

unstructured. This allows the teacher to get to know the students from an academic, social, emotional, and psychological viewpoint. Test scores alone should not dictate instructional placement. For example, a student may technically be on the third-grade instructional level (just barely meeting the criteria), but due to a lack of successful experiences in the reading class, might be better placed at a lower level to ensure success. In addition, test scores do not take into consideration many of the features associated with reading for meaning: experiential/conceptual backgrounds, familiarity with text, purposes for reading, and language features of the text.

Figure 11–1 on page 278 provides a suggested format for collecting information related to students' past reading performances. This display of information provides the teacher with an overview of the students' reading abilities, last year's reading-level placement, and personal information (steps 1 through 3). Variability in the classroom can be noted as well, and significant information for the class is apparent.

Rather than forming reading groups based on steps 1 through 3, the teacher could delay establishing initial groups until the second or third week of school; that is, data for steps 1 through 3 can be collected, but an independent reading program would be organized only for the first few weeks of school. This time would be used for reading informally with students, getting to know their interests, assessing their experiential/ conceptual backgrounds, and collecting data for steps 4 and 5.

During the first few weeks of school, the primary concern should be to determine each student's insructional and independent reading levels. The best means for doing this is through the administration of an IRI in a manner most appropriate for the students with whom the teacher is working (alternative strategies for administering and interpreting an IRI can be found in chapters 5 and 9). This additional information will undoubtedly reveal discrepancies among groups formed according to standardized test information and will require changing the grouping of individual students or perhaps changing the number of groups.

Figure 11–1 also shows the instructional level (step 5) for each student. This information, combined with qualitative analysis of students' miscues and data gathered informally, will help the teacher decide whether or not a student should change to another reading group. The Xs in the bottom row (step 6) indicate actual transfers.

There are several alternatives for determining each student's reading competencies, including the following:

1. Due to time pressures, the teacher could administer the IRI silently to all students to identify those for whom an oral administration is needed. An alternative is to have students read aloud short excerpts from the basal reader while the teacher notes the miscues and estimates the number of words read. Next, the miscues should be analyzed in terms of significance. (Apply the questions found in chapter 5 for the qualitative analysis of miscues.) The percentage of words identified correctly and the qualitative analysis will help identify word-recognition strengths and weaknesses. Comprehension performance can be informally assessed by having students retell the stories read, rating their familiarity with the passages, discussing the important story events, and so forth.
2. A series of two or three cloze passages from different levels of the basal reading program could be administered. From this, teachers can analyze students' performances in terms of correct replacements of words and use of language structure as they read.
3. In the middle grades, Mr. Harris might give a quick group IRI by administering passages for levels four, five, six, and seven for students to read silently. Students can respond in writing to comprehension questions, write a brief summary of what was read, or list key points and ideas.

It is necessary to determine each student's reading levels (independent, instructional, and frustration) if one is to expect reasonable growth in reading. However, it is not enough to simply compute these levels based on quantitative performance; analyzing miscues qualitatively is beneficial in noting specific reading strengths and weaknesses. In addition, if a teacher wishes to avoid misplacement of students in reading groups, information related to the students' experiential/conceptual backgrounds, concepts of reading, vocabularies, knowledge of text organization, and purposes for

	Ms. Turner, Grade 2					**Mr. Harris, Grade 6**				
	Bob	**Mike**	**Sharon**	**Wendy**	**Jerome**	**Harold**	**Bill**	**Anne**	**Maria**	**Tom**
Step 1. Stanine from standardized test	6	4	4	7	3	6	6	5	5	3
Step 2. Last book in basal (level)	1^2	1^2	P	1^2	2^1	5	5	3	5	3
Step 3. Significant personal information	Eye problem		LD referral					Title I reading		LD resource room
Step 4. Initial level placement	2^1	2^1	1^1	2^1	2^2	6	6	4	6	3
Step 5. IRI instruction level	2^1	1^1	1^1	1^1	2^1	4	5	4	5	2^2
Step 6. Students assigned to another group		X		X	X	X	X		X	

FIGURE 11–1 Data Collection

reading should be gathered. Misplacement is often a basis for a student's difficulty in learning to read. Independent reading and homework assignments should be on a student's instructional-independent level and the frustration level avoided. Nevertheless, the job is not finished when these steps have been completed. Some students with the same instructional and independent levels may differ in the amount and type of instruction required if they are to demonstrate and apply various facilitative and functional reading abilities. Diagnosis in relation to each student's strengths and weaknesses is required for effective instruction. To accomplish this goal (step 7, figure 11–2), both Ms. Turner and Mr. Harris have the following options to choose from:

1. If a specific standardized test must be administered early in the school year, the results can be analyzed by using many of the alternative interpretation techniques detailed in chapter 5. This will assist the teachers in evaluating the validity of their instruction and will help identify areas in need of reteaching or continued emphasis.
2. If a criterion-referenced reading test must be administered during the school year, attention should be given to its validity and its overall quality. If the test is deemed appropriate, information related to levels of mastery can be used to identify instructional areas in need of attention.
3. To aid in the ongoing assessment of students' reading growth, the teachers can keep checklists on each student during the first few weeks of school and at appropriate intervals thereafter. Observation of students' performance is a powerful tool, and, combined with teacher-

developed assessment techniques, it can assist teachers in maintaining quality reading instruction.
4. The teachers can categorize strengths and weaknesses in the areas of word-recognition and comprehension from opportunities given to students to read orally excerpts from their reading materials (basal and library books). This can be done individually and at times that the teachers feel such information would be helpful in evaluating a student's reading development.

Both Ms. Turner and Mr. Harris are required by their school district to administer a criterion-referenced test during the first month of the school year. The test is valid in terms of the reading instructional program and is used to assist teachers in evaluating the placement of students in reading groups and identifying areas of needed instruction. Figure 11–2 provides a format with examples for showing the quantitative results of a criterion-referenced test.

Both teachers should try to obtain additional information. For some students it may be helpful to obtain an estimate of their optimum reading levels. Both teachers could use the techniques suggested in numbers three and four of the previous list to gather additional data on their

Step 7. Class Profile	Ms. Turner, Grade 2					Mr. Harris, Grade 6				
	Bob	Mike	Sharon	Wendy	Jerome	Harold	Bill	Anne	Maria	Tom
Instructional level	2^1	1	1	2^1	2^1	4	4	5	5	5
Consonants	+	√	√	+	+	+	+	+	+	+
Vowels—Long	+	√	√	+	+	+	+	+	+	+
Vowels—Short	+	−	√	+	+	+	+	+	+	+
Vowel principles	√	−	√	−	√	√	√	+	+	+
Syllabication	−	−	−	−	−	−	−	√	√	−
Consonant blends	√	−	√	√	−	√	+	+	+	√
Consonant digraphs	√	−	√	√	−	√	+	+	√	+
Vowel digraphs	−	−	−	−	−	−	√	√	√	√
Prefixes and suffixes	−	−	√	√	√	√	−	√	√	−
Root words	−	−	−	√	√	−	−	√	−	−
Endings	−	−	√	√	√	√	√	+	√	√
Basic sight vocabulary	√	−	−	√	√	+	+	+	+	+
Literal comprehension	−	−	−	√	√	√	√	+	+	√
Interpretive comprehension	−	−	−	−	−	√	√	−	√	√
Critical comprehension	−	−	−	−	−	−	−	−	−	−

+ very good √ adequate − needs help

FIGURE 11–2 Results of Criterion-Referenced Reading Test

students. While many schools and local media are concerned with the percentage of students reading at grade level, this is really irrelevant. The important point is whether or not all students are reading up to the limits of their abilities.

INDIVIDUALIZED INSTRUCTIONAL PROGRAM

The remaining steps in the process of diagnostic instruction can be viewed in terms of the four instructional variables—learner style, task conditions, resource attributes, and teacher style—needed to individualize reading instruction. At this point in the diagnostic process, both teachers are ready to identify individual students' strengths and weaknesses and to design an appropriate program of instruction.

Priority Decision Making

As a result of the previous steps, each teacher is aware of the range of instructional levels in the class, specific strengths and weaknesses in the various facilitative and functional reading abilities, and those students in need of corrective instruction. Using the information gathered, analyzed, and summarized for the students, both teachers are now ready to make decisions about each individual's strengths and weaknesses (learner style). Both teachers must also decide on instructional goals (based on individual strengths and weaknesses) for their students. This involves identifying those specific objectives that each student should be able to accomplish following instruction (task conditions).

In addition, the teachers are ready to decide on the number of reading groups based on the instructional reading levels of the students. To ensure an optimum amount of direct instruction and student time-on-task, a maximum of three or four groups for developmental reading purposes should be formed. Within these reading groups, specific skills and abilities, based on students' strengths and weaknesses, should be targeted for instructional emphasis. Strict adherence to a commercial reading system's sequence of reading skills and application is not recommended. Group instruction should be guided by student needs.

The teachers must now organize small instructional groups to teach specific skills and abilities to students in need of corrective help. It is axiomatic that students reading the same developmental reader will have different strengths and weaknesses. This type of grouping fulfills an instructional need and also increases student time-on-task.

Besides identifying specific instructional needs, the interests and attitudes of students will affect the mode of instruction. The decisions made in this step of the diagnostic process are labeled **diagnostic hypotheses**. These hypotheses are based on the students' learning needs and the teacher's ability to synthesize these needs into appropriate goals of instruction.

Preparation of Learning Environment and Teaching Approaches

Individualized instruction is implemented by translating diagnostic hypotheses into corrective hypotheses through the right combination of materials and teaching approaches. In this way, approaches and materials (resource attributes) will have nearly a one-to-one correspondence with diagnostic findings. Each classroom should have an abundance of instructional and recreational materials to meet the needs of students (learner style). When selecting resources to use in the classroom, the eight questions presented in chapter 3 can serve as a guide.

Both teachers are using the basal reading series as the primary method of instruction. However, the basal is not and should not be thought of as a complete reading program, regardless of the supplemental materials that accompany most programs. Both Ms. Turner and Mr. Harris might consider programmed reading, a language-experience approach, individualized reading, linguistic readers, and multimedia approaches as supplements to the basal program.

Whatever combination of approaches fits instructional goals, classroom organization should capitalize on different grouping patterns. Variety is essential for meeting goals and motivating students. Some types of grouping patterns that provide this variety are whole-class, small instructional groups, individual conference, interest groups, friendship groups, peer tutoring, and research groups.

Supplemental materials and approaches for learning facilitative and functional reading abilities should get particular attention in the primary grades. Since the basal will not be appropriate for all students' learning styles, an effort should be made to have programmed materials; additional phonic programs; multimedia materials, such as a language master, audiotapes on phonics, and sandpaper letters; language-experience materials; and books for recreational reading.

To meet the wide range of abilities in the content areas in the intermediate grades, supplemental materials should be obtained in the form of multigraded texts on similar topics and audiovisual equipment to supplement instruction.

Continuous Diagnosis

It has been stressed that diagnosis is the heart of all good teaching. A diagnostic attitude is necessary to collect relevant data on students during the first month of school. However, the need does not end there. This same diagnostic thinking is required every day of the year. A flexible reading program means that initial decisions regarding student strengths and weaknesses, materials, groups, approaches, and high-priority areas for instruction can and do change several times throughout the year (teacher style). Interacting with students and noting their styles and rates of learning will inevitably mean reshaping individual and group instructional goals.

The concept of continuous diagnosis depends on a team approach. Decisions regarding a student's program in reading should have input not only from the teacher but also the student, other people having significant contact with the student in the school (such as speech teacher, social worker, reading teacher, special education teacher, and principal), and the home. Folders on all students can be kept that contain samples of their work and notes on progress in the various facilitative and functional reading abilities. The samples in this folder may be used in an individual conference with the student to help assess past work and set new goals. This same folder could be shared with parents to inform them of progress and solicit their help with new goals. Open communication with all specialized teachers affecting the lives of students is a priority. Effective input regarding teaching approaches and materials can be attained by working closely with specialized personnel.

☐ SUMMARY

The diagnostic process of instruction was applied in this chapter through two classroom reading programs. Although the processes are identical for any grade level, the application of the model differs for primary and intermediate grades. Realizing that the teacher is the key to an effective reading program, teachers should first look at themselves and their programs before looking at their students. After looking inward, both example teachers collected and synthesized relevant data about their students before setting instructional goals. They reached initial decisions regarding reading levels, reading groups, and priority areas for instruction. A variety of materials and approaches were then selected to carry out instructional goals. Continuous diagnosis was seen to be an integral part of diagnostic teaching—beginning with the initial decisions and carrying through the year. Alternative ways of fulfilling various steps in the process were presented to illustrate the fact that there are numerous avenues for achieving a desired result. The individualization model was viewed as the guiding force in the actual "doing" of the diagnostic teaching of reading. Throughout the chapter, a flexible, thinking attitude characterized both teachers' implementations of the diagnostic process to accommodate varied student abilities.

☐ *IN-TEXT ASSIGNMENTS*

FIELD-BASED ACTIVITY

After obtaining permission from a local school, administer an IRI based on the school's reading program to a reading group in one classroom. Synthesize your data on each student and make recommendations for instruction.

LIBRARY ACTIVITY

The need of the classroom teacher to accommodate a wide range of learner needs was increased by the passage of the Education for All Handicapped Children Act (P.L. 94–142) of 1975. Read articles in the ERIC file and *The Reading Teacher* dealing with alternative ways of organizing instruction for meeting the needs of "gifted," "normal," and "'handicapped" students in the regular classroom. Report your findings to the class.

DISCUSS AND DEBATE

Have students react to the following statement:

While it is important to project a positive attitude and have high expectations for students, it is equally important to realize that some students may never read on "grade level."

Is this statement true or false? What is your opinion? What does this say to the classroom teacher?

12

Selection and Use of Instructional Resources for Corrective Reading Instruction

☐ OVERVIEW

Most of the students who need corrective reading instruction do not necessarily need to start over again from the beginning in their problem areas. Instead, they may need only short-term instruction in a particular area of reading development. This chapter focuses on the classroom teacher's selection and use of instructional resources (approaches, materials, and methods) for corrective reading instruction. It must be remembered, however, that methods, materials, and approaches alone do not determine the success of a reading program (see chapter 2). At present there is no set of materials, specific approach, or one best method that ensures that all students will read at their ability level. The major factor that determines a student's success in reading is the teacher's knowledge and use of instructional resources.

There are a number of resources for corrective reading instruction. It is important to critically evaluate, select, and modify these resources based on a student's individual reading needs. Through critical evaluation, teachers can review resources and select or adapt those that are best for particular students. Such a procedure allows for individualized corrective reading instruction. Resources can be selected for instruction because they match learning needs, not because they happen to be available in the classroom.

After reading this chapter, the teacher should be able to

☐ select analytically materials for corrective reading instruction by applying criteria.

☐ evaluate the major features of instructional resources and match these to the needs of students.

☐ select and combine instructional resources from a variety of sources.

☐ identify and use a variety of sources to stay current with available materials, approaches, and methods.

CRITERIA FOR SELECTING INSTRUCTIONAL RESOURCES

This text has emphasized the use of an individualized program that accommodates reading strengths *and* weaknesses. When selecting instructional resources, each part of a student's individualized program must be considered.

Learner Style

Resources chosen for corrective reading instruction should match the individual learner's style. Even though several students may experience similar reading problems, each may need different instructional resources. For example, both Kathy and Jim have problems comprehending literal information. Neither student can determine the main ideas of a story. Because their reading strengths and weaknesses are similar, their teacher could assume that both students would benefit from identical instructional resources. Jim, however, learns best in highly structured situations. Kathy, on the other hand, learns best when instruction focuses on the discovery of relationships. Instructional resources chosen for one student may not be appropriate for the other, even though they have similar reading problems. Therefore, materials, methods, and approaches should be evaluated and selected in relation to each student's specific needs.

Task Conditions

Task conditions are learning outcomes that students are to demonstrate. Instructional resources should deal specifically with behavioral objectives. The following instance illustrates the importance of evaluating resources to determine if they (1) deal directly with the desired reading outcome (product) and (2) match, or can be modified to match, the instructional procedures that are best for a student and the classroom environment.

Roger had problems comprehending the sequence of literal events in stories and their relationships to each other. One of the behavioral objectives identified by his teacher was correctly identifying the sequence of literal events occurring in given stories. An instructional activity to help Roger meet this objective was a seat-work task aimed at reinforcing and evaluating learning taught in a small-group setting. The seat-work task consisted of several short stories (two or three paragraphs in length), each on a separate sheet. Following each story were several literal events that Roger was to arrange in proper sequence by numbering them in their order of occurrence in the story. The first criterion—that the instructional resource deal directly with the desired reading outcome—was met. However, the instructional procedure was not the most suitable for Roger. One of the instructional procedures on Roger's individualized program noted that he learns best when provided with immediate feedback about his performance. Roger's teacher was not able to discuss his performance on the seat-work task until the next day. As a result, he was anxious about his performance and would often interrupt the teacher at inappropriate times to ask whether or not he had correctly completed his work. Thus this particular instructional resource was not best for Roger or the classroom environment.

Roger's teacher corrected the problem by simply preparing answer keys for each worksheet. After completing a worksheet, Roger scored his own performance and received the immediate feedback that he needed. In conjunction with scoring his own work, Roger's teacher found that he could correct many of his errors immediately. During discussion periods, Roger was better able to state why he had placed story events in a particular order.

Resource Attributes

Chapter 3 presented eight questions that teachers should ask themselves when selecting instructional resources. The important features of these questions can be used in a checklist. Figure 12–1 shows such a format.

The left-hand column of the cheklist contains general features of most instructional resources. Students in need of corrective reading instruction can be listed in the remaining columns. What features best meet individual students' needs are determined from the evaluation of diagnostic information. A check mark indicates a feature that instructional resources should possess if they are to meet an individual student's needs.

For example, based on Ann's individualized program, she needs to be introduced to a specific reading skill. The specific skill or skills, such as syllabication, would be noted on her program under reading weaknesses. It can be seen from the checklist that instructional resources have to allow for immediate application of the skill as it is taught. Furthermore, Ann learns best when resources are highly structured and emphasize relationships, and provisions need to be provided for extrinsic motivation either by the materials themselves or by teacher modification. The teacher will need to evaluate resources to determine if they do set specific purposes for learning (or can be made to do so) and if they show Ann how to apply what is taught. Finally, concrete examples should be an integral feature of the instructional resources selected.

By specifying features of instructional resources before they are selected, the teacher is better prepared to evaluate them. Ann's teacher can compare approach *A* with approach *B*, selecting the one that contains the necessary features or making whatever changes are needed. Such a process helps the teacher to focus on specific features of instructional resources in relation to the student's needs and to select them analytically.

Basic Features of Instructional Resources	Students
Purpose	Ann
1. Introduce	√
2. Reintroduce	
3. Extend	
4. Reinforce	
5. Repeat	
6. Apply	√
7. Verify (Diagnosis)	
Organization	
1. Small group	√
2. Large group	
3. Individual	√
4. Flexible	
5. Integration into new group	
Format	
1. Structured	√
2. Minimum structure	
3. Relationships	√

FIGURE 12–1 Checklist for Matching Features of Instructional Resources with the Needs of the Student

Teacher Style

Teacher style refers to the design of a plan of instruction that incorporates the information already gained about learner style, task conditions, and resource attributes. As daily instruction based on this plan is offered, the teacher continually assesses the students' learning. A major feature of such instruction is the selection of resources in terms of their appropriateness to the instructional plan.

Teachers must also take into account limiting conditions such as cost, time, availability, and familiarity. Often such limitations can be overcome, but they are important considerations having to do with the selection and use of instructional resources.

READABILITY

Readability is the approximate level of difficulty of a given text. It is important to be aware of the readability concept and attempt to match a

Basic Features of Instructional Resources	Students
4. Differences	
5. Sequential	√
6. Nonsequential	
7. Intermittent	
Motivation 1. Extrinsic	√
2. Intrinsic	
3. Set specific purposes for learning	√
4. Allow for immediate application	√
Learning mode 1. Concrete	√
2. Vicarious	
3. Abstract	
4. Visual	√
5. Auditory	√
6. Haptic	√
7. Integration of above	

FIGURE 12–1 *(continued)*

student's instructional level with the difficulty level in a particular text. What does it mean, for example, if a text has a 4.0 level of readability? It means simply that an average fourth grader with a known instructional level of fourth grade in that particular text could answer 70 percent of the questions a teacher might ask after he or she reads the material. The key phrase in the previous sentence, however, is "in that particular text."

In order to gauge the approximate level of difficulty of printed material, the teacher can employ both formal and informal means. There are numerous formulas to assess formally the readability of printed materials. The following are the most popular readability formulas in use today: Fry (1968), Dale-Chall (1948), Spache (1974), and Flesch (1948). These formulas usually estimate readability by examining sentence length and word difficulty. While formulas have the aura of precision about them and are relatively quick and easy to use, it is imperative to realize that formulas do not assess all factors that make texts difficult. For this reason, both the use of a formula and an informal appraisal of a text's readability are recommended. Cautioning against using readability formulas exclusively because formulas only look at sentence length and word length or difficulty, Koenke (1987) stated,

> The difficulty that readers have comprehending text is influenced by a myriad of factors, including syntactic complexity, concept density, abstractness, organization, coherence, sequence of ideas, page format, length of line of print, length of paragraph, punctuation, illustrations, color, and—most importantly—student interest. (p. 673)

Informal appraisal of a text's difficulty can more readily take into account several of Koenke's concerns in addition to your estimation of sentence length and word length or difficulty than can formal appraisal. An informal method of estimating the appropriateness of textbooks is recommended by Irvin and Davis (1980). Their readability checklist includes a means for rating the areas of understandability, learnability, reinforcement, and motivation.

As important as the concept of readability is to teachers of reading, the one major factor not included in most formal and informal means of appraisal is a determination of the type and quality of instruction to be provided by the teacher. This instruction will, to a large degree, affect how readable and thus how successful a student will be in reading a particular content text. An example of combining knowledge of a specific text characteristic with a teacher's ability to teach strategies to students to enhance understanding is McNeil's (1984) description of factors that impede sentence description. McNeil describes how sentences with passive voice patterns, appositives with commas, anaphoric relationships, connectives, punctuation, and figurative language can cause students difficulty in understanding sentences. With student awareness of these factors and explicit attention to these characteristics, text understanding can be increased. Another example of how the quality of instruction will affect readability is a teacher's attention to the readiness or motivation phase of teaching. The teacher's attention to motivating students to read a text by capitalizing on student interests, reviewing background experiences related to the text, reviewing key vocabulary and concepts, providing a purpose or purposes for reading, and using a graphic organizer will affect how well students read a particular text. Likewise, the teacher's ability to monitor the actual reading of the text, explain a concept to a student, and provide a summary statement of a section of text will also affect student success in reading a text. The effective teacher of reading modifies and adjusts educational materials to fit the needs of students. This last point clearly emphasizes the diagnosis-of-instruction step in the process of diagnostic teaching (see chapter 11).

RELATIONSHIP BETWEEN MATERIALS AND ACADEMIC LEARNING TIME

As discussed in chapter 2, academic learning time (ALT) involves three factors: allocating sufficient time for students to learn targeted content, ensuring that students are actively working at the task at hand, and ensuring that students are experiencing a high success rate with the materials in which they are working. Also, high-achieving classrooms in basic reading skill acquisition are characterized by having a high percentage of ALT. The ability to achieve a higher percentage of ALT is directly dependent on the proper selection and use of instructional materials. If students are to be actively engaged and experiencing a high success rate with their reading materials, the materials themselves must be on an appropriate level of difficulty (i.e., the student's instructional or independent level). Without attention to this consideration, it is virtually impossible for students to successfully complete assigned activities. Especially in the areas of corrective and remedial instruction, students need practice in which they experience a high amount of success. A high success rate means that students will answer at least 80 to 90 percent of practice items correctly. To achieve this goal, the materials chosen for practice should be on an easy level of understanding.

In addition to the readability or difficulty level of reading materials, teachers need to monitor students' work in reading materials. The benefits of monitoring students' progress in completing reading exercises include assessing which students are understanding the task and those having difficulty, providing corrective feedback immediately, and maintaining a high percentage of time-on-task.

Student mastery of reading skills and the ability to transfer such skills to independent situations are directly related to the effective use of instructional materials. A helpful framework in which to view the proper use of materials to achieve your instructional goals centers on the three areas of planning, delivering, and evaluating practice activities (Blair & Rupley, 1988). The following is a list of these three areas with key concerns for each area.

Planning

Matching materials to instructional goals

Varying the type of organizational structure in which the material will be used in relation to student needs

Delivering

Completing a few practice items with students to ensure clarity and understanding

Setting up beforehand a means by which students can get help when needed

Monitoring student completion of assigned tasks

Evaluating

Determining if students accomplished the intended instructional goal

Noting a student's pattern of incorrect responses

ADDITIONAL CONSIDERATIONS IN CHOOSING RESOURCES

All instructional resources should possess certain features. Materials that take into account students' interests and background experiences help to motivate and encourage attention to the learning task and better ensure that students will comprehend what they read. Approaches that address students' needs by building on reading strengths will probably be more successful than those that focus only on weaknesses. Finally, the effectiveness of instructional resources should be determined through ongoing diagnosis, which helps the teacher determine the effectiveness of instructional resources in relation to each student's progress. Minimal progress could relate directly to loss of interest, confusion, and other problems resulting from a poor choice of resources. When students exhibit minimal progress, the teacher should re-evaluate instructional resources; then, based on the re-evaluation, the teacher can modify resources or select different resources.

COMPUTERS IN THE CLASSROOM

Computers have become an integral part of our lives. With the advent of **microcomputers** (self-contained terminals with a keyboard, a display unit, and a computer), the microcomputer revolution is sweeping through classrooms across the country (Blanchard, Mason, & Daniel, 1987). Educational software (computer programs on a variety of subjects) range from business management to recreational games to educational programs in reading, math, and science.

Microcomputers in educational settings can be used as both a management tool and a medium of instruction. In a management function, microcomputers can be used by teachers to do descriptive statistics, administer diagnostic tests, score and store test data, and prescribe an individualized program for students detailing instructional objectives and materials. As a medium of instruction (commonly referred to as computer-assisted instruction or CAI), the microcomputer can be used to reinforce basic skills in reading by providing varied drill-and-practice activities; these simulation and problem-solving programs foster critical thinking. Initial research findings indicate that CAI does have a positive influence on student achievement (O'Donnell, 1982; Schaudt, 1987).

In providing extra practice on basic skills in reading, a typical sequence on a microcomputer would include the presentation of an exercise to be completed by the student, the student's response to the question, and immediate feedback regarding the accuracy of the response. Depending on the correctness of the student's response, either a new exercise appears or the computer provides further practice. This sequence is not carried out until a pretest has been given and an individual prescription has been designed for each student.

Microcomputers will never replace teachers, but they can greatly assist teachers in the instructional process. Advantages of the microcomputer include:

- ☐ Enhancing student interaction and motivation
- ☐ Providing immediate feedback
- ☐ Providing record-keeping capabilities
- ☐ Providing needed reinforcement
- ☐ Allowing self-paced instruction
- ☐ Freeing the teacher to work with other students while some students work on the computer
- ☐ Increasing academic learning time
- ☐ Enhancing the automacity level for decoding skills

The necessity for an abundance of drill and practice on basic word-identification and comprehension skills in a corrective or remedial situation is greater than average. Students need to know the basic reading skills on an automatic level in order to attend more fully to comprehending the ideas of the writer. While workbooks and dittos can provide practice to foster automacity, drill-and-practice software programs for microcomputers have advantages over the traditional workbook. Rude (1986) feels that two of these advantages are (1) CAI allows students on different instructional levels to work simultaneously on the same software package, and (2) computer software has the ability to randomly select items for various practice sessions in different sequences which reduces the chance of boredom.

Reading teachers should realize that the microcomputer has an extraordinary capacity to help them and their students if it is used correctly. As is the case with any new material or resource, the microcomputer should be viewed as a facilitator in the learning process directly under the control of the teacher. The microcomputer can and should be used when it can assist in the fulfillment of instructional goals based on student needs. Also, as it the case with any new material, the quality and capability of educational software should be assessed by teachers trying out the programs before subjecting their students to them.

Figure 12–2 on page 295 presents a reading software guide, examining the type of program, ease of use, instructional design, content accuracy, and special features. Computers are becoming commonplace in many schools; teachers of reading need to exercise control over how they are used to meet instructional goals.

CATEGORIES OF READING MATERIALS

Materials for teaching reading may be grouped into five main categories: (1) the core program and accompanying materials (usually the basal reader, workbooks, word and picture cards, and related activities); (2) supplemental commercial reading kits, dittos, and games; (3) literature books; (4) functional materials (i.e., newspapers, magazines, periodicals); and (5) teacher-made materials. With the great variety of materials available, it takes careful planning to select the appropriate mixture of materials to advance instructional goals.

USING THE NEWSPAPER

Oddly enough, of the five major types of materials to use in corrective and remedial situations, functional materials such as the newspaper are utilized the least as supplemental materials. Yet, functional materials are an

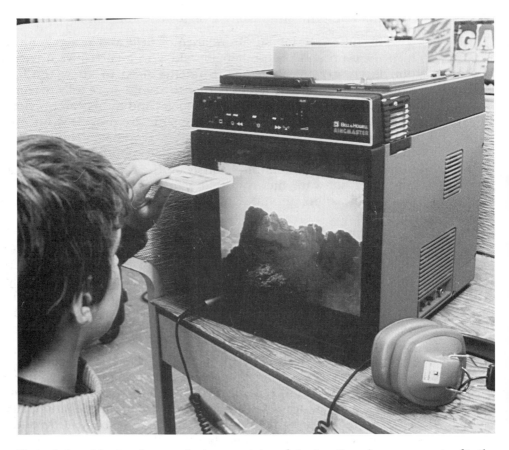

Knowledgeable teachers select a variety of instructional resources to fit the reading needs of their students. (Bell & Howell/Merrill)

excellent source for teaching and practicing reading skills and aiding the transfer of reading skills to new situations. Rowls (1987) feels that the use of the newspaper helps teachers deal with the crucial issues of "currency

	Poor	Good	Adequate
Type of Program			
____drill and practice	____	____	____
____tutorial	____	____	____
____simulation	____	____	____
____learning game	____	____	____
Ease of Use/User Friendly			
clear directions	____	____	____
exit capabilities	____	____	____
control of pacing	____	____	____
provision of help	____	____	____
Instructional Design			
objective made clear to student	____	____	____
introductory explanation of skill	____	____	____
sample exercises	____	____	____
number of practice exercises	____	____	____
immediate and varied feedback	____	____	____
branching capability	____	____	____
built-in assessment of progress	____	____	____
monitoring of student responses	____	____	____
corrections made by reteaching, giving clues, or explaining skill	____	____	____
summary statement	____	____	____
length of program	____	____	____
appropriate difficulty level	____	____	____
Content Accuracy			
direct correspondence between lesson objective and lesson procedures	____	____	____
accuracy	____	____	____
procedures reflect what a reader has to do in the process of reading	____	____	____
correct sequence used in presenting skill	____	____	____
Special Features			
animation	____	____	____
speech	____	____	____
music	____	____	____
laser videodiscs	____	____	____
touch screen	____	____	____
graphics	____	____	____
audio	____	____	____
color	____	____	____

FIGURE 12–2 Reading Software Evaluation Guide

and timeliness (and therefore interest level) of materials and teachers' tendencies to be over-reliant on textbooks and packaged programs for teaching reading." The daily newspaper is not only a wealth of useful information on a range of subjects, but also is an excellent supplemental material to use in the teaching of reading. Aaron (1984) concurs with this idea: "Newspapers are among the best supplementing instructional materials available to teachers of reading and teachers in subject areas."

The major areas of reading instruction that can be developed using the newspaper include:

Word meaning (synonyms, antonyms, homonyms, vocabulary growth)

Word analysis (plurals, prefixes, suffixes, root words, contractions, abbreviations, contextual clues, phonic analysis)

Literal comprehension (recalling facts, main ideas, sequence of events)

Interpretative comprehensive (making inferences, identifying relationships)

Evaluative comprehension (determining fact and opinion, identifying an author's purpose, criticizing data, forming an opinion)

Study skills (locating information; scanning and skimming; reading charts, graphs, and maps)

Also, students can pursue personal interests (i.e., stock market; sports; advertising; science; weather forecasting; entertainment; local, state, national, and international events) and perhaps most important, using the newspaper as a reading tool may encourage students to develop the habit of daily newspaper reading. Direct-instruction lessons on specific skills can be developed around the newspaper and other abilities can be illustrated, practiced, and extended using various parts and/or features of the newspaper.

An excellent source for how to use the newspaper for teaching reading, which includes numerous practical suggestions, is the IRA publication *Teaching Reading Skills through the Newspaper* by Cheyney (1984). In addition, the American Newspaper Publishers Association (Reston, VA) distributes various materials to help teachers use newspapers to teach reading; this resource includes creative ideas and lesson and unit plans for various grade levels. In most cases, individual newspaper publishers will distribute educational packets free of charge and offer a special school subscription rate.

COMMERCIAL MATERIALS

When deciding which materials to select for corrective or remedial instruction, it is helpful to have available a sample listing of materials for various purposes. The following is a partial listing of commercial materials designed for specific purposes.

Reading Readiness

Alpha Time (Artista Corporation)

Sesame Street Pre-Reading Kit (Addison-Wesley)

Peabody Language Development Kit (American Guidance Service)

CAI Software

Getting Reading to Read and Add (Minnesota Educational Computing Consortium [MECC])

Letter Recognition (Hartley)

Computer Animated Reading

Instruction System (Britannica Computer-Based Learning)

Early Words (Merry Bee Communications)

Core or Main Programs

Basal Reader Systems (e.g., basals published by Houghton Mifflin, Ginn, Harper & Row, Scott Foresman)

Reading Skill Builders (Reader's Digest Services)

Merrill Linguistic Reading Program (Merrill)

Language Experiences Approach (*See* Hall, M. [1981]. *Teacher reading as a language experience*, Columbus, OH: Merrill.)

High Interest–Low Vocabulary Series

Breakthrough (Allyn and Bacon)

Jamestown Classics (Jamestown Publishers)

Young Adventure Series (Bowman)

Racing Wheels Series (Benefic)

Pacemaker True Adventures (Fearon)

CAI Software

Pal Reading Curriculum (Universal Systems for Education)

Reading Curriculum (Computer Curriculum Corporation)

Windows To Reading (Micro-Ed)

Micro-Read (American Educational Computer)

Word Identification

Primary Phonics (Educators Publishing Services)

Consonant Lotto (Garrard)

Phonetic Word Analyzer (Milton Bradley)

63 Webster Word Wheels (Webster/McGraw-Hill)

Merrill Phonics Skilltext Series (Merrill)

Phonics Is Fun (Modern Curriculum Press)

Working with Sounds (Barnell Loft)

Schoolhouse Kits (Science Research Associates)

Context-Phonetic Clues (Curriculum Associates)

CAI Software

MECC-Elementary (MECC)

SAT Word Attack Skills (Edu-Ware)

Homonyms (Hartley)

Homonyms (Milliken)

Vowels (Hartley)

Word Master (Developmental Learning Materials)

Vocabulary-Dolch (Hartley)

Vocabulary-Elementary (Hartley)

Antonyms and Synonyms (Hartley)

Homonyms in Context (Random House—School Division)

Computer Drill and Instruction: Phonics (Science Research Associates)

Context Clues (Learning Well)

Comprehension

Reading for Understanding (Science Research Associates)

SRA Reading Laboratories (Science Research Associates)

Starting Comprehension: Stories To Advance Reading and Thinking (Educators Publishing Service)

Beginning Reasoning and Reading (Educators Publishing Service)

Sports Reading Series (Bowman/Noble)

Reading Skills Kit (Zaner-Bloser)

Clues for Better Reading (Curriculum Associates)

Reading Reinforcement Skilltext Series (Merrill)

Reading Comprehension Series (Steck-Vaughn)

Specific Skill Series (Barnell-Loft)

Single Skills: A Concentration and Comprehension Series (Jamestown Publishers)

Reading Reinforcement Skilltext Series (Merrill)

CAI Software

Cloze Plus (Milliken)

Sentence Combining (Milliken)

Comprehension Power (Milliken)

Troll's Tale and Dragon's Keep (Sierra On-Line)

Story Machine (Spinnaker)

Story Maker (Bolt, Beranek, and Newman)

Critical Reading (Borg-Warner Educational Systems)

Four Basic Reading Skills (Brain Box)

Getting the Main Idea (Learning Well)

Descriptive Reading (Educational Activities)

Vocabulary

Worldly Wise (Educators Publishing Service)

Vocabulary Fluency (Curriculum Associates)

Talking Picture Dictionary (Troll)

Picto-Vocabulary Series (Barnell-Loft)

Basic Sight Words (Garrard)

CAI Software

Vocabulary-Elementary (Hartley)

Vocabulary-Dolch (Hartley)

Create-Vocabulary (Hartley)

The Vocabulary Game (J&S Software)

Vocabulary Skills (Milton Bradley)

Word Prep (Micro Power and Light)

Study Skills

EDL Study Skills Library (Educational Development Laboratories)

Research & Study Skills Centers (Curriculum Associates)

Organizing and Reporting Skills Kit (Science Research Associates)

Target Purple—Study Skills Kit (Addison-Wesley)

CAI Software

How To Read in the Content Areas (Educational Activities)

Library Skills (Micro Power and Light)

Recreational Reading

Pleasure Reading Books (Garrard)

Illustrated Classics (Pendulum Press)

New American Library (Books For Young Adverts)

Gold Dust Books (Bowman/Noble)

Quicksilver Books (Bowman/Noble)

Walker Plays (Curriculum Associates)

Scholastic Literature Kits (Scholastic Book Service)

Scholastic Pleasure Reading Library (Scholastic Book Service)

CAI Software

Reading Is Fun (Tandy/Radio Shack)

Magic Wand Books (Texas Instruments)

Newberry Winners (Sunburst Communications)

INFORMATION ON INSTRUCTIONAL RESOURCES

Teachers can stay current with new materials, keep informed about the effectiveness of reading approaches, and identify promising methods through a variety of sources.

Professional Associations and their Publications

The International Reading Association (800 Barksdale Rd., Newark, DE 19711) publishes several professional journals including *The Reading Teacher, Journal of Reading,* and *Reading Research Quarterly.* Also available are professional books, including the Reading Aids Series, which offer practical suggestions for improving instructional practices.

The journal *Reading Research and Instruction* and other monographs addressing topics of particular interest to the classroom teacher are published by the College Reading Association (Rochester Institute of Technology, One Lomb Memorial Drive, Rochester, NY 14623).

The National Council of Teachers of English (1111 Kenyon Road, Urbana, IL 61801) publishes the journal *Language Arts* and other books that offer practical suggestions for classroom reading and language arts instruction.

Professional Textbooks

Some excellent professional textbooks discuss the use and features of various instructional resources. They include *Principles and Practices of Teaching Reading* (Heilman, Blair, & Rupley, 1986); *Teaching Them To Read* (Durkin, 1983); *Approaches To Beginning Reading* (Auckerman, 1984); and *Self-correcting Learning Materials* (Mercer, Mercer, & Bott, 1984).

In addition, most commercial publishing companies are more than willing to put teachers on their mailing lists. Catalogs and informative brochures that describe available materials are an invaluable source for staying current with the large number of reading instructional materials available. Many publishing companies will also send a sales representative to demonstrate and describe their materials to interested teachers.

Another valuable source of information on instructional resources is the ERIC Clearinghouse on Reading and Communication Skills. Transcripts of speeches, papers, program descriptions, inservice and preservice workshop materials, conference proceedings, research reports, experimental studies, and educational journal articles are included in monthly publications of *Resources in Education* (RIE). A large number of these documents detail the use, selection, and evaluation of instructional resources.

A useful, two-volume report to aid teachers in the evaluation and selection of instructional materials is published by the Educational Products Information Exchange (EPIE) Institute (475 Riverside Drive, New York, New York 10027).

Reading Conferences

Reading conferences at the state, local, and national levels are other valuable sources of information. Papers presented by reading authorities, classroom teachers, and school administrators frequently address the selection, use, and effectiveness of many instructional resources.

Commercial publishers of reading materials often display their products at reading conventions. Representatives are available to demonstrate the use of these materials, distribute informative literature and catalogs, and answer questions.

☐ SUMMARY

Instructional resources are chosen and used for corrective reading instruction because they match students' learning needs. The process of selection is an analytic one. Diagnostic evaluations of individual students are used to determine the necessary features of instructional resources. Criteria that are applied to the available instructional resources come from each portion of the individualized program developed for each student or group of students. Information about learner style, task conditions, resource attributes, and teacher style is matched as closely as possible to the instructional resources.

Staying current with instructional resources can be accomplished by reading professional journals and interacting with other professionals. When teachers consider whether or not to use a specific approach or to buy a set of materials, they should ask several questions:

☐ Can it be used with individuals as well as groups?
☐ Would it motivate student interest?
☐ Is it structured or unstructured?
☐ Does it contain concrete or abstract examples?

☐ Could it be used as a basic means of instruction or as a supplement?
☐ Can it be modified or must it be used as suggested?

Such questions go beyond face value and lead to an analytical evaluation of instructional resources.

☐ IN-TEXT ASSIGNMENTS

LIBRARY ACTIVITY

Have students examine the ERIC files for recent investigations regarding the basal reader approach, the language-experience approach, and the use of CAI to teach reading. Students should summarize five reports on 3″ × 5″ cards and share their findings with the class.

FIELD-BASED ACTIVITY

Arrange an interview with a local elementary teacher. Let the teacher provide the class with actual data on three or four corrective readers in their class. A discussion should follow detailing approaches and materials to use with each student.

ROLE-PLAYING ACTIVITY

Divide students into several small groups to critically examine a basal reader series. In a role-playing situation, have each group represent the company's salespeople and argue for the adoption of their series. Encourage the rest of the class to ask critical questions of each basal promoter.

DESIGN ACTIVITY

Have students design and produce a series of self-correctional games and activities for either word-identification or comprehension skills. Students need to specify an objective for each game or activity and intended grade level (primary or intermediate).

☐ REFERENCES

Aaron, I.E. (1984). *Teaching reading skills through the newspaper* (2nd ed.). Reading Aids Series. Newark, DE: International Reading Association.

Aukerman, R.C. (1984). *Approaches to beginning reading.* New York: Wiley.

Blair, T.R. & Rupley, W.R. (1988). Practice and application in the teaching of reading. *The Reading Teacher, 41,* 536–539.

Blanchard, J.S., Mason, G.E., & Daniel, D. (1987). *Computer applications in reading* (3rd ed.). Newark, DE: International Reading Association.

Cheyney, A.B. (1984). *Teaching reading skills through the newspaper* (2nd ed.). Reading Aids Series. Newark, DE: International Reading Association.

Dale, E. & Chall, J.S. (1948). A formula for predicting readability. *Educational Research Bulletin, 27,* 11–20, 28, 37–54. Columbus, OH: Bureau of Educational Research, Ohio State University.

Durkin, D. (1983). *Teaching them to read.* Boston: Allyn & Bacon.

Flesch, R. (1948). A new readability yardstick. *Journal of Applied Psychology, 32,* 221.

Fry, E. (1968). A readability formula that saves time. *Journal of Reading, 11,* 513–516.

Hall, M. (1981). *Teaching reading as a language experience.* Columbus, OH: Merrill.

Heilman, A.W., Blair, T.R., & Rupley, W.H. (1986). *Principles and practices of teaching reading.* Columbus, OH: Merrill.

Irwin, J.W. & Davis, C.A. (1980). Assessing readability: The checklist approach. *Journal of Reading, 24,* 124–130.

Koenke, K. (1987). ERIC/RCS: Readability formulas: Use and misuse. *The Reading Teacher, 40,* 672–677.

McNeil, J.D. (1984). *Reading comprehension: New directions for classroom practice.* Glenview, IL: Scott, Foresman.

Mercer, C.D., Mercer A.R., & Bott, D.A. (1984). *Self-correcting learning materials for the classroom.* Columbus, OH: Merrill.

O'Donnell, H. (1982). ERIC/RCS: Computer literacy, part II: Classroom applications. *The Reading Teacher, 35,* 614–619.

Rowls, M. (1987). Personal communication, University of South Carolina.

Rude, R.T. (1986). *Teaching reading using microcomputers.* Englewood Cliffs, NJ: Prentice-Hall.

Schaudt, B. (1987). Selected research in computer-assisted instruction in reading. In R. Zellner, J. Denton, M. Berger, & R. Kansky (Eds.), *Technology in education: Application and implications* (pp. 60–65). College Station, TX: Instructional Research Laboratory, College of Education, Texas A&M University.

Spache, G.D. (1974). The Spache readability formula. In G.D. Spache (Ed.), *Good reading for poor readers.* Champaign, IL: Garrard.

13

Exceptional Children in the Classroom

☐ *OVERVIEW*

Found in almost every classroom, exceptional children range from those with moderate to severe learning problems to those with advanced learning abilities. For such students to receive maximum benefits from their instruction, classroom programs that contain additional or different features are generally necessary.

The importance of meeting the needs of exceptional children is reinforced by growing emphases on learning disabilities, mainstreaming, and gifted programs.

This chapter focuses on diagnostic procedures and instructional planning for children with learning problems and for intellectually gifted children. With modification, most of the diagnostic and instructional procedures already presented in this text are appropriate for exceptional children.

After reading this chapter, the teacher should be able to

☐ identify the characteristics of exceptional children.
☐ select analytically and use diagnostic instruments and procedures to identify exceptional children's reading strengths and weaknesses.
☐ evaluate critically materials appropriate to the reading needs of exceptional children.
☐ organize reading instruction to meet the needs of exceptional children.
☐ develop an individualized program appropriate to the reading strengths and weaknesses of exceptional children.

CHILDREN WITH LEARNING PROBLEMS

Emphasis on learning problems as a possible cause of reading problems has broadened within the last 20 years. To understand this trend and its importance in classroom reading diagnosis, teachers must know what characteristics are associated with the general term *learning problems* and the more specific term *learning disabilities.* Many conditions, such as a mild hearing or visual impairment, may certainly result in learning problems. Likewise, conditions of economic or environmental deprivation may result in a learning problem. However, these conditions do not fall under the umbrella of learning disabilities because they point to a "cause" of a learning problem. The term *learning disabilities* only designates a result—usually poor academic performance—not a cause (Gearheart & Weishahn, 1980). The following sections present an overview of learning problems and learning disabilities with a focus on descriptions, evidence to support various theories, the nature of the treatments suggested, and the difference, if any, between these treatments and corrective reading instruction for the "normal" child.

MAINSTREAMING EXCEPTIONAL CHILDREN

The practice of placing exceptional children in special, segregated classes is being replaced by the growing trend toward **mainstreaming**—or placing them in regular classrooms. The Education for All Handicapped Children Act of 1975 (P.L. 94–142) mandates that specially designed instruction to meet the unique needs of handicapped children can and should include, when appropriate, instruction in a regular classroom. Under this law, the term *handicapped* includes the deaf, deaf-blind, hard of hearing, mentally retarded, multihandicapped, orthopedically impaired, other health impaired, seriously emotionally disturbed, specific learning disabled, speech impaired, and the visually handicapped. The law states:

> Handicapped children, including children in public or private institutions or other care facilities, are educated with children who are not handicapped, and that special classes, separate schooling, or other removal of handicapped children from the regular educational environment occurs only when the nature or severity of the handicap is such that education in regular classes with the use of supplementary aids and services cannot be achieved satisfactorily.

Thus, the law requires that handicapped children be placed in the "least restrictive environment" in which they can succeed. Many times this means placement in the regular classroom; however, mainstreaming does not mandate the wholesale return of all exceptional children to regular classrooms. An integral part of the law is the requirement for an Individual Educational Plan (IEP) to be developed for each handicapped child. The IEP must include a statement of the student's present level of achievement, annual goals, instructional objectives, materials needed to achieve the objectives, educational services to be provided to the student, and evaluation procedures.

The success or failure of mainstreaming rests with the classroom teacher. Of course, a team approach including the parents, reading specialist, special education specialist, principal, and classroom teacher is absolutely necessary in planning and delivering appropriate instruction. However, the classroom teacher's attitude and skills—his or her ability to accommodate all students successfully in the classroom—is the key difference. Classroom teachers and reading teachers need not feel unqualified to deal successfully with handicapped children. The same good diagnostic strategies and techniques used with "normal" children can form the basis for instruction geared to the needs of exceptional children. The model of individualization described in chapter 3 and illustrated throughout the text is an excellent guide for writing an IEP for each student in the classroom.

LEARNING DISABILITY CHARACTERISTICS

There is a general lack of agreement on what constitutes a learning disability. In 1977, the U.S. Congress adopted a definition of learning disabled children that highlights some of the basic characteristics associated with learning disabilities. **Learning disabled children** are those who have disorders in one or more of the processes involved in using language, spoken or written, which may manifest itself in an imperfect ability to listen, think, speak, read, write, spell, or do mathematical calculations. Such disorders include conditions such as perceptual handicaps, brain injury, minimal brain dysfunction, dyslexia, and developmental aphasia. The term *learning disabled* does not include children with learning problems that are primarily the result of visual, hearing, or motor handicaps; mental retardation or emotional disturbance; or environmental, cultural, or economic disadvantage (Meier, 1980).

Because this definition uses terms that are vague and poorly defined in the existing literature (*dyslexia, minimal brain dysfunction, perceptual handicaps,* and so forth), it is difficult for teachers to apply it, with any degree of reliability, to children in their classrooms. However, this definition does exclude children whose problems are related to factors such as cultural and physical impairments (sight and hearing). Despite this lack of any specific consensus, there is some sense of general agreement among special educators that children with learning disabilities have a discrepancy between their expected and actual achievement (Blackhurst & Berdine, 1981).

Due to the fact that a variety of signs and symptoms are assumed to characterize learning problems and learning disabilities, teachers should be sensitive to the fact that there is no set of symptoms that clearly define a learning disability. Signs and symptoms of a learning disability may be apparent in some children and yet not indicate a learning disability. Conversely, symptoms are often hidden in other children. Bright children who are working only at an average level may be using their above-average abilities to mask a learning disability. Nevertheless, foremost in diagnosing learning problems and learning disabilities is discovering the significance of observed symptoms and their relationship to a student's learning performance.

Motor Development

Some children may respond to all environmental stimuli. They are often totally involved with their environment and, as a result, appear to be impulsive. Impulsive behavior of this type has been frequently called **hyperactivity.** Such behavior may be exhibited in instructional settings by a short attention span, distractibility, restlessness, and exaggerated behavior. It deviates noticeably from what is considered average for other children at the same specific age level. It is important to remember that all children exhibit such behaviors from time to time; however, when these behaviors become excessive and occur frequently over periods of time, they can indicate a learning problem. Whether or not the children who exhibit such behaviors are identified as learning disabled is really not the issue. Such hyperactive behavior can be a contributing factor to a child's lack of success in learning to read. Teachers of reading should be concerned about hyperactivity, because some students having reading problems are also hyperactive (Weinberg & Rehmet, 1983).

Treatment for hyperactive children varies from drug treatment to diet management. The most commonly recommended treatment is using the drug Ritalin (Cotter & Werner, 1987). Ritalin (methylphenidate) is a stimulant that conversely has the effect of a depressant on some hyperactive children. The manufacturer of the drug, however, indicates that when used to treat hyperactivity that is a result of environmental problems or psychiatric disorders, its use is inappropriate. There is little evidence that the use of Ritalin improves students' reading performance (Gittelman, 1985). As a matter of fact, its use is insignificant in relation to minimizing the effect of hyperactivity on the student's reading development.

Because the use of Ritalin in treating hyperactive children is so widespread, reading teachers should be aware of the following implications (Cotter & Werner, 1987):

1. Teachers should recommend to parents that the use of Ritalin might be beneficial only after careful and extended observations of a student's behavior in various settings and his or her performance in a variety of learning situations.

2. Teachers should play an active role in communicating to parents and physicians all available diagnostic information to assist in making a careful and accurate diagnosis.
3. Teachers should be aware of and monitor closely the differential effects of various dosages on the child's classroom behavior and performance. The child should be continually observed so that the doctor and parents can be informed if the prescribed dosage is inappropriate.
4. Teachers should fully realize that the use of Ritalin will not automatically improve reading performance, and can, in some instances, even inhibit reading performance. The student will require quality reading instruction in a supportive environment for his or her reading capabilities to improve.

Reading instructional strategies and practice for hyperactive students should be developed within a highly structured environment. Attention should be given to timed activities that students can complete in a structured fashion and in which immediate feedback and reinforcement of appropriate behaviors can be provided. In addition, many of the features discussed in chapter 2 are appropriate for helping such students attend to instructional tasks: (1) setting purposes and modeling the appropriate reading skill or ability; (2) using extraneous rewards to enhance attention to tasks; (3) developing activities that progress in small, highly related steps; and (4) monitoring closely the amount of engaged time so that the task matches the student's ability to attend to it.

Specific strategies for improving the reading abilities of hyperactive students are based on teaching them to self-monitor their problem-solving strategies and to modify their attention problems (Gentile, Lamb, & Rivers, 1985). Strategies such as providing students with a list of steps to follow when completing reading activities, charts that graphically display both their learning and behavior performances, checklists to use in evaluating completed activities, and questions to help determine what is known or not known about a story or task have been shown to be effective in helping to improve hyperactive students' academic performance (Douglas, 1980; Keogh & Barkett, 1980).

Behavior that is the exact opposite of an impulsive child's reaction to the environment can also signal a learning problem. **Hypoactivity,** or an activity level that is less than average, can affect the way children learn. While hypoactivity is a less common form of learning disability, such behavior, when it deviates extremely from the average student's behavior for a specific age, can suggest the presence of a learning problem. In the school setting, hypoactive children often exhibit a diminished response to their environment; they are difficult to motivate and appear uninterested in the majority of classroom activities. Furthermore, such children may be rejected socially. They frequently learn as little from their social experiences as they do from their school experiences. Often these children are labeled as intellectually slow or retarded. Their problem is not generally due to an intelligence deficiency, however, but to a learning problem necessitating instructional practices that differ from those typically used with the majority of children.

Another area of motor behavior that may signal a learning problem is poor coordination. Children who often appear to lack coordination in large muscle tasks may have a learning problem. They may exhibit problems in synchronizing their large muscles and so "stand out" from the rest of the students as being clumsy. Jerry, for example, was noticed by his gym teacher as a child who lagged considerably behind the average second grader in coordination. Jerry's arm and leg movements were not synchronized when he ran. The gym teacher described him as a child whose whole body just seemed to be out of control. In addition, when asked to bounce or catch a ball, he would let the ball pass by him or roll away and would remain standing with his arms outstretched to catch it or his hand moving up and down as if he were still bouncing it.

Difficulty with fine muscle tasks is also often associated with learning problems. Children who cannot perform fine motor tasks, such as writing, printing, drawing, copying, and tracing, may have learning problems. Brandy's inability to coordinate her fine motor skills was the major factor that led her teacher to suspect she had a learning problem. Figure 13–1 presents an example of Brandy's performance in a copying task. Although it is never wise to rely on only one example as justification for referring a child for extensive diagnosis, it does show that Brandy's ability deviates considerably from the average first grader. Furthermore, P.L. 94–142 requires the use of several evaluation instruments and the opinions of several trained individuals to identify a child with a learning handicap.

Brandy's copying performance could be due to a lack of fine muscle control or to an inability to interpret visual stimuli. Difficulties with buttoning a shirt, sorting marbles into jars, placing pegs in a pegboard, and other fine motor tasks would substantiate that her problem is related to a lack of fine muscle control. However, if problems are not noted with fine motor tasks, her copying performance could result from an inability to interpret visual stimuli.

Inability to coordinate fine muscle movements can be related to visual perception problems that make it hard for children to interpret accurately what they see. Often learning disabled children have problems judging the relationship of objects to each other and themselves (Brutten, Richardson, & Mangel, 1979). For example, Abrams (1970) cites problems in directionality and difficulties in concentration when dealing with words or abstract stimuli. The child may be unable to tie the individual stimulus parts into a whole. Characteristic of this is a lack of integration between vision and movement. Each sense seems to operate independently of the others, and no one sense serves as an adequate guide for integration.

Objects to copy:

Brandy's performance:

FIGURE 13–1 Sample Drawings by a Child with an Inability to Perform Fine Motor Tasks

Language Development

Disorders of language and thought development are among the more serious behaviors that characterize a learning problem. As discussed in chapter 4, the related processes of language and thought develop together in most children. Conclusions and representations children form about their environment are based on the concepts and ideas they receive through their senses. These conclusions and representations are important in their cognitive development. In some children, sensory impressions do not form into meaningful information. This problem is due, in a large part, to language problems related to auditory-perceptual difficulties.

Several symptoms are indicative of learning difficulties associated with language problems. The major difficulties include linking what was heard with what the message means, remembering what was heard, patterning or modeling the speech of others, and finding words to express ideas.

Children who have difficulty linking what they hear with the meaning of a message are said to have a **central auditory imperception.** Symptoms associated with this problem are evidenced by a difficulty with oral language comprehension. There may not, however, be a loss in hearing acuity. Thus the problem is not hearing what is said, but processing it. An example of this problem is described by Hirt (1970, p. 307). She relates an incident that occurred during the diagnostic evaluation of a child when he was asked to describe his mother. The examiner asked the child, "What is your mother like?" The child replied "Steak." Hirt comments, "In another context this would be perfectly appropriate. He was not getting the contractual, 'What is your mother like?' He was hearing 'What does your mother like?' and did not realize it was inappropriate to the line of questioning."

Another symptom of auditory imperception is **auditory span**, which refers to the ability to remember what is heard. Children who have impaired auditory span recall only a minimal number of words in a spoken message. In reading, this may manifest itself as an inability to remember the sequence of sounds within a word. Wilkin's research (1969) indicates that there are considerable interrelationships among auditory discrimination, auditory synthesis, and auditory span. This suggests that children experiencing severe difficulty with auditory span will not make much progress with a reading approach that emphasizes letter-sound relationships (that is, phonics) unless they are given intensive auditory training. Wilkin also observes that variability in auditory perception is present not only among children with learning disabilities, but also among normal children; therefore, caution should be exercised in concluding from a limited assessment of auditory perception that a child has a learning problem. Tests can help identify children who need to be closely observed in various language settings. Those children who differ drastically from the average-age child would require further diagnosis by a speech therapist.

Auditory imperception is a perceptual problem that does not allow children to comprehend spoken language. Often such problems are misinterpreted by parents and teachers, who may believe that such behavior is due to inattention or to never listening. An auditory-perceptual problem does not mean that children do not hear what is said. In fact, the auditory acuity is usually within normal range, but the children have problems processing the message. Both of these problems relate to the receptive features of language. There are, however, productive language features that can also characterize a learning problem.

Two areas of language production that characterize learning problems are speech clarity and word-finding difficulties. **Speech clarity problems** are evidenced by the inability to pattern or model the speech of others. As a result of this inability, children cannot critically analyze and compare their speech with the speech of others. In essence, these children are unaware of the fact that their speech differs considerably from the speech of others. Symptoms of speech clarity problems include frequent mispronunciation or slurring of words, poor phrasing, poor enunciation, and a monotone voice.

Word-finding difficulties may or may not accompany speech clarity problems. Children with this difficulty will often express themselves with a limited number of words. They often have the most difficulty with abstract words and usually omit all but the basic nouns and verbs. Both of these language production problems are best identified through observation. Children who exhibit language behavior that differs noticeably from that of their average-age-level peers should probably be referred to a speech therapist for further diagnosis.

For those children who have language development problems, several general recommendations can be found in the literature. Among these recommendations are: (1) Approach print first as a nonlinguistic task where students are allowed to recognize correct responses by pointing to them rather than using oral recall (Lipa, 1983). (2) Use specialized instructional methods (see chapter 16), such as VAKT (Visual, Auditory, Kinesthetic, Tactile). (3) Base reading instruction around a holistic approach, such as the language-experience approach, that focuses on students' existing language capabilities (Gentile, Lamb, & Rivers, 1985). (4) Use audio- and videotapes, films, filmstrips, pictures, field trips, and other concrete activities as means to supplement printed text (Weinberg & Rehmet, 1983).

In addition to these general recommendations, specific techniques for use with learning disabled students are available in the area of comprehension. One such technique focuses on the logical connections among different pieces of text information, specifically, causal relationships between a story character's goals and his or her attempts to satisfy those goals (Varnhagen & Goldman, 1986). The reasoning upon which this technique is based is that learning disabled readers do not have a basic understanding of the relationships found in story episodes. The technique was successful with 10 children from a class for learning disabled readers who ranged in age from approximately 10 to 13. The features of this instruction included:

□ An initial phase of approximately one week to help students begin thinking about stories as consisting of different parts. This was accomplished by having students read stories aloud and identify words, sentences, and paragraphs in stories that they read.

□ A two-week phase that progressed from identifying different causal relationships in sentences to distinguishing between different story parts (setting, beginning, goal, try (attempt), outcome, and ending). Students were taught the meanings of these terms and were given instruction in applying the terms to story parts of one-episode stories.

□ The third phase occurred during the fourth, fifth, and sixth weeks of instruction. In this phase, students were taught to apply causal reasoning to information within simple, one-episode stories containing familiar content. The activities were then extended to more complex stories with multiple episodes. Accompanying the instruction on causal reasoning was the creation of story trees (similar to story mapping presented in chapter 9). The students made up different episodes about story characters using common information and were then directed to develop different beginning events, goals, actions, and consequences. Story trees were also used in macrocloze exercises—the teacher removed a card from a tree and the students had to construct or remember the appropriate information. As students became more capable in filling the single story gaps, multiple story information cards were removed from the story tree and students again supplied the missing information.

□ The final phase lasted two weeks. Students were assisted in constructing more complex story trees and completing more complex macrocloze activities. They also began to come up with causal questions for the teacher and other students to answer. This phase focused on students internalizing the questioning procedures as a way of identifying causal relationships between story events.

The students involved in this instructional program made significant progress in their reading comprehension. Varnhagen and Goldman indicated that "teaching children about the causal relations within and between story episodes appears to be a worthy (and not too time consuming) endeavor for teachers of reading disabled children" (p. 903). They did, however, recommend that such a technique with story grammar (see chapter 9) is most beneficial for learning disabled students who are reading on at least the second half of the third-grade level or above.

Emotional and Social Development

Emotional disorders and problems with social development are generally the result, rather than the cause, of learning problems. They are secondary to the basic problems already outlined. As children with learning problems appraise themselves in relation to others, they often see that they fall short in terms of achievement. They are usually members of the low-reading group, and reading—or any academic subject—becomes a stress-filled, anxiety-producing situation. As a result, these children are more vulnerable to stress and pressures exerted by their environment. They attempt to minimize these pressures by developing varying defense mechanisms. One defense mechanism is withdrawing from participation in classroom activities and social activities; another is to become loud and aggressive, finding ways to be irritating and upsetting. Both of these avoidance techniques serve to mask a fear of failure. By emphasizing one behavior, such as acting out, attention can be distracted from other areas of inadequacy. Examples can be seen in the defense mechanisms employed by two strikingly different children with learning problems.

Paul, a third grader, was often described as "shy" and "introverted" by his teachers, and on the playground or in a group activity he was most often found alone. Paul had no real friends and spent most of his time watching television. Very rarely would he respond to questions or participate in class discussions. In academic subjects he was far behind all of the other students, and his teacher said that nothing she did seemed to bring him out of his shell. His parents said that before going to school he was a normal, active child who played with neighborhood friends and was even "talkative." Apparently, Paul had discovered that by avoiding any interaction with his educational environment, he could minimize the likelihood that he would be subject to embarrassment and failure.

Mike was the exact opposite of Paul. He was a sixth grader who had been a disruptive influence in all his classes since the middle of second grade. He responded to teachers' requests by saying "I don't have to," "You can't make me," "I hate school," and "I wish you were dead." When requested to read a story or answer a question, he often reacted by slamming his book to the floor, tearing up his paper, or turning over desks and chairs. Mike had spent as much time in the hall and in the principal's office as he had in the classroom. His mother indicated that she was at a loss about what to do with him. She had tried everything from attempting to reason with him to punitive measures.

Fortunately, both of these children received help. When Paul was given a complete diagnostic screening, it was discovered that he had a learning problem related to language comprehension. As his teacher and the learning disability resource teacher adapted their instruction to meet his needs, Paul began to experience success in school. A direct result of his improved performance was an accompanying change in behavior. Although he was still reserved, he was becoming more communicative with his teachers and classmates.

Mike went on to junior high school, where he was encouraged to take vocational courses. He was placed in a program that included such courses as woodworking, metal shop, and drafting. His behavior changed drastically—no longer did he rely on disruptive behavior as a means to avoid a learning situation. Although he still had a tendency to revert to disruptive behavior in classes that dealt with abstract content, he was experiencing success in school. Since many of his teachers understood that he had a problem with reading and math, they attempted to relate both of these to woodworking and metal working, which helped him to better conceptualize the information. They had discovered that Mike could experience success when his individual needs were met.

Many children with learning problems are socially immature in comparison with their age-level peers. They are often uneasy and uncertain about social situations, classroom situations, and peer relationships. Basically, these children do not know how to cope with the daily anxieties and failures that they encounter in school. For them, teacher understanding and guidance is just as important as a diagnosis of their learning problems.

Specific Behaviors Related to Classroom Performance

In addition to the characteristics already mentioned, there are specific classroom learning behaviors that relate to learning disabilities. Johnson and Morasky (1980) asked a group of elementary teachers who were experienced in working with learning disabled children to list the problem behaviors that they most frequently encountered. The teachers listed the following 11 behaviors:

1. Atypical spelling errors
2. Auditory discrimination problems
3. Letter recognition problems

4. Initial sound-in-words confusion
5. Counting and number recognition difficulties
6. Auditory memory deficits
7. Visual memory deficits
8. Gross motor incoordination
9. Spatial disorientation
10. Articulation errors
11. Fine motor problems—usually in handwriting (pp. 31–32)

Another listing of behaviors was developed by Meier (1971) in a study with over 3,000 second-grade children. Again, any child can exhibit one or more of these behaviors and not have a learning disability; the behaviors should be evaluated in terms of their persistence and relationship to a child's age-level peers. Each of Meier's behaviors that was indicative of learning disabilities, as determined by one-half or more of the teachers sampled, is included in the following list:

1. Does not seem to listen to daily classroom instructions (often asks to have them repeated, whereas rest of glass goes ahead).
2. Cannot recall correctly oral directions when asked to repeat them.
3. Is slow to finish work (does not apply self, daydreams a lot, and falls asleep in school).
4. Shows unusually short attention span for daily school work.
5. Is easily distracted from school work (cannot concentrate even with the slightest disturbances from other students).
6. Exhibits poor drawings of people compared with peers' drawings.
7. Demonstrates poor handwriting when compared with peers' handwriting.
8. Reverses or rotates letters, numbers, and words (writes *p* for *q*, *saw* for *was*, *2* for *7*, or *16* for *91* far more frequently than peers).
9. Reads silently or aloud far more slowly than peers (word by word when reading aloud).
10. Makes articulation errors.
11. Substitutes words that distort meaning (*when* for *where*).
12. Cannot sound out or "unlock" words.
13. Possesses a reading ability at least three-fourths of a year below most peers.
14. Has trouble telling time.
15. Cannot follow written directions, which most peers can follow, when reading orally or silently.
16. Has trouble organizing written work (seems scatterbrained, confused).
17. Repeats the same behavior over and over.

Characteristics that can indicate learning problems are numerous and include persistent problems with behavior, language, motor development, and academic performance (see pages 307–316). It is when behavior in these areas differs noticeably and consistently from that of the average child that further diagnosis is warranted.

Reading diagnosis and classroom observation can substantiate the probability of a learning problem. Classroom diagnostic procedures used to identify learning disabled children do not differ drastically from those discussed in earlier chapters. The same tools for diagnosis of reading abilities are used, and similar quantitative and qualitative evaluation decisions are made. And, instructional procedures and guidelines for the areas of word analysis, sight vocabulary, and comprehension are used to fit the specific needs of the child.

The purpose for diagnosis is not simply to determine whether or not a child has a learning problem. As stressed throughout this text, the purpose of diagnosis is to help the teacher develop the best possible instructional program for a child who is experiencing reading problems. Labeling a child as learning disabled (LD), educable mentally retarded (EMR), or emotionally disturbed (ED) serves no real purpose. This point has been well-stated by Hallahan and Kauffman (1985):

> The real danger occurs when one uses labels that are vague. The overlap in characteristics among LD, ED, and EMR children makes the use of such terms as "learning disabled," "emotionally disturbed," or "educable mentally retarded" relatively meaningless. The teacher is in need of descriptive terms that define the specific attributes of the child in his class. If a child is labeled an "auditory learner," for example, we are a step beyond the indication that he is learning disabled. . . . Using tests for the purpose of looking for educationally meaningful data on children is warranted and should be the primary justification for doing any testing at all. (p. 47)

If the child exhibits behavior characteristics such as those outlined earlier, and if these occur frequently, then a medical referral through the school nurse is recommended. The following set of guidelines outline a diagnostic procedure:

Behavioral Assessment in the School Setting

1. Academic history
   a. Observe classroom behaviors, focusing on characteristics discussed on pages 315–316.
   b. Review anecdotal records (if available), noting patterns of behavior that substantiate classroom behaviors and past performances on reading and general achievement tests.
   c. Administer and interpret survey and diagnostic tests to further substantiate observations and past indicators of performance.
2. Parent conferences
   a. Ask about behavior at home and expressions of attitudes toward social and educational aspects of school.

b. Obtain details of childhood illnesses (symptoms, severity, and care), which may be shared with the school nurse and/or physician.

c. Gain insights about acculturation factors, family dynamics, and emotional stress (ridicule by brothers or sisters, parental pressure to achieve, comparisons with other family members).

3. Individual intelligence test
   a. Have the test administered by the school psychologist or psychometrist.
   b. Note any discrepancy between the IQ (obtained on individual test—most often the *Wechsler Intelligence Scale for Children—Revised [WISC-R])* and grade achievement scores (obtained from achievement test results found in academic history), which is a bench mark of learning disability (McCarthy & McCarthy, 1969).

Evaluation of Medical History

1. Obtain medical history including pre- and postnatal information (age of child, symptoms—both those noted by parents and teachers—severity, and care).
2. Note motor development, language development, personal-social development history (in school and home environments, supported by teacher observation and parent observation).

Physical Examination

1. General health
2. Neurological evaluation—function and integrated motor acts

Special Examinations

1. Vision—acuity, fields, and discrimination (supported or warranted by teacher observations, testing, and recommendation)
2. Hearing—acuity and discrimination (supported or warranted by teacher observations, testing, and recommendations)
3. Allergy testing—food, drugs, inhalants, animals, and so on
4. Nutritional evaluation—early deprivation may indicate subsequent impairment to central nervous system

This procedure may vary depending on the resources available and the professional judgment of individuals gathering the diagnostic information; however, preliminary identification of children with learning problems often rests with classroom teachers. Information that relates to children's academic and social performance in the classroom is a valuable asset to the specialists who will help to complete the diagnostic process. The following specific case study shows how such information is gathered in the classroom and how instructional decisions are made.

Case Study: Wayne

Analysis

Wayne, a second grader, has a very short attention span and is easily distracted from a learning activity. He may read a sentence and start to tell a story about something completely unrelated to what is being read. Wayne often gives the impression that he is in a daze and seems to live in his own world. While he can follow simple verbal directions, he must be reminded time and time again to finish his work.

When the *Gates-MacGinitie Reading Test: Readiness Skills* battery was administered to Wayne, the results indicated that he has trouble with vowel sounds. He confuses short vowel sounds and sometimes forgets what particular sound a short vowel records. He can sound out words if he is prompted with the correct vowel sounds, which must often be repeated for him several times. He verbally refuses to try to sound out words longer than four letters.

An IRI was administered to substantiate his performance on the readiness test and to provide further diagnostic information. Wayne's performance on the graded-word list did not go beyond the preprimer level. He guessed at words he did not know, and there was no apparent pattern to his guessing; that is, he appeared to say any word that came to mind and none of the words he substituted began with the same letter or had a similar shape as the words on the list.

On the oral reading of the preprimer passage, similar behavior was noted. He again substituted words for those he did not know and had problems sounding out words. He pronounced the word *cat* as *kāt* on several occasions. Wayne made several substitutions. It did not bother him when the word substituted did not make sense. He appeared to be unconcerned about meaning because there were no regressions or self-corrections. Wayne reached the frustration level for word recognition on the preprimer passage.

Although Wayne did not answer any of the comprehension questions correctly, he did exhibit a behavior observed previously in classroom reading activities. He responded by talking about a story the teacher had read to the class two days earlier when he was asked, "What was the pet's name in this story?" and "Do you think that the author wrote this story about things that really happened?"

Wayne was administered the *Wechsler Intelligence Scale for Children-Revised* by the school psychometrist. Significant strengths were noted in practical judgment, visual sequencing, comprehension (listening), and spatial relationships. Areas of weakness included psychomotor speed, visual discrimination, and numerical reasoning ability. He demonstrated a significant visual perceptual problem in copying designs; in addition, his overall functioning was consistently in the average range of intellectual ability. However, his academic achievement based on the *Metropolitan Achievement Test* and the reading tests was approximately one and one-half years below estimated potential.

Individualized Instructional Program

Learner Style

Wayne's reading strengths as identified through the use of classroom observation, the *Gates-MacGinitie Reading Test: Readiness Skills*, and performance on the IRI include the following:

☐ Knows sounds represented by consonants and consonant combinations in initial position of words
☐ Is highly verbal, but does not always relate to topic of discussion
☐ Has a sight vocabulary of approximately 50 to 60 words
☐ Recognizes whole-to-part relationships, which could form basis for discussing similarities and differences of new words to known words
☐ Shows good listening comprehension
☐ Exhibits some literal comprehension of information found in the beginning of stories

The following reading weaknesses were also identified:

☐ Exhibits poor visual perception
☐ Has problems with visual discrimination of words
☐ Lacks any well-developed strategy for identifying a minimum of words to get at meaning
☐ Shows difficulty associating the sound recorded by a letter or group of letters with graphic representation
☐ Demonstrates limited reading comprehension and gives little attention to meaning as he reads
☐ Exhibits weak literal comprehension for relationship of ideas throughout stories; has difficulty making inferences
☐ Exhibits limited understanding that reading is getting meaning

The following motivational characteristics were noted through classroom observation and Wayne's responses to interest inventory:

☐ Enjoys fast-paced, board-type instructional games
☐ Responds well to task-related comments and teacher praise
☐ Values special privileges, such as collecting lunch money, closing windows, and taking messages to principal's office
☐ Enjoys personal recognition from teacher and other adults
☐ Likes drawing and painting activities
☐ Is interested in small pets, especially his dog and cat
☐ Responds well to symbols, such as stars, smiling faces, and rocket ships, used on written work to highlight correct responses

Additional motivational characteristics and attitudes noted for Wayne in classroom instruction and interaction with peers include the following:

☐ Works best in tasks that require no more than 10–15 minutes to complete
☐ Does well on tasks that are presented in a step-by-step manner and are illustrated with concrete examples
☐ Performs satisfactorily when provided with immediate teacher feedback
☐ Responds well when the teacher or another student models the desired learning with several examples
☐ Works well when given opportunity for *much* repeated practice for each step of learning
☐ Understands concepts that are illustrated with many examples related to his background of experience
☐ Easily distracted from both group and independent learning tasks that take more than 10–15 minutes
☐ Unwilling to participate actively in tasks without direct teacher attention
☐ Short attention span
☐ Needs visual reinforcement of what he hears to learn auditorily

☐ Reluctant to work in groups if he perceives that other students will not "do things his way"

☐ Hesitant to complete a learning activity that he perceives as being too much to do

Task Conditions

Behavioral objectives established for Wayne include the following:

☐ Will identify correctly words from the Dolch list when they are flashed as word cards

☐ Will discriminate visually a given word from other word choices

☐ Will identify the main idea of a short story or paragraph by discussing the ideas with the teacher or by drawing an appropriate picture of them

☐ Will use syntax to determine and predict both words and meaning found in given passages and stories

☐ Will retell short reading selections in his own words

Resource Attributes

Instructional materials, approaches, and formats include the following:

☐ Basal reader readiness book and first reader

☐ Pictures and visuals for introducing new words, for discussing his experiences in terms of story content, and for setting meaningful purposes for reading

☐ Workbook activities and worksheets to reinforce and extend skills covered in individual and small-group settings

☐ Art activities for reinforcing and extending sight vocabulary and summarizing the main ideas of experience stories read in the first reader

☐ Teacher-made games to reinforce and extend individual and small-group instruction

☐ Language-experience approach

Teacher Style

The following instructional procedures were identified for use with Wayne:

☐ Structure short, individual sessions to present new words, review words, and demonstrate use of these words in reading situations

☐ Use independent seat work dealing with highly structured short activities

☐ Focus small-group instruction on the reinforcement and extension of skills introduced in individual sessions

☐ Use games and informal groupings with other children to reinforce application of skills and reward appropriate behavior

☐ Reward appropriate responses and reading behaviors with verbal praise; ignore all inappropriate responses

☐ Use special privileges, such as collecting lunch tickets, taking enrollment count to the office, and closing windows, to reward learning and effort

☐ Take advantage of free time for drawing; drawing and painting can also be used in instructional sessions for improving comphrension of literal information, representing ideas, and illustrating inferential comprehension outcomes

☐ Develop competitive games that are fast-moving and easy to play that can be used for reviewing new words, for comprehension instruction, and for reinforcing small-group instruction

☐ Present highly organized instruction in small steps and build on each step

☐ Introduce and discuss new words to associate meaning with them; activities such as rhyming words, constructing short sentences, and copying a word several times should help Wayne recall new words and develop visual perception

☐ Utilize workbook pages and teacher-made activities, to be completed under close supervision by the teacher, to reinforce and extend learning
☐ Take advantage of interest in drawing to introduce new words, motivate writing of language-experience stories, and guide the rereading of language-experience stories for comprehension purposes
☐ Emphasize literal comprehension of information by providing an overview of the story content, relating content to past experiences, and setting purposes
☐ Set specific purposes for reading and skill introduction; relate these to previous learning and discuss how the things he already knows will help him to understand what he reads
☐ Use pictures to introduce the concept of *same* and *different* for visual discrimination skills; tape recording of different sounds can introduce the concept of *sounds the same* or *sounds different* for transfer to letters, groups of letters, and words

Instructional Strategies and Procedures

In addition to the instructional procedures and techniques already described, there are others that teachers may wish to use. The following are adaptations of Mangano's (1978) instructional ideas for meeting the reading needs of children with learning problems:

☐ *Curriculum bank:* This is an area of the school where teachers can donate copies of teaching units, materials, packets, and ideas that have succeeded with students who have learning problems. All teachers are free to check these materials out and use them with their students.
☐ *Taped texts:* Students and volunteers can tape texts for students who have learning problems that interfere with their reading. In this way students with learning problems can keep up with the information in an auditory fashion while instruction is given to improve their reading ability. Students can even answer questions on a tape.
☐ *Behavior modification techniques:* These are not only helpful in controlling behavior, but can also be used as a motivational tool for incorporating positive learning behavior in all aspects of corrective remedial instruction.
☐ *Peer tutoring:* This not only cuts down on the teacher's teaching time but can also be useful for developing social skills. Sometimes letting a so-called "trouble maker" tutor the child who has learning problems benefits both children. Trouble makers often feel important because of the added responsibility and modify their behavior. Children with learning problems benefit from direct individual instruction.
It is also valuable for the child who has a learning problem to tutor younger children. This tends to build a more positive self-image and reinforces skill learned in class instruction.
☐ *Listing steps:* Children with learning problems often forget from step to step. Listing important steps for reading activities on 3″ × 5″ cards for students to refer to helps them to focus on the activity rather than being frustrated with the task.
☐ *Reference charts:* Students can utilize reference charts placed around the room instead of always asking for assistance. Charts can help students

familiarize themselves with words commonly used in particular subject areas. For example, reference charts could present definitions for the parts of speech, define high-frequency words, and list frequently occurring content-area words in context.

☐ *Organize a volunteer program:* Students who have learning problems have had tremendous success and progress as a result of instruction that they receive from volunteers. There are two types of volunteers—student and parent.

Particularly at the secondary level, students can serve as an elementary teacher's aide as an elective. Sign up for these students and utilize them. They can tape-record texts, make reading materials, tutor students, and help with an assortment of other activities.

The second type of volunteer is the parent. Organize a program where parents come at a convenient time to work with specific students. Be sure to train the parents in tutoring techniques and inform them of the nature of the student's reading problem. Working with a special parent not only gives students who have learning problems one-to-one attention in developing cognitive skills, but also affords them the chance to receive personal attention.

☐ *Adopt a class grandparent:* There is an emphasis in our society on "Gray Liberation." It may be feasible to team up with an organization for the elderly. Possibly they can assist in reading instruction with students who have learning problems; students, in turn, can fulfill older Americans' needs. Students can learn to value the elderly, and this has the potential for bringing tremendous satisfaction to both parties.

☐ *Colleagues:* Never underestimate the worth of colleagues. Share materials and ideas. By sharing, one can decrease the load in schools today and also acquire teacher-tested ideas. (pp. 33–36)

The diagnostic and instructional procedures discussed in this section do not differ considerably from suggestions presented throughout this text. One apparent difference, however, is referral to a physician for a complete examination. The primary purpose for such a referral is to confirm that the child is physically healthy.

GIFTED CHILDREN

The skills and abilities of intellectually gifted children challenge many teachers. Programs that meet the needs of the gifted increase the discrepancy between their performance and the average performance and often require special instructional features. Early identification of gifted children ensures that a reading instruction program can be developed to nurture their abilities.

Identification of gifted children is a multifaceted process. It comprises teacher observation, standardized and informal testing, and the input of special resource people. One characteristic of giftedness is advanced language skills, which often allow for rapid development of reading ability.

There are, however, gifted children who experience reading problems and do not read up to their potential. Identification of the gifted within the reading program enables the classroom teacher to plan a program that both meets the needs of intellectually gifted children who are reading at a level equal to their ability and helps gifted students who are having problems begin to reach their appropriate reading level.

The following sections describe the characteristics, diagnostic procedures, and instructional programs for the gifted child. The tools of diagnosis, instructional procedures, and materials are similar to those presented in previous chapters, but there is a noticeable difference in how the diagnostic information is interpreted, how information is used in instructional planning, and what the level of instruction is.

Identification of Gifted Children

It is easier to identify and develop an instructional program for the gifted if one has a conceptualization of giftedness. A definition offered by the advisory panel to the U.S. Office of Education provides a general overview:

> Gifted and talented children are those identified by professionally qualified persons and who, by virtue of outstanding abilities, are capable of high performance. These are children who require differentiated educational programs and/or services beyond those normally provided by the regular school program in order to realize their contribution to self and society. (U.S. Congress, Senate Subcommittee on Labor and Public Welfare, 1972, p. 10)

The key points of this definition are *the identification of gifted children* and, following identification, *the development of educational programs that meet their needs.* Identification can be facilitated by considering some of the characteristics that are common to gifted children.

Seagoe's (1974) list of learning characteristics presents the traits of intellectually gifted children and also some of the problems which such children may experience:

Characteristics	**Concomitant Problems**
1. Keen power of observation; naive receptivity; sense of the significant; willingness to examine the unusual	1. Possible gullibility
2. Power of abstraction, conceptualization, synthesis; interest in inductive learning and problem-solving; pleasure in intellectual activity	2. Occasional resistance to direction; rejection or remission of detail
3. Interest in cause-effect relationships, ability to see relationships; interest in applying concepts; love of truth	3. Difficulty in accepting the illogical
4. Liking for structure and order; liking for consistency, as in value systems, number systems, clocks, calendars	4. Invention of own systems, sometimes conflicting

Exceptional children are found in almost every classroom. (David Strickler)

Characteristics	Concomitant Problems
5. Retentiveness	5. Dislike for routine and drill; need for early mastery of foundation skills
6. Verbal proficiency ; large vocabulary; facility in expression; interest in reading; breadth of information in advanced areas	6. Need for early specialized reading vocabulary, parent resistance to reading; escape into verbalism
7. Questioning attitude, intellectual curiosity, inquisitive mind; intrinsic motivation	7. Lack of early home or school stimulation
8. Power of critical thinking; skepticism, evaluative testing; self-criticism and self-checking	8. Critical attitude toward others; discouragement as a result of self-criticism
9. Creativeness and inventiveness; liking for new ways of doing things; interest in creating, brainstorming, free-wheeling	9. Rejection of the known; need to invent for self

Characteristics	Concomitant Problems
10. Power of concentration; intense attention that excludes all else; long attention span	10. Resistance to interruption
11. Persistent, goal-directed behavior	11. Stubbornness
12. Sensitivity, intuitiveness, empathy for others; need for emotional support and a sympathetic attitude	12. Need for success and recogniton; sensitivity to criticism; vulnerability to peer group rejection
13. High energy, alertness, eagerness; periods of intense voluntary effort preceding invention	13. Frustration with inactivity and absence of progress
14. Independence in work and study; preference for individual work; self-reliance; need for freedom of movement and action	14. Parent and peer-group pressures and noncomformity; problems of rejection and rebellion
15. Versatility and virtuosity; diversity of interests and abilities; many hobbies; proficiency in art forms such as music and drawing	15. Lack of homogeneity in group work; need for flexibility and individualization; need for help in exploring and developing interests; need to build basic competencies in major interests
16. Friendliness and outgoingness	16. Need for peer-group relations in many types of groups; problems in developing social leadership (pp. 20–21)

Each of the behaviors listed could be displayed by gifted children in the reading program, since the majority of the characteristics are related to reading ability and would surely help children to become competent advanced readers. Some of the concomitant problems listed may also be exhibited by gifted children in the reading program. They may, however, be mistakenly perceived as adjustment problems or disruptive behavior rather than as problems related to giftedness.

As the list suggests, gifted students have needs similar to those of all children. The major difference is that they are advanced in the level at which these needs must be met. Concomitant problem behaviors probably develop as a result of the teacher's failure to adapt instruction to meet their needs. In addition, other behaviors relate directly to reading and highlight the importance of developing a reading program that accommodates the intellectually gifted child.

Admittedly each gifted child is different; however, common reading behaviors include the following:

1. A rich, well-developed vocabulary and an interest in words
2. Early reading ability prior to entering school
3. An advanced linguistic ability in sentence construction, expression of ideas, and listening vocabulary

4. An interest in trade books and reading (The student often keeps a list of books read and takes the initiative to write summaries without being required to do so.)
5. An early interest in learning to write and in writing creative stories
6. Frequent use of information sources, such as the dictionary, encyclopedia, and information texts, to explore areas of interest
7. Comprehension abilities at early grade levels (that is, kindergarten or first grade) that go beyond the literal level and are evidenced by an understanding of the relationship of story ideas
8. Well-developed reading skills and abilities by the end of first grade

These reading behaviors and characteristics are those most often exhibited early in school by gifted children. Through noting such behaviors, potentially gifted children can be identified for further diagnosis.

Usually, standardized tests are used in conjunction with informal observation and informal screening devices to identify intellectually gifted children. Standardized group achievement and reading tests serve as screening instruments to point out potentially gifted students. In addition, the results from these tests can indicate areas of special concern, which may be in need of further diagnosis.

Most authorities stress that individual intelligence tests are more appropriate for identifying intellectually gifted children than are group tests. Not only do individual tests provide a more accurate assessment of ability, but they also allow for gathering information about attitudes, interests, and background. The importance of using an individual assessment instrument is most apparent when intelligence is a criterion for determining intellectual giftedness.

Both the *Wechsler* and the *Stanford-Binet* are frequently recommended for identifying the gifted. Martinson (1974) points out that research comparing the two favors the *Stanford-Binet*. The advantage of the *Stanford-Binet* is that it has a higher IQ range than that of the *Wechsler*. Martinson states: "The *Wechsler* scale does not encompass either extremely high or extremely low IQs and thus is limited for the gifted" (p. 58).

It is interesting to note that many classroom teachers feel that identifying gifted students in the area of reading should also be based on a teacher's judgment as well as on the use of standardized test procedures. In a survey of 116 teachers of high-ability reading students (Gaug, 1984), all the teachers reported that they used at least two of the following criteria to determine gifted students' reading placement: teacher's judgment, textbook publisher's placement test, students' previous year's performance, and teacher-developed tests. The survey results show that the role of the teacher is extremely important in identifying and developing instruction for gifted readers. There are many school districts nationwide that either do not have a specified program for gifted readers or do not identify gifted readers until the second grade or later. As a result of either situation, many students who are gifted in their reading capabilities would not be provided with appropriate instruction without the classroom teacher identifying them and developing an appropriate reading program to meet their advanced reading needs.

Instructional Practices and Strategies

One of the major characteristics of intellectual giftedness is advanced reading ability, which includes fluent oral reading abilities, excellent recall of text, competent language capabilities, superior reasoning strategies, and well-developed abilities to make inferences (Carr, 1984). However, many gifted readers often fail to achieve their potential (Boothby, 1980). Simply requiring more from these readers does not guarantee that their advanced reading abilities will continue to develop at a level equal to their capabilities. Many of the reading problems exhibited by intellectually gifted students are a direct result of poor instruction decision making on the part of the teacher. The following recommendations detail some important instructional features to help in teacher decision making.

Instructional Features of Reading Programs for the Intellectually Gifted Student

Reading instruction for gifted students should be adjusted to fit their advanced reading abilities. The instructional program should be based on meaningful content; the pace and coverage of instruction should be greater than those used in the regular reading program; and the focus should be on critical and creative thinking. Teachers should keep in mind, however, that individual differences exist among gifted readers, and should therefore evaluate the effectiveness of their reading instruction in relation to the students' reading progress. Some recommendations for teaching reading to gifted students have been identified by Carr (1984) and are presented in the following list:

☐ *Pacing of instruction:* Because gifted students often quickly understand basic skills and are fluent oral readers, drill exercises may be inappropriate for them. Through the use of informal assessment procedures (IRIs, interviewing, oral reading of selected excerpts from texts, and so forth), teachers can identify students' instructional reading levels and then accelerate students to the appropriate reading level. Teachers will usually discover that only a few minutes of instruction are necessary for teaching gifted students a particular skill even at their instructional level.

☐ *Content:* Because of gifted students' ability to comprehend materials that are usually beyond that of average students, a wide variety of children's books should be available for them to read. Students' interest and motivation in reading can be better sustained by having them read library books than by using a basal reader series for their reading.

□ *Integration with other language arts:* Integrating writing with reading can stimulate students' curiosity and exploration of many topics through reading. Most gifted children do well in writing their own books and expressing themselves through writing. Through such writing interests, teachers can guide children to further explore the topics about which they write by using encyclopedias, almanacs, content texts, and other reference sources.

□ *Thinking skills:* Teacher guidance is still needed to maximize gifted students' development and application of their thinking skills in dealing with complex concepts. Discussing with gifted students the background and inferential features of what they read both prior to and following reading will help them reach their potential. Discussions and activities should be developed around interpretative questions ("Why do you think. . .?" "How is this. . .?"), analysis (comparing character traits, story events), synthesis ("What would happen if. . .?"), and evaluation (debate why an ending is appropriate).

Similar recommendations have been offered by Cassidy (1981):

□ Word-recognition and comprehension instruction should be appropriate to an advanced reading level, even though not all reading skills appear to be well-developed. A key question to ask as a guide about whether or not a gifted student would benefit from instruction in a reading skill area is "Will the student's comprehension capabilities be enhanced as a result of learning this skill?" If the answer is no, then teaching the skill is not warranted.

□ Reading instruction and materials that meet the needs of the gifted student should be used; the student should not be forced to meet the demands of the instruction and the materials.

□ A large number of trade books should be included in the classroom, and the teacher should guide and encourage the selection of books that appeal to each student's interests without requiring a written book report.

□ There should be an emphasis on the individualized reading approach (student self-selects what is read, paces his/her reading, and shares what is read in a personal conference with the teacher), the language-experience approach, and reading interest groups (see chapter 12).

□ Opportunities should be available for developing long-range interest in given topics through reading in various resource materials, such as science, social studies, and history texts.

□ Various activities (writing, art, dramatics, and oral sharing) should focus on creative reactions to books and texts read.

□ Instruction and experience is needed to develop research skills with an emphasis on reading (library skills, dictionary skills, and experiences with a variety of reference materials).

☐ The teacher should stimulate curiosity by posing problems that can be solved through reading books, reference materials, magazines, and other sources of informational literature.

☐ There should be many varied opportunities to relate and apply concepts acquired through reading to other areas (solving social problems, performing science experiments, identifying world issues, etc.).

☐ There should be an ongoing assessment of reading progress with instruction focusing on specific areas as indicated by the students' reading performance and interests.

Providing gifted readers with enrichment activities is recognized by teachers as one of the most important features of their reading program. Primary-grade and intermediate-grade teachers reported the use of the following techniques and activities as ways to enrich the reading program for gifted students (Gaug, 1984).

☐ Primary teachers recommended the use of contracts (a written agreement between the student and teacher to complete a given task), creative writing activities (stories, books, poems, drama, and so forth), library research, computer activities, library reading, interest projects, and mini units as independent types of enrichment activities for reading. In addition, these teachers also used higher level questioning techniques to stimulate students' thinking and interaction with what they read.

☐ Intermediate-level teachers reported using similar enrichment practices with the addition of research projects, tutoring younger students, analyzing authors' styles, investigating different types of literature, and reading newspapers and magazines. In addition, they engaged advanced readers in compare-and-contrast discussions of text and often worked with them in increasing their reading speed and efficiency.

The importance of using children's literature and library books is a common thread running through most of the instructional recommendations for teaching reading to gifted students. Children's literature books offer gifted readers a variety of quality reading materials and a wide range of writing styles. The appeal of children's trade books to gifted readers can provide teachers with an excellent means for developing vocabulary strategies in a stimulating and enriching manner. The following strategies adapted from Howell (1987) are suggestions for combining vocabulary development with good library books.

☐ Although gifted students may be extremely capable in decoding words, they may not always know their meanings. The highly descriptive style found in many storybooks provides varied opportunities for teachers to illustrate learning from context. Teachers can direct students to apply strategies to help them figure out words found in their library books by asking questions that encourage students to look at sentence and picture clues, to think of opposite meanings for unknown words, and to imagine what the word depicts. Teacher guidance is done with appropriate library books and the use of initial examples with which students are familiar.

□ Library books can be used with gifted students to expand their vocabulary knowledge by exploring collective terminology. Searches for collective nouns, for example, could be done in a story book and then extended to textbooks, magazines, newspapers, television guides, and so forth. Students can keep a file for sharing and referencing when writing creative stories or poems.

□ Because synonyms are a means for authors to help the reader develop images about what is read, they provide an excellent source for expanding the gifted student's vocabulary. Students can be directed to find words that are highly descriptive and to think of substitutes that don't change the author's meaning. Students can also discuss the word pictures that they form for a descriptive word's synonyms.

□ Students can be introduced to the study of antonyms concurrently with their study of synonyms. Gifted students can represent their interpretations of antonyms by drawing pictures of how they are used in their storybook. The pictures can be used to help them generalize the function of antonyms (comparing objects, ideas, people, places, things, and conditions) to develop and strengthen mental images.

□ To help students better understand the use of figurative language and idioms, examples excerpted from popular storybooks can be used. Howell (1987) notes that figurative language and idioms will probably need specific clarification for gifted students. Discussion of figurative language and idioms can focus on the real (literal) meaning of the text and the character's interpretation. Students can construct their own examples of figurative language and idioms and can illustrate them with pictures or share them with classmates.

□ Because many gifted readers have a fascination with words, the study of word origins and history is often highly motivating for them. Words for study can either be selected by the students from their books or identified by the teacher for presenting a "word a day." Students can be encouraged to construct trivia games, to explore how words have changed and to classify the changes, to trace the origin of modern slang terms, and to investigate old words that are no longer used today.

A list of children's books that provides teachers with a collection appropriate for many of the activities recommended has been developed by Howell and is presented in figure 13–2.

Intellectually gifted students can experience the same reading problems that any other student might experience. Diagnosis and instructional planning are necessary to identify their reading strengths and weaknesses. Procedures identical to those presented throughout the text should be

Basil, Cynthia. *How Ships Play Cards: A Beginning Book of Homonyms.* New York, N.Y.: Morrow, 1980.

Burchfield, R.W., ed. *A Supplement to the Oxford University Dictionary.* Oxford, England: Oxford Unviersity Press, 1976.

Gwynne, Fred. *A Chocolate Moose for Dinner.* New York, N.Y.: Windmill/Dutton, 1976.

Gwynne, Fred. *The King Who Rained.* New York, N.Y.: Windmill, 1970.

Hoban, Tana. *Push-Pull Empty-Full.* New York, N.Y.: Macmillan, 1972.

Hunt, Bernice K. *The Whatchamacallit Book.* New York, N.Y.: G.P. Putnam's Sons, 1976.

Lobel, Arnold. *Frog and Toad Are Friends.* New York, N.Y.: Harper and Row, 1970.

Maestro, Guilio. *What's a Frank Frank? Tasty Homograph Riddles.* New York, N.Y.: Clarion, 1984.

Merriam, Eve. *A Gaggle of Geese.* New York, N.Y.: Knopf, 1960.

Moscovitch, Rosalie. *What's In a Word? A Dictionary of Daffy Definitions.* Boston, Mass.: Houghton Mifflin, 1985.

O'Dell, Scott. *Island of the Blue Dolphins.* Boston, Mass.: Houghton Mifflin, 1960.

Oxford English Dictionary. Oxford, England: Oxford University Press, 1933.

Parish, Peggy. *Amelia Bedelia.* New York, N.Y.: Harper and Row, 1963.

Sperling, Susan K. *Murfles and Wink-A-Peeps: Funny Old Words for Kids.* New York, N.Y.: Clarkson N. Potter, 1985.

Spier, Peter. *Fast-Slow, High-Low: A Book of Opposites.* Garden City, N.Y.: Doubleday, 1972.

Steig, William. *The Amazing Bone.* New York, N.Y.: Farrar, Straus and Groux, 1976.

Steig, William. *Sylvester and the Magic Pebble.* New York, N.Y.: Simon and Schuster, 1969.

Terban, Marvin. *Eight Ate: A Feast of Homonym Riddles.* New York, N.Y.: Clarion, 1982.

Terban, Marvin. *In A Pickle and Other Funny Idioms.* New York, N.Y.: Clarion, 1983.

Terban, Marvin. *Too Hot to Hoot: Funny Palindrome Riddles.* New York, N.Y.: Clarion, 1985.

Viorst, Judith. *Alexander and the Terrible, Horrible, No Good, Very Bad Day.* New York, N.Y.: Atheneum, 1972.

FIGURE 13–2 Children's Books for Vocabulary Study

Source: From "Language, Literature, and Vocabulary Development for Gifted Students" by H. Howell, 1987, *The Reading Teacher,* 6, p. 504. Copyright 1987 by the International Reading Association. Reprinted with permission of Helen Howell and the International Reading Association.

employed, but the instructional program must contain more individual and self-directed learning activities.

☐ SUMMARY

Diagnostic procedures and instructional planning for both learning disabled and intellectually gifted children focus on identification and accommodation of their reading strengths and weaknesses. The tools of reading diagnosis are those used for all children, except that an individual intelligence test should be administered.

Children with learning problems often require a corrective/remedial reading program that extends over a longer period because of problems associated with language processing. A team approach for providing needed instruction and ongoing diagnosis should be developed cooperatively by the classroom teacher, learning disability resource teacher, and/or the reading resource teacher.

Intellectually gifted children are often advanced in their reading abilities. They can, nevertheless, make minimal progress in reading if the teacher does not provide for their advanced reading level. Negative attitudes toward reading can develop when gifted children are forced to meet the reading curriculum demands rather than modifying the curriculum to meet their needs.

Identification of both learning disabled children and intellectually gifted children early in their school experiences is the best practice to ensure that reading growth occurs as those children progress through school.

☐ IN-TEXT ASSIGNMENT

FIELD-BASED ACTIVITY

Visit an elementary classroom in your area and review the characteristics of intellectual giftedness with the teacher. Discuss with the teacher what procedures he or she uses to identify a gifted reader and what procedures the school district uses. Offer to work with a gifted reader for two or three days using some of the reading instructional strategies presented in this chapter. Prepare a short report to share with your classmates about the instructional strategies you used and their effectiveness in working with the gifted reader.

DISCUSS AND DEBATE

Form several small groups and discuss the development of an instructional lesson based on the case report for Wayne presented in this chapter.

Include in the lesson the materials for instruction as well as strategies for introducing, teaching, and evaluating your lesson. Share your recommendations with the other groups and discuss your rationale for including features that are different from the other groups' recommendations.

RESOURCE ACTIVITY

Invite a learning disabilities resource teacher to visit your class and discuss how students are identified and what the basic instructional techniques are for teaching reading. Follow up the resource teacher's visit with a visit by a reading resource teacher from a local school district. Ask the reading resource teacher to discuss how students are identified and what instructional strategies are used in teaching reading. After the visits, compare and contrast the procedures discussed by each resource teacher and analyze the information for areas of duplication and differences. A variation of this is to have both individuals speak on the same day and then discuss the similarities and differences in the services they provide.

☐ REFERENCES

Abrams, J. C. (1970). Learning disabilities: A complex phenomenon. *The Reading Teacher, 23,* 299–303.

Blackhurst, A. E. & Berdine, W. H. (1981). *An introduction to special education.* Boston: Little, Brown.

Boothby, P. C. (1980). Creative and critical reading for the gifted. *The Reading Teacher, 33,* 674–676.

Brutton, M., Richardson, S. O., & Mangel C. (1979). *Something's wrong with my child* (2nd ed.). New York: Harcourt Brace Jovanovich.

Carr, K. S. (1984). What gifted readers need from reading instruction. *The Reading Teacher, 38,* 144–146.

Cassidy, J. (1981). Inquiry reading for the gifted. *The Reading Teacher, 35,* 17–21.

Cotter, R. B. & Werner, P. H. (1987). Ritalin update. *Reading Psychology, 8,* 179–187.

Douglas, V. I. (1980). Treatment and training approaches to hyperactivity: Establishing internal or external control. In C. K. Whalen & B. Henkar (Eds.), *Hyperactive children: The social ecology of identification and treatment* (pp. 136–148). New York: Academic Press.

Gaug, M. A. (1984). Reading acceleration and enrichment in the elementary grades. *The Reading Teacher, 37,* 372–376.

Gearheart, B. R. & Weishahn, M. W. (1980). *The handicapped student in the elementary classroom* (2nd ed.). St. Louis, MO: Mosby.

Gentile, L. M., Lamb, P., & Rivers, C. O. (1985). A neurologist's view of reading difficulty: Implications for remedial instruction. *The Reading Teacher, 39*, 174–182.

Gittleman, R. (1985). Controlled trials of remedial approaches to reading disability. *Journal of Children, Psychology and Psychiatry, 26*, 843–846.

Hallahan, D. P. & Kauffman, J. M. (1985). *Introduction to learning disabilities: A psycho-behavioral approach* (2nd ed.). Englewood Cliffs, NJ: Prentice-Hall.

Hirt, D. M. (1970). Teaching children with severe learning disabilities. *The Reading Teacher, 23*, 304–310.

Howell, H. (1987). Language, literature, and vocabulary development for gifted students. *The Reading Teacher, 40*, 500–504.

Johnson, S. W. & Morasky, R. L. (1980). *Learning disabilities* (2nd ed.). Boston: Allyn & Bacon.

Keogh, B. K. & Barkett, C. J. (1980). An educational analysis of hyperactive children's achievement problems. In C. K. Whalen & B. Henker (Eds.), *Hyperactive children: The social ecology of identification and treatment* (73–89). New York: Academic Press.

Lipa, S. E. (1983). Reading disability: A new look at an old issue. *Journal of Learning Disabilities, 16*, 543–557.

McCarthy, J. J. & McCarthy, J. F. (1969). *Learning disabilities.* Boston: Allyn & Bacon.

Mangano, N. (1978). The effects of Public Law 94–142 on the teaching of reading to students with learning disabilities. Mimeograph. Texas A&M University, College Station, Texas.

Martinson, R. A. (1974). *The identification of the gifted and talented.* Ventura, CA: Office of the Ventura County Superindent of Schools.

Meier, J. (1971). Prevalence and characteristics of learning disabilities found in second grade children. *Journal of Learning Disabilities, 4*, 1–16.

Meier, J. (1980). *New vistas in special education.* Princeton, NJ: Educational Testing Services.

Seagoe, M. V. (1974). Some learning characteristics of gifted children. In R. Martinson (Ed.), *The identification of the gifted and talented* (pp. 20–21). Ventura, CA: Office of the Ventura County Superintendent of Schools.

U. S. Congress, Senate Subcommittee on Labor and Public Welfare. (1972). *Education of the Gifted and Talented* (92nd Cong., 2nd sess.).

Varnhagen, C. K. & Goldman, S. R. (1986). Improving comprehension: Causal relation instruction for learning handicapped learners. *The Reading Teacher, 39*, 896–904.

Weinberg, W. & Rehmet, A. (1983). Childhood affective disorders and school problems. In D. P. Cantwell and G. Carlson (Eds.), *Affective disorders in childhood and adolescence—An update* (pp. 109–128). Jamaica, NY: Spectrum Publications.

Wilkin, B. R. (1969). Auditory perception—Implications for language development. *Journal of Research and Development in Education, 3*, 53–71.

14

Culturally and Language Diverse Children in the Classroom

☐ OVERVIEW

Improving the success in school of culturally diverse children and language minority children in the classroom is based on modifying the means used to achieve learning outcomes, not on changing the intended outcomes themselves. The underachievement in reading among culturally diverse and language minority students continues to move downward due to a lack of understanding on the part of school personnel concerning cultural values, orientations, and perceptions that differ radically from those of the middle-class white American student (Gilbert, 1985). For example, studies on black children of low socioeconomic status (SES) indicate that the major challenge for educators in helping them become more successful is to stop trying to use their home environments or social status as an excuse for poor achievement. Focusing instead on understanding the *real importance* of the school system, the classroom environment, and the teaching activities used will create classroom climates that promote high achievement (Gilbert, 1985).

Culturally and language diverse children have many linguistic and cultural needs that the classroom climate should accommodate in the teaching/learning context. Among the academic needs of these children is the importance of reading achievement. Teachers need to know how to accommodate these needs as well as gain an understanding of any cultural

Dr. Viola Florez, Texas A & M University, contributed major portions of this chapter.

attitudes, values, and behaviors that directly affect the reading instructional process. This chapter is designed to help teachers better understand the culturally and language diverse student. It is felt that through a better understanding and awareness of these children, diagnosis and corrective/remedial instruction will better meet their academic needs.

After reading this chapter, the teacher should be able to

☐ identify linguistic and cultural characteristics that influence language learning of the culturally diverse child.

☐ discuss specific characteristics in relationship to dialect interference in reading.

☐ identify major characteristics common among some dialects and standard English and utilize this information to diagnose children's reading difficulties.

☐ understand the culturally diverse child and utilize this information to plan and implement corrective/remedial reading instruction.

☐ identify and implement specific instructional strategies that apply directly to the learning styles of culturally diverse children.

☐ understand the process of acquiring a second language for the language minority student and its relationship to reading in a second language.

SCHOOL EXPECTATIONS

Culturally and language diverse children have one thing in common—their cultures and/or ethnic backgrounds are *different* from those of their typical American counterparts. Rather than capitalizing on this, many schools have handled this difference as a deficit. Thus, labels such as "culturally deprived," "disadvantaged," "language deficient," and "slow learner" have sometimes been used to refer to these children. Such children are frequently described as having low self-images, language deficits, apathetic attitudes, unpredictable behaviors, low motivation, and limited experiences. Labels and terms such as these are the result of tunnel vision and ignorance. Many teachers and administrators who use derogatory labels for language and culturally diverse children have a limited understanding of the cultures and life-styles of the children they teach. This is not to say that none of these students possess such characteristics; however, it is the cumulative effect, year after year, of living a different life-style outside of school and of the school not recognizing these differences in terms of its programs that often results in these children's reading difficulties. It is also appropriate to note that children who are not culturally or language divergent also exhibit some of these previously mentioned characteristics.

Culturally diverse students come to school just as eager to learn as any other student. They bring with them language patterns, experiences, and sociological and psychological problems, however, that are different from some of these other students. But these differences can be recognized and capitalized on in the school setting. The conception of readiness as the adequacy of students' capacities in relation to the demands of learning tasks respects both hereditary and environmental factors. Some culturally diverse students have experienced environments that place little emphasis on emerging literacy (reading experiences within home and so forth) to which most average preschoolers have been exposed. For example, reading as a social tool is highly regarded in most middle-class homes, but this is not so in many low-SES homes.

Reading readiness is an integral part of an effective reading program. Data concerning a student's background and experiences, amount of reading readiness training, and reading abilities, as well as knowledge of the culture of the student and of nonstandard dialects (phonology, morphology, and syntax) are imperative. The type and quality of instruction rests on teachers' specific knowledge of their students and their ability to use diagnostic findings in planning an appropriate instructional program. The cumulative effect of students entering school with different backgrounds and teachers expecting that such students adapt to an "average" American background (rather than the school adapting its instruction to these students) means that many culturally and language diverse children experience reading problems.

The concept of readiness is crucial to understanding underachievement. With a readiness factor that may be deficient in terms of success in average curriculums taught by average teachers, culturally and language diverse students can experience great difficulty from the onset if adaptive instruction is not offered. Key factors in adapting instruction are knowledge of the student's culture, values, language, learning behaviors, and level of readiness. Teachers need to also understand the relationship of teacher attitudes and expectations to reading achievement for these children (see chapter 2). Studies by Trueba (1986) indicate that teachers' low expectations and negative attitudes contribute significantly to students' lack of academic achievement. Understanding and believing in the culturally diverse student while encouraging him or her to perform at the student's highest potential can provide the support and encouragement every child needs academically.

DIALECTS AND STANDARD ENGLISH

It is a widely documented fact that both language minority and black students score lower on reading tests than do standard-English speaking white students of similar socioeconomic and residential status. Traditionally, the former group of children have been evaluated in standard English with instruments whose standardization populations include few representatives of minority groups. (The importance of the norming population and interpretation of test results is presented in chapter 5.) As a result, language minority students and black students have sometimes been labeled as retarded readers, language deficient, and/or mentally retarded. These labels imply a language and cultural deficit so great that only minimal progress in reading can be expected. This is an illogical assumption. Children whose language differs from standard English can become succesful readers.

Black Dialect and Reading Achievement

One hypothesis explains the reading difficulties experienced by many black children as the result of a mismatch between the language structure of black English and the language structure of standard English used in schools. This interference effect makes learning to read a more difficult task. These language differences are semantic, syntactic, and phonological; therefore, many black students are, in a sense, involved in learning a new variety of their language, as well as in learning reading skills.

The linguistic interference hypothesis has not won unanimous support. Those in opposition maintain that differences between oral language and written language are sufficient to cause problems for all beginning readers, and dialect does not add significantly to the task for groups whose dialect differs from standard English (Weber, 1970).

Labov (1970) believes that a primary cause of reading difficulties for black children is the conflict between the vernacular culture and the middle-class culture of the classroom rather than linguistic differences. However, Labov accepts the idea that there might be indirect interference resulting from poor communication between the teacher and black students, due to areas such as learning styles, interactional styles, communication styles, and perceptions of involvement. In addition, it has been suggested that a lack of confidence in the alphabet as a systematic representation of black children's speech contributes to their difficulties in learning to read.

It is yet to be established that black dialectal interference is responsible for black children's difficulties in learning to read. In a review of research, Harber and Bryen (1976) examined the relationship between reading and black dialect usage. They concluded that the literature supports dialect interference in terms of black children's performance on oral reading tasks, but large evidence gaps exist to support the relationship between black English and reading difficulties. Specifically, they noted several unresolved issues concerning the teaching of reading to black urban students.

1. There is no clear-cut evidence that a child's use of black English interferes with the entire reading process.
2. No conclusive empirical evidence supports the use of dialectal-based texts in place of standard English instructional materials.

3. Not enough is currently known about black English phonology to identify how extreme the differences are between it and the English of commercial textbooks.
4. There is a lack of training for teachers in teacher preparation programs about how to teach culturally diverse students adequately and how to use instructional materials effectively with these students.
5. No effective means has been found to develop in teachers the attitude that black English is not inferior but is instead an acceptable style of speech that adequately meets the user's communicative needs.
6. There is a lack of information concerning other variables that affect reading development in relation to using black English, such as intelligence, cultural background, and social issues.

Although there are still more questions than answers about the effect of black dialect on reading difficulties, linguists and educators stress the need for teachers to be more accepting of black English, to allow children to use linguistic variety in the classroom, and to be more knowledgeable about specific differences between black English and standard English. The importance of this knowledge to being able to help black children become better readers is stated by Somervill (1975):

> Whether the teacher's attitude is that the black child's language must be changed or that his language should be incorporated into the school setting, the importance of the teacher's knowledge of specific differences between her own language and the language of the black child cannot be underestimated. (p. 248)

Familiarity with the systematic differences between black English and standard English is necessary for an accurate diagnosis in an oral reading situation, such as administering an IRI. Dialectal differences that are attributed to reading difficulties may not be interfering with comprehension, and, as such, are not really reading problems. A guide (Fryberg, 1974) to the principal pronunciation and syntactic differences between black nonstandard English and standard English follows. Its purpose is to facilitate accurate diagnosis and instructional planning for children who speak black nonstandard English.

1. In all variables of spoken English, the sounds at the ends of words, as represented in their written form, may not be articulated. Black English speakers may weaken the final sounds *r, l, t, d, s,* and *z* more than other English speakers: for example, "too" for "tool," and "they" for "their."
2. Sounds represented by *v* may be substituted for voiced *th*: for example, "muvver" for "mother."
3. Sounds represented by *f* may be substituted for voiceless *th*: for example, "toof" for "tooth."
4. Sounds represented by *d* and *t* may be substituted for both voiced and voiceless *th*: for example, "dis" for "this" and "brudder" for "brother."

5. Sounds represented by *t, d,* and *s* may be omitted when indicating inflectional markers in English: for example, "jump" for "jumped," "stop" for "stopped," "cent" for "cents," and "miss" for "missed." Omission of sound recorded by *ed* in past tense usually occurs for regular verbs. Irregular verbs often indicate past tense with vowel changes and words such as "told," "gave," and "run" would usually be pronounced as written.
6. Sounds represented by final consonant clusters *sk, sp,* and *st* are frequently simplified; for example, "des" for "desk" and "tes" for "test."
7. Sounds represented by initial consonant clusters *thr, shr, str,* and *pr* at the beginning of words may be pronounced differently: for example, "th'ow" or "t'row" for "throw," "srimp" or "swimp" for "shrimp," "skreet" for "street," and "p'tect" for "protect."
8. Syntactic differences may be noted for agreement of third person singular subject with present tense verb—"Mary pay" for "Mary pays"; noun plurals—"seven cent" for "seven cents"; noun possessives—"Susan chair" for "Susan's chair"; simple past tense—"they walk" for "they walked"; linking verb—"Sam a good boy" for "Sam is a good boy" or for "Sam's a good boy"; invariant verb *to be* to express general or habitual action—"she be here" for "she is generally here"; formation of compound pasts— "Sarah done play" or "Sarah been play" for "Sarah has played"; and negation—"Mom never goes nowhere" for "Mom never goes anywhere," "They ain't got no car" or "They don't got no car" for "They don't have a car." (Fryberg, 1974, pp. 191–195)

Familiarity with phonological and syntactic differences between standard English and black English enables the teacher to distinguish between a child who has a reading difficulty and one who just differs in dialectal pronunciation. Grammatical variables, such as syntax, and their effect on comprehension should be the focus of diagnosis. Dialectal differences in pronunciation only become important when they interfere with the child's comprehension of the materials read.

Several alternatives have been suggested for helping black children experiencing reading difficulties to become better readers. Among these are (1) emphasizing standard English prior to or during reading instruction, (2) using dialect readers, (3) using the language-experience approach, and (4) allowing a dialect reading of traditional English texts. Somervill (1975) examined each of these alternatives with an emphasis on relevant research and concluded that none of these alternatives demonstrated marked superiority in producing reading achievement gains.

A review of research on black English and reading conducted by Harber and Bryen (1976) supports Somervill's conclusion:

Educational alternatives (dialect-based reading materials) may be premature when one considers the existing research that explores the relationship between black English and reading. Studies indicate that the relationship between black English usage and reading continues to remain unclear. (p. 391)

Diagnosis for black children experiencing reading difficulties is based on the same procedures recommended for children who speak standard English. Interpretation of oral performance considers the dialectal features outlined earlier and also investigates other factors such as those discussed in chapter 4. Dialectal variation cannot be considered as the single cause of a black child's reading difficulties. Corrective and remedial instruction must be based on a program that meets the child's individual needs, focuses on reading strengths, and emphasizes comprehension as the goal of instruction.

Language Minority Children and Reading Achievement

Language minority children (bilingual as well as non-English speaking) are faced with many expectations when they enter a formal education setting. They are expected to adjust not only to a different cultural and social environment, but also to understand and to speak another language (English) different from their own. These children are expected to read and comprehend English with competency as part of their school curriculum. It is not possible to read in a language one does not know, if reading involves the act of making intelligible to oneself written texts of any complexity beyond that of street signs (Fillmore, 1987). True, individuals can be taught to "decode" a printed text with a minimal knowledge of the language in which it is written; that is, they can be taught to reproduce the speech sounds that have been given a written representation in a language they do not know. Hence, most literate English-speaking adults could, with some training, learn to associate letters and letter combinations in written Vietnamese with creditable approximations to their phonetic value, and could possibly in that manner "decode" a Vietnamese text. Being able to do this task, however, is clearly distinct from knowing what the text is about. Such readers would find this task demanding and not intelligible. A motivated, mature reader with effective study skills could go even further with this type of effort and decipher the text by looking up each word in a bilingual dictionary. However, this is still decoding and not reading. Decoding is only one aspect of reading; not many of us would call it "reading." By reading, we refer to the act of reconstructing the meaning of a text as intended by the writer, and through this process, gaining access to the information that is written in the text. It appears, then, that a prerequisite for true reading is a fairly high level of knowledge of the language in which the text is written. Therefore, language minority children cannot be expected to read and comprehend texts written in English if they are not proficient in the new language involved.

Reading and Special Language Programs

Presently, bilingual education and English as a Second Language (ESL) programs are attempting to meet the linguistic needs of these children. Meanwhile, the controversy exists about using students' native languages for reading instruction throughout bilingual programs in the southwestern part of the United States. There has been a number of studies showing the hardly surprising result that students find it easier to learn in a language they already know than in one they are just learning (Fillmore, 1987). In a study conducted in the Chiapas highlands of Mexico, Modiano (1973) studied the effects of initial reading instruction in a first language (L1) and in a second language (L2). She compared a large sample of Mexican Mayan children, some of whom were being taught to read in their first language (Mayan), and some in their second language, Spanish. The study revealed that the children who learned to read first in L1 were more successful in becoming literate in L2 than those children who learned to read directly in Spanish, a language they were learning at the same time that they were learning to read. At the end of the third grade, a significant difference was found between the two groups in Spanish reading skills and in the transfer of these skills as they learned to read in Spanish.

Another study by Rosier (1977) compared the effectiveness of initial reading instruction given to Navajo-speaking children in their native language to the effectiveness of reading instruction given in English. Students who were taught reading in English were concurrently given instruction in ESL. Those who were taught to read in their L1 were given assistance in developing oral proficiency in English, and at the third grade were transferred to English reading. At the end of the third year, Rosier found that the group taught to read in L1 scored significantly higher than the L2 reading group on the English achievement tests used in the study (the *Stanford* and the *Metropolitan Achievement Tests*). These studies by Rosier show that initial reading instruction in L1 has the effect of later success in L2 reading; the skill of reading, once acquired through the process of first-langauge reading, is transferable.

The question of when and how to introduce reading instruction in the L2 is more of an important issue in bilingual education programs today than is whether or not to begin with native-language reading instruction. The research evidence supports the usage of L1 in initial reading programs for language minority students, but many questions remain on when and how to introduce reading instruction in L2. There exist several practices being observed in special language programs. One is that of teaching reading in the L1 and L2 simultaneously, with students learning to read in two languages. Studies (Barik & Swain, 1976) reveal the dangers of language interference if the languages share the same orthography, such as English and Spanish. Barik and Swain, however, feel that the interference of two systems can be overcome in time, but it does present problems in the early stages of reading instruction.

A second practice is to introduce reading instruction in L1, but switch to L2 reading as soon as students give evidence of being able to speak the second language (English). The difficulties with this approach are that many times these children have not gained a cognitive level of L2 proficiency that allows them to make sense of written text in English; and more important, they have not learned to read in L1, and therefore do not have the necessary transferable skills from one language to another.

A third practice of reading instruction is to teach L2 reading from the beginning, but use it as a kind of ESL instruction. The concept here is that written text can serve as a means by which students are taught a new language. Studies by Goodman, Goodman, and Flores (1979) indicate that it is possible to introduce English reading to students before they have mastered the language; however, it is important that these students can deal with the new language at a receptive level and can handle reading instruction. They feel that in this way language minority students could gain useful data about the new language which might not be available to them otherwise. However, they also state that this practice works better when the learners are already literate in their first language.

Even though discussion continues about how and when English reading should be taught to language minority children, educators need to be aware of the difficulties related to the process of learning to read in a new language and be sensitive to the approaches used to teach initial reading instruction. Language learning is influenced by all the factors surrounding a child in the classroom setting; therefore, the child must be motivated by a desire to participate and to learn a new language. The desire to learn the new language in an educational setting can be seriously impeded if the teacher is not aware of the child's cultural and linguistic background along with his or her value systems and learning behaviors. Culture or value conflicts between the child's culture and a new language, along with the demands of acquiring English, can cause the child to withdraw socially, psychologically, and academically from the educational setting.

Learning to read in a second language requires the same skills and abilities as learning to read in a native language. The process of reading is the same and must only be learned once. Therefore, the same facilitative factors and functional reading factors apply to both language minority children and monolingual, English-speaking children. However, the role of facilitative reading factors becomes an area of primary focus for teachers helping ESL children who are experiencing reading difficulties. Providing extensive vocabulary development; context-embedded, knowledge-based language experiences; and conceptually comprehensible printed text is necessary in helping the language minority student who is learning to read or is having reading difficulties with the new language. Many times language minority children may have deficient literacy skills in their first language, and this can inhibit learning to read in English.

Many of the reading problems of language minority students are unwillingly created by their teachers whenever these children are assigned reading tasks and materials patently incompatible with their language backgrounds (Barrera, 1983). An example of this is the frequent expectation that bilingual students can perform English phonic instructional tasks and sequences as well as monolingual, English-speaking students. Many children have difficulty in this area and so perform very poorly; for example, some bilingual students cannot produce certain English sounds. The typical reaction is not to question the relevance or appropriateness of such training of bilingual learners, but to respond instead with more instruction of the same kind.

Another disregard for the language backgrounds of these children is the use of commercially produced English reading tests to measure students' reading progress and academic achievement. Many of these tests contain items and English labels unknown to children from different backgrounds. Also, these tests assume a knowledge of English grammar that is incomprehensible to second-language students. Other types of evaluation measures should be used to provide more information on a child's reading abilities instead of academic achievement.

The classroom practices previously described make it clear that much more work is needed if more effective instruction is to be realized for the language minority child. Helping teachers become aware of the developmental nature of second-language learning may limit the impositions of monolingual standards of bilingual children's reading. Teachers need to understand the process involved as these children learn to control English phonology, grammar, orthography, lexicon, and idiomatic expressions. Obviously, these children are progressing toward a command of the English language that is influenced by their native languages; they are not progressing toward an adult grasp of the language. Teaching teachers to sort out differences in L2 reading patterns that are a natural outcome of students' language backgrounds is important for successful reading achievement.

Classroom Applications

There are some important considerations for working with second-language learners who are experiencing reading problems. First, it is important to develop the child's language exposure through extensive oral language opportunities, such as reading aloud, storytelling, using puppetry and fingerplays, reading poetry, and using drama (such as role playing). Exposure to the new language in this way is necessary in order for the child to hear the new linguistic system. If the materials being utilized to develop a second language are comprehensible and worthwhile, the student will be motivated to learn English, and therefore will begin to merge second-language reading with second-language oral development. Integrating both reading and oral language development for these children is much more effective than is separating them from each other. Such development should focus on both factual and fictional language. **Factual language** is used in such situations as reporting, explaining, conversing, discussing, questioning, evaluating, and debating. **Fictional language** is most often used for telling about prose or poetry, restructuring prose or poetry, interpreting oral communication of others, role playing, dramatizing school and life incidents, and telling creative stories. Each language type should be practiced on a continuum from informal to formal, and children should get instruction in using various styles appropriate to the situation (Buckley, 1976).

A second consideration in working with second-language learners is that it is important for these children to continue to develop conceptually. Introducing concepts through the language-experience approach (LEA) is extremely useful due to its utilization of context-embedded language familiar to the child. This process allows children to talk about personal and familiar experiences; then their statements can be used to help them acquire the ability to understand written language and to read. Children's motivation to read their own stories is high. Recognizing their own words in print is easier than dealing with the unfamiliar language of many basal readers and textbooks (Dixon, 1976).

Third, accept the transfer of the reading process from L1 to L2 as an interdependent process instead of as separate, distinct processes. Strategies for processing written text to get at meaning are carried over from one language to another. In essence, one reading process is operative across all languages, regardless of their surface forms, and is kept in motion by the reader's ongoing drive to gain meaning and understanding (Barrera, 1983). If the teacher understands the process of transfer from one language to another, then the child's knowledge base will be utilized and the probability of reading improvement will increase.

Finally, in teaching second-language learners, teachers must realize that correcting and remediating reading difficulties does not always mean attending to the pronunciation of sounds or to letters representing particular sounds. Research has shown that the mispronunciation of sounds or letters does not automatically interfere with the comprehension of meaningful, connected texts (Barrera, 1978; Goodman & Goodman, 1978). Many teachers of language minority children continue to treat mispronunciations as errors disruptive of meaning, and therefore they spend a tremendous amount of time drilling sound pronunciations and concentrating only on these "problems." Correcting and remediating word-recognition difficulties are important, but not at the expense of impeding the comprehension of the intended text meaning. Concentrating on a language-based approach to teaching sound/letter relationships will benefit bilingual children more as they become familiar with a new language system. By using this approach, language minority children will be able to make sense of what they hear and read in printed text.

Teachers of language minority children need to recognize that other characteristics, such as differences in conceptual schemata and cultural backgrounds, might present more formidable barriers in reading for these children than will pronunciation patterns (Joag-Dev & Steffensen, 1980).

Teachers need to direct more attention to other variables instead of only word-recognition or pronunciation skills.

It is important for classroom and resource teachers to understand and be aware of the differences and similarities of speech sounds and grammatical features from one language to another. This knowledge allows for accurate diagnosis of some reading difficulties and helps ensure that linguistic interferences are not viewed as reading difficulties. Having this knowledge helps the teacher of the linguistically diverse child to understand the process of interference in transfer from L1 to L2 as the child acquires the new languages. The following description of linguistic features common to Navajo, Spanish, and Vietnamese speakers who are learning English should prove beneficial for diagnostic and instructional purposes.

NAVAJO LINGUISTIC FEATURES

Phonology

Studies show that there are many differences between English and Navajo in the pronunciation of sounds in the two languages (Troike, 1978 and Young, 1973). Since there is no distinction between /p/ and /b/ in Navajo, Navajo speakers usually do not distinguish these sounds and often substitute their own slightly different /b/ for both. Since in Navajo these sounds never occur at the end of a syllable, children often substitute /ˈ/ (a glottal stop) for final /p/ or /b/ or reduce all final stops to the Navajo /d/. This /d/, which sounds like the /t/ in /stop/, is also typically substituted for the English /t/ or /d/ in initial position. The /ˈ/ is frequently substituted for stop consonants and is added before initial vowels, making Navajo speech sound choppy to speakers of English. In Navajo there are no sounds corresponding to /f/, /v/, /o/, /ð/, and /ŋ/, so all of these sounds constitute learning problems for the Navajo child learning English.

The primary differences between the vowel systems of Navajo and English are that vowel length and nasalization are used to distinguish meaning in Navajo, and that English exhibits a greater variety of vowel sounds. The vowels /æ/ and /ɔ/ do not occur in Navajo and are the hardest for students to learn. Navajo students must also distinguish between English /ow/ and /uw/.

Consonant clusters (blends) present a major problem for Navajo students learning English. Navajo children usually have difficulty with noun and verb inflections because they fail to hear or produce final consonant clusters in English.

Mastery of the sound systems of both languages is essential for the Navajo child. If an appropriate English oral language program is implemented in the school curriculum for these children, they can master both

English Phonemes						Navajo Phonemes				
/p/	/t/			/k/			/t/	/k/	/k/	
							/t'/	/k'/	/'/	
/b/	/d/			/g/	/b/	/d/		/g/		
			/č/			/ts/	/č/	/tł/		
						/ts'/	/č'/	/tł'/		
						/dz/	/ǰ/	/dl/		
/f/	/θ/	/s/	/š/	/h/		/s/	/š/	/h/	/x/	
/v/	/ð/	/z/	/ž/			/z/	/ž/		/x̣/	
/m/		/n/	/ŋ/		/m/	/n/				
/w/	/l/	/y/	/r/		/w/	/l/	/y/			
			/u/			/ł/				
/iy/		/uw/								
/i/		/u/			/i/		/o/			
/ey/	/ə/	/ow/								
/e/					/e/					
/æ/	/a/	/ɔ/				/a/				

FIGURE 14–1 Comparison of Navajo and English phonemic systems

sound systems and, as a result, increase their English proficiency and reading capabilities.

Figure 14–1 shows the differences and similarities between Navajo and English phonemic systems; circled English phonemes signify that they do not exist in the Navajo language system.

Syntax

The Navajo grammatical system includes all the elements necessary to form complete sentences. Navajo children learn that English syntax is different from their own; through oral language instruction these children can learn to function within both syntactical systems. Gleason and Cook (1961) indicate that several areas seem to give Navajo children who are learning English more difficulty with language acquisition, therefore causing academic difficulties, especially in the areas of reading and writing. The following are major areas of linguistic differences for the Navajo child.

Nouns. Most Navajo nouns do not show number; instead, the verb form conveys this information.

Pronouns. Navajo pronouns do not change in form the way English pronouns do. In English, the pronoun changes form according to number, case, and gender; in Navajo, the pronoun *bi* is used for all third person genders, numbers, and cases. As a result, the Navajo child has trouble learning to use the various English pronouns correctly or may use just one form of a pronoun for all third person situations.

In Navajo, object pronouns occur as prefixes of the verb rather than as independent forms. Possessive pronouns also give Navajo children difficulty —in Navajo, the marker for possession goes with the possessed rather than with the possessor, as in English. This pattern, carried over into English, accounts for such nonstandard phrases as "the boy his hat."

Plurals. With few exceptions, nouns in Navajo do not change form to express singular or plural. Plurality of the subject is usually indicated in the verb. As a result, the Navajo child may say "the horse are running" instead of "the horses are running."

Word Order. The normal order in Navajo is subject + object + verb. When an indirect object is added, it must precede the direct object. English not only has a different order of elements, but the arrangement of elements is somewhat flexible. Most of the inflectional elements of words occur as prefixes in Navajo but as suffixes in English. Usually Navajo children who are learning English may consequently omit inflectional suffixes.

Prepositions. There are forms in Navajo that roughly correspond to English prepositions but that are postpositions following the word modified. Occasionally prepositions are omitted altogether, as in "go school" or "go home."

Articles. There are no words in Navajo that correspond exactly to English definite and indefinite articles (although there are forms that can be used to show definiteness and indefiniteness). Navajo children usually omit articles in English when expressing themselves orally, producing sentences such as "Joe has red hat" or "Book on table is red."

Adjectives. With only a few exceptions, there are no adjectives in Navajo. The closest form to the adjective as it is used in English is a neuter verb which occurs after the noun. Navajo children will usually say "the pretty girl" before they can produce "The girl is pretty."

Verbs. The Navajo verb system is based on aspects rather than tense; in other words, the concern lies with the state of completion, contour, and duration rather than with the time of the action. Navajo children learning English have difficulty with all English verbs, mainly because English tenses change the meaning of what is said. This gives Navajo children great difficulty when attempting to learn to read. The teacher's sensitivity to this issue while teaching reading will help Navajo children perform more effectively.

Lexicon

According to Young (1973) and Harvey (1974), the lexicon is considered a major system within a language. Their studies indicate that Navajo children learning new English words try to superimpose on these words the same categories into which experiences are classified in their native language. Navajo children find it difficult to express ideas in English that relate to English concepts, such as *to cause, to force, to compel, to make, to order,* and so forth, which have no Navajo referents; therefore, Navajo children learning these concepts in English must learn the appropriate referent in Navajo.

Basic categories are sometimes different in English and Navajo. The English concept of *rough* is perceived as a series of different attributes, each having different labels (*dighol, digoon,* and *dich' iizh*) depending on whether the roughness is perceived as the texture of a road, a rock, or a file; the last category (*dich' iizh*) actually includes the rough texture of both a file and a bumpy surface. A Navajo speaker learning English must learn to make verbal distinctions among different types of rough surfaces.

Every child learns a great deal of language from his peer groups. A child learns the subtle meanings of words by trial and error, testing words among other members of his or her group in actual communication; therefore, an extensive oral language program before initial reading can help Navajo childen experience and learn more about the two languages involved. Such a program will bring about a better attitude toward reading. As comprehension and understanding in the new language are developed, reading improvement will increase.

SPANISH LINGUISTIC FEATURES

The classroom teacher needs to be alert to the linguistic features of the Spanish language that may cause Spanish-speaking children difficulty in acquiring language as it relates to reading. The following are some of the speech sounds that are difficult for Spanish-speaking children as well as examples of nonstandard usage forms most common to Spanish-speaking children.

Phonology

1. Voiceless Spanish sounds are frequently substituted for voiced English sounds:

   f for *v*   *t* for *d*   *s* for *z*   *k* for *g*

   This substitution is likely to occur at the end of words; for example, "ret" for "red" and "bus" for "buzz."
2. Sounds represented by *s, p,* or *t* are sometimes substituted for voiced *th*: for example, "tum" for "thumb."
3. Sounds represented by *z, v,* or *d* are sometimes substituted for voiced *th*: for example, "dan" for "then."
4. Sounds represented by *b* and *v* are sometimes interchanged.

5. Sounds represented by *ch, sh,* and *zh* are often interchanged: for example, "shair" for "chair," and "choes" for "shoes."
6. Sounds represented by *j* are sometimes substituted for sounds represented by *y*: for example, "jellow" for "yellow."
7. Sounds represented by *ng* are sometimes made with an added *k* or *g* following the sound: for example, "sing-ging."
8. Sounds represented by short *i* and long *e* are interchanged frequently, with the *e* being most often substituted for the *i*: for example, "sheep" for "ship."
9. Sounds represented by vowels in words like "cat," "cup," and "brother" are made to sound like *ah* while the vowel in "put" is usually made to sound like *oo* (Frey, 1970, pp. 49–50).

Grammatical forms

1. Using double negatives
   Example: I don't see nobody.
2. Using double comparisons
   Example: My brother is more taller.
3. Confusing simple preterit with past participle
   Example: He should have gone.
4. Consistently misusing third person singular, present tense
   Example: He come to school every day.
5. Using double subjects
   Example: My mother she is home.
6. Adding an unnecessary *s* to possessive forms
   Example: He took mines and his.
7. Adding an unnecessary *s* to plural forms
   Example: The mens came to work every morning.
8. Using possessive forms of nouns
   Example: This is the dress of my sister.
   (In Spanish, the form for "my sister's dress" is not found. Literal translation from the Spanish language results in such things as "the nest of the bird" instead of "the bird's nest.")
9. Confusing word order in sentences and questions
   Example: "Where I am?" instead of "Where am I?"
10. Confusing verb forms—both tense and number
    Example: Yesterday my mother tell me to be good.
11. Confusing word order of adjectives and nouns
    Example: I want that flower red.
    (In Spanish the adjective always comes after the noun.)
12. Using direct translations of Spanish idioms
    Example: He is sick of the eye.
13. Using words interchangeably and incorrectly (some—any; much—many; like—want; say—tell; make—do; all—every)
    Example: I have many money in my pocket.

14. Using *me* instead of *I*
    Example: Me have shoes.
15. Pronouncing final *d* as *t*
    Example: bad vs. bat
16. Using *he* and *she* to differentiate males and females
17. Omitting *-s* from third person singular, present tense verbs.
    Example: "He play" vs. "He plays"
18. Using *don't* instead of *doesn't*
19. Omitting *Do* when it begins a question
    Example: "You go there?" instead of "Do you go there?"

VIETNAMESE LINGUISTIC FEATURES

Teachers may have Vietnamese students in their classrooms who speak little or no English. Teachers who are aware of the linguistic features present in the Vietnamese language will be able to help Vietnamese children overcome major reading problems as they acquire the English language. Teachers' awareness and sensitivity to differences in language characteristics can help with corrective/remedial or diagnostic instruction.

The present writing system of the Vietnamese is a modified Roman alphabet system devised by European missionaries in collaboration with the Vietnamese more than two centuries ago. Its spelling system is closely related to the spoken form of Vietnamese. Due to close geographical proximities and cultural influences, the Vietnamese language contains a high percentage of vocabulary borrowed from Chinese, just as English has borrowed extensively from Latin and French (Thuan, 1962).

The Vietnamese language is invariable in form. In other words, to express the notion of past versus nonpast, or plural versus singular, Vietnamese does not use inflectional suffixes such as *play* in contrast to *played* or *book* in contrast to *books.* Instead, as a reflection of its culture (Thuan, 1962), the Vietnamese language uses a set of particles to express time-relationships (the occurrence of one event in relationship to that of another event or other events) rather than to express definite time. This does not mean that the Vietnamese langauge is not capable of expressing definite time; but it does mean that the Vietnamese concept of time and ways of expressing it will influence how a Vietnamese child uses English as the process of acquisition develops.

An area of major concern for the Vietnamese child developing a new language and learning to read is the area of phonology. The pronunciation of sounds in the final position of a word such as *s* (in consonant clusters), and final *es, t,* and *d* are unfamiliar to the Vietnamese child. Vietnamese children have never heard these sounds; therefore, when speaking English, they will often ignore the unfamiliar sounds. A Vietnamese child, for example, might say something like "I work har on my tes las nigh," instead of "I worked hard on my test last night." Because such differences in speech sounds will affect the reading performance of Vietnamese students, it is important that the teacher is aware of the differences and similarities of the English and Vietnamese languages in order to help these children succeed in all areas of language learning. Teaching reading from a language-based approach is essential if understanding and comprehension in reading is to occur. Integrating the pronunciation skills and other reading skills with relevant and meaningful language will help Vietnamese children increase their reading capabilities.

Developing and implementing an instructional reading program for language minority children is based on the same consideration as is a program for English-speaking children. Diagnosis takes into account the influence of factors that can inhibit reading development. Language minority children's reading difficulties usually stem from factors other than language differences. Causes of reading problems (cultural backgrounds, auditory defects, social/emotional problems, educational factors, and the like) also must be investigated in the diagnostic process. Instructional programs that recognize individual reading strengths and weaknesses are more likely to bring about reading improvement. Although it is probable that much instructional emphasis will be aimed at further English language development, reading instruction should be built on each child's existing reading strengths. Reading instruction that builds on potential, interests, cultural diversities, and strengths will go a long way in facilitating reading growth (Cheyney, 1976).

CULTURALLY DIVERSE CHILDREN

America has long been considered the cultural "melting pot" of the world. Persons of all cultures were, in a philosophical sense, assimilated into and contributed to the existing culture, which benefited from this unique blending. The melting pot philosophy, however, has not always been readily apparent in either American society at large or in middle-class American schools. Many teachers, because they possess Anglo backgrounds, perceive this culture as the most appropriate and give little recognition to other cultural backgrounds. Currently, educational policies based on the melting pot philosophy force the culturally diverse child to either seek cultural identity with the home or with the school (Ramirez & Castandeda, 1974). Children who choose the culture of the home are typically those who experience learning problems. There is, however, a third alternative, which is developing a bicultural identity that "permits the child to enjoy satisfying relations in more than one cultural world and to identify with aspects of both of those cultures" (Ramirez & Castandeda, 1974, p. 16).

Culturally diverse students come to school just as eager to learn as any other students. (Bruce Johnson/Merrill)

Black Culture

Reading difficulties experienced by many black children can be the result of forcing a reading curriculum on them that does not recognize and build on their culture. The cultural background of black children is often a different one from the cultural background the school expects. Those who view this difference as a learning impediment say that learning problems tend to result from this "cultural deprivation." However, such a simplistic explanation does not help the black child become a better reader. The term *cultural deprivation* implies that black children possess *no* cultural background rather than a cultural background *different* from that which the school expects. Black children *do not* lack a cultural background! Instead, they have a different range of experiences, values, and language abilities. Building on what they bring to reading instructional settings is more likely to result in reading growth than are attempts to force them into a curriculum based on cultural values they do not possess.

In Johnson's (1977) opinion, black children who have reading difficulties are likely to become more proficient readers if teachers attempt to understand and build on these students' cultural backgrounds. Teachers who interpret black children's behavior in light of their cultural background can better meet these students' reading needs.

Johnson notes several cultural aspects of black children's behavior that are frequently misinterpreted by teachers:

> Black children crave affection (especially physical contact) because they are denied affection in their culture. Instead, the correct interpretation . . . is that black children are accustomed to receiving attention in their culture, and they are looking for the same thing in the school culture. Black children . . . do better in a highly structured classroom situation conducted by an authoritarian teacher. Instead, the correct interpretation is that black children view the teacher as a surrogate mother, and . . . they are confused by the role discrepancy between the permissive teacher ("let's all plan what we want to do") and their authoritarian black mothers ("you will do this"). Or, black children are described as "nonverbal" when, in fact . . . they are taught in their culture not to carry on or discuss with authority figures as equals. (p. 147)

Cultural differences alone cannot explain reading difficulties that black students may or may not experience. However, if corrective and remedial reading diagnosis and instruction are to be effective, the teacher must consider what the child brings to the reading act (learner style). One unquestionable variable that cannot be overlooked is the the child's cultural background.

Mexican-American Culture (Bilingual/Bicultural)

As with black children, failure to recognize the cultural background of bilingual children may lead to reading problems. A corrective or remedial reading environment will be effective only if it recognizes and encourages the language minority child's cultural values. Several major cultural factors and their instructional implications are discussed by Dixon (1976). These variables should be considered when teachers gather and interpret information on learner style.

1. Children of Mexican-American culture tend to identify closely with their families. Not only do they identify with parents, but with other siblings as well. The extended family of uncles and aunts is very important to the family unit. Reading activities that stress the improvement of skills in a group situation and cooperative learning are more successful than activities that stress self-improvement in an individual or competitive setting.
2. Motivation is enhanced for Mexican-American children if it is related to the achievement of the group rather than the individual child. (This is in agreement with the recommendations for motivation in chapter 3). Teachers should not assume that all motivation and reinforcement techniques have the same effect on all students. What one child views as an appropriate reinforcer may have no effect or might possibly inhibit motivation for another.
3. Reading activities that encourage cooperation rather than competition are usually more motivating for Mexican-American children. This is not

to suggest that these children are not competitive or that competition should be totally removed from reading instruction; rather, teachers should analyze the level of competition most appropriate to motivate learning.

4. Finally, the human environment in the instructional setting is important. Mexican-American children generally benefit from settings in which they can relate directly to other students and to the teacher. In all probability, working with other children who are in roles of authority will not negatively affect Mexican-American children's reading performance. According to Dixon, this tack "may be viewed as natural and desirable in the classroom as a result of . . . the generalization from the use of other children as authority figures in the 'home' culture" (1976, p. 143).

Reading experiences that rely on paper-and-pencil tasks may be less effective than those that allow for group interaction. For this reason, corrective and remedial reading instruction should not emphasize written drill in seat-work situations. Allowing for interaction on written tasks with other students is more appropriate for Mexican-American students than asking them to complete and hand in written assignments. As mentioned earlier, the LEA seems to be the best choice for bilingual children experiencing reading problems. It recognizes and builds on their language skills and cultural backgrounds and allows for specific skill instruction when weak areas are noted. Skill instruction is then more meaningful because it relates to the child's langauge background and evolves from observed performance in an actual reading situation.

Cultural differences are never the single cause for bilingual children's reading difficulties. Such differences may contribute to the problem, but other causes, such as those discussed in chapter 4, must also be investigated. If needed, they must be accommodated in corrective or remedial instruction. However, classroom and reading resource teachers who are aware of a bilingual child's cultural differences and adjust their reading instruction accordingly will probably be more effective in correction and remediation than those who do not make such adjustments. Ramirez and Castandeda (1974) summarize the major cultural differences between Mexican-American and American children of which teachers need to be aware.

> Mexican-American culture is composed of four major value clusters: (1) identification with family, community, and ethnic groups; (2) personalization of interpersonal relationships; (3) status and role definition in family and community; and (4) Mexican-Catholic ideology. Mainstream American middle-class values . . . can be categorized under the value clusters: (1) sense of separate identity; and (2) individual competitive achievement. (p. 56)

Failure to recognize such differences in reading instruction will surely minimize reading growth for Mexican-American children.

INSTRUCTIONAL IMPLICATIONS

Corrective and remedial reading teaching practices and materials for culturally and language diverse children must be based on diagnostic information to meet these children's needs. While much research is yet to be done before exact recommendations can be made, reading instruction should be grounded on the cultural and language backgrounds of the students and on the premise that each child's language is to be respected, not rejected (Barnitz, 1980; Padak, 1981). Teachers who have a thorough knowledge of the cultural backgrounds of their students and who accommodate these in their corrective/remedial instruction will aid reading improvement.

Understanding the role of dialects is important to the teaching of reading in all situations. Barnitz (1980) discussed the following implication of dialectology on the teaching of reading:

Reading for the child's natural dialect in oral reading situations.

Use of contextual analysis to extend word meanings.

Careful use of auditory discrimination test items because of dialectal differences.

Phonic instruction should vary for children because of dialectal differences.

Since meaning is integral to all dialects, reading instruction should focus on meaning through a language arts approach. (pp. 783, 784)

Recommendations for specialized instructional approaches for those teachers with culturally and language diverse children can be summarized in the following major points.

1. Respect the student's own language and build on it.
2. Use instructional materials that reflect the child's own culture, not middle-class American culture.
3. Focus reading skill development on improving reading comprehension.
4. Use the LEA, because it allows for identification of words in context, builds on the child's experiences and language, and helps conceptualize the purpose of reading.
5. Know thoroughly the child's dialect and be able to detect dialect features that impede comprehension.
6. Provide many varied opportunities for the acquisition of English.
7. Relate existing language skills to reading skills in actual reading tasks.
8. Develop language flexibility that recognizes the child's dialect but that also helps the child realize the need for developing English language skills, for example, using role playing and experience stories that highlight various language situations, such as who is speaking to whom for what purpose, and so on. Children's language usage may also provide insights into how they view adult roles and the need for language flexibility.

Reading problems for the language minority child are complex. They relate to many linguistic and cultural factors that influence language learning. Herbert (1987) provides the following suggestions for reading programs for second-language learners:

1. Teach vocabulary in context. The context should be interesting and pertinent to children. Isolated words lists will not be remembered or learned.
2. Present and pattern grammatical structure in a systematic fashion and in context to content that is meaningful and relevant. Children must learn to read structures if they are to gain real understanding.
3. Use reading materials that have a written language similar to that of the children's listening comprehension and speaking skills.
4. Utilize visual materials to help develop concepts that are included in the reading materials. Too often visuals are not included at all; if present, they are more decorative than useful. Visual materials help clarify and understand meaning in the written text.
5. Use meaningful and relevant lessons. That is, beginning reading materials should develop the skill of understanding and comprehension versus the decoding of sounds and pattern drills of single letter = single sounds. Build upon reading skills from a schematic base for greater understanding and success in reading.
6. Use materials that are meaningful and sequentially organized to enhance the reading process. In other words, materials should emphasize and integrate the oral skills of listening and speaking before these materials are attempted.
7. Provide numerous contexts and associations, including sensory-motor activities, to further develop perceptions.

Knowledge of children's cultural backgrounds is also imperative to providing appropriate instruction. Teachers should communicate their concern for culturally and language diverse students and build positive self-concepts as much as possible. The following strategies, adapted from Ching (1976, pp. 11–12), are suggestions for increasing bilingual children's motivation to learn and for improving their self-concepts:

1. Develop a bond of trust and friendship between teacher and pupil.
2. Provide an atmosphere which will encourage each child to share home and daily experiences and talk about him or herself, personal interests, and aspirations.
3. Provide books in the classroom library and display pictures and various artifacts relating to the cultural heritage of the child in order to reinforce self-identification.
4. Use a camera (Polaroid, if possible) to take photos of class activities and to photograph individual pupils.
5. Provide live models of achievement by having men and women of the child's cultural background, who have succeeded in various lines of endeavor, speak to the class.

6. Develop a unit of study relating to the cultural heritages of the bilingual children.
7. Give bilingual children many opportunities to be recognized by their peers not only through sharing but also through academic accomplishments.
8. Involve parents and siblings in class activities whenever possible; for example, invite parents to share their knowledge and materials relating to their culture and ask siblings to class activities to share their hobbies or personal interests with the children whenever possible.

☐ SUMMARY

Reading problems in today's schools are acute, to say the least. Teachers need to understand children who are culturally and/or linguistically diverse to help them become better readers. Instruction is more effective when teachers adjust to diversity rather than try to force a child to adapt to the cultural and language values of the school.

This chapter identified several unresolved issues concerning the teaching of reading to black children. Collectively, these issues suggested that too little is known about black dialect and its relation to reading to offer clear-cut diagnostic and corrective/remedial guidelines; however, it is emphasized that the teacher working with black students should know the basic syntactic and pronunciation differences between black dialect and standard English. Fryberg's guide should assist teachers in recognizing these language differences. Also, awareness of other factors such as culture, learning styles, behaviors and values should influence the teaching of black children.

Bilingualism and reading instruction is another topic that requires considerable attention for developmental reading instruction as well as for corrective or remedial instruction. The research reviewed suggested guidelines for the teaching of language minority children by building from the unknown to the known in the new language. Factors that affect the learning of a second language, such as desire, teacher expectations, cultural background, socioeconomic status, and so forth, were presented in terms of the teacher's domain of influence and responsibility. Some specific instructional guidelines for helping language minority children become better readers were emphasized, such as the utilization of the language-experience approach (LEA). In addition, the basic linguistic differences between English and second languages in areas such as speech sounds and grammatical forms were presented. These differences should not be viewed as reading errors, but as important features contributing to the failure or success of language minority children learning to read.

Cultural differences were discussed in relation to their potential impact on reading development. It was stressed that cultural differences can lead to or be related to reading difficulties; however, if teachers attend to individualizing corrective and remedial reading instruction, they can accommodate these differences in instructional practices.

Major instructional implications for correcting or remediating reading difficulties of language and culturally different children were summarized. Specific recommendations for black children and language minority children were built on an individualized approach. Teachers were encouraged to capitalize on the children's knowledge base before expecting them to meet the demands of the established reading program. Intensive development of the English language was emphasized as crucial to the development and improvement of reading.

□ IN-TEXT ASSIGNMENTS

LIBRARY ACTIVITY

Select two or three of the instructional practice recommendations presented in this chapter. For example, you may wish to reread the sections on instructional practices of ESL and black students. Using these instructional practice recommendations, develop an individualized instructional plan (see chapter 3) for the areas of task conditions, resource attributes, and teacher style. You may wish to consult recent journal publications in popular reading and language arts journals (e.g., *The Reading Teacher, Reading Psychology, Reading Research and Instruction,* and *Language Arts*) to identify teaching recommendations for culturally and language diverse students. Using the information you gathered for the areas of the individualized instructional plan, prepare a direct-instruction lesson to promote students' reading growth. Share this information with your classmates and professor.

FIELD-BASED ACTIVITY

Visit an elementary-school classroom containing language and culturally diverse students. Observe and note language and cultural similarities and differences presented in this chapter. Observe the classroom and/or reading resources teachers' atempts to accommodate these similarities and differences in their instructional practices. Prepare a brief report of your observations to share and discuss with your classmates.

SHARING AND BRAINSTORMING ACTIVITY

Listed are some examples of dialectal and language differences that are used often by "average" American speakers. Based on the information presented in this chapter, determine if these would interfere with communication of meaning. "Crick" for "creek," "howz come" for "how come," "runnin" for "running," and "me too" for "I too." Other examples include "don't have none" for "don't have any," "he/she don't" for "he/she doesn't," "'idear" for "idea," "might could have" for "might" or "maybe," "ceb" for "cab," and "fixin to" for "about to" or "going to."

RESOURCE ACTIVITY

Invite an educator (either public school or higher education) from another cultural and linguistic background to speak to your class. Discuss with this person how he or she feels reading should be taught to culturally and linguistically diverse students. Focus your discussion on such things as the impact of cultural differences on students' reading comprehension, ability to take standardized tests, diagnosis of students' reading, and so forth. Additional discussion could focus on linguistic differences in this individual's culture and the influence these might have on students' decoding and comprehension abilities.

☐ REFERENCES

Barik, H.C. & Swain, M. (1976). English-French bilingual education in the early grades: The Elgin study through grade four. *Modern Language Journal, 60,* 3–17.

Barnitz, J.G. (1980). Black English and other dialects: Sociolinguistic implications for reading instruction. *The Reading Teacher, 33,* 779–786.

Barrera, R.B. (1978). *Analysis and comparison of the first-language and second-language oral reading behavior of native Spanish speaking Mexican American children.* Doctoral Dissertation, University of Texas at Austin.

Barrera, R.B. (1983). Bilingual reading in the primary grades: Some questions about questionable views and practices. In T. Escobedo (Ed.), *Early childhood bilingual education: A Hispanic perspective* (pp. 164–184). New York: Teachers College, Columbia University.

Buckley, M. (1976). A guide for developing an oral language curriculum. *Language Arts, 53,* 621–627.

Cheyney, A. (1976). *Teaching children of different cultures in the classroom: A language approach.* Columbus, OH: Merrill.

Ching, D. (1976). *Reading and the bilingual child.* Newark, DE: International Reading Association.

Cook, M.J. (1973). Problems of Southwestern Indian speakers in learning English. In P. Turner (Ed.), *Bilingualism in the Southwest* (pp. 159–165). Tucson, AZ: University of Arizona Press.

Dixon, C. (1976). Teaching strategies for the Mexican American child. *The Reading Teacher, 30,* 141–145.

Escobedo, T. (1983). *Early childhood bilingual education: A Hispanic perspective.* New York: Teachers College, Columbia University.

Fillmore, L.W. (1987). *A comparative study of two approaches of introducing initial reading to Navajo children: The direct method and the Native Language Method.* Unpublished doctoral dissertation, Northern Arizona University, Flagstaff, AZ.

Frey, E.B. (1970). *Basic helps for teaching English as a second language.* Tucson, AZ: Palo Verde Publishing.

Fryberg, E. (1974). Black English: A descriptive guide for the teacher. In Bernice Cullinan (Ed.), *Black dialects and reading* (pp. 190–196). Urbana, IL: National Council of Teachers of English.

Gilbert II, S. (1985). Improving success in school of poor black children. *Phi Delta Kappan, 11,* 36–42. Bloomington, IN.

Gleason, H.A., Jr. & Cook, M.J. (1961). *An introduction to descriptive linguistics.* New York: Holt, Rinehart & Winston.

Goodman, K. & Goodman, Y. (1978). *Reading of American children whose language is a stable rural dialect of English or a language other than English* (Final report, Project NIE–00–3–0087). Washington, DC: Department of Education.

Goodman, K., Goodman, Y., & Flores, B. (1979). *Reading in the bilingual classroom: Literacy and biliteracy.* Rosslyn, VA: National Clearinghouse for Bilingual Education.

Harber, J.R. & Bryen, D.N. (1976). Black English and the task of reading. *Review of educational research, 46,* 387–405.

Harvey, G. (1974). Dormitory English: Implications for the teacher. In Garland Bills (Ed.), *Southwest Area Linguistics* (pp. 144–158). San Diego: Institute for Cultural Pluralism.

Herbert, C. (1967). English as a second language: The fringe of meaning. In Malcolm Douglass (Ed.), *33rd Yearbook Claremont Reading Conference* (pp. 153–157). Claremont, CA: Claremont University Center.

Joag-Dev, C. & Steffensen, M.S. (1980). Studies of the bicultural reader: implications for teachers and librarians. *Reading Education report, 12.* Champaign, IL: Center for the Study of Reading.

Johnson, K.R. (1977). Accountability and education: Black children in reading and the language arts. *Language Arts, 54,* 144–149.

Labov, W. (1970). Language characteristics: Blacks. In Thomas Horn (Ed.), *Reading for the disadvantaged: Problems of linguistically different learners* (pp. 139–159). New York: Harcourt Brace Jovanovich.

Modiano, N. (1973). *Indian education in the Chiapas highlands.* New York: Holt, Rinehart & Winston.

Padak, H.D. (1981). The language and educational needs of children who speak black English. *The Reading Teacher,* 144–153.

Ramirez, M. & Castandeda, A. (1974). *Cultural democracy, bicognitive development and education.* New York: Academic Press.

Rosier, P. (1977). *A comparative study of two approaches of introducing initial reading to Navajo children: The direct method and the Native Language*

Method. Unpublished doctoral dissertation, Northern Arizona University, Flagstaff, AZ.

Somervill, M.A. (1975). Dialect and reading: A review of alternative solutions. *Review of Educational Research, 45,* 247–262.

Thuan, N. (1962). An approach to better understanding of Vietnamese society: A primer for Americans. In *Hints for Dealing with Cultural Differences in School* (pp. 38–63). Arlington, VA: Published by Center for Applied Linguistics.

Troike, S. (1978). *Handbook of bilingual education.* Washington, DC: Center for Applied Linguistics.

Trueba, H. (1986). *Success or failure: Learning and the language minority student.* Cambridge, MA: Newbury House.

Weber, R. (1970). Some observations on the significance of dialect in the acquisition of reading. In J.A. Figurel (Ed.), *Reading Goals for the Disadvantaged* (pp. 124–131). Newark, DE: International Reading Association.

Young, R.W. (1973). The development of semantic categories in Spanish-English and Navajo-English bilingual children. In Paul Turner (Ed.), *Bilingualism in the Southwest* (pp. 238– 251). Tucson, AZ: University of Arizona Press.

PART FOUR

Clinical Diagnosis and Remediation

15

Sources of Information for Diagnosis and Correction of Noneducational Factors

□ *OVERVIEW*

Although the primary cause of a reading problem may be poor word-recognition skills or gaps in past learnings, other noneducational factors may be related to it. Treatment aimed at correcting or lessening the effect of a noneducational factor often makes reading instruction more beneficial. Students with behavior problems, for example, may not benefit from remedial instruction until provisions are made to correct or lessen these problems. A knowledge of noneducational factors that may interfere with reading development helps the resource teacher to identify problems and to develop an effective individualized reading program.

Several procedures for gathering and evaluating the effects of noneducational factors on reading development were presented in chapter 4. These procedures were intended for use in diagnosis and instruction by both the classroom and the reading resource teacher. Several additional sources of information help the teacher to gather and evaluate the effects of noneducational factors on students' reading abilities. Information sources can range from informal observation forms to evaluations by medical specialists.

This chapter discusses several procedures for gathering information about noneducational factors that may hamper students' reading progress. Once this information has been gathered and evaluated, instructional resources and practices can be identified.

After reading this chapter, the teacher should be able to

☐ gather and evaluate information about physical factors that may impede students' reading progress.

☐ compile and evaluate information about intellectual factors that can hamper reading progress.

☐ gather and evaluate information about social and emotional factors that may stand in the way of reading progress.

☐ select and interpret diagnostic instruments to provide information about noneducational factors.

☐ select and use instructional procedures based on diagnostic information.

SOURCES OF INFORMATION

Both classroom teachers and reading resource teachers use a variety of information sources to gather and evaluate the effects of noneducational factors on students' reading problems. These information sources may be informal screening devices, information gathered from specialists (hearing, vision, medical, and/or psychological), or formal diagnostic instruments administered by a teacher or by specialists. Among the major sources of information available for gathering information about students' reading problems are the following:

☐ Classroom teachers', reading resource teachers', and specialists' observations, anecdotal records, and informal screening reports.

☐ Parent interviews, both written and in person.

☐ Results from diagnostic instruments.

☐ Reports from medical specialists and special school personnel, such as school nurses, speech and hearing teachers, and school psychometrists or psychologists.

A Team Approach

Gathering and evaluating information about noneducational factors possibly contributing to a student's reading problems should be done in a team manner as much as possible. A team approach means that all individuals who are directly involved in the assessment of a student's noneducational factors should communicate with each other and assist in the interpretation of data. Members of such a team include the student's classroom teacher, special teachers (art, music, physical education), reading resource teacher, language disability teacher (if the student is eligible for or is receiving LD instruction), parents, and specialists (if they have been directly involved in gathering diagnostic data). It is extremely important that the classroom and reading resource teachers coordinate their efforts in gathering information about noneducational factors related to a student's reading. Research has indicated that all too often the classroom teacher and the reading resource teacher do not coordinate their efforts and fail to adequately communicate with each other (Allington, Stuetzel, Shake, & Lamarche, 1986). Furthermore, if the learning disabilities teacher is involved in working with a student, important information about noneducational factors will probably be overlooked if he or she is not a member of the team (Schneider, German, & Johnson, 1986). The parents' role in helping to evaluate and identify possible noneducational factors that could contribute to the student's reading problems is of paramount importance; information about a student's home background and reading can lead to the identification of these contributing noneducational factors. Specifically, parents can provide information about a student's verbal interactions (language development), intellectual activities, general health, hearing, vision, personality factors, and so forth (Greaney, 1986). In addition, other professionals, such as physicians, optometrists, and school psychologists or psychometrists who have worked with the student should be directly involved in interpreting and assessing the impact of noneducational factors on the student's reading development.

The involvement of all individuals directly related to the assessment and interpretation of interfering noneducational factors better ensures that all sources of information have been explored. Furthermore, each team member's contributions can be evaluated to determine the presence of noneducational factor(s) that are in need of attention or to recommend referral for additional diagnosis. The coordinated efforts of the team will also lead to planning an effective instructional program that complements the instructional efforts of all teachers involved.

Classroom Teachers' Observations and Informal Screening Procedures

Classroom teachers' observations and informal screening reports are a valuable source of information for identifying possible noneducational factors that impede students' reading development (Rupley, Wise, and Logan, 1986). Because classroom and special teachers (art, music, and physical education) are with students for varying lengths of time and in various situations, they can provide important information about the students with whom they are working. Classroom and special teachers who gather information about vision, hearing, general health, and social-emotional adjustment can assist in evaluating the effects of such noneducational factors on a reading problem. Specific problems are often noted by classroom and special teachers that may not be noted by the resource teacher, parents, or specialists.

Checklists can be used by teachers for gathering information about individual students. The purpose and use of each checklist should be thoroughly understood before teachers actually complete them. Several examples of checklists that can be used by classroom and special teachers are presented on the following pages.

Name: _____ Grade: _____ Age: _____

Teacher: _____ Date: _____

Directions: Place a check beside each descriptive item or phrase that best describes this student's behavior or abilities. Additional information that would benefit the reading resource teacher in diagnosis and instructional planning should be noted. Only check those items that accurately describe this student.

I. When Participating in Class Discussions and Giving Oral Reports:

Vocabulary:
_____ Rich
_____ Words often mispronounced
_____ Lacks appropriate vocabulary
_____ Meaningful

Speech:
_____ Distinct, clear enunciation
_____ Stuttering and/or stammering
_____ Incorrect sounds or distortion of sounds
_____ Monotone voice
_____ Expressive

Language Patterns:
_____ Complete sentences
_____ Simple sentences
_____ Complex sentences
_____ Good organization

Reactions of Peers:
_____ Interested
_____ Uninterested
_____ Sympathetic
_____ Friendly
_____ Critical
_____ Hostile

Emotional Factors:
_____ Poised
_____ Relaxed and at ease
_____ Tense and anxious
_____ Self-confident
_____ Shy and embarrassed
_____ Antagonistic
_____ Unhappy

Additional Information:_____
_____
_____
_____
_____

FIGURE 15–1 Checklist of Classroom Observations of Student Reading

Informal Checklists Figure 15–1 is an example of a checklist that is easy for teachers to complete, yet provides important information about non-educational factors observed in a classroom setting. Completing the checklist can aid other team members in evaluating specific noneducational factors and determining their possible relation to a reading problem. For example, if the following items were checked by the classroom teacher, further exploration in a number of areas could be warranted.

Vocabulary: Words often mispronounced; **Reaction of peers:** Critical, hostile; **Speech:** Incorrect sounds or distortion of sounds; **Emotional factors:** Tense and anxious; **Language patterns:** Repetition of ideas

This student could have a speech problem, a hearing problem, an information-processing problem or could view class discussions and oral reports as tense situations. If the teacher does not have specific information showing that

_____ Repetition of ideas

_____ Interpretation of ideas

_____ Imaginative

II. Reading Interests and Activities

_____ Reads at home

_____ Brings reading materials
from home

_____ Has own home library

_____ Special collection

_____ Hobbies

_____ Sports

_____ Clubs

_____ Trips with family

_____ Science activities

_____ Art activities

_____ Music activities

Additional Information: Please note special interests and activities that this child enjoys. Be as specific as possible, yet brief (e.g., "enjoys painting and working with clay").

III. Peer Relationships and Classroom Behavior:

_____ Gets along well with girls

_____ Gets along well with boys

_____ Works alone only

_____ Works well with one or two children

_____ Works well in small groups (six to ten children)

_____ Works well in large groups (more than ten children)

_____ Is reluctant to participate in most activities

_____ Respects the ideas and opinions of others

Additional Information:_____

_____

_____

_____

_____

Source: Based on checklist form developed by Charles Welch, Department of Elementary Education, Fort Wayne Community School, Fort Wayne, Indiana. Copyright 1971. Used by permission.

one or all of these possibilities could be ruled out, then further diagnosis should be conducted. Additional diagnostic information can then be gathered by the classroom teacher through observation, by the resource teacher through observation and testing, and by specialists through referral.

The checklist categories of Reading Interests and Activities and Peer Relationships and Classroom Behavior can serve several purposes. Information about students' attitudes and interests in reading can be evaluated in relation to encouragement from home. Information about interaction with classmates and attitudes toward instructional settings helps teachers match instructional procedures to students' needs. Also, both categories provide information that the classroom and resource teachers can use to motivate interest and participation in reading activities.

Figure 15–2 is a more detailed checklist than is figure 15–1. It provides the resource teacher with specific information about a student's

Name: _____ Grade: _____ Age: _____

Teacher: _____ Date: _____

Directions: Check the appropriate space for each item listed. *If you have not had an opportunity to observe a specific behavior, leave that space blank.*

	Behavior noted:		
	Often	Seldom	Never
Vision			
1. Loses place when reading	_____	_____	_____
2. Rigid body posture for far-point visual tasks	_____	_____	_____
3. Holds book too close to face	_____	_____	_____
4. Distorts face on both near- and far-point tasks	_____	_____	_____
5. Rubs eyes as if trying to see more clearly	_____	_____	_____
6. Avoids near-point visual tasks	_____	_____	_____
7. Moves head during reading rather than eyes	_____	_____	_____
8. Assumes poor sitting posture for visual tasks	_____	_____	_____
9. Thrusts head forward during visual tasks	_____	_____	_____
10. Appears tense during near-point visual tasks	_____	_____	_____
11. Covers or closes one eye on visual tasks	_____	_____	_____
12. Turns one eye or both eyes inward on visual tasks	_____	_____	_____
13. Eyes appear watery and inflamed	_____	_____	_____
14. Complains of headaches during visual tasks	_____	_____	_____
Hearing			
1. Inattentive during listening tasks	_____	_____	_____
2. Turns ear in the direction of the speaker	_____	_____	_____
3. Fails to follow simple directions	_____	_____	_____
4. Distorts facial expressions when listening	_____	_____	_____
5. Speaks too loudly for most speaking situations	_____	_____	_____
6. Has speech difficulties	_____	_____	_____
7. Cups a hand behind an ear	_____	_____	_____
8. Speaks in a monotone voice	_____	_____	_____
9. Complains of headaches and/or buzzing in the ears	_____	_____	_____
General Health			
1. Complains or appears to be tired	_____	_____	_____

FIGURE 15–2 Checklist of Classroom Observations of Student Physical Factors

	Behavior noted:		
	Often	Seldom	Never
2. Sleeps during class	___	___	___
3. Complains of being hungry early in the school day	___	___	___
4. Participates actively in playground and physical education activities	___	___	___
5. Is often absent from school	___	___	___
6. Has persistant cold or flu symptoms	___	___	___
7. Complains of pains and not feeling well	___	___	___

Information Processing

1. Poor and erratic performance when copying geometric figures	___	___	___
2. Difficulties with figure-ground discrimination	___	___	___
3. Difficulties on abstract learning tasks	___	___	___
4. Problems perceiving whole-part relationships	___	___	___
5. Easily distracted from most learning tasks	___	___	___
6. Problems performing fine motor tasks, such as copying, writing/printing, tracing, etc.	___	___	___
7. Unusually short attention span for daily school work	___	___	___
8. Problems following directions (that most peers can follow) when reading orally or silently	___	___	___
9. Repeats the same behavior over and over	___	___	___
10. Asks to have daily classroom instructions repeated, whereas the rest of the class goes ahead	___	___	___

Additional Comments: _____

_____

_____

Information Screening: Check the following informal screening procedures that were adminstered. Note your findings beside those that were administered.

Skiffington String Test: _____

Saccadic eye movement: _____

Pencil or penlight for coordinated eye movement: _____

Whisper test: _____

Student's Work: Please attach to this checklist examples of the student's written work that illustrate information-processing problems.

Source: Based on checklist form developed by Charles Welch, Department of Elementary Education, Fort Wayne Community School, Fort Wayne, Indiana. Copyright 1971. Used by permission.

| | Name: _____ Grade: _____ Age: _____ |
| Teacher: _____ Date: _____ |

Directions: Check the appropriate space for each item listed. *If you have not had an opportunity to observe a specific behavior, leave that space blank.*

Behavior noted:

	Often	Seldom	Never
I. Language			
Oral			
1. Uses a rich and wide choice of words to express ideas	_____	_____	_____
2. Uses sentence structure equivalent to that of the other children	_____	_____	_____
3. Organizes ideas well when expressing self orally	_____	_____	_____
4. Is hesitant to participate in language activities	_____	_____	_____
5. Speaks clearly and distinctly	_____	_____	_____
6. Speaks in a monotone voice	_____	_____	_____
7. Can be described as lagging behind age-level peers	_____	_____	_____
8. Stutters or stammers when speaking	_____	_____	_____
Written			
1. Spelling patterns indicate an attempt to use rules (e.g., appearance of final *e*, vowel digraphs, etc.)	_____	_____	_____

FIGURE 15–3 Checklist of Classroom Observation of Student Language and Emotional-Social Behavior

vision, hearing, general health, information processing, and performance on informal screening tests. It can be completed by the student's classroom teacher and by any special teachers who work with the student regularly, such as music, art, and physical education teachers.

Based on the teacher's response to each category, the reading resource teacher is in a better position to judge whether noneducational physical factors are related to a student's reading problems. Further diagnosis, if necessary, can be conducted in those areas where teachers have noted problems. Also, additional diagnosis may be appropriate if teachers have not had an opportunity to observe a student's behavior in one or several areas.

A similar form for gathering information about noneducational factors

	Behavior noted:		
	Often	Seldom	Never
2. Syntax reflects an attempt to use rules (e.g., *rided* for *rode, runned* for *ran*, etc.)	___	___	___
3. Word choices indicate an attempt to vary ideas communicated and are used appropriately	___	___	___
4. Sentence structures are similar to those of the majority of children at a comparable level	___	___	___

II. Social and Emotional

1. Withdraws from participation in group activities	___	___	___
2. Appears confident with most learning tasks	___	___	___
3. Behaves in a manner that disrupts class activities	___	___	___
4. Works best in a one-to-one teaching situation	___	___	___
5. Displays outward aggressiveness toward other children	___	___	___
6. Responds well to verbal praise	___	___	___
7. Appears relaxed, happy, and at ease	___	___	___

Additional Information:_____

_____

_____

_____

_____

is shown in figure 15–3. Language and emotional-social problems that are noted by the student's teachers could be related to his or her reading problems.

Language features are divided into the categories of oral and written. The oral language behaviors reflect those detailed in chapter 4. Written language behaviors are based on students' writing products and on information concerning textual features of written language and relationships between reading and writing. For example, Clay (1975) has noted that writing enables students to learn important features of written language. Furthermore, there is evidence to suggest that what students learn from their interaction with language becomes important background information for future interaction with language (Wilson, 1981).

Commercially Published Checklists Another important source of information for identifying and evaluating the effect of noneducational factors on students' reading problems is commercially published checklists and interviews. The *Burks' Behavior Rating Scale* (Burks, 1968a) is an example of a checklist that is used as a screening device to identify students with particular problems that may be related to difficulties with reading. Twenty categories of behavior are included in the scales:

1. Excessive self-blame	11. Poor impulse control
2. Excessive anxiety	12. Poor reality contact
3. Excessive withdrawal	13. Poor sense of identity
4. Excessive dependency	14. Excessive suffering
5. Poor ego strength	15. Poor anger control
6. Poor physical strength	16. Excessive sense of persecution
7. Poor coordination	17. Excessive sexuality
8. Poor intellectuality	18. Excessive aggressiveness
9. Poor academics	19. Excessive resistence
10. Poor attention	20. Poor social conformity

There is a total of 116 items on the rating scale. Figure 15–4 presents an example of the items and of the scoring procedures. Each category of items is arranged so that the vertical rows of squares are added together and the total is then compared with an accompanying profile sheet. For example, vertical row one totals 10, vertical row two totals 4, and vertical row five totals 5. Each vertical row on a page assesses one of the 20 behaviors listed.

During both the development and actual use of the scales, Burks concluded that the scales have shown some ability to

1. identify patterns of disturbed behavior which distinguish between several groups of children.
2. show changes in behavior patterns over a period of time.
3. indicate areas in a child's personality where further evaluation might advantageously take place.
4. provide a source of information useful to school personnel for conferences with parents.
5. predict which children will do well in special education classes and which will not.
6. be of practical value when used by parents as well as teachers. (1968b, pp. 1–2)

The major advantages of Burks' scale are that each of the 20 behaviors measured is defined, possible causes for each behavior are listed, procedures for interpretation are given, and suggested intervention techniques are discussed.

Another instrument that provides information on a student's developmental history, past medical problems, and his or her own perceptions of problems and strengths is the ANSER System (Aggregate Neurobehavioral Student Health and Educational Review) developed by Levine (1981) and

BURKS' BEHAVIOR RATING SCALES
DEVISED BY HAROLD F. BURKS. PH.D.

Name _____ Age _____ Grade _____

School _____ Date _____

Rated by _____ _____

RELATIONSHIP TO CHILD

Please rate **each** and **every** item by putting the number of the most appropriate descriptive statement in the box opposite each item. The 5 descriptive statements are given below:

Number **1.** You have not noticed this behavior at all.
Number **2.** You have noticed the behavior to a slight degree.
Number **3.** You have noticed the behavior to a considerable degree.
Number **4.** You have noticed the behavior to a large degree.
Number **5.** You have noticed the behavior to a very large degree.

1. Shows erratic, flighty or scattered behavior. `3`

2. Questions indicate a worry about the future. `1`

3. Maintains other children pick on him. `3`

4. Does not ask questions. `2`

5. Upset if makes a mistake. `1`

6. Has trouble holding on to things. `1`

7. Perseverates, cannot shift responses. `1`

8. Is easily distracted, lacks continuity of effort and perseverance. `3`

9. Complains he never gets his fair share of things. `1`

10. Shows poor coordination in large muscle activities. `2`

11. Gives inappropriate responses. `2`

12. Shows overremorse for wrong doing. `1`

13. Attention span not increased by punishment or reward. `2`

14. Handwriting is poor. `2`

15. Does not show imagination. `2`

16. Will not forgive others. `1`

17. Is upset if things do not turn out perfect. `1`

18. Attention span is short. `2`

19. Drawings and paintings are messy. `2`

20. Has trouble remembering things. `2`

21. Accuses others of things they actually did not do. `1`

22. Shows poor vocabulary. `2`

23. Complains others do not like him. `1`

FIGURE 15–4 Selected items from Burks' Behavior Rating Scales

Source; From *Burks' Behavior Rating Skills* (p. 1) by F. Burks, 1968, Huntington Beach, CA: Arden. Copyright 1968 by Harold F. Burks. Reprinted with permission.

published by Educators Publishing Services. The ANSER is intended to provide a systematic way for gathering information in four areas: education, health, development, and behavior. The system includes: (1) three parent questionnaires, (Form 1P—ages 3 to 5, Form 2P—ages 6 to 11, and Form 3P—ages 12 and above); (2) three school questionnaires (Form 1S—ages 3 to 5, Form 2S—ages 6 to 11, and Form 3S—ages 12 and above); (3) a self-administered student profile (Form 4— ages 9 and above); and (4) an examiner's manual.

All three forms of the parent questionnaire have a similar format and request information for the following areas: possible pregnancy problems; possible newborn infant problems; health problems; functional problems (early-life behavioral problems); early development (motor skills, language acquisition, and self-help skills); family history; early educational experiences; skills and interests; activity-attention problems (current behavior problems); associated behaviors (aggressiveness, withdrawal, stress); and associated strengths (positive behaviors). The items in each area are easy to follow and are arranged in checklists.

The school questionnaires are aimed at recording important observations within a school setting. The student's classroom teacher or teachers, reading resource teacher, school psychologist or psychometrist, or anyone familiar with the student's school performance completes this questionnaire. Each form of the school questionnaire has open-ended items for the respondent to note the student's strengths and weaknesses, identify special services provided by the school, and describe the student's reading program. Following these sections are three checklists. The first checklist asks the respondent to rate the student's performance in subject areas, developmental areas, motor output, visual perception functions, and memory. The second checklist requests a rating for attention deficits (hyperactivity, distractibility, impulsiveness, and disorganization). Checklist number three is for rating associated behaviors, which include withdrawal, aggressiveness, anxiety, and coping strategies. Because there is a close relationship between the items on the parent questionnaire and the school questionnaire, comparison between the student's behavior at home and at school can be made.

The last feature of the ANSER System is the student profile, which students who are 9 years of age or older complete. There are three parts to the student profile. The first part is an inventory of what the student perceives as his or her strengths in academic and nonacademic areas. Part two surveys the student's interests by requesting him or her to check those activities that he or she "likes to do a lot." The third part of this section contains 60 direct quotations from students who have learning or adjustment difficulties. The student responds to each item by selecting either "Very true of me," "Little true of me," or "Not true of me." The items are arranged in groups of 10 that represent areas such as motor skills, memory, language, attention, academic performance, and social interaction. Last, there is space provided for the student to write "other things about me in school."

The ANSER System can provide a systematic means for collecting background information from parents, teachers, and older students to use in the evaluation of students' learning and behavioral problems (Jongsma, 1982). Its emphasis on a team approach is effective because it directly involves a number of significant individuals in the evaluation and interpretation of noneducational factors that could impede a student's reading development.

Standardized Tests of Language Development

Additional information about students' language development can be gathered through the administration of language assessment instruments. Such instruments, used to complement information gathered through informal means, can assist team members in interpreting the impact of students' language capabilities on their reading development. Identification of potential language problems should be addressed early in students' educational programs so that appropriate instructional accommodations can be made if necessary. Two tests that are available for gathering information about language development are discussed in the following paragraphs.

The Test of Early Language Development (TELD) is intended for children ages 3 through 7 years, 11 months. It is an untimed, individually administered test and requires approximately 15 to 20 minutes to administer. The following purposes have been suggested for TELD (Hresko, Reid, & Hammill, 1981): (1) to identify children who are significantly behind their peers in language development, (2) to document children's progress in language, and (3) to suggest appropriate instructional procedures.

The test consists of a 39-page manual, 12 picture cards, and 50 record sheets. The manual details how to administer the test and how to score a child's response for each question. The score sheet identifies the starting point by the age of the child, and the questions are arranged so that they increase in difficulty.

The TELD can be used as a source of information about children's language development. As with any standardized test, its value lies in its interpretation. Therefore, when the TELD is used with other formal and informal measures, it can help both classroom and reading resource teachers make informed decisions about children's language development (Bartlett, Slade, & Bellerose, 1987).

Another test, the Receptive One-Word Picture Vocabulary Test (ROWPVT), is intended to estimate a student's receptive vocabulary learned at home and in school. The test is intended for children 2 years old to 11 years, 11 months old. The test does not require any verbal responses. The student is provided with a brief introduction to the test and practice examples.

Groups of four black-and-white, hand-drawn pictures are presented, one at a time, and the student either points to a picture or to a number that best matches an orally presented stimulus word. There is a total of 100 test-plate pictures. A basal level of eight consecutive correct responses is identified and the administration of the test ends when the student misses six out of eight consecutive items.

Although the ROWPVT appears to be a good measure of a student's ability to associate meaning with a given stimulus picture, the norms are limited to children from the San Francisco area. Therefore, using the norms for children in other areas would be inappropriate. A recommended approach to interpretation would be to explore the results qualitatively regarding an individual student's receptive vocabulary (Amster, 1987). The major value of such a test is to help teachers screen young children for vocabulary problems that might limit their success when beginning reading instruction.

Parent Interviews

Information gained from parents, in both written and personal interviews, provides important information for both diagnostic and instructional planning. Patterns of performance noted at school may or may not be noted at home. Specific problems, such as poor hearing or vision, that are observed both in a school setting and at home may warrant referral to a specialist. Behavior patterns that are observed only in a school setting could indicate that certain school factors are causing the behavior. For example, language problems exhibited in school such as stammering, mispronunciation of words, and lack of participation in language activities may not be exhibited in the home; thus, the child's language problem may be school-related rather than developmental. The reading resource and classroom teachers could then investigate school factors, such as learning demands, grouping procedures, and reading materials. A modification of school factors could lessen or remove the cause of the language problem, allowing reading instruction to be more beneficial.

Written Interviews   Teachers may wish to either develop their own parent interview form or supplement the form presented in figure 15–5 on pages 382–383. A teacher-developed interview form has the advantage of focusing on information that would be the most beneficial for a particular student. Areas of important consideration on a teacher-developed form are similar to those found in figure 15–6 on page 385, with the possible inclusion of the following considerations (Greaney, 1986).

> *Verbal Interaction.* Parents can describe how they interact verbally with their child in the home environment by providing examples of topics talked about, language development of their child in comparison with siblings and other children of the same age, and the verbal interaction of the child with other children.

Ordinal Position and Sex. Parents sometimes treat children differently according to their birth order and sex. For example, parents may interact more with and provide a more stimulating environment for first-born children and may provide more school-related activities for girls than for boys. Gathering this type of information from parents is important; questions that ask them to detail their interactions can provide insights into factors associated with the child's home environment.

Personal Factors. The child's home environment can also affect both the level of his or her reading skill development and amount of recreational reading. A positive home situation that associates value with and encourages reading for pleasure has a direct impact on students' reading. Overcrowding and noisy conditions in the home can nega-

Personal parent interviews can provide teachers with information about students' reading. (Bruce Johnson/Merrill)

Student's name_____

Age _____ _____ Date of birth _____ Place of birth _____
     Year Month

Father's name _____ Mother's name _____
Address _____ Telephone _____
Father's age _____ Mother's age _____
Parents are (check one): Living together _____ Separated _____
Divorced _____ Dead _____ _____
                                          Father   Mother

Put a ring around the last school grade attended by:
  Father: Grades 1 2 3 4 5 6 7 8   High School 1 2 3 4
           College 1 2 3 4 5 6
  Mother: Grades 1 2 3 4 5 6 7 8   High School 1 2 3 4
           College 1 2 3 4 5 6
Father's occupation _____
Mother's occupation _____
Names and ages of other children _____
_____

Language(s) spoken in home _____
Schools the child has attended (Years attended) _____
_____

Has your child repeated a grade? Yes _____ No _____ What grade? _____
What are child's special abilities? _____

What are your plans for the child's future? _____
_____

When did the child begin to walk? _____
When did he or she begin to talk? _____
Has the child had any speech troubles? _____

When does the child go to bed? _____ Get up? _____
Does he or she watch television? _____ What are his or her favorite programs?
_____

FIGURE 15–5 Home Information Report

tively impact reading performance and contribute to a student's reading problems. Therefore, it is important that teachers gather information about the home situation to evaluate possible negative influences on reading performance.

The use of written parent interview forms should precede a personal interview; however, simply asking parents to complete an interview form without communicating to them the importance of doing so as accurately

How much of the child's evening is spent viewing T.V.? _____

Has your child ever been treated at a private Reading Center?

    Yes ____ No ____ If so, when? Year ____ Semester: Sum. ____ Spr. ____

    Fall ____

Address of Center: _____

What does he or she do with free time? _____

Does the child like to read? _____ Does he or she read at home? _____

With whom does he or she like to spend time? (Check one)

    Children own age _____ Younger children _____

    Older children _____ Parents _____ Other adults _____

    Self _____

Which newspapers are in the home? _____

Magazines? _____

How many books? _____

Does the child have his or her own books? _____ How many? _____

Did you read to your child during his or her preschool years? ____ Now? ____

General health of child (Circle):   good   fair   poor

List child's sicknesses _____

    High fever _____

    Operations _____

    Accidents _____

    Others _____

Has he or she had a recent physical examination? _____

Physician's name and address _____

_____

Does he or she wear glasses? _____ When were his or her eyes last checked?

_____

Please describe the child's problem _____

_____

In your opinion, what has caused the child's problem? _____

_____

How do you try to help your child with school work? _____

_____

How does he or she react to your help?_____

_____

Source: From form developed by Karl Koenke, University of Illinois.

as possible may limit the completeness of their responses. Therefore, it is necessary to help parents understand as fully as possible their child's reading performance and the reasons for requesting specific information from them. One way to alert parents to their child's reading problem and to communicate that written and personal interviews would assist in helping plan a quality reading program is providing them with a progress report (Vukelich, 1984). A progress report can be either verbal or written and should contain information that (1) details explicitly their child's reading level, (2) provides examples of the child's reading capabilities (rather than just reporting test results), (3) explains the child's reading development in relation to classmates' development and his or her own capabilities, and (4) avoids labeling the child. (Parents will often misinterpret labels such as *dyslexic, reading disabled,* and *learning disabled.*) The meanings of such labels are vague and do not communicate accurate information to the parents.

Personal Interviews   Conducting a personal interview serves several important purposes. First, it communicates to the parents that the school is making a sincere effort to help their child become a better reader. Second, personal interviews help reduce anxieties that many parents often have when their children are not doing as well as they think they should. Third, it allows the reading resource teacher to gather additional diagnostic information in areas that a written interview does not cover in depth. Fourth, personal parent interviews enable the reading resource teacher to suggest to the parents how they can help their children at home.

There is no set procedure to follow when personally interviewing parents. In all likelihood each interview will be unique, because each child will have different reading problems. Also, parents of one child will respond differently to the interview than will the parents of another child (Auten, 1981). There are, however, some general guidelines to follow:

1. Explain thoroughly the purpose of the interview. Attempt to set a positive mood and do not lead the parents to believe that only their child's problems will be discussed. The interview is an information-gathering process to plan an instructional program to help the child become a better reader. Therefore, information about what the child can do well will also be useful in program planning.

2. Do not ask questions about information that is already available. If information about other schools the child has attended is listed in his or her anecdotal records or the written parent interview, do not ask for this information again. However, it may be desirable to gather additional information about a certain area by asking such questions as: "I see that Timmy attended Sunnyside School for two years. What can you tell me about his experiences at that school?" Or, "You noted on the written interview that Mary likes to make clothes for her dolls. What kind of help do you offer her? Do you give her verbal directions, do you show her what to do, or does she use a pattern?

3. Ask open-ended questions as often as possible, rather than questions that can be answered simply "yes" or "no." For example, the question "Does Bob like school?" calls for a "yes" or "no" response. However, "What things about school does Bob seem to like?" encourages the parents to respond with specific information.

4. If the parents respond to questions too briefly or appear reluctant to discuss an area of concern, restating their response will often encour-

---

Directions: Draw a ring around one of the four figures: 1 means high, 2 means average, 3 means low, ? means you are not sure.

General Health

1 2 3 ? General health
1 2 3 ? Eyes
1 2 3 ? Free from colds and sickness
1 2 3 ? Hearing
1 2 3 ? Strength
1 2 3 ? Sleep habits

Peer Relationships and Attitude

1 2 3 ? Takes part in school activities
1 2 3 ? Popular at school
1 2 3 ? Plays with many children
1 2 3 ? Kind and thoughtful with other children
1 2 3 ? Is dependable
1 2 3 ? Interested in school
1 2 3 ? Shares with others
1 2 3 ? Polite

Capabilities

1 2 3 ? Intelligent
1 2 3 ? Directs self
1 2 3 ? Ability in music or art
1 2 3 ? Ability with machines
1 2 3 ? Talks well
1 2 3 ? Does school work well
1 2 3 ? Understands readily

Emotional Factors

1 2 3 ? Happy
1 2 3 ? Calm
1 2 3 ? Tells truth
1 2 3 ? Free from nervous habits
1 2 3 ? Can see a joke
1 2 3 ? Easily frustrated

Work Habits

1 2 3 ? Works hard
1 2 3 ? Orderly and neat
1 2 3 ? Works well alone
1 2 3 ? Works well with others

FIGURE 15–6 Parent's Rating of the Child

age them to provide more information. If the parents said, for example, "Mike just can't read and doesn't like to," the teacher can respond by saying, "What you are telling me is that Mike doesn't know how to read and doesn't like reading." In this instance, the parents might indicate that Mike has read some books, but reading causes him problems in school (Della-Piana, 1968).

5. Discuss with the parents what additional diagnosis may be necessary. Explain accurately why you think referral to a specialist is needed. If referral to a physician or eye specialist seems necessary, offer to assist the parents with the referral. The school nurse, school physician, or a community agency can help parents locate a specialist.

6. Try to end the interview on a positive note, but do not make unrealistic promises. Suggest ways that the parents can help at home. These should be offered only as suggestions and not as orders. The teacher might say, "If you have time once or twice a week, you might read to Mark or maybe he could read to you." Attempt to set a specific date on which the parents can get in touch with you about the progress of outside referrals. Encourage the parents to call or make an appointment to see you about any questions or concerns they might have. Let the parents know that you will keep in touch with them about their child's progress.

SUMMARIZING DIAGNOSTIC DATA

Information from the teacher's checklists, rating scales, observations, and diagnosis should be summarized to identify problem area patterns. The summary should also include information obtained from both the written and personal parent interviews. Figure 15–7 illustrates one method of summarizing diagnostic information about noneducational factors. Problem areas that are noted in both the school and home help the resource teacher to decide what additional diagnosis may be necessary. Furthermore, the summary can serve as a guide for sharing information with the child's parents. Problem areas noted in school or in home situations can be discussed with the parents and areas that require further diagnosis by a specialist can be pointed out to them.

Earlier in this text, screening procedures for visual or auditory problems were discussed. The following section presents other procedures that reading resource teachers can use.

SCREENING TESTS FOR IDENTIFYING PROBLEMS

Visual Screening

Several batteries of tests are available for visual screening. These screening devices are not intended to yield an accurate diagnosis of visual deficiencies, but to facilitate referral of students to eye specialists. Three of the more popular and easy-to-use screening batteries are

□ The *Ortho-Rater* screens for acuity defects, depth perception, and binocular vision. It was recently adapted for use with intermediate-age schoolchildren.
□ *Keystone Visual Screening Test* screens for astigmatism, myopia, hyperopia, fusion, depth perception, and color blindness. Similar to most telebinocular tests, it is easy to administer and to interpret.
□ *Eye Trac 106* screens for horizontal and vertical positions of both eyes during reading. Fixations, regressions, breadth of fixations, length of

Factor	Anecdotal Records by Classroom Teacher	Special Teachers	Resource Teacher	Parents	Diagnosis
Vision	Problems noted often on near-point tasks. Often complains of headaches during prolonged near-point tasks. Poor posture, tenseness, and inflamed eyes.	Art teacher noted problems with near-point vision, poor posture, tenseness, and inflamed eyes.	Identical symptoms noticed as noted by classroom and art teachers. Results of *Keystone Visual Screening Test* suggests near-point vision problems.	No problems noted. No recent eye exam indicated.	Discuss with parents problems noted. Recommend referral to eye specialists.
Hearing	No problems noted. Administered audiometer test three years ago in kindergarten.	No problems noted.	No problems noted. Whisper test and audiometer sweep check administered.	No problems noted.	Additional diagnosis does not appear necessary.
General health	No problems noted.	No problems noted.	No problems noted.	No problems noted.	Additional diagnosis does not appear necessary.
Information processing	Unusually short attention span. Problems following directions. Poor handwriting and copying.	Both art and physical education teachers noted poor coordination in comparison with peers. Poor drawing and copying noted by art teacher.	Short attention span, problems following directions, and poor handwriting. Burks' scale suggests poor coordination and poor attention.	Easily distracted and has poor coordination.	Refer to school psychometrist for individual intelligence testing.
Language	No problems noted.	No problems noted.	No problems noted.	No problems noted.	Additional diagnosis does not appear necessary.
Social-emotional	Within a range similar to peers.	Seldom causes problems. Plays and participates well with others.	Eager to please and participate.	Happy, well-adjusted.	Additional diagnosis does not appear necessary.

FIGURE 15–7 Sample Summary Sheet of Diagnostic Information on Noneducational Factors

fixations, percentage of left-to-right movement, and rate are recorded on a graph.

☐ *Spache Binocular Reading Test* is a screening test designed to assess the relative participation of both eyes in reading. Test cards for preprimary, primary, and intermediate students can be used with any stereoscope.

The *Keystone Visual Screening Test* and the *Ortho-Rater* are stereoscope visual testing instruments. For example, the Keystone telebinocular is a machine that weighs aproximately 14 pounds and can be carried to most testing situations. The complete screening test set consists of the telebinocular instrument; an occluder, which allows for testing of one eye at a time to screen for suppressed vision; a rapid screening test series, which makes possible rapid screening of simultaneous perception and fusion, normal depth perception, and color blindness; a test for fusion and vertical posture; a test for near-point vision at reading distance (16 inches); and a comprehensive test battery. The comprehensive test battery provides a more detailed analysis of vision for those children who fail one or more of the rapid screening tests. Also included in the materials is a two-part record form. One part of the record form is for the school records. The second part of the form is for reporting the visual screening results to the child's parents. The back of the parents' form describes each of the individual screening tests and discusses the importance of good vision.

The major reason for using binocular testing to screen children with reading problems for possible vision defects is that more than good visual acuity is necessary for reading. Visual acuity is measured in many schools with the Snellen Chart. This chart consists of lines of letters that are sized to correspond with a given distance: 20/20, 20/30, 20/15, and so forth. The first number refers to distance in feet at which testing is done. The second number is the distance at which the letters of a given size are distinguished by most individuals.

The Snellen Chart measures far-point vision at 20 feet and has little application to the near-point vision required of the reader. Many children can perform within a normal vision range of the Snellen Chart and still have a vision defect that interferes with reading development. Children who are slightly nearsighted or who have an astigmatism often learn that they can make out the 20/20 line of the Snellen Chart if they squint. As a result, the children for whom an accurate visual screening is most important often escape detection (Vetterli, 1959).

The importance of screening children who have reading problems for possible visual defects cannot be overstated. As pointed out in chapter 4, observation is a powerful diagnostic procedure for identifying children who have possible visual problems. Visual screening test batteries are easily and quickly administered; however, they are intended to identify gross visual problems and have limitations for evaluating skills needed for reading. Teachers should not hesitate to recommend that students with reading problems be given a thorough eye examination by a specialist (Rabin, 1982).

Auditory Screening

In addition to observation and informal screening procedures such as the whisper test (see chapter 4), auditory acuity can be screened with the use of an audiometer. An audiometer provides information about a person's ability to hear sounds of varying pitch at varying degrees of loudness. Testing is available in most schools through the school nurse or speech and hearing teacher. Many reading resource teachers also have audiometers available in their classrooms. Audiometers are easy to learn how to use, and portable models are available from Maico, Zenith, Belton, and Eckstein.

The purpose of using an audiometer for auditory acuity screening is to identify children who may have hearing problems. Referral to a hearing specialist is necessary for those children who exhibit problems with auditory acuity.

REFERRAL REPORTS

When referral to medical specialists and/or special school personnel, such as the nurse, speech and hearing teacher, or psychometrist, is necessary, there are several important points to consider. First, the parents should, if at all possible, handle the referral to a physician, eye specialist, or hearing specialist. The process of referral can be coordinated through the school nurse if parents need assistance in identifying competent specialists. Second, the parents should be notified about referrals to school personnel so they understand why their child is being referred and how the results will be used. Third, the resource teacher should get the name of the specialist to whom a child is referred. A release form signed by the parents may be necessary before outside specialists will send information to the school.

Consultations with the specialists are recommended as supplements to a written report of diagnostic findings. Through personal consultation, the reading resource teacher can ask questions about ways to help the child become a better reader that may not be suggested on a written report. In addition, many of the written reports use terminology that is difficult to understand and interpret by someone not trained in that field.

INSTRUCTIONAL CONSIDERATIONS FOR CHILDREN WITH NONEDUCATIONAL PROBLEMS

Her teacher's observation and the results obtained by the reading resource teacher's administration of the Keystone telebinocular suggested that Sue had a visual problem. She was taken to an eye specialist by her parents and fitted with corrective lenses, which corrected her visual problems. The reading resource teacher felt that Sue's reading problem was a direct result of her vision defects, which had interfered with reading development. Since Sue's vision defect has been corrected, reading instruction should now be more beneficial for her and the reading resource teacher expects rapid progress.

Mike's teachers noted social-emotional problems in both instructional settings and peer interactions. Mike's parents had commented that he exhibited social-emotional problems in the home as well. Mike was withdrawn, overdependent on his parents and teachers, and lacked self-confidence. He was referred to a physician for a complete physical examination. The results of the examination indicated that there were no physical problems. The physician felt that the possibility that school factors were causing Mike's behavior should be explored. The resource teacher knew that instructional practices must accommodate Mike's problems, and that lasting changes in his behavior would take considerable effort and planning. Mike's reading resource teacher, classroom teacher, and parents discussed cooperatively some techniques that should help him adjust better to social and instructional activities.

These two examples of children with noneducational problems illustrate an important factor to consider when planning remedial reading programs: the speed with which detrimental noneducational factors can be corrected. Some noneducational problems, such as vision or hearing defects, may be corrected quickly. In a sense, the factor that may have caused the reading problem in such cases is removed or minimized. Even though severe reading problems still exist after the noneducational factor has been corrected, reading instruction will most likely be more beneficial. Other noneducational factors that interfere with reading development, such as problems with behavior, language, and information processing, are not as easily corrected. Problems in these areas often require a long time to correct, and in some instances correction is not possible. Remedial reading instruction must, therefore, be planned so that the effect of the problem on reading development is minimized.

Most instructional procedures and programs discussed in this text are appropriate for use with children who experience noneducational problems. Chapters 7, 8, 12, and 16 offer specific instructional suggestions that can minimize the effects of noneducational factors on children's reading problems. Instructional considerations for children who have hearing, visual, social-emotional, and language problems are presented in the following sections.

Hearing Problems

Even after children with hearing problems have been fitted with a hearing aid, some hearing problems may persist. Many hearing defects are of a medical nature, and although a hearing aid often improves hearing, it may not completely correct the problem. For this reason there are several important instructional points to consider when teaching reading to children with hearing problems:

☐ Minimize distracting sounds during reading instruction.
☐ Encourage the child to look directly at the speaker to get information from facial expressions and gestures.
☐ Seat the child close to the speaker and as far away from distracting sounds as possible.
☐ Use visual materials to illustrate oral information and directions.
☐ Employ an approach to reading instruction that relates oral language to written language, such as language experience and creative writing in conjunction with a code-breaking approach.
☐ Build on existing sight vocabulary to introduce and illustrate phonic generalization. Reinforce and extend phonic generalization learning in actual reading situations.
☐ Experiment with several types of instructional procedures to determine those with which the child learns best. (Teaching procedures that incorporate the use of visual, auditory, kinesthetic, and tactile [VAKT] pathways to learning; cloze procedure; and writing can be used with the child to identify those that are most successful.)

Teachers often ask whether or not children with hearing losses will benefit from phonics instruction. Many children who have a hearing loss not only have difficulty hearing some sounds, but also misarticulate letter sounds, especially if the hearing loss occurred early in life. How then can children who have difficulty hearing sounds and who may also misarticulate letter sounds benefit from phonics? Some advice for teaching phonics to such children follows:

> Even though a child may misarticulate sounds or mispronounce them from printed symbols, if he has has a constant association or enunciation for each symbol, he can read and he can use phonic clues reasonably effectively. His exact enunciation of the sound for consonant or blend does not really matter, if he uses that sound-symbol association consistently. (Spache, 1981, pp. 55)

Visual Problems

There is no adequate substitute for referring students with vision problems to an eye specialist and using the following suggestions for improving their reading instruction. Teachers can compensate for visual problems in the classroom, but compensation will not correct a structural defect. The following suggestions compensate for, rather than correct, visual defects.

☐ Provide well-lighted work areas for reading instruction and minimize glare on the chalkboard and book pages.

□ Minimize the use of reading tasks that require quick and accurate refocusing of the eyes from near-point to far-point tasks and vice versa.

□ Use short, varied periods of reading instruction rather than longer periods of sustained reading.

□ Seat children who have problems with far-point vision close to chalkboards, word charts, and other visual displays.

□ Write instructional information larger than normal for the child who has problems with near-point acuity.

□ Check to make sure that the child who has been prescribed glasses wears them. Sometimes children do not wear their glasses because they do not fit properly or because their vision has changed since the glasses were prescribed.

□ Incorporate auditory activities with visual activities and explain fully what the child is to learn rather than relying on visual representation alone to illustrate instructional information.

Social and Emotional Problems

Research (Rupley, 1971) and classroom experiences indicate that social-emotional problems can improve with reading growth. Children who exhibit excessive withdrawal, poor self-concepts, poor peer relations, and excessive aggressiveness show marked improvement when reading instruction accommodates their particular problem.

Many children's social and emotional problems are closely related to the academic environment and learning demands. For example, poor self-concept, which is a learned behavior by definition, may result from a student's continued failure to reach established learning standards. We have found that lowering achievement standards, focusing on reading strengths, individualizing instruction, minimizing comparisons with other children, and helping parents learn how to encourage their child's performance have a positive influence on children's self-concept. Likewise, withdrawal from instructional activities is a normal behavior for many students who continually face the probability of failure. These students often find reading frustrating and, as a defensive technique, refuse to participate in reading instruction.

Most of these children need a teacher who understands and recognizes their problems. Some instructional procedures that often accommodate children's social-emotional problems include the following:

□ Employ behavior modification techniques that focus on rewarding only appropriate behavior. Inappropriate behavior should be ignored, yet every opportunity to praise a child verbally for appropriate behavior should be taken.

□ Modify the expectations of the learning situations so that they are challenging but still allow the children to experience some success.

☐ Avoid the use of activities that the child might view as threatening to self-concept or to peer relationships.

☐ Help the parents learn how to encourage their child in both school and home activities.

☐ Individualize reading instruction in the manner discussed throughout this text.

☐ Use small increments of instruction with the child that provide positive feedback about performance.

☐ Identify and use motivation activities that encourage active participation in learning.

☐ Eliminate distracting stimuli as much as possible from instructional settings.

☐ Provide a warm, accepting environment that communicates to the child that he or she is an important, worthwhile person.

Language Differences or Problems

As pointed out in chapter 4, a child's language problems could be developmental, dialectal, or pathological in nature. Children with severe language problems of a pathological nature should receive special instruction from a speech pathologist and specially trained teachers. However, children who exhibit a developmental lag in language (either receptive or productive) or language problems related to dialectal differences can benefit from teacher instruction. Some specific instructional techniques might include the following:

☐ Minimize placing the student in language situations that might be viewed as threatening, such as giving an oral presentation to the class or reading aloud from a book to several students.

☐ Encourage the student to fully describe a requested object he or she wants to use. Regarding this technique, Hallahan and Kauffman (1985) indicate that teachers can use this as a means of contingent access to materials or activities. By encouraging the student to describe objects or activities, teachers are facilitating the student's acquisition of functional language responses.

☐ Focus instruction on comprehension of both oral and written language, as well as production of language. Dwyer and Raver (1986) recommend that students can frequently substitute written language for spoken language by employing word cards in natural situations. For example, the student might ask, "May I sharpen my _____?" and use a word card for "pencil." Longer written requests can also be used throughout the school day in both instructional and classroom situations in which students communicate with each other and the teacher.

☐ Utilize language situations for reading that are meaningful to the student and do not focus on isolated sounds or words. The language-experience approach is ideal for providing meaningful language situations. In addition, talking books, in which the student follows along in the book as he or she listens to a tape recording of the text, are an excellent means to emphasize the communicative features of print.

☐ Focus instruction on getting meaning, whether it is receiving a message (hearing or reading) or producing a message (speaking or writing). Help the student realize that comprehension, or understanding the message, is the purpose of language. Some activities could include (1) having students retell stories that are told to them, (2) having students provide a different ending or provide an ending for an unfinished story, (3) having students listen to an oral description of a concrete object or event and represent what is described by drawing a picture of it, (4) using puppet plays as a means to encourage students to use oral language, and (5) giving students simple oral directions to follow in the classroom for projects in art and social studies.

☐ Incorporate all language skills—reading, writing, listening, and speaking— into classroom or clinic situations. Techniques for doing this include group language experience stories; creative dramatics; puppet plays; group projects in art, science, and social studies; and guest speakers.

☐ SUMMARY

Gathering diagnostic information to determine whether or not children have noneducational problems that interfere with their reading development is an important part of the teacher's role. One of the more powerful diagnostic procedures for gathering such information is observing a student's behavior both in school and in home situations. Additional diagnostic information can be obtained through screening—using, for example, the *Keystone, Ortho-Rater*, whisper test, audiometer, and behavior rating scales. While screening procedures are not intended to yield accurate diagnoses, they can assist in identifying students who need to be referred to a specialist.

After gathering and evaluating diagnostic information, the teacher must decide how individual problems can best be accommodated in the reading program. The effect of noneducational factors on reading development should be minimized through the use of individualized programs that meet each child's needs. In a sense, such an approach recognizes that noneducational problems are teacher problems rather than student problems. Reading instruction that fits the needs of the child often lessens or eliminates the effect of many noneducational problems on reading development.

□ *IN-TEXT ASSIGNMENTS*

FIELD-BASED ACTIVITY

Visit an elementary school and discuss with the classroom and/or reading resource teacher how information about noneducational factors is gathered. Focus your discussion on the formal and informal procedures that are used to gather information, how information is communicated to the student's parents, how referrals are made to specialists, whether or not a team approach is used in gathering and analyzing data, and how students are involved in the process of gathering and evaluating data on noneducational factors. Share the checklists presented in this chapter with the teacher and ask him or her to compare and contrast them with those he or she uses.

RESOURCE ACTIVITY

Ask an ophthalmologist and/or a speech and hearing specialist to visit your class. Ask them to discuss how they conduct a diagnosis and what recommendations they would offer for classroom screening or visual and/or hearing problems. Request that they make available to your class copies of reports that are sent to teachers and parents and any literature that they give to parents and teachers about vision and hearing problems.

GROUP ACTIVITY

Form several small groups, two or three students to a group, with each student assuming one of the following roles: classroom or reading resource teacher and parents of a child with a reading problem. The people who are role playing the parents can complete the home information report (see figure 15–5) with hypothetical information. After the written interview is completed, cooperatively evaluate the information on it. Following the evaluation, role play the personal interview of parents and teacher. Critique the personal interview by following the guidelines presented in this chapter. You will probably want to audio tape-record the interview for critiquing purposes.

□ **REFERENCES**

Allington, R., Stuetzel, H., Shake, M., & Lamarche, S. (1986). What is remedial reading? A descriptive study. *Reading Research and Instruction, 26*, 15–30.

Amster, J. B. (1987). Test review: Receptive one-word picture vocabulary test. *The Reading Teacher, 40*, 452–457.

Auten, A. (1981). Effective parent teacher conferences. *The Reading Teacher, 35,* 358–361.

Bartlett, A., Slade, D., & Bellerose, P. C. (1987). Test review: The test of early language development. *The Reading Teacher, 40,* 546–549.

Burks, H. F. (1968a). *Burks' Behavior Rating Scale.* Huntington Beach, CA: Arden.

Burks, H. F. (1968b). *Manual for Burks' Behavior Rating Scale.* Huntington Beach, CA: Arden.

Clay, M. (1975). *What did I write?* London: Heinemann.

Della-Piana, G. M. (1968). *Reading diagnosis and prescription: An introduction.* New York: Holt, Rinehart & Winston.

Dwyer, C. & Raver, S. A. (1986). Teaching resistent readers: A new paradigm for instruction. *Reading Psychology, 7,* 101–110.

Greaney, V. (1986). Parental influences on reading. *The Reading Teacher, 39,* 813–818.

Hallahan, D. P. & Kauffman, J. M. (1985). *Introduction to learning disabilities: A psycho-behavioral approach.* Englewood Cliffs, NJ: Prentice-Hall.

Hresko, W. P., Reid, D. K., & Hammill, D. D. (1981). *The test of early language development.* Austin, TX: Pro-Ed.

Jongsma, E. A. (1982). Test review: The ANSER system. *The Reading Teacher, 35,* 934–937.

Levine, M. D. (1981). *The ANSER system.* Cambridge, MA: Educators Publishing Service.

Rabin, A. T. (1982). Does vision screening tell the whole story? *The Reading Teacher, 35,* 524–527.

Rupley, W. H. (1971). Relationships between behavioral problems and reading retardation. *Indiana Reading Quarterly, 3,* 4–9.

Rupley, W. H., Wise, B. S., & Logan, J. W. (1986). Effective teaching of reading: An overview of its development. In J. Hoffman (Ed.), *Effective Teaching of Reading: Research and Practice.* Newark, DE: International Reading Association.

Schneider, M. F., German, D., & Johnson, B. (1986). Service overlap for the reading disabled student: A survey of learning disability and remedial professionals. *Reading Psychology, 7,* 153–162.

Spache, G. D. (1981). *Diagnosing and correcting reading disabilities.* Boston, MA: Allyn & Bacon.

Vetterli, C. H. (1959). How good is 20/20 vision? *Education, 80,* 16–19.

Vukelich, C. (1984). Parents' role in the reading process: A review of practical suggestions and ways to communicate with parents. *The Reading Teacher, 37,* 472–477.

Wilson, M. J. (1981). A review of recent research on the integration of reading and writing. *The Reading Teacher, 34,* 896–901.

16

<hr>
<hr>

Clinical Implementation of the Diagnostic Process

□ OVERVIEW

For a variety of reasons, some students need additional reading instruction outside the regular classroom. Besides having a reading program geared to their needs, these students often require further diagnosis and instruction provided by a reading resource teacher in a small-group setting outside the classroom. Some debate exists about the effectiveness of specialized reading classes. Major determinants of effectiveness are (1) the manner in which students are selected for further diagnosis and remediation, and (2) how closely the remedial program is tied to the regular classroom program. If effective screening takes place and if reading personnel are properly trained, reading instruction outside the regular classroom can be successful. The purpose of this chapter is to illustrate the diagnostic model of instruction when used in a clinical situation.

After reading this chapter, the teacher should be able to

□ apply the diagnostic process of instruction in a clinical setting.

□ select students who will benefit from extra reading instruction.

□ explain the different types of severe reading problems.

□ understand the need for a team approach in working with students who have severe reading problems.

□ design an individual plan of instruction that indicates strengths, weaknesses, and appropriate remedial instruction for a student.

□ write an efficient case study report on a student referred for extra instruction.

□ design and implement instruction sessions in a clinical situation.
□ apply specialized methods to use with students who cannot learn to read successfully using the traditional auditory-visual approach.

INCIDENCE OF READING DISABILITIES

It is reasonable to say that every teacher has at one time or another encountered students having extreme difficulties in learning to read. The incidence of severe reading problems is estimated to range from 10 to 80 percent of the school population, depending on the definition of the term *reading problems*, a particular school, a particular group of students (that is, school dropouts), and various socioeconomic groups. While severe reading problems will continue to exist due to factors outside a teacher's influence, it is our belief that a great many reading problems could be prevented or corrected with early identification and effective instruction. The success or failure of a student learning to read in a clinic situation depends on the resource teacher. Severe reading problems are often quite complex; however, the effort reading resource teachers expend in efficiently diagnosing and implementing a program based on a student's needs does make a difference. Besides highlighting the importance of the teacher, other realizations concerning reading disability in the schools are these:

□ Severe reading problems occur at all levels of intelligence.
□ Students with extreme reading problems may have problems emotionally and socially.
□ Extreme reading problems occur at all grade levels.
□ Students reading at a level appropriate to their grade may still have major reading problems.

SELECTING STUDENTS FOR THE READING CLINIC

Team Approach

The decision about which students should receive additional reading instruction outside the regular classroom should be a team effort. Professionals in the field need to acknowledge the expertise of other professionals and pool their resources, especially since diagnostic procedures have not reached the level of precision necessary to ensure 100 percent accuracy in student selection. Information required to make this decision should come from the child, his or her parents, the classroom teacher, the principal, and other specialized personnel, such as psychologists, social workers, speech teachers, special education teachers, and resource teachers. Students selected for remedial reading must have the capability of reading at higher levels to ensure that they will indeed profit from extra help. Both the reading resource teacher and the classroom teacher should assume the leadership roles in determining whether or not a student will profit from such instruction. In addition to combining the necessary data on a student's reading abilities, both teachers should discuss the feasibility of remedial instruction with other staff members and the child's parents. Information concerning the child's attitudes, motivations, learning style, social and emotional adjustment to placement outside the regular classroom, and ability to profit from special instruction should also influence the decision.

As stated previously, the incidence of reading disability in a particular population depends on how the term is defined. Earlier, we discussed the importance of detecting whether or not students are reading within the limits of their abilities. One method discussed was the administration of a listening comprehension test to estimate a student's reading expectancy or potential. Reading expectancy is "a level of reading performance that a given student should be able to reach" (Harris & Hodges, 1981). Another common method relies on various reading expectancy formulas. These formulas yield an expectancy level, which can then be compared to the reading achievement score of a student. Further diagnosis and placement in a remedial reading class is recommended if the expectancy is significantly greater than the student's reading achievement scores and his or her reading performance in class. Two popular formulas are the Bond and Tinker formula (Bond, Tinker, Wasson, & Wasson, 1984) and the Harris reading expectancy formula (Harris & Sipay, 1985).

Bond and Tinker Expectancy Formula

$$\text{Expected Reading Grade} = (\text{years in school} \times \frac{IQ}{100} + 1)$$

This formula uses the variables of the number of years a child has spent in the school, the IQ of the child, and the constant 1.0. The number of years in school are calculated beginning in grade one. The criteria for determining a significant discrepancy between the average reading score on a norm-referenced standardized test and the expected reading grade varies with the student's grade level.

Grade 1.5–2.4: Greater than or equal to 0.5 years (½ school year)

Grade 2.5–3.4: Greater than or equal to 0.75 years (¾ school year)

Grade 3.5–5.4: Greater than or equal to 1.0 (1 school year)

Grade 5.5 and above: Greater than or equal to 1.5 school years

Example: Student in grade five, second month (no repetition): 4.2
IQ: 95
Average reading grade score: 3.0
Expected reading grade $= (4.2 \times 0.95) + 1$
$= 3.99 + 1$
$= 5.0$
Comparison with average reading score yields a discrepancy of 2.0

Conclusion: Reading disability exists and student is a possible candidate for remedial reading.

Harris Expectancy Age Formula

$$\text{Reading Expectancy Age (REA)} = \frac{2\ MA\ +\ CA}{3}$$

$$\text{Mental age formula if only IQ is given: MA} = \frac{IQ\ \times\ CA}{100}$$

The expectancy age formula uses the variables of mental age (MA) and chronological age (CA). To determine the discrepancy between a student's average reading score and expectancy, the reading expectancy age is compared to the reading age (RA), which is the average reading score plus 5.2. Criteria for noting a significant discrepancy is completed by computing the reading expectancy quotient as follows:

$$\text{Reading Expectancy Quotient (REQ)} = \frac{RA\ \times\ 100}{REA}$$

Criteria: REQ = 90 to 110: No disability
REQ = Less than 90: Disability
REQ = Greater than 110: Overachievement

Example: Pupil in grade three
MA = 8.3
CA = 8.7
Average reading grade score: 2.2
REA = 2(8.3) + 8.7
$= \dfrac{16.6\ +\ 8.7}{3}$
$= 8.4$

RA = 2.2 + 5.2
$= 7.4$
Discrepancy between REA and RA is 1.0
REQ $= \dfrac{7.4\ +\ 100}{8.4}$
$= 88$

Conclusion: Severe reading problems exist and student is a possible candidate for remedial reading.

The concept of reading disability used in this text involves in part a comparison of potential or expectancy level to present achievement level. A student is said to be disabled in reading if a significant discrepancy exists between his or her capacity and present achievement. However, additional important considerations concerning a student's need and ability to profit from instruction outside the regular classroom should influence the decision. A student with the capability to read at a higher level may not be a candidate for remedial reading if proper instructional modifications can be made in the regular classroom. Likewise, a student might be a candidate for remedial reading if it is determined that the child would profit from specialized diagnosis and instruction even in the absence of a significant discrepancy between performance and potential.

Furthermore, reading expectancy formulas are not totally reliable. Different formulas sometimes yield different results even though they use the same data. This fact is a caution against relying 100 percent on such a calculation. On the other hand, the formulas do yield one measure which, coupled with other observations, helps in identifying students who might profit from a reading clinic situation. The disagreement over what constitutes a "significant discrepancy" between performance and potential shows the need for subjective judgment.

Various authors use different criteria in comparing potential and performance. Since there is no generally accepted criterion for significant discrepancy, differences should be treated carefully. However, this does not necessitate abandonment of the concept. While current measures have flaws, the concept of reading disability is important. Grade-level placement and chronological age have little connection with reading ability. Slow learners might be classified as disabled readers just because they are reading below grade level. These students are perhaps functioning within the limits of their abilities and need a corrective program in the regular classroom—not extra help simply because they are reading below grade/age norms. In contrast, gifted students might be reading at grade level but have the capability to read at a much higher level. These students are, in fact, disabled in reading and need proper corrective programs. Gifted children have special needs that should be recognized and acted upon.

Kaufman has made a significant departure from the use of traditional reading expectancy formulas to select students for remedial reading. He feels that current formulas predicting present reading achievement from an aptitude or capacity measure do not reflect a student's ability to profit from a particular program of instruction. Kaufman, in a personal communication, stated: "The only valid reading expectancy formula would be one that predicts *future* achievement after a defined remediation program of a definite duration." His criteria for placing students in remedial reading are whether or not they are reading "significantly below average for [their] grade placement" and whether or not students "would gain more from remedial instruction than from developmental instruction alone." The second criterion would be determined through program evaluation. (For a detailed explanation of interpreting expectancy by predicting future achievement through multiple regression procedures, see Burg, Kaufman, Korngold, and Kovner, 1978.)

In conclusion, deciding whether or not a student is disabled in reading is only important in terms of identifying students who might benefit from extra reading help. The determination that a student has a reading disability is not a final decision—it is the beginning of further inquiry. Such a determination should be a team decision and only implies the need to look more closely at a particular student and at the individualized instruction designed for him or her.

CLASSIFICATION OF READING PROBLEMS

Inherent in any classification system of reading problems is the tendency to fit every problem into a labeled category. It must always be remembered that each student is unique. While adhering to this position, it is beneficial to discuss types of reading problems and the corresponding treatment for each type. Overlap exists, but it is important to gain a broad understanding of types of reading problems. Table 16–1 depicts types of reading problems for both classroom and clinic. Classroom reading problems as discussed in chapter 6 are corrective in nature and include students who are reading within tolerable limits of their reading expectancy, but who lack various reading abilities. These problems are handled within the regular classroom with minor organizational modifications by the classroom teacher. Reading disability cases (students having a significant discrepancy between potential and performance along with additional supporting evidence) are divided into two sections: (1) those students for whom the auditory-visual (A-V) approach is recommended, and (2) those for whom the traditional A-V approach is not recommended. In the first instance, students recommended for a clinic situation indicate their ability to progress with a developmental reading method that incorporates the A-V approach. There are several developmental approaches from which to choose, including analytic basals, synthetic basals, linguistic readers, modified alphabet, language experience, programmed readers, and individualized reading.

To determine which method is appropriate for each student, a teacher must assess learner style, task conditions, and resource attributes. An initial decision may be changed after a trial period. A **trial period** includes short trial lessons that can be completed in a clinic setting to predict informally whether or not a student is likely to achieve success with a

TABLE 16–1 Classification of Reading Problems

Type of Reading Problem	Characteristics	Broad Areas of Reading Ability
Corrective (within the classroom)	1. One or two specific reading deficiencies (mild)	• Basic sight vocabulary • Word recognition • Comprehension • Study skills
Reading disability (outside the regular classroom)	1. Use of A-V approach is warranted (reading deficiencies in several areas) 2. Use of A-V approach is not warranted (reading deficiencies in several areas)	• Basic sight vocabulary • Word recognition • Comprehension • Study skills

particular approach. In the second instance, students recommended for a clinic situation have not previously learned by methods using the A-V approach and give evidence that they cannot associate meaning to printed symbols using this approach. Reading problems in this category include, for example, word blindness, dyslexia, alexia, and so forth. Specialized remedial approaches that have demonstrated success with remedial readers of this type are discussed later in the chapter.

Disabled readers' problems can be mild to severe depending on the complexity of the problem. The possible combinations of deficient facilitative and functional reading abilities are endless. In order to help disabled readers, the reading resource teacher must examine all relevant physical, educational, intellectual, emotional, and cultural factors and try to determine which areas are contributing to the problem. A team approach that involves parents, school psychologists, speech teachers, social workers, special education teachers, and guidance counselors is an absolute necessity in planning an appropriate educational plan.

INSTRUCTIONAL GUIDELINES

The success of clinic instruction depends on a host of outside influences as well as on the program, teacher, and student variables (see chapter 2). Two of the more crucial variables are direct instruction by the teacher and sufficient instructional time for students to learn.

Successful remedial reading programs are characterized by allowing students to have more quality reading time accompanied with providing excellent instruction. This is in contrast to the philosophy of providing remedial reading with a different curriculum and different teacher attributes. Instead, the same characteristics of effective reading instruction described in chapter 2 only need be given greater emphasis in a remedial

Remedial instruction needs to directly complement the student's reading instruction in the regular classroom. (Kevin Fitzsimons/Merrill)

classroom. In this light, a remedial reading program is directly linked to the regular classroom program. Through this linkage, the remedial program actually enhances the instruction given in the regular classroom because in both situations are similar goals and curricula materials (Allington & Shake, 1986). Obviously, for this to occur, classroom teachers and remedial reading teachers must be in close communication and must cooperatively plan a student's instruction. Speaking about the need for a close relationship between the regular classroom program and the remedial reading program and to the roles of the teachers involved, Chall and Curtis (1987) state:

> An overall instructional plan for the student should be made—and coordinated, as much as possible, with the regular curriculum. Some if not most of the work will require direct teacher instruction and reinforcement. Poor readers, especially, need teacher direction, guidance, confirmation, and response. Independent tasks are usually not enough. Generally, the younger the student and the lower the reading level, the more direct the teaching should be. Older students and those reading at higher levels can usually do more on their own, but they too need instruction and guidance. (p. 788)

In a clinic situation, it is important that students know where they stand in relation to their strengths and weaknesses. Most will not have to be told they are having difficulties in reading, but the reading teacher should outline specific areas of strengths and weaknesses. As much as possible, students should help plan their own program of instruction. Given a choice of materials to achieve an objective, the student might choose one particular set of materials over others. Capitalizing on students' strengths means that the reading teacher will concentrate on the positive to teach a weakness. For example, highlighting a student's knowledge of long vowel sounds when teaching short vowel sounds can be very effective. Also, teachers can capitalize on a student's interests in designing games to reinforce a weak skill area. Related to this point of capitalizing on a student's strengths, Milligan (1986) identified through interviews and observation the following seven instructional procedures that worked *against* having an effective remedial reading program:

> insufficient time spent on actual reading by students
>
> too heavy an emphasis on decoding skills in diagnostic testing
>
> too much instructional time allocated to phonic skills
>
> too heavy an emphasis on sounding out unfamiliar words to the exclusion of other word-identification techniques
>
> inordinate emphasis on requesting poor readers to correct oral reading miscues
>
> lack of attention to the importance of background knowledge in choosing reading materials
>
> inordinate emphasis on correcting students' reversals of letters or words

The importance of students knowing why they are doing what they are doing is universally acknowledged. It is essential in a clinic situation—so many of these students have experienced continual failure that they aimlessly complete assigned work. These students must become involved with their own progress and understand the reason behind each activity. The concept of providing instruction on a level where students will be successful is crucial in a clinic situation. The student must have confidence from the outset that work can be done successfully in prescribed materials. If in doubt, reading teachers should always start at an easy level of difficulty. It is much easier to jump to a higher level than to go back. Students will know if they must move to easier material, and this kind of mistake can add to their feelings of failure and frustration.

Unlike some classroom situations, the clinic setting often demands a structured learning experience for the child. Once priority areas for instruction are identified, a variety of approaches and materials can be used to achieve the teacher's objectives and to avoid boredom. Chapters 7 and 8 on word recognition discussed the need to use many different means to achieve one goal. This principle is important in a clinic situation. For example, if a student needs instruction on vowel principles, the following procedures might be employed:

1. Short, direct lessons
2. Game using vowel principles
3. Independent worksheets on vowel principles
4. Use of media, that is, listening tapes on vowel principles, language masters
5. Oral and silent reading with the student, making sure skills are being applied in context and that the focus is on comprehension

To accomplish a teaching objective (for example, student knows and applies vowel principles), the teacher must teach and reinforce the skill in many situations and in a variety of ways.

There is no one lesson format to be followed in each clinic situation. While student and teacher preferences and styles will differ, it is possible to outline components that deserve attention. However, the components of effective clinic instruction mirror those of effective classroom instruction.

1. *Introduction:* Reviewing, setting purpose, talking with students about nonreading subjects (5–10 minutes)
2. *Word-analysis or comprehension instruction:* Instruction, supervised practice (15–20 minutes)
3. *Comprehension:* DRA followed by meaningful oral reading (20–25 minutes)
4. *Independent reading:*
   a. Read aloud to student; material should be fun and based on past experiences
   b. Student selects own book and reads silently
5. *Vocabulary:* Basic sight vocabulary, words in content areas, words in story (DRA), tachistoscope (10 minutes)
6. *Game time:* Reinforce word-recognition and comprehension skills (10–15 minutes)
7. *Extras*
   a. Machine time: Tape recorders, records, filmstrips, typewriters, controlled readers, language masters
   b. Art activities
   c. Physical exercises
   d. Science experiments
   e. Spotlight time: Discuss things of interest to the child and use LEA to record these for future discussion and instruction
8. *Review purpose for activities completed:* Illustrate with familiar examples and show how this learning will help in future learning

The overriding concerns for clinic sessions are that they be structured, be diagnostic in nature, consist of short direct lessons, and be highly flexible depending on the mood of the students. Once priority areas of facilitative and functional reading abilities are identified, clinic lessons should provide direct instruction on needed skills. While direct instruction on needed abilities is essential, the sessions themselves must be interesting and must contain activities designed to allow the teacher to get to know students better and motivate them to want to improve. An atmosphere of concern for the whole child must be conveyed—not just a concern narrowly focused on reading instruction.

Continuous Diagnosis

Throughout instruction in a clinic setting, there is a need for continuous diagnosis of educational and noneducational factors affecting a student's performance. Unlike the problems encountered with a large group of students in a regular classroom, the opportunity for immediate changes in a student's program is readily available in an individual or small-group clinic setting. Every lesson can and should be both instructional and diagnostic in nature. Initial corrective hypotheses concerning a student's individualized plan can be altered on the spot if reading teachers respond to a student's reactions and progress through prescribed approaches and materials. This process requires some type of record keeping to take place (refer to chapter 11 for sample forms). While it is important to closely monitor a student's progress in the reading resource room, clinic teachers must also monitor the student's progress in the regular classroom and with other important persons, (e.g., parents, speech teachers, social workers, psychologists, and learning disability teachers). Progress or lack of progress in these other areas can have a definite effect on a student's performance in a reading resource room. This team approach requires communication between the reading teachers and a number of other persons. If the reading teacher attempts to operate in a vacuum, the best laid individualization plans will fail.

INSTRUCTIONAL RESOURCES

Although there is no sharp line of demarcation, it is often possible to identify two groups of students who experience major reading problems: (1) those students who profit from instruction in the traditional A-V mode and (2) those students who do not. For both types of children, there are basically three available avenues of instruction: (1) a begin-over approach to fill in major gaps, using different materials from those employed in the classroom; (2) specialized approaches for those students who have shown an inability to profit from traditional approaches, methods, and materials; or (3) a combination approach utilizing aspects of both the begin-over and specialized approaches.

The types of methods and materials used to achieve success are important determinants of student achievement. It is only logical for a reading resource teacher to ask, "Are there specialized reading instructional resources to use with disabled readers?" In fact, there is little actual difference in materials, except for severely disabled readers. With proper instruction, most children (both corrective and disabled) can learn to read using traditional instructional resources. Surely a clinic situation affords a more individualized and personalized setting; however, the same teaching procedures recommended for classroom instruction apply in clinic situations. The problems are often greater, but both classroom and reading resource teachers should be sensitive to individual differences and capitalize on a variety of instructional resources to teach students what they need to know. Both situations demand the right instructional resources at the right time for the right student.

In discussing specific methods of teaching reading, one important fact must be realized: all methods of teaching reading have failed to teach some children to read. Skillful reading teachers, then, must adapt their instruction to the particular learning style of each student, utilizing a variety of approaches and materials to be successful. This adaptive instruction should be highlighted by a high percentage of direct instruction and a high percentage of time provided for mastery and transfer of targeted reading skills and abilities.

Options for Selecting Instructional Resources

Students recommended for specialized help in reading who can learn through an A-V approach often do not need specialized instructional resources. Many children can profit from remedial instruction with classroom-type resources that include varied and interesting materials. Depending on students' strengths and weaknesses, this may necessitate using a linguistic, language-experience, or adapted-basal approach combined with and supplemented by any of these other approaches plus any one of a number of phonic programs on the market. The point is that while these students are able to acquire reading skills through the usual A-V mode of presentation, a modified approach working with resources other than those previously used is warranted. The basic reason for selecting resources other than those used for past instruction is that the student has not learned to read with these; more instruction with the same resources will not ensure reading improvement. A relatively new avenue for reading instruction in both classroom and clinic is computer-assisted instruction (CAI). Relying primarily on a programmed reading approach, CAI can be successful if used properly. Computers and their use are discussed later in this chapter (also see chapter 12).

The list of possible combinations of materials and approaches is endless and depends on the strengths and weaknesses of the learner. Specific activities that are appropriate for both a classroom and a reading resource room were discussed in earlier chapters. Any one of these instructional resources, or a combination of them, may help a child become a better reader; however, the key to selection and use is matching the instructional resources as closely as possible to the learner's individualized program.

A second avenue open for reading resource teachers is to use specialized instructional resources with those severely disabled readers who are unable to acquire reading abilities through the conventional A-V approach. Methods developed for these readers involve a multisensory approach incorporating the use of visual, auditory, kinesthetic, and tactile (VAKT) pathways to learning. Such instructional resources are usually recommended only for those students who are experiencing major problems with reading.

A third option for working with problem readers incorporates a specialized method, for example, VAKT or VAK, with conventional classroom-type reading materials. This is a common avenue inasmuch as it combines a multisensory approach for word learning with needed practice in materials that utilize the auditory-visual aspects of learning. Most multisensory approaches aim at bringing a child back to the point of learning words through an A-V method. This combination approach is generally preferable to a strict adherence to a specialized approach.

These alternatives deal primarily with instructional resources aimed at improving a child's word-recognition skills. However, as we have emphasized, the child must have opportunities to apply these skills in actual reading situations. Such instruction should focus on applying the word-recognition skills to get at meaning. All of these options can and should lead a child to improve comprehension if the teacher provides activities and situations that emphasize comprehension, such as those discussed in previous chapters.

Selection of Instructional Resources

The importance of diagnosing instruction has been emphasized throughout the text. Reading resource teachers should look at instructional resources in relation to student needs to determine if modification must be made. Although there is a multitude of reading materials, approaches, and methods currently available, each one should be evaluated in terms of the individual child's needs.

Chapter 12 presented and discussed five criteria that classroom teachers should consider when selecting resources for corrective reading instruction. Briefly, the criteria suggested were that instructional resources should (1) match the individual learner's style; (2) deal specifically with the behavioral objectives and be appropriate to the instructional procedures; (3) be evaluated before use by first specifying features that are best for the students; (4) be considered in terms of limitations, such as cost, availability, and teacher familiarity; and (5) be re-evaluated and modified in regard to student progress. These criteria are also applicable to the selection of instructional resources for use with children receiving instruction from a reading resource teacher. Applying the criteria before choosing instructional resources allows the reading resource teacher to match the materials, methods, and approaches to the student's needs, rather than forcing the student to meet the demands of the resources.

SPECIALIZED INSTRUCTIONAL RESOURCES

The Fernald-Keller Method

Many years ago, Dr. Grace M. Fernald and Helen B. Keller devised a specialized reading method for severely disabled readers that is still effective today. This approach, which is multisensory in nature, showed dramatic success with disabled readers who could not learn to read through the usual A-V mode of presentation. This VAKT approach enables the reader to use four sensory modalities in the process of learning words. For example, the child sees the word (visual), hears the word said (auditory), traces the word with a finger (kinesthetic), and feels the word as it is traced (tactile). The approach is a time-consuming one-to-one method that is to be used only with severely disabled readers. The procedure itself is based on a four-stage process (Fernald, 1943) that brings students to the point of identifying unknown words through visual analysis. The technique is outlined in the following stages by Cooper (1964).

Stage 1: Tracing

1. The child is motivated in two ways: First, the child is told that he or she may try a new method of learning words that works. Second, the child is encouraged to learn many words he or she *wishes to use but does not know how to write.*
2. The teacher writes the word with a crayon on a large piece of paper (approximately 3″ × 10″) while the child observes the process. The teacher says the word while writing it. Either manuscript or cursive writing is used, depending on what a particular child has been using. Some teachers prefer manuscript because it more nearly approximates the printed word in the book.
3. The child traces the word with a finger until he or she can reproduce it *without looking at the copy.*
   a. The child uses either one or two fingers for tracing, as he or she wishes. Finger contact is important in tracing. Tracing with chalk, crayon, pencil, or stylus does not produce the desired results.
   b. The child says the word by syllables in a natural tone while writing each part. It is important that the word be said as it would in conversation; no distortion of the sounds of letters or syllables is permitted. No letter-by-letter spelling is permitted.

Some students can profit from specialized reading methods. (Michael Siluk)

    c. The tracing is repeated as many times as necessary in order for the child to write the word without looking at the copy.

4. The child writes the word, saying it by syllables in a natural tone while writing each part. This writing is first done on scrap paper before putting it in a story or record.

    a. The word is written without looking at the copy.

    b. If an error is made, the whole word is traced again and again until it can be written without looking at the copy. Attention is directed to correct form, not to errors.

    c. The word is always written as a unit.

5. The word is always used in context. During the first few periods, the word may not be used in a story. The purpose of the initial activities is to convince the child that he or she can learn words and can remember them. However, the word must have meaning to the child; it must be one that he or she wants to learn. After the first period or so, the child uses this method to learn words that he or she wishes to use in a story or in some type of experience record. The child may ask for words to label diagrams, to label pictures in booklets, or for stories.

6. After the child completes the story or record, the teacher types it immediately so that it can be read in print.

7. After the labeling of the story is completed, the child files the word cards in alphabetical order.

8. Frequent checks on retention are made. Re-reading labels and stories and flash card checks are used as a means of appraising retention.

9. During stage 1, the child makes use of several aids to learning. First, the word has meaning to the child; he or she is motivated by a desire to use the word for communication. Second, the child *sees* the word written by the teacher, *sees* it while tracing, *sees* it while writing, and *sees* it in the final typed form. Third, by using direct finger contact in tracing, the child "*feels*" the word while saying and seeing it. Fourth, by arm movement in tracing and in writing the word, the child "*feels*" the word while saying and seeing it. Fifth, by pronouncing the word while tracing and writing it, the child "*feels*" the word with his or her speech apparatus. Sixth, by hearing the word pronounced, the child is given an additional aid for retention. When all modalities of learning are used, the child should learn.

10. The child is given no systematic help in phonic analysis. The emphasis is on structural analysis, especially syllabication. However, the knowledge of structural analysis is not acquired in the usual manner through systematic and specific instruction.

11. The length of time a child has to stay in stage 1 varies greatly, depending on the severity of the difficulty. Some children move out of stage 1 after only a few words, while others may have to stay with it for one hundred or more words.

Stage 2: Writing from Script

1. Stage 2 has been achieved when words can be learned without tracing. The need for tracing is reduced gradually; that is, the number of retracings required to learn a word is reduced until tracing is no longer necessary. In short, tracing is discontinued when the child can learn without it.

2. In this stage, the children learns a word by looking at it written in manuscript (or cursive), by saying it, by writing it without copy as he or she says each part.

   a. The child indicates the word he or she wants to write but cannot.

    b. The teacher writes it in small manuscript, pronouncing each part as it is written. A small card (perhaps 3″ × 5″) is used. The child observes the teacher write the word.

    c. The child says the word silently while looking at it.

    d. The child writes the word without looking at the copy, saying each part of the word while writing it. At the beginning of this stage some tracing may be necessary. If so, follow procedure for stage 1.

    e. The word is always written as a whole by the child. When an error is made, the child either retraces or looks at it (saying it silently or aloud) until he or she can write it without copy.

    f. The child uses the word in his or her story or composition.

3. The child's composition is typed immediately by the teacher.

4. The child reads the typed copy without delay. Silent reading is used to prepare for fluent oral re-reading.

5. When tracing is not necessary, small cards are used and filed alphabetically in a small box.

6. No attempt is made to simplify the vocabulary, sentence structure, or concepts in the child's composition. The learning and retention of larger words is, in general, better than that of shorter words.

7. Immediate and delayed recall is checked with the flash cards in the small file box.

8. The only modality of learning eliminated in this stage is that of tracing.

Stage 3: Writing from Print (Initial Book Reading)

1. This stage has been reached when the child can *write* the word after looking at the *printed* form of it and being told what it says. It is no longer necessary for the teacher to write the word for the child; instead the teacher pronounces it for the child.

2. At this stage the child begins to read from books.

    a. Words to be taught are taken from the book the child is reading.

    b. Silent reading is always done first.

    c. During the silent reading, the child indicates the words he or she does not know and is told immediately what they are.

    d. After the silent reading is completed, the "new" words are learned as follows:

        (1) The teacher tells the child what a word says.

        (2) The child looks at the printed word and says it silently.

        (3) The child writes the word from memory; that is, without looking at the copy. If the child is unable to make the transfer from print to script, the teacher writes the word for the child. The child then writes the word and identifies it in print.

    e. Immediate and delayed recall of the words is appraised by flash cards or some other means such as re-reading the material in which the words first appeared.

Stage 4: Recognition of Words Without Writing (Book Reading and Visual Analysis Techniques)

1. This stage has been reached when it is no longer necessary for the child to write a word in order to remember it.
2. Phrasing is improved by developing the habit of silent reading to clear up the meaning of new words.
3. During this fourth stage progress is rapid.
4. With this procedure, children always do their own reading; they are never read to.
5. Word recognition is developed by a syllabication approach. Writing the word without copy is used when necessary.

Summary of Method

In stage 1 the child traces the word. Stage 2 has been reached when the child writes the word after looking at a copy prepared by the teacher. In stage 3, the child looks at the printed word and pronounces it; he or she then writes the word without looking at the copy. During stage 4, very little writing of "new" words is necessary. The child gets words by visual analysis.

The following is a modification of VAKT that we have found to be successful in our reading clinics. In this adaptation the child prints the words and then transfers them to actual reading situations.

1. A word the child is to learn is printed by the teacher on a 5" × 8" sandpaper card as the child watches.
2. The word is shown to the child and pronounced by the teacher as the child looks at it. It is extremely important that the child looks at the word as it is pronounced to help associate the oral representation of the word with its written representation.
3. The child and teacher pronounce the word in unison five or six times as the child looks at the word.
4. The child takes the word card, and as the teacher and child say the word together, prints the word in a tray filled with moist sand. A gift box lid, approximately 14" × 18", lined with aluminum foil works well for a sand tray.
5. After the child prints the word in the sand, it is retraced several times as it is pronounced.
6. Following the tracing, the word card is again shown and the child pronounces the word. The child keeps the word card to bring to the next session. During free time the child is encouraged to review the word and trace it in the sand tray.
7. Each word is reviewed daily with this procedure until the child recognizes the word when presented in isolation, in a short list with other words, and in a phrase or short sentence. Words that are recognized are

filed in a "words I know" envelope and reviewed periodically with the child. These words are then used to construct short sentences and stories where the focus of instruction is on comprehension. For example, if a child recognizes the words *the, is, and, red, big, ball, bike,* and *cat,* sentences such as the following can be constructed:

> "The cat is big."
> "The ball is big."
> "The bike is big and red."
> "The big ball is red."

Although these are simple sentences, they can form the basis for activities to help a child better understand that reading is comprehension. For example, one of the sentences could serve as a title to stimulate a language-experience story. Words could be interchanged; for example, "The cat is *big*," could be changed to "The cat is *red*." The effect that changing one word has on the ideas could then be discussed. Pictures could be drawn by the child to illustrate one or several sentences; and the need for learning a new word could be illustrated, for example, "The ball and bike *are* red."

As we have emphasized throughout the text, corrective and remedial reading instruction should build on a child's strengths instead of focusing only on the weaknesses. When using a VAKT approach for teaching words, one student strength the teacher can use is to select words from the child's speaking vocabulary. This ensures that the child has a referent for the words and that they are meaningful to him or her. As the child becomes successful in recognizing some words on sight, this becomes another strength on which the teacher can build to transfer this skill to actual reading situations where the focus is on comprehension.

The Cooper Method

The Cooper method (1964) is a modification of the Fernald-Keller method. The main differences are in the selection of words to be taught, the introduction of book reading from the outset, and the inclusion of both structural and phonic analyses to eventually replace sight-word learning. An outline of the Cooper method follows.

1. Select a series of basal readers, preferably one the child has not had before.
2. Find the child's instructional level in this series by means of an informal reading inventory. (Note: It is assumed here that if this procedure is indicated, the child's instructional level will not be more than primer level and probably lower.)
3. Assess the child's recognition of the total list of words in the first preprimer and make a list of those words that are not known. These become the words to be taught as the book is read.

4. Teach these words to the child, using the appropriate stage of the Fernald-Keller method, and have the child read them in the contextual setting of the book.
5. Practice these words, both in context and in isolation.
6. Repeat steps 3, 4, and 5 with the second preprimer, third preprimer, primer, and so on, moving from one stage to another as the child is able to do so.
7. Parallel the early stages with additional visual discrimination training and auditory discrimination training.
8. At some point in the sequence of stages, depending on the child's readiness, introduce a systematic program of word analysis skills that will eventually replace all sight techniques.

Although the Cooper method incorporates each stage of the Fernald-Keller method, it does not use words of high emotional importance to the child. The words selected come directly from the basal reader. Veatch and others (1973) point out that words which come from children and relate to their experiences are often more easily learned. For this reason, the Cooper method might better serve to help a child make the transition from the Fernald-Keller method to reading in prepared materials.

Although the Fernald-Keller method has proven to be successful with extreme reading disability cases, there are several other specialized approaches and programs available to use in a clinic situation. Reading teachers considering the use of one of these approaches should study the original source and become totally familiar with its philosophy and proper implementation. A number of sources are listed here:

Color Phonics System
Bannatyne, Alex. "The Color Phonics System." *The Disabled Reader*, ed. John Money, Baltimore, Md.: The Johns Hopkins Press, 1966, pp. 193–214.

Gillingham-Stillman Method
Gillingham, Anna, and Bessie W. Stillman. *Remedial Training for Children with Specific Difficulty in Reading, Spelling, and Penmanship*, 7th ed. Cambridge, Mass.: Educators Publishing Service, 1966.

Hegge-Kirk-Kirk Method
Hegge, Thorleif G., Samuel A. Kirk, and Winifred Kirk. *Remedial Reading Drills*. Ann Arbor, Mich.: George Wahr Publishing Company, 1965.

Multisensory Approach to Language Arts for Specific Language Disability Children
Slingerland, Beth H. *A Multi-Sensory Approach to Language Arts for Specific Language Disability Children*. Cambridge, Mass.: Educators Publishing Service, 1974.

Phonovisual Method
Schoolfield, L., and J. Timberlake. *The Phonovisual Method.* Washington, D.C.: Phonovisual Products, 1960.

Unified Phonics Method
Spalding, Romalda Bishop, and Walter T. Spalding. *The Writing Road to Reading.* New York: William Morrow & Company, 1969.

DIAGNOSTIC PROCESS: CLINICIAL IMPLEMENTATION

The reading resource teacher should follow the process of instruction described in chapter 6 with a few modifications. Major differences stem from the possibility of dealing with more severe reading problems, the possible use of a greater number of diagnostic and instructional procedures, and greater involvement with a variety of professionals and parents.

Knowledge about the reading act, of correlates to reading disabilities, and of the teacher's own assumptions about children learning to read are important prerequisites to implementing a clinical reading program. Not to diminish the need for classroom teachers' knowledge in these areas, clinic teachers must have an even more thorough understanding. Students in need of special help in reading often bring with them special problems, which may be emotional, social, physical, cultural, educational, and/or intellectual in nature. Reading teachers should be prepared to respond in an appropriate manner to each child. A correct attitude is crucial. Realizing the social and emotional effects of reading failure, clinic teachers must have a positive attitude that they can make the difference in promoting a successful experience for each child.

Diagnosis of instruction must precede diagnosis of the child in a clinic situation. The same questions asked by classroom teachers (see chapter 6) are appropriate here. The reading resource teacher must also answer these additional questions:

☐ Do I have the necessary supplemental tests to formulate specific diagnostic hypotheses?
☐ Do I have a variety of specialized remedial approaches and materials to meet the varied needs of children?

The remaining steps in the process parallel those described for the classroom teacher with the following major modifications:

1. Additional diagnostic testing is sometimes required (duplication of testing is not recommended).
2. A team approach—involving the cooperation of various specialists and parents—is usually employed. Information gathered from the sources described in chapter 15 are evaluated cooperatively.

3. A personalized instructional plan can be executed without the pressure of handling 25 to 30 other children at the same time.

A case study report of a student referred to a special reading class illustrates the remaining steps of the process. Relevant data are collected (for example, reading levels, specific strengths and weaknesses, and reading expectancy levels), results are interpreted and synthesized (individual profile of performance), environmental and physical limitations are assessed, interests and attitudes are solicited, priority areas for instruction are translated into diagnostic hypotheses, corrective hypotheses are then put in action in terms of materials and approaches, and continuous diagnosis is implemented. This diagnostic process is comprehensive yet economical. Clinical diagnosis and prescription depend on the teacher's skill in responding to children's needs—not the administration and interpretation of a great number of tests.

Case Study: Gary

Analysis of Reading Difficulty

This case report introduces a fifth grader, Gary, who is 10 years, 10 months of age. In order to obtain relevant diagnostic data and plan appropriate instruction, the clinician administered the *Peabody Picture Vocabulary Test* (PPVT), the *Gates-MacGinitie Reading Tests*, and the *Stanford Diagnostic Reading Test*, the results of which follow.

The *Peabody Picture Vocabulary Test*—Revised, Form L was used to obtain an assessment of receptive vocabulary. It consists of a series of 175 plates with four pictures on each plate. The plates are arranged in order of increasing difficulty. The subject is asked to indicate which one of four pictures best illustrates the meaning of a stimulus word pronounced by the examiner.

Gary's scores on the PPVT were as follows:

Raw Score 115

Standard Score Equivalent 102

Percentile Rank 55

Stanine 6

Age Equivalent 11-1

These results fall in the average score range.

Level	Word List	Word Recognition		Comprehension	
		Context	Level	Oral	Level
PP	100%				
P	100%				
1	100%	98%	Independent	100%	Independent
2	80%	92%	Instructional	70%	Instructional
3		89%	Frustration	70%	Instructional
4		87%	Frustration	50%	Frustration

The results show that Gary's independent reading level (the highest level at which he can read fluently without teacher aid) is at the first-grade level. His instructional-reading level is second grade. His most common word-recognition miscues are mispronunciations, having a total of 22 in the four passages read. These mispronunciations increased significantly with the difficulty of the selection. Omissions and unknown words were also found to be somewhat frequent, as were repetitions and spontaneous corrections. Qualitative assessment of the oral reading miscues in the third- and fourth-grade passages indicate that approximately 60 percent of them did interfere with Gary's comprehension. Word-recognition miscues seem to indicate weaknesses in short vowel sounds, vowel principles, syllabication principles, knowledge of structural components of certain words, and the ability to combine syntactic and semantic cues with phonic cues to pronounce a word. Gary's pattern of miscues appears to reflect an understanding of the reading process as "word-calling" rather than communication. An analysis of the types of errors in comprehension shows that Gary is strong in literal comprehension outcomes but somewhat weak in inferential and vocabulary-type outcomes.

The clinician administered the *Gates-MacGinitie Reading Tests* (2nd ed.), Level D, Form 1. This test is a standardized test of general reading ability. It contains two subtests: vocabulary and comprehension. On the vocabulary test, the student is asked to choose the word or phrase that is closest in meaning to the test word. On the comprehension test, the student reads passages and answers questions about them.

Gary obtained the following scores:

	Raw Score	Stanine	Normal Curve Equivalent	Percentile Rank	Grade Equivalent	Extended Scale Score
Vocabulary	13	2	20	8	3.1	443
Comprehension	14	2	23	10	3.0	436
Total	27	2	19	7	3.9	440

The *Stanford Diagnostic Reading Test* (3rd ed.), Green Level, Form G was used to identify Gary's strengths and weaknesses in various word-identification and comprehension skills. It consists of five subtests. In test 1, auditory vocabulary, the student listens to an incomplete sentence and then three words, and then selects the word that best completes the sentence. In test 2, auditory discrimination, the student listens to two words and indicates whether they have the same beginning, middle, or ending sound. Test 3, phonetic analysis, asks the student to choose the word that contains the same sound as the one made by the underlined letters in a given word. Test 4, structural analysis, consists of two tasks, word division and blending. Test 5, reading comprehension, tests both literal and inferential comprehension through the use of a multiple-choice cloze format and passages followed by questions.

Gary's scores were as follows:

Test	Raw Score	Stanine	Percentile Rank	Grade Equivalent	Scaled Score
Auditory vocabulary	35	4	39	4.9	614
Auditory discrimination	28	5	52	8.6	646
Phonetic analysis	25	4	37	3.1	597
Structural analysis	36	2	7	2.7	546
Literal comprehension	21	4	30	3.8	610
Inferential comprehension	17	3	19	3.1	578
Comprehension total	38	4	27	3.1	591

Individualized Instructional Program

Based on the information gathered, the following individualized program was developed for Gary.

Learner Style

The following strengths were evident:

- [ ] Possesses adequate basic sight vocabulary; recognizes short one-syllable words quickly and associates meaning with them
- [ ] Exhibits strong literal comprehension for recall and recognition of facts, main ideas, and sequence of events
- [ ] Knows initial consonant sounds, blends, and long vowel sounds
- [ ] Shows positive attitude toward reading and reading instruction
- [ ] Attempts to get meaning as he reads; however, poor use of context clues impedes progress

The following reading weaknesses were identified:

- [ ] Exhibits problems with inferential comprehension for main idea(s), character traits, and sequence of events
- [ ] Demonstrates difficulty with comprehension for critical outcomes
- [ ] Shows limited use of context clues to get at word meaning(s)
- [ ] Exhibits difficulty with structural analysis skills—prefixes, suffixes, and compound words
- [ ] Displays difficulties identifying short vowel sounds; lacks knowledge of phonic generalizations for short vowel sounds
- [ ] Has syllabication problems with vcv and vccv principles
- [ ] Shows problems with auditory and visual discrimination of word endings in multisyllabic words

Motivational characteristics based on information obtained from the classroom teacher and observation during diagnosis include the following:

- [ ] Shows enhanced learning ability when A-V developmental approach is used
- [ ] Requires immediate feedback regarding correctness of response, particularly when he is unsure of correct word identification
- [ ] Responds well to positive, sincere verbal praise and encouragement
- [ ] Enjoys and participates actively in creative art activities
- [ ] Works best in reading tasks when the purpose for learning is shown to him and illustrated with many concrete examples
- [ ] Responds well when a variety of materials are used for reading instruction

These additional strengths and weaknesses were noted:

Strengths

☐ Attends well to both individual and group tasks that are less than 15 minutes in duration
☐ Responds best to questions that are sequenced in terms of their order of difficulty
☐ Pays more attention to individual seat work tasks when he is given only a portion of the work to complete and then given the remainder after having finished the first part
☐ Performs better when each step of learning is discussed and illustrated in a detailed, structured manner
☐ Responds well to prompts and cues when responding to questions

Weaknesses

☐ Shows reluctance to attend to activities that are longer than 15 minutes in duration
☐ Exhibits a negative attitude toward materials resembling a basal reader in format and is reluctant to participate when such materials are used for reading instruction
☐ Refuses to attempt to complete seat-work activities that he perceives as being "too much work to do"
☐ Hesitant to think about responding to questions if he doesn't immediately have a response
☐ Has short attention span for tasks that are not highly structured
☐ Withdraws from participation in group learning situations.

Task Conditions

Behavioral objectives established for Gary include the following:

☐ Will identify the short vowel sounds occuring in given words, pronounce the words correctly, and use them in oral and written sentences
☐ Will use context clues to get at the meaning of unfamiliar words
☐ Will apply knowledge of syllabication generalizations and then phonic generalizations to correctly identify given words
☐ Will infer main idea from a given story or passage

Resource Attributes

Instructional materials, approaches, and formats include the following:

☐ Language master
☐ Reader's Digest Skill Builders
☐ Games—commercial and teacher-made
☐ Creative art activities for comprehension
☐ Language-experience approach
☐ VAKT method
☐ Teacher-made and commercial worksheets

Teacher Style

The following instructional procedures were established for use with Gary:

☐ Use instructional resources that are structured and that illustrate the development of the skill
☐ Use basic sight vocabulary to introduce and reinforce short vowel generalization in both isolation and application in meaningful content

□ Provide sequential direct-instruction lessons and practice in a variety of situations on the following skills and abilities: short vowel sounds, syllabication principles, structural analysis (especially suffixes), context clues, and inferential comprehension

□ Incorporate a variety of materials, yet focus on a specific skill application

□ Incorporate verbal praise and encouragement with all instruction

□ Use instructional resources that allow for short instructional periods that focus on teaching the same basic skills

□ Incorporate language experience with art activities to illustrate purpose of learning and application to get meaning

□ SUMMARY

The effective implementation of the diagnostic process for instruction in a clinic situation was the focus of this chapter. Reading disability was defined in terms of a significant discrepancy between a student's potential and actual achievement. A team approach was recommended (with the team including the classroom teacher, reading teacher, parents, the student, and various specialists) to decide whether or not a particular student would profit from special reading instruction. While each reading problem is unique, types of reading problems were classified according to the nature and severity of the difficulty. Reading disability cases of two general types were noted: (1) those students who have sufficient auditory and visual abilities to learn through the A-V approach and (2) those students who are unable to learn by a traditional A-V method of presentation.

The teacher is the key ingredient in a clinic situation. While not ignoring various physical, psychological, social, and emotional factors impeding a student's progress, emphasis was placed on effective teacher practices. Rather than providing a different program from the one used in the regular classroom, clinic instruction should be directly related to and actually enhance the regular reading program.

Clinic teachers were encouraged to look at themselves and their programs before looking at the child. Principles for effective instruction in implementing diagnostic findings were discussed and components of clinic lessons were outlined. Most reading disabled students will profit from good classroom practices and materials presented in a direct-instruction framework. For those children who are unable to learn through a traditional auditory-visual approach, the Fernald-Keller multisensory approach, or a modification of it, is recommended.

□ *IN-TEXT ASSIGNMENTS*

LIBRARY ACTIVITY

Search the ERIC files in your library for recent research studies on remedial reading and the application of remedial reading programs. Summarize two or three documents on 3″ × 5″ cards and report orally to the class.

FIELD-BASED ACTIVITY

As a class, arrange a visit with a reading coordinator or director of reading in a local school system. Use the following questions to interview the reading coordinator:

□ How are students selected for special reading instruction?
□ What tests are used in the process?
□ How is the special instruction coordinated with regular classroom reading instruction?
□ What are the qualifications for your reading teachers?
□ What are some ways your reading teachers work to enhance students' self-esteem?

SHARING AND BRAINSTORMING

Break up into small groups and discuss the following:

Many of the best-laid plans for effective reading resource instruction go astray because of poor public relations between the reading teacher and the staff.

List ways to make your program more effective with respect to administration and teachers.

□ *REFERENCES*

Allington, R.L. & Shake, M.C. (1986). Remedial reading: Achieving curricular congruence in classroom and clinic. *The Reading Teacher, 39*, 648–654.

Bond, G.L., Tinker, M.A., Wasson, B.B., & Wasson, J.B. (1984). *Reading difficulties: Their diagnosis and correction* (5th ed.). Englewood Cliffs, NJ: Prentice-Hall.

Burg, L.A., Kaufman, M., Korngold, B., & Kovner, A. (1978). *The complete reading supervisor*. Columbus, OH: Merrill.

Chall, J.S. & Curtis, M.E. (1987). What clinical diagnosis tells us about children's reading. *The Reading Teacher, 40*, 784–789.

Cooper, J.L. (1964). An adaptation of the Fernald-Keller approach to teaching an initial reading vocabulary to children with severe reading disabilities. *The Australian Journal on the Education of Backward Children, 10*, 131–145.

Fernald, G.M. (1943). *Remedial techniques in basic school subjects.* New York: McGraw-Hill.

Harris, A.J. & Sipay, E.R. (1985). *How to increase reading ability.* New York: Longman.

Harris, T.L. & Hodges, R.E. (1981). *A dictionary of reading and related terms.* Newark, DE: International Reading Association.

Milligan, J.L. (1986). The seven most common mistakes made by remedial reading teachers. *Journal of Reading, 30,* 140–145.

Veatch, J. et al. (1973). *Key words to reading: The language experience approach begins.* Columbus, OH: Merrill.

Appendix   Annotated Listing of Tests

Annotated Listing of Achievement Tests, Criterion-Referenced Tests, Intelligence Tests—Individual, Intelligence Tests—Group, Reading Diagnostic Tests—Individual, Reading Survey and Diagnostic Tests—Group, Reading Readiness Tests, Screening Tests, Spelling and Study Skills, Perception Tests, and Language Tests.

Compiled by John W. Logan, Wheeling School District, Wheeling, IL
John E. Booker, Texas A&M University

Achievement Tests

California Achievement Test. A group test for ten levels: K.0–K.9, K.6–1.9, 1.6–2.9, 2.6–3.9, 3.6–4.9, 4.6–5.9, 5.6–6.9, 6.6–7.9, 7.6–9.9, 9.6–12.9. Subtests measure listening for information, letter forms, letter names, letter sounds, visual discrimination, phonic analysis, alphabet skills, visual and auditory discrimination, and mathematics for the early grades. Subtests for grades 3.6 and up measure vocabulary, comprehension, mathematic computation, concepts and problems, language, listening, mechan-

ics of English, English usage and structure, and spelling. Tests are hand- or machine-scored. (California Test Bureau/McGraw-Hill)

Kaufman Test of Educational Achievement, Brief Form. Individually administered test of children's school achievement for grades 1 to 12. No referenced scores in reading, mathematics and spelling are rendered. Many items come directly from or are adopted from the Kaufman Assessment Battery for Children (K-ABC). (American Guidance Service)

Metropolitan Achievement Test. A group test for grades K–12.9 in eight levels. There are two batteries: the Survey Battery, which measures reading, mathematics, and language in the Preprimer and Primer levels, and the Primary, Primary One, Primary Two, Elementary, Intermediate, and Advanced levels, which score reading, mathematics, language, science, and social studies. Each level has three separate tests; reading, language, and mathematics. All tests can be hand- or machine-scored. (The Psychology Corp.)

Peabody Individual Achievement Test. An individually administered achievement test for grades K–12. The purpose of this test is to provide a wide-range screening measure of achievement in the areas of mathematics, reading, spelling, and general information. (American Guidance Service)

SRA Achievement Series. A group test for grades K–12 in eight levels. Scores reading (visual discrimination, auditory discrimination, letters and sounds, listening comprehension, comprehension); mathematics (concepts, computation, problem solving); language arts (mechanics, usage, spelling); reference materials; science, and social studies. May be hand- or machine-scored. (Science Research Associates, Inc.)

Stanford Achievement Test. A group-administered hand- or machine-scored test. Primary Level I (grades 1.5–2.9) has subtests of vocabulary, comprehension, word study, math concepts, math computations and applications, listening comprehension, and spelling. Primary Level II (grades 2.5–3.9) has the previous subtests plus social science and science. Primary Level III (grades 4.0–5.4), Intermediate Levels I (4.5–5.4) and II (5.5–6.9)

have all previous subtests plus language. Each level has two forms. Reading and math subtests may be ordered separately. (Harcourt Brace Jovanovich)

Wide Range Achievement Test. A 15–30 minute test that studies the sensorimotor skills involved in learning processes to determine approximate instructional levels and needs. There are two levels: Level I for ages 5–11 years, and Level II for ages 12 years to adult. Each level has three subtests: *reading*—recognizing and naming letters, pronouncing words; *spelling*—copying marks, writing name, printing or writing words from dictation; *arithmetic*—counting, reading numerals, oral and written computation. Both levels are printed on the same form. Scoring is done by hand and takes approximately 15 minutes to complete. Reading is administered to individuals; spelling and arithmetic to groups or individuals. (Jastok Associates)

Criterion-Reference Tests

Basic Skills Assessment. Assessment tests for grades 7 and above. Scores include Reading (literal comprehension, inference-evaluation), Writers' Skills (spelling, capitalization-punctuation, usage, logic-evaluation); Mathematics (computation, applications); and Writing Sample, A Direct Measure of Writing. (California Test Bureau/McGraw-Hill)

Basic Skills Inventory. A general achievement assessment instrument designed to test common objectives of minimum competencies with three subtests: reading, language arts, and mathematics. Each can be ordered separately. Reading scores phonetic analysis, vocabulary, and comprehension in two forms and eight levels. Language arts scores language analysis, conventions, and expression/comprehension in two forms and eight levels. (Los Angeles County Office of Education)

Brigance Diagnostic Comprehensive Inventory of Basic Skills. An extensive criterion-referenced test including sequences of 203 skills for readiness, reading, listening, research and study, spelling, language, and math for preprimer to 9th grade. Forty-four of the skills have two forms to enable pre- and post-testing. (Curriculum Associates)

Comprehensive Test of Basic Skills: Reading, Expanded Edition. An extensive battery of a reading and reference skills test intended for kindergarten to grade 12 in nine levels. A wide variety of score types is available, ranging from raw scores, national and/or local percentiles, stanines, and grade equivalent scores to the publisher's scale score. Can be either computer- or hand-scored. The *CTBS* is used nationally by many school districts to assess students' basic reading skills at all levels. (California Test Bureau/McGraw-Hill, 1976 edition)

Cooper-McGuire Diagnostic Word-Analysis Test. A group-administered criterion-referenced test with two equivalent forms for grades 1–5. The test focuses on readiness for word analysis, phonic analysis skills, and structural analysis skills. The tests overlap. A spirit-master is available for self-duplication (Croft Educational Service, 1972 edition)

Groups Phonics Analysis. A group-administered criterion-referenced test for children with reading levels of grades 1–3. The test assesses the ability to recognize the following elements: numbers, letters, consonants, alphabetization, vowels, short sounds, long vowel sounds in words, vowel digraph rule, final *e* generalization, open and closed syllables, and syllabication. (Dreier Educational Systems)

Oral Reading Criterion Test. An individually administered oral test for children with reading levels of grades 1–7. The test yields the child's independent, instructional, and frustration reading levels. (Dreier Educational Systems)

Phonics Criterion Test. A group-administered criterion-referenced test for children with reading levels of grades 1–3. The test assesses phonic abilities in the following areas: easy consonants, short vowels, long and silent vowels, difficult consonants, consonant digraphs, consonant second sounds, schwa sounds, long vowel digraphs, vowel plus *r*, broad *o*, diphthongs, difficult vowels, consonant blends, and consonant exceptions. (Dreier Educational Systems)

Prescriptive Reading Inventory. A group-administered criterion-referenced test in four levels. Level A, for grades 1.5–2.5, and Level B, for grades 2.0–3.5, measure recognition of sounds and symbols, phonic analysis, structural analysis, translation, and literal, interpretive, and critical comprehension. Level 3, for grades 3.0–4.5, and Level 4, for grades 4.0–6.5, measure phonic analysis, structural analysis, translation, and literal, interpretive, and critical comprehension. The test yields scores of mastery, needs review, or nonmastery. (California Test Bureau/McGraw-Hill)

Stanford Diagnostic Reading Test. A group of individual criterion-referenced test that assesses a student's instructional needs in reading. This machine-scored test is divided into four levels: Red Level, grades 1.6–3.5; Green Level, grades 2.6–5.5; Brown Level, grades 4.6–9.5 and Blue Level, grades 9.0–13. The subtests cover auditory vocabulary, auditory discrimination, phonetic analysis, structural analysis, word reading, reading comprehension, and rate. (The Psychological Corp., 1976 edition)

Systematic Approach to Reading Improvement (SART). A group-administered criterion-referenced test found within a step-by-step system based on performance objectives. The system is for children with reading levels of readiness to 8. The reading program is divided into main skill areas: vocabulary, word analysis, comprehension, and oral reading. (Phi Delta Kappa)

Wisconsin Test of Reading. An individual or group-administered criterion-referenced test that measures proficiencies and deficiencies in reading skill development in kindergarten through grade 6. This hand- or machine-scored test includes six subtests: word attack, comprehension, study skills, self-directed reading, interpretive reading, and creative reading. Each test can be used independently and is available in two formats: a booklet edition for each of the levels or a single-skill test (separate edition). (National Computer Systems, Inc.)

Woodcock Reading Mastery Test. An individually administered oral test for kindergarten through grade 12. The test assesses ability in letter identification (both manuscript and cursive), word identification, word-attack skills, word comprehension (understanding the relationship of pairs of words), and passage comprehension. The test yields easy reading level, reading grade score, and failure reading level for each subtest. (American Guidance Service)

Intelligence Test—Individual

Detroit Tests of Learning Aptitude. An individually administered 60–95 minute intelligence test for ages 6–18. Subtests are pictorial and verbal absurdities, pictorial and verbal opposites, motor speed and precision, auditory attention span for unrelated words and related syllables, oral commissions, social adjustment, visual attention span for objects and letters, orientation, free association, memory for designs, number ability, broken pictures, oral directions, and likenesses and differences. (PRO-ED)

Full-Range Picture Vocabulary Test. A 15-minute individually administered intelligence test to determine verbal comprehension for ages 2 to adult. There are two forms of sixteen plates with four drawings on each plate; the testee indicates by word or gesture which picture fits the meaning of a given word. Scores are reported by IQ. (Psychological Test Specialists)

Illinois Test of Psycholinguistic Abilities. A test for individuals ranging from ages 2–10 years to specify the student's psycholinguistic abilities and difficulties. The test scores auditory reception, visual reception, visual sequential memory, auditory association, auditory sequential memory, visual association, visual closure, verbal expression, grammatic closure, manual expression, auditory closure (optional), and sound blending (optional). (University of Illinois Press)

Kaufman Assessment Battery for Children (K-ABC). An individual intelligence and achievement test for ages 2.5–12.5. A nonverbal scale for hearing impaired, speech and language-disordered, and non-English-speaking children ages 4.0–12 are also available. Ten mental processing subtests include magic window, face recognition, hand movements, Gestaldt closure, number recall, triangles, word order, matrix analogies, spatial memory, and photo series. The six achievement subtests include expressive vocabulary, faces and places, arithmetic, riddles, reading/decoding, and reading/understanding. (American Guidance Service)

Minnesota Preschool Inventory. An individual test for ages 3–4 and 4–6 in two levels. The test is used to identify children whose development and/or adjustment pose a high risk of failure in kindergarten. Can be hand-scored or scored by Apple II computer program. (Behavior Science Systems, Inc.)

Peabody Picture Vocabulary Test. An individually administered instrument for ages 2.5–4.0. Two equivalent forms are available in a verbal and nonverbal test designed to provide an estimate of a child's receptive language through measuring his or her learning vocabulary. The child indicates which one of four pictures best fits the stimulus word pronounced by the examiner. (American Guidance Service)

Progressive Matrices. A 30–60-minute timed or untimed group or individual nonverbal intelligence test. Used to measure intellectual capacity to form comparisons and reason by analogy. There are two sets of twelve problems of mainly geometrical designs with a "gap" to be filled in from a choice of alternatives. The testee marks answers on a score sheet. *Standard Progressive Matrices* are for ages 6–11; *Coloured Progressive Matrices* are for ages 5 and over and for mentally ill patients and senescents; *Advanced Progressive Matrices* are for ages 11 and over. Scoring is by hand. Percentile figures are

classified into five "grades" ranging from "intellectually superior" to "intellectually defective." (H. K. Lewis and Co. Ltd., England; U.S. Distributor: Psychological Corp.)

Quick Test. A 3–10-minute individually administered intelligence screening test for ages 2 and over. The test attempts to assess visual-perceptual recognition of basic concepts utilized in language. The child is asked to point to one of four drawings that fits a stimulus word pronounced by the examiner. There are three forms of 50 items each. Scores are reported by MA and IQ. (Psychological Test Specialists)

Raven Progressive Matrices. A nonlinguistic test designed to aid in assessing mental ability by requiring the student to solve problems presented in abstract figures and designs. Test can be hand scored. Scores correlate well with comprehensive intelligence tests and are reported to be highly saturated with Spearman's g. The test is designed for individuals ages 8–65 years. *Advanced Progressive Matrices* designed for use with individuals of above-average intellectual ability are available. (Psychological Corp.)

Slosson Intelligence Test. A short, individual screening instrument to evaluate an individual's mental ability. It can be used for all ages from infants to adults. The test usually requires 10–20 minutes to administer and is hand scored. It is administered verbally and the results correlate with the *Stanford-Binet, Form L-M* (Slosson Educational Publications, Inc.)

Stanford-Binet Intelligence Scales. An individually administered intelligence test for ages 2 and over. A specially trained tester marks answers on a score sheet and from the results derives mental age,

IQ, and percentile ranks. Scoring is done by hand. (Riverside Publishing Co.)

Wechsler Adult Intelligence Scale. A 40–60-minute individually administered intelligence test for ages 16–75. Scores are determined for verbal and performance. Verbal includes information, comprehension, arithmetic, similarities, digit span, and vocabulary. Performance includes digit symbol, picture completion, block design, picture arrangement, and object assembly. There is one form hand- or computer-scored by a specially trained tester. Norms are for IQs from 45–159. (Psychological Corp.)

Wechsler Intelligence Scale for Children—Revised. A 40–60-minute individually administered intelligence test for ages 6–16. Scores are determined for verbal and performance. Verbal includes information, comrpehension, arithmetic, similarities, vocabulary, and digit span. Performance includes picture completion, picture arrangement, block design, object assembly, mazes, and coding. These measures must be administered and hand- or computer-scored by a specially trained tester. Norms are in IQs. (Psychological Corp.)

Intelligence Test—Group

California Test of Mental Maturity. A 60–90-minute group intelligence test measuring functional capacities basic to learning, problem solving, and reacting to new situations for grades K–16. Each of six levels has one form. Level 0, K–1, and Level 1, grades 1.5–3, are hand scored. Other levels are machine scorable. Level 2 is for grades 4–6, Level 3 for grades 7–9, Level 4 for grades 9–12, and Level 5 for grads 12–16 and adults. Scores are determined for logical reasoning, spatial relationships, numerical reasoning, verbal concepts, memory, language total, and nonlanguage total. Norms are in IQ, MA, and anticipated grade placement. (California Test Bureau/McGraw-Hill)

Culture Fair Intelligence Test. A group or individual test available in three scales: Scale 1 is for children 4–8 years old and for mentally retarded adults; Scale 2 is for children 8–14 years of age and for adults in the average range of intelligence. Scale 3 is especially designed to discriminate among higher ranges of intelligence from high-school age or through adulthood. Both Scale 2 and Scale 3 have two comparable forms, A and B, that are recommended to be administered together for maximum reliability. The test is hand scored. (Institute for Personality and Ability Testing)

The Henmon-Nelson Tests of Mental Ability. A 35-minute group intelligence test for kindergarten through grade 12, in four levels, hand or machine scored to provide grade level, MA, and IQ. The four levels are Primary Battery (K–2), grades 3–6, grades 6–9, and grades 9–12. (Houghton Mifflin Co.)

Kuhlman-Anderson Test, Eighth Edition. A group-administered intelligence test that yields three scores: verbal, quantitative, and total. This hand- or machine-scored test is available in booklets organized into nine levels. The first seven levels cover kindergarten through grade 6. Level 8 is for grades 7–8 and Level 9 is for grades 9–12. This timed test should take no more than an hour to administer. (Personnel Press)

Lorge-Thorndike Intelligence Test. A group intelligence test for kindergarten through grade 13 in two forms. There is a multilevel edition for grades 3–13 that gives verbal and nonverbal scores. The test for grades 12–13 can be ordered separately. The separate level edition has five test booklets: Level 1 (K–1), Level 2 (grades 2–3), Level 3 (Grades 4–6), Level 4 (grades 7–9), Level 5 (grades 10–12). Levels 1 and 2 give nonverbal scores; Levels 3, 4, and 5 give verbal and nonverbal scores. (Riverside Publishing Co.)

Otis Quick Scoring Mental Ability Tests. A group-administered test, scored by machine or hand, to measure thinking power and maturity of mind. There are two forms for each of three levels. The alpha form, grades 1–4, is 45 sets of 4 pictures where the testee marks the picture that does not belong in the group and then follows teacher-read directions for marking the same 45 items. On the beta form, grades 4–9, and gamma form, grades 9–16, students read the directions for answering questions about word meaning, verbal analogies, scrambled sentences, interpretation of proverbs, logical reasoning, number series, arithmetic reasoning, and design analogies. Scores are reported as MA and IQ. (Harcourt Brace Jovanovich)

Otis-Lennon Mental Ability Test. A group-administered 30–60-minute test to assess general mental ability of scholastic aptitude of students in kindergarten through grade 12. There are two forms on each of the following levels: Primary I (grade 1), Primary II (grade 2–3), Elementary I (grade 4–5). Intermediate (6–8), and Advanced (9–12). No reading is required in Primary I and II or Elementary I. Primary I is hand scored; others can be scored by hand or by machine. (The Psychological Corp.)

SRA Pictorial Reasoning Test. An untimed 30–45-minute or timed 15–20-minute group intelligence test for use with American subcultural groups to measure the learning potential of individuals ages 14 and over with reading difficulties and their ability to learn jobs independent of background and culture. There is one form of 80 items involving reasoning with nonverbal, pictorial materials by selecting the one of five pictures that differs from the other form. The testee marks answers on a sheet that is scored by hand. (Science Research Associates)

SRA Tests of General Ability (TOGA). A 30–45-minute group intelligence test for kindergarten thorugh grade 12 which gives verbal (cultural) and reasoning (noncultural) scores. It can be scored by hand or machine, and a Spanish edition is available. There are five levels: K–2, grades 2–4, grades 4–6, grades 6–9, and grades 9–12. Test items are multiple choice and pictorial in form. Some items measure information, vocabulary, and concepts; others assess reasoning ability. Norms are given for IQ and grade expectancy. (Science Research Associates)

Reading Diagnostic Tests—Individual

Analytical Reading Inventory (ARI). This informal reading inventory has a range of passages from primer to grade 9 and contains graded word lists as well as separate student passages and summary sheets. There are no pictures or illustrations in this inventory. Harris-Jacobsen and Spache readability formulas were used in the construction of the *ARI*. Questions in the graded passsages include literal, inferential, critical-evaluative, main ideas, and vocabulary. Suggested answers are provided. Oral reading and listening comprehension testing are required; silent reading assessment is optional. Types of scored miscues include examiner aids, insertions, reversals, repetitions and substitutions. Three forms of the *ARI* are available. Neither suggestions for diagnostic interpretation, sample cases, nor teaching suggestions are offered to the examiner. Guidance for handling discrepancies in performance is provided. (Merrill Publishing Co.)

The BADER Reading and Language Inventory. A comprehensive assessment battery for preprimer to adult. Scores include word-recognition lists, graded reading passages, phonics and word analysis, spelling and cloze tests, visual and auditory discrimination tests, a test of unfinished sentences, and oral language and authentic tests. Other tests include written expression, writing letters and writing words in sentences, near- and far-point copying, writing from dissertation, and expressing ideas in writing. (MacMillan Publishing Co.)

Basic Reading Inventory. An individual test for grades K–8. Provides independent, instructional, and frustrational reading levels. Scores word recognition in isolation. Word recognition in context, and comprehension. Three forms can be used for silent, oral, and listening tests. (Kendall/Hunt Publishing Co.)

California Phonics Survey. An individual or group-administered test for grades 7 to college; two equivalent forms measure phonic adequacy of students in long-short vowel confusion, confusion of consonants with blends and digraphs, consonant and vowel reversal, configuration, endings, and sight words. Student responds on an answer sheet. (California Test Bureau/McGraw-Hill)

Classroom Reading Inventory. An individually administered oral test for grades 2–8 (two equivalent forms). This diagnostic tool yields information about a child's hearing capacity and frustration, instructional, and independent reading levels. The test consists of three parts: spelling survey (which can be group administered), graded word lists, and graded oral paragraphs. A third form for each of the subtests is available. (Wm. C. Brown Co.)

Cloze Reading Tests. A cloze test for ages 8.0–10.6, 8.5–11.10, 9.5–12.6 (Hodder & Stoughton Educational Publishers, England)

The Contemporary Classroom Reading Inventory (CCRI). Three forms of the *CCRI* are available for use by the examiner. Passages range from primer to ninth-grade levels and graded word lists range from primer to seventh-grade levels. Separate student passages and summary sheets are included. Both pictures and illustrations are in this informal reading inventory. Readability formulas used include the Botel-Granowsky, Dale-Chall, Fry, Harris-Jacobsen, and Spache. Types of questions used in assessing comprehension include literal, inferential, critical-evaluative, main idea, sequencing, and vocabulary. Suggested answers are provided. Oral reading is required, silent reading is not included, and listening comprehension is optional. The types of miscues that can be counted include examiner aids, insertions, reversals, mispronunciations, omissions, repetitions, and substitutions. Suggestions for diagnostic interpretation are provided, and sample cases are demonstrated. No teaching suggestions are offered, but guidance for handling discrepancies in performance is included. (Gorsuch Scarisbrick Publishers)

Decoding Skills Test. An individually adminstered instrument designed to identify children with developmental dyslexia. The test includes three subtests: basal vocabulary, phonic patterns, and contextual decoding. Scores yield instructional, independent, and frustration levels along with specific diagnostic information concerning decoding and comprehension. (York Press)

Diagnostic Reading Examination for Diagnosis of Special Difficulty in Reading. An individually administered diagnostic tests for grades 1–4. The test assesses oral reading, silent reading, spelling, arithmetic computation, letter naming, orientation, mirror reading and writing, number reversals, word discrimination, and sounding. (Stoelting Co.)

Diagnostic Reading Inventory (DRI). The *DRI* is a single-form test that contains a range of passages from first to eighth grades with corresponding graded word lists. Separate student passages and summary sheets are available. Neither pictures nor illustrations are included in the *DRI*, nor are readability formulas. Types of questions from the graded passages include literal, inferential critical-evaluative, and vocabulary. Suggested answers are not offered. Oral and silent reading as well as listening comprehension are all required testing features. The types of miscues that are scored include examiner aids, insertions, omissions, and substitutions. Suggestions for diagnostic interpretation and sample cases are provided. Guidelines for handling discrepancies in performance are recommended. (Kendall/Hunt Publishing Co.)

Diagnostic Reading Scales. A series of integrated tests that provide standard evaluations of oral and silent reading skills and of auditory comprehension intended for use in determining the reading proficiency of normal and disabled readers from elementary through high-school age. The test requires 45 minutes to an hour. The scores render an instructional, independent, and frustration reading level, plus a potential level (expectancy or capacity). The battery includes 3 word-recognition lists and 22 reading passages of graduated difficulty with comprehension questions. Supplementary word analysis and phonics tests include initial consonants, final consonants, consonant diagraphs, consonant blends, initial consonant substitutions; sounds (recognized automatically), auditory discrimination, short and long vowel sounds, vowels with *r*, vowel diphthongs and digraphs, common syllables, and blending. (McGraw-Hill)

Dolch Basic Sight Word Tests. A group or individually administered test to determine students' mastery of the 220 Basic Sight Vocabulary words. The test is presented in Parts 1 and 2 so that young children can take the test in two sittings. Older students may take both parts together. There are four lists of tests words for each part so that four trials can be made and every word on the list tested. This teacher-scored test can be used to assess the Basic Sight Vocabulary of any age student but is especially useful for primary and remedial readers. (Garrard Publishing Co.)

Durrell Analysis of Reading Difficulty (Third Edition). An individually administered series of tests to discover reading weaknesses for grades 1–6; one form. Subtests consist of (a) oral reading tests to check oral reading and comprehension; yields grade level; (b) silent reading tests to check oral recall; yields grade level,

(c) listening comprehension tests with oral comprehension questions, (d) word recognition and word analysis; yields grade-level, (e) visual memory of word forms, primary and intermediate levels, (f) auditory analysis of word elements; primary and intermediate levels, (g) spelling and handwriting; primary and intermediate levels, (h) phonics test of sounds of letters and blends; includes checklist of difficulties with subtests. (The Psychological Corp.)

Ekwall Phonics Survey. An individually administered diagnostic tool used to gather information about a child's abilities with phonics. Knowledge of the sounds recorded by initial consonants, consonant clusters, vowels, vowel teams, and special letter combinations is assessed. The ability to blend sounds presented in isolation is also measured by this instrument. As the child progresses through the test, he or she is required to give the name of specific letters and to pronounce real and nonsense words. (Allyn and Bacon)

Ekwall Reading Inventory (ERI). This informal reading inventory has a range of passages from K–9 with accompanying graded word lists. Separate student passages and summary sheets are provided. There are no pictures or illustrations in this inventory. Dale-Chall and Harris-Jacobsen readability formulas were used in test construction. Literal, inferential, and vocabulary-related questions are incorporated to accompany the graded passages. Suggested answers are provided. Oral and silent reading tests are required; listening comprehension is optional. The types of miscues that can be scored include examiner aids, reversals, mispronunciations, omissions, repetitions, and sequencing. Suggestions for

diagnostic interpretation and sample cases are included, but no teaching suggestions are offered. Guidance for handling discrepancies in performance is provided. (Allyn and Bacon)

Flash-X Sight Vocabulary. An individually administered oral test of word-recognition skills for grades 1 to 2. Sight vocabulary and experience vocabulary are tested with a tachistoscope. (Educational Development Laboratories)

Gates-McKillop-Horowitz Reading Diagnostic Test. An individually administered diagnostic test to be used in analyzing and discovering causes of reading deficiencies. From grades 1–6. The test is available in form, I and II, which contain comparable material of equivalent difficulty. The examiner records and scores the test in the Pupil Record Booklet, which also includes checklists of errors and space for notes and summaries. Tests oral reading, vocabulary, phrase perception, knowledge of word parts, recognition of the visual form of sounds, auditory blending, spelling, syllabication, and auditory discrimination. Each subtest can be used independently. (Teachers College Press, Columbia University)

Gilmore Oral Reading Test. An individually administered, 20-minute oral reading test to analyze oral reading in grades 1–8. Below-average, average, and above-average ratings are given for word accuracy, comprehension, and rate. There are two forms. (Harcourt Brace Jovanovich, 1968 edition)

Gray Oral Reading Test. An individually administered oral reading test to assess the level of oral reading achievement. Reading passages range in level from preprimer to adult and have four literal meaning comprehension questions after each. Errors and time are used to determine grade equivalent. (Bobbs-Merrill Co.)

Informal Reading Assessment. A series of graded word lists and graded passages (preprimer through grade 12, designed to determine independent, instructional, and frustration levels as well as capacity (expectancy) levels. Specific reading problems may also be diagnosed with the test. There are two graded word lists along with graded passages in four forms to facilitate pre- and post-testing. (Houghton Mifflin Co.)

Reading Miscue Inventory. An individually administered oral test for grades 1–7. A tape recorder is used to record a child's reading of a 15–20-minute selection and his or her immediate retelling of what was read. Errors are called miscues to suggest that they are cued by the thought and language of the reader. The reader's performance is scored for retelling, miscues causing comprehension loss, miscues with sound similarity, graphic similarity, grammatical-function similarity, and semantic similarity. (Macmillan Publishing Co.)

Roswell-Chall Auditory Blending Test. A 5-minute, individually administered, hand-scored test for grades 1–4 to evaluate a student's ability to blend sounds to form words when the sounds are presented orally. The teacher marks answers on the score sheet. There is one form of 30 words with three parts—words divided into three sounds, two parts, and three elements. (Essay Press)

Roswell-Chall Diagnostic Reading Test of Word Analysis Skills. A 5-minute, individually administered, hand-scored oral test for grades 1–4 to evaluate word-recognition skills. The teacher marks answers on the score sheet. Two forms are available. Subtests measure single consonants and blends, short vowel sounds, rule of silent *e*, vowel combination, and syllabication. (Essay Press)

Sand: Concepts about Print Test. An individual test for early detection of reading difficulties. Intended for children ages 5–7 years. One test form is available. (Heinemann Educational Books, Ltd.)

Reading Survey and Diagnostic Tests—Group

Botel Reading Inventory. A group of four tests designed to provide estimates of reading levels from grades 1 through junior high school; (a) the word recognition test is an individually administered oral test and yields an independent, instructional, and frustration level; (b) the word opposites test is a group-administered written test that yields an independent instructional and frustration level for comprehension; (c) the phonics mastery test is group-administered and indicates a student's knowledge of key word perception skills; (d) the spelling placement test is a group-administered test that determines independent, instructional, and frustration levels in spelling. Two equivalent forms (Follett Publishing Co.)

Comprehension Tests of Basic Skills: Reading. A group-administered test available in four overlapping levels containing similar content. The four levels are: Level 1, grades 2.5–4; Level 2, grades 4–6; Level 3, grades 6–8; Level 4, grades 8– 10. Level 4 may also be used in grades 11 and 12. This machine-scored test measures reading vocabulary and comprehension (California Test Bureau/McGraw-Hill)

Davis Reading Test. A group, 60-minute written test to indicate level of comprehension and speed of comprehension for grades 11–13 (Series 1) and grades 8–11 (Series 2). Each series has four forms. Five categories are measured: literal meaning, main idea, inference and purpose, tone, and structure. Scoring is done by hand or key machine. (Psychological Corp.)

Doren Diagnostic Reading Test of Word Recognition Skills. A group-administered test for grades 1–9. Provides information about word-recognition skills including letter recognition, beginning sounds, whole-word recognition, words within words, speech consonants, ending sounds, blending, rhyming, vowels, sight words, and discriminate guessing. The test manual includes a section on remedial instruction techniques. (American Guidance Service)

Durrell Listening-Reading Series. A group written test to compare reading and listening abilities. There are three levels: primary (grades 1–3.5), intermediate (grades 3.5–6). advanced (grades 7–9). Depending on the level, these three abilities are tested—vocabulary, sentence, and paragraph comprehension. Scoring is by hand or machine. (Harcourt Brace Jovanovich)

Durrell-Sullivan Reading Capacity and Achievement Tests. A group-administered test that seeks to identify students who are experiencing difficulty with reading but who are capable of reading considerably beyond their level. Two levels measure achievement and capacity. The primary test is suited for grades 2.5–4.5 and comes in booklet form. The intermediate test is available as two separate tests, which cover grades 3–6. This hand-scored test yields five scores: word meaning, paragraph meaning, spelling, written recall, and total. (Harcourt Brace Jovanovich)

Iowa Silent Reading Test. A group-administered written test on the three levels for grades 6–9, 9–14, and academically accelerated 11 to college; there are two forms for each level. All of the levels contain subtests measuring comprehension, vocabulary, reading efficiency, and work-study skills. The test can be hand or machine scored. (Harcourt Brace Jovanovich)

McCarthy Individualized Diagnostic Reading Inventory. Diagnostic test for grades K–12 that reveals three qualitative ratings of reading (independent, instructional, frustration) for placement in reading instruction (fluency, comprehension, and thinking skills; phonics, word-recognition, and study skills). The test includes a questionnaire concerning the student's reading interests and habits. (Educators Publishing Service, Inc.)

McCullough Word-Analysis Tests. A group test to assess phonic and structural analysis skills for students in grades 4 to 6. Students mark answers in a test booklet for the subtests; initial blends, vowels, sounding out words, interpreting phonetics symbols, syllabication, and root words. Scoring is done by hand. (Personnel Press)

McGraw-Hill Basic Skills System. An individually or group-administered series of diagnostic tests and instructional materials for grades 10–13. Two equivalent forms can be administered for pre- and post-test assessment. Subtests, which can be ordered separately, consist of reading, writing, spelling, vocabulary, and study skills. The tests can be hand or machine scored. (McGraw-Hill)

Nelson-Denny Reading Test. A group-administered test for grades 9–16 and adults. The test measures vocabulary, reading comprehension, and reading rate using a multiple-choice question. It can be machine or hand scored, and special adult norms are provided. (Riverside Publishing Co.)

Nelson Reading Test, Revised Edition. A group-administered timed test for grades 3–9. Two equivalent forms are available. Subtests measure vocabulary and reading comprehension. Answer sheets are self-marking. (Riverside Publishing Co.)

Phonovisual Diagnostic Test. A group-administered test for grades 3–12. The tester dictates several words that the children write. The test measures knowledge of consonant sounds, digraphs, blends, and vowel sounds through use of auditory discrimination and knowledge of spelling conventions. (Phonovisual Products, Inc.)

Primary Reading Profiles. A group-administered diagnostic test to evaluate reading skills that a student should have mastered by the end of the second year of instruction. This hand-scored test is divided into five subtests. Test 1 measures reading aptitude, Test 2 evaluates auditory association, Test 3 measures word recognition, Test 4 measures word attack skills, and Test 5 reading comprehension. (Houghton Mifflin Co.)

Rosewell-Chall Diagnostic Reading Test of Word Analysis Skills, Revised and Extended. For reading level grades 1–4. Scores words (high-frequency words), decoding (consonant sounds, consonant digraphs, consonant blends, short and long vowel, sounds, rule for silent *e*, vowel digraphs, diphthongs, and vowels controlled by *r*), syllabication, letter names, and encoding. (Essay Press, Inc.)

Silent Reading Diagnostic Tests. A group written test for students reading at 2–6 grade levels. Eight subtests measure word recognition, context, root words, syllabication, synthesis, beginning sounds, ending sounds, vowel and consonant sounds. Tests are hand scored. (Lyons and Carnahan)

SRA Reading Record. A group-administered written test for grades 6–12. Four subtests measure rate of reading, reading comprehension, everyday reading (reading a telephone directory, indexes, advertisements, and maps), and reading vocabulary (which includes sentence meaning and technical and general vocabulary). Four reading scores and totals can be obtained from self-scoring answer pad. (Science Research Associates)

Stanford Diagnostic Reading Test. A group-administered written diagnostic test on four levels, grades 1–13. Red level grades, 1.6–3.5, scores auditory vocabulary, auditory discrimination, phonic analysis, and comprehension. Green level, grades 2.6–5.5, scores auditory vocabulary, auditory discrimination, phonetic analysis, structural analysis, literal and inferential comprehension. Brown level, grades 4.6–9.5, scores same as above plus reading rate. Blue level, grades 9.0–13, scores literal and inferential comprehension, vocabulary, decoding, and rate. (Psychological Corp.)

Traxler Silent Reading Test. A group-administered test for grades 7–10. The test measures vocabulary, reading rate, story comprehension, and paragraph meaning. A multiple-choice format is used, which can be hand or machine scored. (Bobbs-Merrill Co.)

Reading Readiness Tests

Clymer-Barrett Readiness Test. A group-administered test for first-grade entrants designed to evaluate prereading skills and to diagnose for beginning reading instruction. There are two equivalent forms that measure visual discrimination, auditory discrimination, and visual-motor coordination. Contains a prereading rating scale to be filled out on the basis of classroom observations concerning basic language development. (Brook & Kent)

First-Grade Screening Test. A group test for first-grade entrants. Separate answer booklets for boys and girls, although both can be tested simultaneously. Measures intellectual deficiency, central nervous system, dysfunction, and emotional disturbance. Norms are provided to aid in the evaluation of students' performances. (American Guidance Service)

Gates-MacGinitie Reading Test: Readiness Skills. A small-group (10–15) administered test to be used at the end of kindergarten or at the beginning of grade 1 to measure readiness for beginning reading, to predict rate of development of reading ability, and to diagnose students' needs in several abilities required to learn to read. This hand-scored test consists of eight subtests: listening comprehension, auditory discrimination, visual discrimination, following directions, letter recognition, visual-motor coordination, auditory blending, and word recognition. The administration of the test is divided into four parts, each one-half hour long. Two days are recommended for administration. (Teachers College Press, Columbia University)

Gesell School Readiness Test. An individually administered test for children of ages 5 to 10 to determine their readiness to start school. The child is scored on observation of performance, conversation, and approach to situations. Trained

examiner recommended. (Programs for Education)

Keystone Ready-to-Read Tests. An individually administered visual screening test for school entrants to determine visual readiness to read books at the usual distance. Using a telebinocular, the test measures near-point fusion, usable vision, and lateral and vertical posture. (Keystone View)

Lee-Clark Reading Readiness Test. A group-administered test for children in kindergarten and grade 1 to determine readiness for reading instruction and pattern of maturation for those not ready. The test is taken silently with oral instructions to measure various aspects of visual discrimination and linguistic development. Subtests measure discrimination of letter symbols, vocabulary, following directions, and discrimination of word symbols. (California Test Bureau/McGraw-Hill)

Macmillan Reading Readiness Test. A group-administered test for first-grade entrants to determine readiness for reading instruction. Test includes a rating scale and measures visual discrimination, auditory discrimination, vocabulary, knowledge of concepts, knowledge of letter names, and visual-motor coordination. Takes approximately 90 minutes to administer over several testing periods. (Macmillan Publishing Co.)

Metropolitan Readiness Test. A small-group pictorial test that can be administered orally and taken silently. Two levels, beginning kindergarten (Level I), and ending kindergarten (Level II) to grade 1. Equivalent forms are available for each level. Level I yields scores for visual and language skill areas; Level II yields scores for auditory, visual, language, and quantitative skill areas. (Psychological Corp.)

Monroe Reading Aptitude. An individually administered test for first-grade entrants. The test measures auditory memory, speed and accuracy of articulation, and speed of association. Also measured are motor control, memory of orientation of forms, eye-hand coordination, visual memory, auditory word discrimination, sound blending, and picture vocabulary, each of which can be group administered. (Houghton Mifflin Co.)

Murphy-Durrell Reading Readiness Analysis. A group-administered test to measure skills necessary in learning to read. It measures auditory discrimination, visual discrimination, and learning rate. Each of the subtests can be administered separately to first-grade entrants. The last part of the learning rate test needs to be administered individually. This test is hand scored. (Harcourt Brace Jovanovich)

School Readiness Survey, Second Edition. This readiness test is intended for children ages 4–6 years. It can be administered and scored by parents with school supervision. Eight scores can be derived in the areas of number concepts, discrimination of form, color naming, symbol matching, speaking vocabulary, listening vocabulary, total, as well as unscored general readiness checklist. (Consulting Pscyhologists Press)

Screening Tests

The BADER Test of Reading Spelling Patterns. Individually administered reading disability screening test that provides information that may be used for prescriptive reading instruction for grades K–12 and adults. Scores for reading include reading level, reading age, and reading quotient. Spelling scores are for known words correct and unknown words/good phonetic equivalents. Grune & Stratton, Inc.)

Carrow Auditory-Visual Abilities Test. An individual test for ages 4–10. The visual abilities battery subtests include visual discrimination matching, visual discrimination memory, visual-motor copying, visual-motor memory, and motor speed. The auditory abilities battery subtests include picture memory, picture sequence selection, digits forward, digits backward, sentence repetition, word repetition, auditory blending, auditory discrimination in quiet, and auditory discrimination in noise. (D L M Teaching Resources)

Diagnostic Screening Test: Reading, Third Edition. An individual diagnostic test for grades 1–12. The test scores comfort reading level, instructional reading level, and frustration reading level; listening level; phonics/sight ratio; word attack and skill analysis. (Facilitation House)

Dyslexia Determination Test. An individual test for preschool to college. Scores dysnemkinesia (writing of numbers, writing of letters), dysphonesia (decoding, encoding), dyseidesia (decoding, encoding). I-Med)

Goldman-Fristoe-Woodcock Test of Auditory Discrmination. An individually administered test to identify the listener's ability to distinguish among speech sounds. This test for ages 4 and over is administered under two conditions: quiet, and background noise supplied by a tape. The use of earphones is recommended. The *GFW* is hand scored. (American Guidance Service)

Harris Test of Lateral Dominance. An individual test used to discover eye, hand, and foot dominance for ages 6 to adult. Monocular sighting, binocular sighting, knowledge or right- and left-hand preferences, visual acuity, and total eye dominance are measured. Approximate test administration time is only 5 minutes and is offered in a single form. The A-B-C Vision Test for Ocular Dominance is included in this hand-scored test. (Psychological Corp.)

Keystone Visual Screening Tests. An individually administered visual screening test for ages preschool through adult, using a Keystone Telebinocular, a lay person can test far-point and near-point vision and fusion for referrals to eye specialists. (Keystone View)

Learning Methods Tests. An individually administered test for grades 1–3 that measures comparative effectiveness of four methods of teaching new words; visual, phonic, kinesthetic, and combination. (Mills School)

Maico Audiometer. An individually administered screening test of auditory acuity for kindergarten through adult. Using an audiometer, a lay person can test auditory acuity at several frequencies to determine referrals to specialists. One form is available for recording learning levels. (Maico hearing Instruments)

Marianne Frostig Developmental Test of Visual Perception, (DTVP). This test can be administered individually or to groups of children ages 3–8. Five perceptual skills are measured: eye-motor coordination, figure-ground discrimination, form constancy, position in space, and spatial relations. Each of the five subtests can be used independently. The *DTVP* is hand scored. (Consulting Psychological Press)

Ortho-Rater. An individual visual screening device, this test can be administered by a lay person to children and adults. Screens both far-point and near-point vision, binocular action of the eyes or the ability to use both eyes to see an image, depth perception, and color discrimination. Used for referral to eye specialists. (Bausch and Lomb)

Purdue Perceptual Motor Survey. An individual test used to identify children age 6–10 who are lacking perceptual motor abilities necessary for acquiring academic skills. This test is hand scored (Merrill Publishing Co.)

The Reading Eye II. An eye-movement camera, which yields five scores related to reading: fixations, regressions, average span of recognition, average duration of fixation, and rate of comprehension. This test, which is suitable for students in grades 1–16 and adults, has three ratings (grade level of fundamental reading skill, relative efficiency, directional attack, left to right eye movement while reading, and two diagnostic categories (visual adjustments and general adjustment to reading). (Educational Developmental Laboratories)

Slingerland Screening Test for Identifying Children with Specific Language Disability. An individually administered test for children in grades 1–4. The subtests assess visual-motor coordination, visual memory, visual discrimination, and visual memory to motor coordination. Also measured are auditory-visual discrimination and auditory memory to motor ability, ability to recall and pronounce words, and ability to express organized ideas in oral and written form. (Educators Publishing Service)

Spache Binocular Reading Test. An individually administered visual screening test for grades 1 to adult. Using a stereoscope or telebinocular and specially prepared slides, this test measures the extent to which each eye participates in the reading act. (Keystone View)

Valett Developmental Survey of Basic Language Disabilities. An individually administered screening instrument for ages 2–7. The test is largely an adaptation of items from many scales. Measures motor integration and physical development, tactile discrimination, auditory discrimination, visual-motor coordination, visual discrimination, language development and verbal fluency, and conceptual development. (Consulting Psychologists Press)

Wepman Auditory Discrimination Test. An individually administered instrument for age 5–10. An oral test designed to give a quick analysis of a child's auditory abilities (two equivalent forms). The examiner repeats two words, which the child must identify as same or different. (Language Research Associates)

Spelling and Study Skills

California Study Method Survey. A group test that is designed to determine study habits of individuals ages 12–18 years. The test comes in a single form, and approximate administration time is 40 minutes. (California Test Bureau/McGraw-Hill)

Lincoln Diagnostic Spelling Tests. This test includes three separate but overlapping levels to measure spelling ability. The *Lincoln Primary Test* is available in forms W, X for fall testing and Y, Z for spring testing for grades 2–4 in independent schools and grades 3–5 in public schools. The *Lincoln Intermediate Test* is for grades 4–8 and comes in Forms A, C for fall testing and B, D for spring testing. The *Lincoln Diagnostic Spelling*

Test is available in Form A for students in grades 8–12. (Educational Records Bureau)

Survey of Study Habits and Attitudes. A group of individual test that is designed to (1) provide a survey of study habits and study attitudes that do not provide a basis for good academic performance, (2) provide a basis for counseling students in improving study methods, and (3) predict academic success. Scoring key and a special counseling key are provided for interpreting the results. (Psychological Corp.)

Perception Tests

Marianne Frostig Developmental Test of Visual Perception, (DVTP). This individual or group test is prepared in one available form to assess various aspects of visual perception. The test is designed for children ages 3–8 years and take approximately 30 minutes for individual administration and 60 minutes for group administration. (Follett Publishing Company)

Purdue Perceptual Motor Survey. An individual test of perceptual motor skills; the test is prepared in one form and has an approximate administration time of one hour. (Merrill Publishing Co.)

Language Tests

Assessment of Children's Language Comprehension. A group or individual test that identifies receptive language difficulty in children and indicates guidelines for correction. Expressive ability in children is not required in this test. The test also measures students' ability to identify pictures that contain one, two, three, or four verbal components. Intended for preschool through elementary grade level students. (Consulting Psychologists Press)

Boehm Test of Basic Concepts. A group or individual test for kindergarten through second-grade students intended to measure the basic vocabulary of quantity, space, and time. Two alternative test forms are available. (Psychological Corp.)

Carrow Elicited Language Inventory. An expressive language test to examine a student's productive control of grammar. The test provides for an analysis of students' miscues on verbs and is intended for administration to children ages 3–8 years (Learning Concepts)

Clinical Evaluation of Language Functions. A test for students kindergarten through 10 years that accesses a wide range of language functions, including forming sentences, understanding words, word relationships, and memory of spoken discourse as well as word retrieval and fluency. Subtests are intended to assess features of language that create difficulties for learning disabled students. (Merrill Publishing Co.)

Detroit Tests of Learning Aptitude. A test that can be administered from ages 6–18. It is intended to identify strengths and weaknesses in faculties directly or indirectly associated to language that is considered important for the performance of academic tasks. Eleven subtests assess reasoning and comprehension, as well as verbal and auditory attentive abilities. (PRO-ED)

Goldman-Fristoe Test of Articulation. A quick test to assess a student's ability to articulate speech sounds. The test is intended for individuals age 2 or older and measures speech sound articulation in initial, medial, and final positions in

words and sentences. (American Guidance Service)

Houston Test of Language Development. A test for individuals ranging from ages 6 months to 6 years. Numerous expressive and receptive language and language-related activities are included to assess a person's developmental language capabilities. Subtests measure syntactical complexity, intonation, vocabulary, comprehension, and self-identity. The test also includes a checklist for parents and teachers to identify items at the age they were first noticed in the student. (Houston Press)

Language Comprehension Tests. This test is designed to assess the comprehension of linguistic aspects of language comprehension of preschool children. The examiner asks a child to respond to real objects and attempts to delineate the child's use of active sentences, singular/plural verbs, inflections, adjectival modifications, negative affixes, comparatives, and so forth. (University of Illinois Press)

McCarthy Scales of Children's Abilities. A test intended for individuals ages 2.6–8.6 years to test word knowledge. There are six scales included that specify verbal, perceptual-performance. Quantitative, general cognitive, memory, and motor information. The purpose of the test is to identify faculties associated with intellectual functioning. (Psychological Corp.)

Ordinal Scales of Psychological Development. This test is designed to assess cognitive correlates of the language and communication of children ages 2 weeks to 2 years. The test examines six areas of sensorimotor intelligence—object permanence, initiation, means of achieving desired ends, casualty object relations of space, and schemata for relating to objects. (University of Illinois Press)

Porch Index of Communicative Ability in Children. Two batteries for this test are available, basic (15 subtests) and advanced (20 subtests), to be administered from ages 3–12. It is intended to assess general communication ability involving verbal, gestural, and graphic tasks related to 10 common objects serving as stimuli. (Consulting Psychologists Press)

Templin-Darley Test of Articulation. This test is for children ages 3–8 and screens for articulation diagnosis. There are 25 consonant blends, 12 vowels, and 6 diphthong sound elements that are used in assessing for articulation diagnosis. (Bureau of Educational Research and Service, State University of Iowa)

Test for Auditory Comprehension of Language. An individual auditory comprehension test for children ages 3–6 years. This test of vocabulary, morphology, and syntax is used to measure receptive language in English or Spanish by having a child select appropriate drawings from a set of 101 pictorial stimuli plates. (Learning Concepts)

Test of Language Development (TOLD). This receptive and expressive language test assesses such aspects as vocabulary, syntax, and phonology. The test is intended for children ages 4–9 years and is brief and simple to administer. Five principal subtests—including speech sound discrimination and articulation—are incorporated in the test. The subtests correlate with criterion tests, with reliability coefficients usually in the 0.70s. The subtests are internally consistent and sound. The purported purpose of the test is to provide some indication of students' overall language strengths and weaknesses. The intermediate level, 8.6–12.11, includes five subtests. Scores include sentence combining, characteristics, word ordering, and grammatic comprehension and five composite scores (syntax, semantics, listening, speaking, and total spoken language). (PRO-ED)

Glossary

Achromatic vision: Total color blindness resulting in complete loss of color sense.

Adaptable resources: Special instructional resources intended for use with children experiencing severe reading problems and can be used with existing resources.

Affective comprehension: Personal and emotional responses to material that is read.

Amblyopia: Monocular vision apparently caused by suppression of the image coming from the less effective eye.

Analytic phonics: Method of teaching phonics beginning with words taught by the whole-word approach and then applying phonic analysis to these words.

Arousal: An individual's state of motivational activity in relation to internal and external stimuli.

Astigmatism: Blurring of vision due to a defect in the curvature of the refractive surfaces of the eye. Light rays are diffused rather than focused to a single point.

Auditory acuity: Sharpness or clearness of sounds transmitted to the brain.

Auditory blending: Ability to analyze and blend parts of words together to form words.

Auditory discrimination: Ability to discriminate likenesses and differences of sounds represented by a letter, group of letters, and/or words.

Auditory memory span: Ability to recall related sounds after hearing them.

Basal approach: Reading instruction that is given through the use of a series of basic readers. Sequence of skills is determined by the basic readers and accompanying manuals and materials.

Basic study skill: Organized method of reading a content chapter which includes previewing steps, followed by line-by-line reading for total understanding.

Bilingual: Ability to communicate in two languages.

Binocular vision: Use of both eyes together to see clearly. Also referred to as fusion, which is the coordination into one image of the separate images of the same object in the two eyes.

Central auditory imperception: Difficulty in linking what is heard with the meaning of a message.

Central processing dysfunction: Impaired processing of incoming information received from one or a combination of the auditory, visual, or haptic sensory channels.

Cloze procedure: Mutilating a 250- to 300-word freestanding passage by deleting every *n*th word and administering the mutilated passage to a reader who attempts to make it whole again.

Cognitive clarity: Reader's clear conceptualization of the communication purpose of written language, the symbolic function of writing, the concepts and terminology of linguistic terms, and what it means to "read."

Cognitive confusion: Inability to realize and to understand the nature of reading and what it means to "read."

Compound word: Word consisting of two or more independent words that combine their meanings to make a new word.

Construct validity: Degree to which test performance can be interpreted in terms of certain psychological behaviors.

Content validity: Degree to which test results reflect the subject matter and behaviors being considered.

Context clues: Method of determining the meaning of a word from other words in a passage.

Contraction: Shortening of a word or words by omitting one or more sounds or letters within a word or between words.

Corrective reading instruction: Usually a program of regular classroom instruction aimed at correcting a child's reading problems.

Criterion-referenced test: Test designed to measure specified behaviors performed by an individual toward mastery of a specific skill.

Criterion-related validity: Degree to which test results predict future performance or estimate present performance on a related task.

Critical comprehension: When a reader analyzes, evaluates, and/or judges the merits of written information.

Crossed dominance: When the preferred eye is opposite of the preferred hand.

Culturally divergent students: Children who come from cultural backgrounds that are *different* from the school culture.

Decoding: Analysis of written symbols into speech elements to determine pronunciation.

Deductive approach: Method of teaching by first stating the conclusion and then soliciting examples to support the conclusion.

Descriptive linguistics: Branch of linguistics that deals with the structure of language including phonology, morphology, syntax, and semantics.

Developmental reading instruction: Instruction designed to meet the reading needs of those students who are progressing satisfactorily in relation to their capacity. Focus of instruction is on systematic development of reading ability.

Dialect: Regional or ethnic variety of spoken language.

Discipline: Process of directing behavior to gain desired result.

Exceptional children: Children who have special needs that a typical classroom reading program usually does not accommodate.

Facilitative reading factors: Skills and abilities that facilitate reading for meaning but by themselves are not reading.

Fixation: Stops that the eyes make as they progress along a line of print for the purpose of seeing a word or words.

Frustration reading level: The reading level at which students would be frustrated in their attempts to understand what is read.

Functional reading factor: Actual reading abilities where the focus is on comprehension.

Gifted children: Children identified by qualified professionals who, by virtue of outstanding abilities, are capable of high performance.

Graded word list: A list of words that are given a grade level in terms of their difficulty and frequency of use. Used for determining a student's placement in the graded passage of an IRI, assessing sight vocabulary of words in isolation, and identifying word-recognition strategies.

Grade level standardized tent score: Standardized score that indicates the relative position of a student's raw score with the raw score of the average student at a certain grade level in the norming population.

Grapheme: A visual symbol (letter[s]) that represents a phoneme.

Graphonic similarities: Symbol/sound relationship for the initial, medial, and final portion of a word.

Group experience stories: Language experience stories composed by a group of children based on a common experience.

Handedness: The preferred use of either the right or left hand for most manipulation.

Haptic stimuli: Information received through the touching and feeling of an object.

Heterogenous grouping: Classification of students characterized by a high degree of disparity.

Higher order spelling units: Spelling patterns that have invariant spelling-to-sound correspondence.

Hyperactivity: Excessively active behavior that deviates regularly and frequently from a level of activity that would be considered within a normal range.

Hyperopia: Farsightedness; lack of eye refracting power to focus parallel rays on the retina.

Hypoactive: A less-than-average level of behavior that deviates regularly and frequently from a level of activity that would be considered within a normal range.

Incentive: Factor that motivates one to act in a particular way.

Independent reading level: The level at which a student can read materials without teacher assistance.

Individualized reading instruction: An instructional program that is developed to meet a student's specific reading needs. Diagnostic information is used to make decisions about what to teach, when to teach, how to teach, and how much to teach to best ensure that a child's reading will improve. The four phases of an individual reading instructional program are learner style, task conditions, resource attributes, and teacher style.

Inductive approach. Method of teaching by providing examples that lead to a conclusion.

Inferential comprehension: The reader infers meaning that goes beyond explicitly stated story information.

Inflectional ending: Suffix added to a word to change grammatical intent.

Informal assessment: Procedures used to assess a child's reading that have no established norm for comparing him or her performance with a group.

Informal reading inventory (IRI): A series of grade-level passages ranging usually from preprimer through grade 6 or higher with one or two passages at each level. Word-recognition miscues and responses to comprehension questions are used to identify independent, instructional, and frustration reading levels.

Instructional reading level: The reading level at which the material to be read is challenging and the reader needs teacher assistance in reading it. Thus, the material is neither too easy nor too difficult.

Instructional resources: Materials, methods, and approaches used for reading instruction.

Interest grouping: Grouping of students for reading instruction based on their similar interests in reading material topics.

Interest inventory: Informal procedure for identifying topics and activities in which a child is interested.

Interfixations: Point at which eyes are shifting from one fixation to the next along a line of print.

Irregular words: Words that are not spelled as they are sounded or do not adhere to regular spelling patterns.

Item analysis: Analyzing students' responses to each item of a test to identify patterns of performance. Also, reviewing each item of a test prior to administration to determine whether or not the test has content validity.

Language experience approach: Approach for teaching reading that is built on a child's experiences. The child dictates his or her experiences and the teacher writes them or the child writes his or her own story. The child's story is the basis for reading instruction.

Lateral dominance. The preferred and more skilled use of one side of the body.

Learner style: Phase of an individualized corrective or remedial reading program based on diagnostic findings. A student's reading strengths and weaknesses and attitudes are evaluated to identify appropriate instructional settings and motivation strategies.

Learning disability: A disorder in one or more of the processes involved in using language, spoken or written, which may manifest itself in imperfect ability to listen, think, speak, read, write, spell, or do mathematical calculations.

Linguistic geography: Branch of linguistics that focuses on dialect variations in our language.

Linguistics: The study of language.

Listening capacity: The highest level at which a child is able to understand material that is read aloud to him or her.

Literal comprehension: Recalling or recognizing information that is stated explicitly in materials read.

Miscue analysis: Examination of a reader's oral reading miscues to better understand his/her use of graphic, phonological, syntactic, and semantic information.

Miscues: An observed response in oral reading that does not match the expected response.

Monocular vision: Vision with only one eye.

Morphemes: Smallest unit of meaning in a language. For example, *cats* consists of two morphemes—*cat* and *s.*

Morphology: Study of the structure of words.

Motivation: Reasons that sustain, intensify, and direct a person's goal-seeking behavior.

Multilevel reading kit: A set of reading materials that is given a level according to reading difficulty and skill development.

Myopia: nearsightedness; light rays reflected from an object beyond a certain distance are focused in front of the retina.

Neurological impress method: System of unison reading between a student and a teacher.

Normative population: Population on which a standardized test was normed.

Orthographic encoding: Identification of the letters and groups of letters that form words.

Paraphrased comprehension questions: Paraphrased questions that have no nouns, verbs, or modifiers in common to the information presented in a reading passage.

Passage dependency: Refers to comprehension questions that can only be answered correctly by comprehending information presented in a given piece of reading material.

Percentile rank: A standard score that refers to an individual's rank in some particular group.

Phoneme: Smallest unit of speech that distinguished one sound from another.

Phonetics: Study of speech sounds.

Phonics: Body of knowledge regarding letter-sound correspondence in order to pronounce unknown words.

Phonological encoding: Process of rendering words into implicit (silent) or explicit (oral) speech.

Phrase grouping: Representing the information presented in sentences by separating the information into phrases containing one basic piece of information.

Prefix: Meaningful element attached to the beginning of a root word.

Psycholinguistics: Study of the relationship between language and characteristics of children learning to read.

Qualitative analysis: Analyzing a student's test performance to better identify reading strengths and weaknesses.

Quantitative analysis: Computing a student's raw score and converting it to a standardized score of levels of reading competence.

Raw score: Number of points received on a test when the test has been scored according to the directions.

Reading comprehension: Both what a person remembers and understands about what he or she has read. The four levels of comprehension include literal, inferential, critical, and affective.

Reading disability: Condition in which there is a significant discrepancy between a student's reading potential and actual performance.

Reading expectancy: Optimum reading level of a student.

Reading readiness: The adequacy of existing reading capacities in relation to the demands of a given reading task.

Reading resource teacher: Teacher who is trained and certified to teach reading to children who experience severe reading problems.

Recall: To remember an idea or information presented in a story. The reader recalls an idea or ideas stated by the author to respond to a comprehension question.

Recognition: The reader is required to recognize specific information presented in a story.

Recreational reading: Reading solely for the purpose of enjoyment or entertainment.

Regressions: When the eyes shift to the left along a line of print to return to a word or words to get meaning.

Regular words: Words that are sounded as they are spelled or adhere to regular spelling patterns.

Reliability: The degree to which the results of a measurement instrument are consistent.

Resource attributes: A phase of an individualized corrective or remedial reading program that focuses on matching available materials, methods, and approaches to learner style.

Response availability words: Words that have a high degree of association with each other, for example, small–big, bread–butter, and knife–fork.

Return sweep: Diagonal sweep of the eyes at the end of a line of print to begin reading on the next line of print.

Root words: Element of a word remaining after all prefixes and suffixes have been removed.

Saccadic eye movement: Jerky movement of the eyes along a line of print during reading; fixations, interfixations, and return sweeps make up saccadic movement.

Scanning: Quick method of reading for the purpose of locating a specific piece of information.

Self-fulfilling prophecy: Hypothesis stating that one's expectation of a student influences what he or she becomes

Semantic: Relating to the meaning of a word or group of words within a pharse or sentence.

Semantic encoding: The meaningful interpretation of words the reader sees or hears himself or herself pronouncing.

Service words: Words that appear with a degree of frequency in written materials.

Sight vocabulary: Words that a reader recognizes instantly on sight and has meaning for.

Skimming: Quick method of covering a reading selection for the purpose of obtaining a general idea of the content.

Specialized instructional resources: Resources intended for use with children experiencing severe reading problems. Such resources often require a one-to-one instructional setting and incorporate the sensory modes of vision, hearing, touch, and movement.

Standard error of measurement: An estimate of the amount of variation in a test score.

Stanines: A single-digit standard score that divides a distribution of raw scores into nine parts.

Strabismus: A squint deviation of one eye or both eyes from a proper direction. *Absolute* occurs at all distances for a fixation point. *Relative* occurs for some and most other distances. *Convergent* is when the eye or eyes turn inward when focusing. *Divergent* is when the eye or eyes turn outward when focusing.

Structural analysis: Method of determining the meaning of pronunciation of a word by identifying the meaningful units.

Study skills: Specific skills required to read content materials.

Study-type reading: Purposeful and deliberate reading of a selection for the purpose of complete understanding.

Suffix: Meaningful element attached to the end of a root word.

Syllable: Basic unit of pronunciation in the English language.

Syntax: The ordering of words to construct phrases and sentences.

Synthetic phonics: Method of teaching phonics beginning with direct instruction in grapheme-phoneme correspondence.

Tachistoscope: Mechanical device that rapidly exposes reading material at varying rates of exposure.

Task conditions: A phase of an individualized corrective or remedial reading program. This phase specifies what the learner should be able to do following a period of instruction (behavioral objectives) and identifies instructional procedures appropriate to the product.

Teacher style: A phase of an individualized corrective or remedial reading program. This phase deals with the teacher synthesizing the information about learner style, task conditions, and resource attributes to begin a student's corrective or remedial reading instruction.

Validity: The degree to which test results serve the uses for which they are intended.

Visual acuity: Sharpness or clearness of a visual image transmitted to the brain. *Nearpoint acuity* is the clearness of the image at reading distance. *Farpoint acuity* is the clearness of the image at 20 feet.

Visual, Auditory, Kinesthetic, Tactile (VAKT): A method of teaching word identification that uses the sensory modes of seeing, hearing, tracing, and feeling a word.

Visual discrimination: Ability to note visual similarities and differences of a letter, letters, and/or words.

Visual imagery: The formation of mental images of a story information.

Visual perception: The ability to perceive visual similarities and differences.

Word banks: Student-kept files of words taken from his or her language experience stories. The student selects the words he or she wishes to include in the word bank.

Author Index

455

Subject Index

WE VALUE YOUR OPINION—PLEASE SHARE IT WITH US

Merrill Publishing and our authors are most interested in your reactions to this textbook. Did it serve you well in the course? If it did, what aspects of the text were most helpful? If not, what didn't you like about it? Your comments will help us to write and develop better textbooks. We value your opinions and thank you for your help.

Text Title _____ Edition _____

Author(s) _____

Your Name (optional) _____

Address _____

City _____ State _____ Zip _____

School _____

Course Title _____

Instructor's Name _____

Your Major _____

Your Class Rank _____ Freshman _____ Sophomore _____ Junior _____ Senior

_____ Graduate Student

Were you required to take this course? _____ Required _____ Elective

Length of Course? _____ Quarter _____ Semester

1. Overall, how does this text compare to other texts you've used?

_____ Superior _____ Better Than Most _____ Average _____ Poor

2. Please rate the text in the following areas:

	Superior	Better Than Most	Average	Poor
Author's Writing Style	_____	_____	_____	_____
Readability	_____	_____	_____	_____
Organization	_____	_____	_____	_____
Accuracy	_____	_____	_____	_____
Layout and Design	_____	_____	_____	_____
Illustrations/Photos/Tables	_____	_____	_____	_____
Examples	_____	_____	_____	_____
Problems/Exercises	_____	_____	_____	_____
Topic Selection	_____	_____	_____	_____
Currentness of Coverage	_____	_____	_____	_____
Explanation of Difficult Concepts	_____	_____	_____	_____
Match-up with Course Coverage	_____	_____	_____	_____
Applications to Real Life	_____	_____	_____	_____

3. Circle those chapters you especially liked:
1   2   3   4   5   6   7   8   9   10   11   12   13   14   15   16   17   18   19   20
What was your favorite chapter? _____
Comments:

4. Circle those chapters you liked least:
1   2   3   4   5   6   7   8   9   10   11   12   13   14   15   16   17   18   19   20
What was your least favorite chapter? _____
Comments:

5. List any chapters your instructor did not assign. _____

6. What topics did your instructor discuss that were not covered in the text?_____

_____

7. Were you required to buy this book? _____ Yes   _____ No

   Did you buy this book new or used? _____ New   _____ Used

   If used, how much did you pay? _____

   Do you plan to keep or sell this book? _____ Keep   _____ Sell

   If you plan to sell the book, how much do you expect to receive? _____

   Should the instructor continue to assign this book? _____ Yes   _____ No

8. Please list any other learning materials you purchased to help you in this course (e.g., study guide, lab manual).

_____

9. What did you like most about this text? _____

_____

10. What did you like least about this text? _____

_____

11. General comments:

   May we quote you in our advertising? _____ Yes   _____ No

   Please mail to: Boyd Lane
                     College Division, Research Department
                     Box 508
                     1300 Alum Creek Drive
                     Columbus, Ohio 43216

   Thank you!